Renaissance Poetry
and Drama in Context

Renaissance Poetry and Drama in Context: Essays for Christopher Wortham

Edited by

Andrew Lynch and Anne M. Scott

Cambridge Scholars Publishing

Renaissance Poetry and Drama in Context: Essays for Christopher Wortham,
Edited by Andrew Lynch and Anne Scott

This book first published 2008 by

Cambridge Scholars Publishing

15 Angerton Gardens, Newcastle, NE5 2JA, UK

British Library Cataloguing in Publication Data
A catalogue record for this book is available from the British Library

ISBN (10): 1-84718-610-6, ISBN (13): 9781847186102

Contents

List of Illustrations

Editors' Foreword

Andrew Lynch and Anne M. Scott

This collection has been assembled by the colleagues, friends, students and admirers of Christopher (Chris) Wortham. The title's choice of the term 'Renaissance' rather than the more usual 'Early Modern' suits the man, for Chris's interests and expertise are broad; to hear him lecture is to evoke the concept of 'the Renaissance individual'. His international influence and global scholarship are reflected in the range of essays and diversity of contributors, which, in turn, endorse Chris's equal respect for senior researchers and emerging scholars. In their prefatory appreciation, with reference to very different stages of Chris's life and work, Geoffrey Cooper and Bob White pay full tribute to him as a colleague. We can add our own gratitude for his extraordinary contribution in many contexts: as a former editor of *Parergon*, founder and long-time presiding genius of the Perth Medieval and Renaissance Group, major figure in planning the ARC Network for Early European Research, and a dynamic participant for many years in the Australian and New Zealand Association for Medieval and Early Modern Studies. Above all, this volume has been undertaken to honour Chris as an inspired and inspiring teacher at UWA, where we look forward to his long continuance as Professor Emeritus. The last words of the book are given, fittingly, to Chris and Anne themselves.

The editors have grouped the scholarly essays chronologically and thematically to reflect Chris's influence as editor, critic and teacher of early English drama and poetry. The volume begins with explorations of the influence of late medieval plays on scenes of cruelty in Shakespeare (Blake), the social context of early Tudor drama (Welna), and marginal but menacing social groups—the insane (Daalder), the hirsute feminine (Hirsch) and the Turk (Vella Bonavita). Marchant and Newman then examine the spatial discourse of Shakespeare's *Henry IV* and Marlowe's *Tamburlaine*, with close reference to contemporary cartography and cosmology, in this reflecting some of Chris's current research interests. Other essays bring new and original insights to bear on well-studied material—Brissenden (*As You Like It*), Bradshaw (*Othello*), Miller (Ben Jonson), Dubrow (Donne's poetry), Southwood (the Diana myth). Riley challenges existing assumptions about the authorship of the Dialogues of the Little Academy at Little Gidding, cogently arguing that these were written by the daughters, rather than the father, of the Ferrars family, and adding further to the body of knowledge concerning women's role in classroom drama. Kelly's critique of Lady Grace Mildmay's letters and diaries forms a neat doublet with this article, giving modern readers further and corroborative insight into how English women of the seventeenth century strove to derive moral and spiritual capital from their circumscribed lives and expectations.

Chris Wortham's work in editing the poems of Marvell draws direct responses from Condren and Bladen, each of whom contextualizes specific poems in terms of contemporary political issues and events. Finally, the afterlife of Shakespeare's plays, such an enduring part of Chris's critical, dramatic and teaching life, is represented by essays from Stevenson, Wright and White. Special thanks to the two anonymous referees who read and commented on all the scholarly essays, with extensive notes for revision.

The editors and contributors offer this volume as a tribute to Chris and Anne Wortham whose grace and generosity to generations of students and colleagues have immeasurably enriched Medieval and Renaissance studies in Australia and far beyond.

Chris Wortham: an Appreciation

Geoffrey Cooper and Robert White

Many of Chris Wortham's friends and colleagues have contributed to this volume: it is a palimpsest of many hands. It is fitting that it should be a result of our collective experiences of Chris as he himself is a great collaborator, both in work and play. Though this introduction necessarily honours the academic Chris, it also recognizes the man, and his family, that lie at the root of his achievements.

Christopher John Wortham, a born Rhodesian who undertook an Honours and Master's degree in South Africa at Rhodes University, and his Australian-born wife, Anne, began their academic careers in 1967 at the University College of Rhodesia and Nyasaland, (now the independent nations Zimbabwe and Malawi), Chris in the English department and Anne in Applied Linguistics.

To the uninitiated this may appear to be an inauspicious start to Chris's otherwise illustrious career, like a twentieth-century Beowulf or Prince Hal. However, UCRN was not, as *Yes, Minister* may have called it, a 'TPLAU', A Tin Pot Little African University. It was one of the best, if not the best, of the African universities at that time: from its incorporation by Royal Charter in 1955 to 1970 when it became the University of Rhodesia, it had a 'Scheme of Special Relation' with the University of London whose rigorously examined degrees were awarded to UCRN graduates. Early Professors of English included internationally recognized authorities such as Norman MacKenzie, a Gerard Manley Hopkins scholar, and Bernard Blackstone, a Blake and Romantics scholar. After the special arrangements with London were dissolved, high standards of graduation, equivalent to the best British universities', were maintained throughout the 1970s by external examiners, such as, for English, Professors Norman Sherry (Lancaster University) and Jim Boulton (Birmingham University).

Throughout Chris's time at the College/University (1967–76), Rhodesia became increasingly troubled and politically dangerous following the unilateral declaration of independence from Great Britain in 1965 by the Rhodesian Front Government (led by Prime Minister Ian Smith). These were formative years in Chris's career, and the political context should be understood in order to appreciate Chris as both the man and the academic.

By 1967, many senior academics had been deported by the Smith government or had resigned from the College in anticipation of deportation or because of the political situation. One was imprisoned for allegedly conspiring to overthrow the government by violence. They were usually replaced by younger staff, many of whom, such as Chris, were commencing their brilliant careers. (Two at the antipodes that now spring to mind are Sir Malcolm Rifkind, the distinguished British politician, and Conal Condren, Emeritus Professor of Politics and International Relations at The University of New South Wales). The English department, as more senior lecturers resigned, was youthful and inexperienced but Chris and his new colleagues enthusiastically embraced their new careers.

All in all, it was not an easy introduction to an academic life but Chris and Anne thrived despite the problems. The country was as culturally isolated as it was politically so the Worthams, missing the rich culture of London where they had met, decided to make their own and threw themselves into musical and dramatic performance. While Chris played viola with the Salisbury Municipal Orchestra, Anne organized and played recorder and cello following the tradition of European 'hausmusik'. Both of them acted in a number of plays, especially Shakespeare, and Chris went on to direct several productions including a fine interpretation of *Waiting for Godot*.

Meanwhile, Chris, remarkably given his diverse commitments (to say nothing of cricket and liar dice!), completed a University of London PhD on Lovelace in 1974—a testimony to his academic determination.

In the face of the difficulties the country as a whole was undergoing within the University, and the English department in particular, a strong common bond was forged which sustained a general, though perhaps somewhat youthfully idealistic, belief that the University, as a multiracial institution, and increasingly so as time passed, was the best medium to combat racialism, encourage mutual understanding among its racial groups, and educate tolerant students who would at a later stage lay the foundations of a fully enfranchized and independent nation.

This bond of collegiality increased as the political situation worsened during the 70s, and the latter increasingly impacted upon the University and its staff. The rift between the Smith government and its supporters and the University and its staff grew ever wider: the latter being vilified, with little originality though much venom, as the 'Kremlin on the hill'. Much worse, as the Smith regime became more and more besieged by African nationalist forces, more and more of the academic staff were pressed into 'defensive' service by the Rhodesian government for at least two months at a time in a year, regardless of their beliefs or nationality, or of the needs of the University. The alternative was imprisonment. Some staff were given front-line duties: others were drafted to release manpower for the war. Chris's particular burden was to act as a representative of government in a 'protected' African village in the bush which was caught between the conflicting forces. One of his main duties, accompanied by armed soldiers, was to probe the dirt roads for landmines (fortunately not managing to find one!). More than the physical danger he was much disturbed by the experience of his helplessness to assist the disaffected villagers in any real way, as well as by his consciousness that he was implicitly supporting a regime many of, or most of, whose policies and practices he detested.

As a consequence of such disruptions to what were small departments, academics had to cover for their colleagues by undertaking additional teaching duties (most already had a teaching load of seventeen hours per week), often in areas where they did not have particular expertise and often at very short notice.

The situation demanded qualities of collaboration, of flexibility and willingness to teach beyond the narrow confines of a particular specialization, to say nothing of an earnest desire to share knowledge with colleagues and students, to teach to the best of one's ability, to treat all people with respect no matter their creed or colour, and the determination to maintain these values against all odds. Above all, stamina, academic and personal, was needed.

All the above are epitomized by Christopher Wortham.

Those of us who have had the privilege of working alongside Chris, together with his numerous students, recognize the earnest, controlled passion for his work and the profound love of literature that characterize him and his dealings with both students and colleagues.

Chris has always been a committed teacher and a great communicator with students who invariably talk of him with a mixture of admiration and affection. This comment is from one of his former Rhodesian students, Clayton MacKenzie, now Professor of Literature at Hong Kong Baptist University:

> It was not simply an honour but a commonly understood delight to be a student in one of his classes. Affable, witty, insightful, his lectures brought a plethora of collateral disciplines into the literary classroom—among them music, history, art, architecture, philosophy, politics, religion, science. No subject was taboo; no intellectual avenue for learning barred or discouraged.

Chris's teaching has always been collegial and student-focused, long before such concepts became educationese catch-cries. His approach may have developed naturally from his early experience of teaching students for whom English is a second language: their needs are greater than native English users, both linguistically and culturally. Whatever the cause, besides understanding and anticipating the needs of students, Chris has always treated all students, the pedestrian as well as the gifted, with respect, and has given generously his time at all times to assist them even when his other manifold commitments in academia must have placed great pressure on his time. No student has ever had to chase after Chris in order to get his advice and assistance.

His early experiences of academia may also partly explain why Chris is such a good colleague (it's of course his character too). In those days everyone in the

English department had to support each other, in some ways due to their collective lack of experience, in others due to the political circumstances, and also perhaps due to the fact that the English department from 1968 until Zimbabwean independence did not have a Professor in charge, so all were equal: the head was simply 'primus inter pares', and decisions were made collectively. Whatever the reason, the fact is that Chris has always been involved in collaborative projects, as will be demonstrated time and again in this introductory essay.

One of his earliest collaborative ventures would later result in his first major publication, an edition of *The Summoning of Everyman*, that was prepared with Geoff Cooper while they were working together at the UR, though not published until they were subsequently reunited at the University of Western Australia. Again, the context is significant. Teaching at UR was paramount: the idea of scholarship in the form of published research was not only of lesser importance but also difficult to pursue given the isolation of the University, the strained political circumstances and call-up duties. Neither author really envisaged the project as a 'research' undertaking that would enhance their reputations and lead to promotion or better prospects. Rather, it was a response to a teaching need: second-language students needed more help in understanding the play than was provided in the edition they were reading. So Chris, with an interest in early modern English literature and drama (MA on Arthur Miller) and Geoff with an interest in medieval/early modern English literature, decided to edit the text so as to provide an introduction and textual notes that would explain the context of the work historically and culturally and evaluate its importance critically. The initial workload was divided: Chris responsible for the critical introduction and Geoff for the text and its variants and the textual notes. In fact, there was a great deal of stimulus and cross-fertilization of knowledge and expertise in the process of consulting and deciding, from a *student's* point of view, what to or not to address—one of the great benefits of collaboration. At the same time, the edition exemplifies their naïveté at the time: they did all the work and only later began to seek out a publisher.

In the meantime, the political and military situation was deteriorating rapidly. Periods of optimism when negotiations between the Smith government, Great Britain's Wilson government and national leaders such as Bishop Muzawera and Joshua N'komo appeared to herald a peaceful transition to majority rule were increasingly dispersed by ones of gloom and depression when no solution between the protagonists eventuated and when the carnage was increasing daily. By 1976 to venture outside the capital Salisbury was to risk one's life.

At this point a major event for the Worthams occurred, the advent of a daughter, Miranda, a significant Shakespearean name given the tumult in the country. The risk of a baby's life in the midst of a civil war was the most critical reason for the Worthams' decision in 1977 for Chris to accept a lectureship offered by The

University of Western Australia and to leave Rhodesia. For Anne it was a return to her own country: for Chris, having visited Australia on sabbatical leave, it was a promise of peace and opportunity.

At UWA Chris was involved in a number of collaborative efforts. The first was the publication by the UWA Press in 1980 of *Everyman* (with Geoff Cooper, who had arrived there in 1978). The critical reception of the edition first established Chris's scholarly reputation.

It was that year too that Chris returned from a trip from Sydney enthused with the prospect of founding a society for the promotion of early English and European studies which he proposed to call the Perth Medieval and Renaissance Group. The name is significant: the Sydney group was more narrowly focused and comprised only academic specialists from the same university. The Perth group was intended to be much more inclusive and eclectic, open to anyone who had an interest in the period, including not only academics and students from all the Perth universities but also the general public. As he was the prime mover, Chris was naturally elected as the founding President, an office he has held several times as he has always been the driving force of the organization. For over a quarter of a century the PMRG has been a remarkable success: it has always maintained a strong membership (bigger and more various than any of the other groups that form the Australian and New Zealand Medieval and Renaissance Society) and has offered a varied and stimulating programme of some dozen events each year. This success is a tribute to Chris's foresight in initiating a forum where individuals and disciplines with different but complementary foci can interact and collaborate to their mutual benefit.

Geoffrey Cooper

There is another magician saying goodbye today,[1] though I know he won't bury his books, and he might take heart that we are still talking about the first Prospero some four centuries after his play was performed.

I want to honour the retirement of Chris Wortham from UWA, and say frankly that we will be the poorer for his absence from the teaching role. I suspect he won't be so deprived of opportunities, since academics don't ever really retire—they just take honorary fellowships, write books and articles, give guest lectures, travel the world to conferences—all the things in fact which they don't have time to do when they are being paid to do them. And I know that Chris will also continue teaching since it is his special vocation. Born teachers who retain such passion and commitment are rare indeed.

Chris is a remarkably inspiring teacher, even amongst the many other demands on his time, because of his unique, personal fusion of deep learning and intellectual vitality. Even quoting the lines of Shakespeare's characters reveals Chris's early days as an actor, as he slips into dialect and roles. He has been respected and loved by generations of students, for the energy, time and attention he has put into every encounter with individual students and groups. He has been anxious to coax the very best out of each one of you, for over many years, and he has genuinely rejoiced over every student's success and achievement, grieved over the rare failures, and always done his very best to try every way of helping you all achieve your goals. Chris has the true teacher's instincts, as he can make even the most complex ideas very clear and exciting through the urgent desire to share and communicate his ideas. As I said about academics not retiring, these also are gifts that are innate and lifelong and will be shown in new ways in the future.

As a close colleague who has taught many times with Chris, I have seen not only these facets of him but others as well—his efficiency in administration, his personal kindnesses even when the recipient has been unaware of them, and also his international reputation as a scrupulous scholar, writer, editor and critic, respected at the highest level of Renaissance learning. His commitment has been to the discipline itself, the field of Renaissance and medieval literature and history, and he has for many years sustained the PMRG, the journal *Parergon*, and more recently the huge enterprise of the Network for Early European Research, NEER, which has put UWA on the national and international map of cutting edge scholarship. His own particular research interests are wide and deep, extending well beyond writers such as Shakespeare and Marlowe (whose *Doctor Faustus* he has edited in a best-selling volume), the anonymous writer of *Everyman* and Andrew Marvell (whose poems have also been edited by Chris in a very handsome edition), and reaching out to early cartography, acting conventions, and stately homes. In many ways his editions show the full breadth of his skills. They are meticulous in profound scholarly detail presented with unobtrusive succinctness, while being full of sound critical insight. 'User friendly' and designed for students, they enthuse as well as enlighten, while also reaching the highest standards of scholarship. When many other works of criticism will disappear over time, Chris's fine editions will remain as beacons.

So, Chris, from us all, thank you—hail, but NOT farewell—we won't let this magician say goodbye to our magic island.

Robert White

Notes

1   After giving a lecture on *The Tempest* entitled 'The Magician Says Goodbye', Bob White made these comments, on the occasion of Chris Wortham's retirement.

Shakespeare and the
Medieval Theatre of Cruelty

Ann Blake

An old Westmoreland man, questioned in 1644 by the Puritan cleric John Shaw about his knowledge of the doctrine of redemption, replied that 'he had once seen a play "where there was a man on a tree, and blood ran down"'. This startling anecdote, quoted by Helen Cooper[1] in a review of Michael O'Connell's investigation into the Puritan conviction that all forms of theatre, religious and secular, were idolatrous, is, as Cooper argues, a testimony to a pervasive after-life of the medieval religious cycle plays long after their discontinuance in the sixteenth century. More generally, it points to what one might expect, that is, continuity between pre- and post-Reformation England in people's memory and imagination of their immediate past. The case for this persistence specifically in the consciousness of post-Reformation dramatists writing fifty years after the break with Rome, and put by Cooper in her review, has from time to time been presented in the works of scholars who have looked back to the medieval theatre to explore what might be seen as the 'origins' of Shakespeare. Early English religious drama is not conventionally considered among his sources. It goes unmentioned in Muir's one-volume study, and in Bullough's *Narrative and Dramatic Sources* attention to cycle plays is minimal, extending little beyond citing the Wakefield (Towneley) *Harrowing of Hell* in relation to the Porter in *Macbeth*. Relations with the morality plays have been better served, by Alan Dessen's *Shakespeare and the Late Moral Plays* (1986) for instance, and before that by Bernard Spivak's *Shakespeare and the Allegory of Evil* (1958). Within that field of Shakespeare studies devoted not to sources but to the broader category of forerunners, or 'origins', most attention has gone to classical works, though medieval connections have been consistently suggested. Charles Lamb hints at a possible connection when he recognizes in the suffering of Calantha, in the catastrophe of John Ford's *The Broken Heart* (1625), an echo of the Crucifixion:

> The expression of this transcendent scene almost bears me in imagination to Calvary and the Cross; and I seem to perceive some analogy between the scenical sufferings which I am here contemplating, and the real agonies of that final completion to which I dare no more than hint a reference.[2]

Perhaps here Ford (b. 1586), and some in his audience, at this point had in mind not only the Gospels' narrative of the Crucifixion but also what they had heard, or even seen, of its staging in the cycle plays of the Passion.

For substantial examinations of such connections, one turns first to A. P. Rossiter, especially to the chapter 'Gothic Drama' in *English Drama from Early Times to the Elizabethans* (1950), and to Glynne Wickham, in his discussion of cycle play sources in *Shakespeare's Dramatic Heritage* (1969). To these writers, and to others familiar with medieval drama, including Cooper,[3] aspects of Shakespeare's histories and tragedies call to mind similar qualities in the cycle plays, and of course in those other biblical plays which were never part of cycles: their grand historical scope, their blending of the tragic and the comic, their flexible locations, and, in scenes of murder and humiliation, their dramatic exploitation of presented action. Writing of 'Comic Relief' in Shakespeare, Rossiter identifies a mingling of tones resembling the cycle plays' 'habit of juxtaposing the religious and the farcical'. Shakespeare writes in 'the same spirit' as the cycle plays, but, Rossiter cautions: 'the direct dramatic connection is non-proven'.[4] Wickham writes of Shakespeare's awareness of 'the dramatic possibilities' of the cycle plays, and examines what he sees as a specific debt to them in *Macbeth*. Emrys Jones in *The Origins of Shakespeare* (1977) goes further, arguing that Shakespeare found in these plays 'dramatic paradigms', that is, structures for the dramatization of powerful human situations, and presents detailed evidence of their influence on his early plays.

History and historicism have dominated Shakespeare studies for the last forty years. Writers have viewed the plays in the context of their contemporary social history, and of prevailing ideologies of power within the state and the home. The plays have been read in relation to court politics, colonial expansion, religious conflict and the Gunpowder Plot. Simultaneously, but looking through the telescope from the opposite historical perspective, other studies have centred on understanding the meaning of Shakespeare today and in the immediate past, by investigating appropriations, re-inventions, and adaptations for the stage, film and other media. Scholars and critics, we can say, have been, predominantly, looking at Shakespeare in our time, and in his own.[5] But what of Shakespeare in relation to what came *before*, rather than Shakespeare now, and Shakespeare then.

To take this viewpoint means following those scholars who have resisted the notion of two eras of dramatic activity, medieval and Renaissance, cut off from each other by the Reformation. In terms of playing places, Glynne Wickham plausibly argued that 'a stage of mediaeval invention' survived, with some modifications, until the theatres were closed in 1642.[6] This view accepts the notion that the cycle and other biblical plays, though suppressed during the sixteenth century, but persisting at various locations until well into the second half of the century, and even later in more remote areas, did not at once vanish from the memory. An awareness of them could reverberate in the minds of playwrights of Shakespeare's generation, perhaps even as late as Ford. We might think of their awareness of that material, no longer acted and not in print, as roughly analogous to that of the relation of the music hall to writers in the 1960s and 70s.

But did Shakespeare actually see the cycle plays? Shakespeare biographers (also writers of history) now speculate on what theatrical experiences the young lad might have enjoyed. These, they suggest, would include traditional popular rituals such as Robin Hood's Day (May Day), and plays performed in Stratford by visiting professional players. Perhaps the eleven-year-old Shakespeare slipped into the lavish Kenilworth Entertainments presented to the Queen in 1575. And if he failed to get there in person he may have read of them in Robert Langham's pamphlet, *A Letter*, 'a work so obviously aimed at a wide and popular market'.[7] Some of the speculation about what Shakespeare saw can now be given substance thanks to the discoveries of the *REED* project which has contributed so much to understanding relations between the Elizabethan theatre and its immediate predecessors. In the area of religious drama the *REED* volumes chart the end of the cycles, as they disappear from the centre of a city's dramatic life, often not so much simply suppressed as falling into decay due to a combination of economic forces and Protestant pressure. As already mentioned, this was a process which met with varying degrees of resistance through the country. In Cornwall religious plays were performed 'at the end of Elizabeth's reign' and in Kendal as late as 1603.[8] In Coventry the last cycle was presented in 1579, but enthusiasm for presenting plays based on biblical themes did not vanish: it burst out again with a spectacular performance in 1584 of a new play, *The Destruction of Jerusalem*.[9] Thus it remains possible that Shakespeare went to Coventry to see the cycle plays, more than once perhaps, before they were discontinued when he was fifteen. It is not just romantic speculation to think this was the case. As the *REED* editor points out, the Coventry Council presided over what 'was a national and not merely a local event ... a sacred entertainment which drew people from all over England. Casual reference proves the fame.'[10] Two of the recent biographers, Stephen Greenblatt and Peter Ackroyd, both see the 'mark' of these plays on Shakespeare. Greenblatt writes:

> Something of their power—their way of constructing a shared community of spectators, their confidence that all things in the heavens and the earth can be represented onstage, their delicious blending of homeliness and exaltation—left its mark upon him.[11]

Alongside this possible indebtedness to medieval dramatic art, the late sixteenth century provides plenty of evidence implying that the medieval literary heritage, the art of 'that misty time', as Sidney calls it, was perceived as either amusingly old hat, quaint, or to be discarded, condemned, and even persecuted. In the romantic world of Shakespeare's late plays, with their self-consciousness about 'old tales' and miraculous happy endings, the presence of 'Old Gower' as Chorus in *Pericles* (1606–08) associates that story with a specific long-gone, indeed medieval past, and thereby casts upon it a heightened, even 'authentic', air of romance. As for Spenser, his archaic diction, real and invented, and tales of chivalry can be seen as late sixteenth-century tributes to Chaucer and medieval romance.[12] But simultaneously scholars and grammarians were writing treatises disparaging such works as the *Morte d'Arthur*, and encouraging English writers to cast off their native heritage and take up the genres of the European Renaissance. In the sphere of drama, Sir Philip Sidney's neoclassicist condemnatory judgements of his contemporaries' efforts in *An Apology for Poetry* (1580, published 1595) furnish a catalogue, one after another, of precisely those qualities, 'gross absurdities', which are carried over from the native medieval plays. Where the stage should represent one place and one day, instead 'many places and many days [are] inartificially imagined', and tragedy and low comedy are clumsily mixed, 'mingling kings and clowns'.[13] Instances spring to mind of this last criticism as readily from cycle plays as from Shakespeare: the Second Shepherds' play, or Mrs Noah refusing to enter the ark, the Porter in *Macbeth,* the man with the basket of figs in *Antony and Cleopatra.*

Other forms of continuity with the medieval were of course much more dangerous. Any persistence in the practice of the old religion was subjected to fierce suppression, in the persecution of priests, recusants, and the obliteration of religious imagery. One instance of the destruction of images, the order for the painting over of the Doom picture in the nave of the Guild Chapel in Stratford, given by John Shakespeare, is now regularly mentioned in biographies of his son. Nevertheless, some pre-Reformation painted glass and sculpture survived, as did some wall paintings, with some subsequently uncovered, while others perhaps were never obliterated. At the time, the whitewash itself must have reminded the congregation of what could no longer be seen. Similarly, at the end of the sixteenth century traces of the medieval religious theatre remained, not so much in the few play scripts which were not destroyed but preserved by chance in council records and elsewhere, but in details in church windows and wall paintings and in the less vulnerable carvings which depicted the cycles' staging of some biblical event,[14] and above all in sayings and allusions, in short, in the cultural memory. That Shakespeare had some awareness of these plays and their most memorable images is testified by those few passages which unmistakably recall them. There is none alluding to the onstage Crucifixion, recalled by the man in Westmoreland, but when Richard II presents himself in the deposition scene as Christ betrayed by Judas, and then as arraigned before Pilate, his lines might well have reminded some of the audience of the old plays. Moreover, when Richard asks: 'Did they not [sometimes] cry 'All hail' to me?'(IV. i. 169),[15] 'All hail' repeats the words of the York Judas, not the Gospels' 'Hail, master'.[16]

There are even clearer allusions in the reference to the ranting tyrant in *Hamlet*: 'it out-Herods Herod' (III. ii. 13–15) and to children being tossed on the pikes of soldiers in *Henry* V (III. iii. 38-41). Both hark back to versions of the slaughter of the innocents.[17]

To some scholars and critics it has seemed that the plays of Shakespeare and his contemporaries reveal a substantial underlying presence of the cycle plays, beyond the allusions cited here. What follows is an attempt to examine the evidence for a conceptual and structural continuity between a particular group of medieval and Shakespearean scenes: those which present violence against children. These episodes form part of what might be called a medieval theatre of cruelty. The phrase, borrowed from the title of Jody Enders' study,[18] of course also suggests Artaud's conviction that violent action is the essence of theatre, a belief which led to his enthusiasm for 'the bloody spectacle of Renaissance melodrama', but not for Shakespeare, where, according to Artaud, the visceral impact of violence was obliterated by narrative and psychological interest.[19] Here, however, the phrase is borrowed to draw attention to the prominence and frequency of those violent episodes enacted before the spectators. In the cycle plays, the Passion—the buffeting, scourging, and Crucifixion of Christ—presented the most harrowing spectacle. Others remarkable for their violence were Cain and Abel, and—instances of violence specifically against children—Abraham and Isaac, and the slaughter of the innocents; all three episodes according to traditional medieval exegesis prefigured Christ's Passion; equally all three presented the spectators with reflections of the cruelty and violence of their own world.

Scenes of violence, as R. A. Foakes notes in *Shakespeare and Violence*, are characteristic of the earlier plays of Shakespeare, *1, 2 and 3 Henry VI, Titus Andronicus* and *Richard III*. These are indeed plays of murdered sons, brothers and fathers, and of grieving mothers, as Brian Boyd observes, writing of that pre-eminently distressed father, Titus Andronicus. Some of these murdered sons are also young, they are children: young Rutland in *3 Henry VI*, and the princes in the tower, and they foreshadow the fates of children in plays to come, Arthur in *King John,* and Young Macduff.

The outstanding biblical instances of the threatened or actual killing of innocent children are the story of Abraham and Isaac and Herod's slaughter of the innocents. Both memorably combine horror and pathos in incidents which have become archetypal images of adult violence against children. The slaughter of the innocents, an episode in the traditional life of Christ, appears in each of the complete cycles, Towneley, York, and Chester, in the N-Town and Digby plays, and forms part of one of the two surviving Coventry plays. The story of Abraham and Isaac is in the three cycles, in N-Town, and in two single plays, Brome and Northampton. All present the horror of the threatened killing and the pathetic circumstances of father and son, with Abraham torn between his desire to obey God and love for his son. In

Northampton, however, a prologue between God and an angel makes God's testing of Abraham 'something of a controlled experiment'.[20] Versions of the slaughter of the innocents offer their own affecting juxtapositions, the ruthless raging of Herod, and the brutality of his soldiers as they spear the babes and attack the mothers set against the mothers' terror and grief. In some versions the women's plight becomes something close to grotesque farce as they struggle with the soldiers to protect their children. In the Digby 'The Killing of the Children' farce nearly runs away with the play, as the cowardly soldier Watkyn meets the distaff-wielding women. It is precisely this combination of strong dramatic effects, appealing to a range of feelings in the spectators in quick succession, which, Rossiter argues, is characteristic of the 'gothic drama' with its 'disturbing doubleness of tone and point of view'.[21] It is powerfully disconcerting, and with, for instance, certain scenes of *Titus Andronicus* in mind, also recognizably Shakespearean. These are effects close to that 'sublime incongruity' or 'comedy of the grotesque' which, for Wilson Knight, pervades *King Lear*.[22] To some the effect is too disconcerting, and to be deplored. Writing of the Coventry, York and Digby slaughter scenes, T. W. Craik remarked: 'Every spectator … will naturally pity the mothers, and it is unseemly to make their sorrow take the form of grotesque and comic violence.'[23]

There are strong resemblances among the biblical plays, not just in the overall design of the matter chosen for presentation, but the effect of cross-fertilization between versions of the episodes as they were rewritten over the years. The slaughter plays nevertheless show considerable variation of detail in their presentation of the events related in St Matthew. All put the tyrant Herod at the centre. In some versions, York and Towneley for instance, the slaughter is suggested by Herod's counsellors; in Chester and Coventry Herod makes the plan himself. His soldiers are more or less content with their task. One Chester knight claims killing a 'shitten-arsed shrowe' is work for a lad (157),[24] but he stops protesting when his fellow goes along with Herod's plan. In contrast to Herod's brutal tirades, their cruelty is more casual. When they threaten and abuse the mothers, their colloquial language, along with their boasting, cowardice, and petty competitiveness, brings their part in the event down to an everyday level of human nastiness. The three Towneley soldiers play out a ninety-line scene with the mothers who cry out, threaten vengeance and attack them: 'thy skalp shall I clefe' (510), 'Have at thi groyn' (554). The soldiers' abuse, 'hags', 'trots', 'stry' and 'whore',[25] matches their ruthless energy in killing. They remain untouched by conscience, arguing after the slaughter about who is the best soldier and who should speak to Herod first. The Chester soldiers threaten the women, resisting their distaff blows and pleas, and urge themselves on with ghastly jokes:

Dame, thy son in good faye,
hee must of me learne to playe:

hee must hopp, or I goe awaye
upon my speare ende.

(321–24)

In contrast, the Coventry soldiers go through with the killing but regret it and fear
its consequences.

All versions present the spectacle of the slaughter. In N-Town it is acted out
without dialogue: '*Tunc ibunt milites ad pueros occiendos, et dicat Prima Femina*'.
First and Second Woman then speak only sixteen lines of mourning: 'Gon is all my
good game! / My lytyll childe lyth all lame / þat lullyd on my pappys' (98–100).[26]
Coventry, Towneley and Chester also present the women's protests before the killing.
In the Chester version the First Woman and First Soldier exchange threats and pleas
until the child is stabbed, and the whole sequence is then repeated by Second Soldier
and Second Woman. As in Chester, N-Town soldiers *impale* the children: 'Upon
my spere / A gerle [male child] I bere' (109–10). In these versions, as in Towneley,
stuffed dummies were probably used to resemble the naked infants.[27] This is the
image which appears in medieval church paintings and windows,[28] and is recalled
for Shakespeare's audience when Henry V at the siege of Harfleur depicts the horrors
of war in his appeal to the citizens to surrender:

Your naked infants spitted upon pikes,
Whiles the mad mothers with their howls confus'd
Do break the clouds, as did the wives of Jewry
At Herod's bloody-hunting slaughter-men.

(*Henry V*, III. iii. 38–41)

At Coventry the staging presumably provided its own touch of realistic horror, given
the soldiers' lines referring to the 'waynis and waggyns fully fryght' with bodies
which they say they must take to Herod: 'Loo! Eyrode, kyng, here mast thow see /
How many [thousand] thatt we haue slayne' (884–85).

The flight into Egypt establishes the ineffectuality of Herod's attempt to kill the
King of Kings. In York and Coventry the women, with an omniscience more choric
than realistic, know of the flight even as their children are being slaughtered, and
foretell Herod's frustration: 'The same þat þei have soughte / Schall þei neuere come
till' (232–33).[29] They find some consolation, a sense of just revenge, in this idea. At
the end of the York play Herod, not satisfied that he has killed the king to be, sets off
for more killing. In N-Town and Chester he suffers immediate punishment. Chester
Herod learns that his own son has been slain in the slaughter, and the Devil appears
to carry him off to hell. In N-Town the figure of retribution is Mors who joins Herod,
like Banquo's Ghost, Emrys Jones suggests, at his own feast.[30]

Of all the versions, Coventry, the version Shakespeare is most likely to have seen, is arguably the most compelling. From the start there is a sense of common human feeling. The soldiers here are neither comic braggarts nor simply eager to perform Herod's commands: they argue against them. The first soldier declares: 'To see soo many yong chylder dy ys schame'; the second argues against the plan on political grounds: 'So grett a moder to see of yong frute / Wyll make a rysung in thi noone cuntrey' (795 ... 800).[31] He already has a picture of the terror they will create: 'Thatt make many a moder to wepe an be full sore aferde / In owre armor bright when the hus see' (812–13). After the slaughter, when other soldiers look for reward and are indeed given fields and lands, they speak of the women's cries and foresee evil to come (870–76). The mothers too are especially affecting because they express a greater variety of feeling. Before the slaughter they enter singing lullabies to their babies, the famous Coventry carol. It is clear from their song that they know already of Herod's decree: the soldiers' arrival will be no surprise. As they lull their babies to sleep their song becomes a farewell, their tenderness and dread sharpening the impending horror. After the lullaby each still prays that her child may escape its fate. The soldiers then arrive, the women plead for their children, the first appealing to the Soldier's 'curtessee' and 'chivaldre' to pity an innocent (847–49). The vulnerability of the child is stressed in a way unparalleled in other versions:

> For a sympull sclaghter yt were to sloo
> Or to wyrke soche a child woo,
> þat can noder speyke nor goo
> Nor neuer harme did.
>
> (851–54)

The second woman abuses and threatens the soldiers in the fierce tones of the Chester women; the third helplessly threatens blows with her 'pott-ladull'. After the careful pacing of the suspense and the heightening of horror with tender feeling, this final blending of pathos, violence and comic impotence is strikingly poignant. The desperate woman, driven to flout all conventions of behaviour, like Shakespeare's Paulina pleading before Leontes for the infant Perdita she brings before him, knows that she will appear mad, 'wode', that all she has are a woman's weapons, 'thys same womanly geyre' (867). But Paulina too must plead, and Leontes abuses her in the language of cycle play soldiers: 'Out / A Mankind witch' ... 'bawd' ... 'Dame Partlet' ... 'crone' (*The Winter's Tale*, II. iii. 68–77).

These versions of Herod's slaughter of the innocents, alluded to in *Henry V* and *Hamlet*, seem to be present in the background of Paulina's appearance, and the dramatic shaping of the episodes is even more detectable in scenes in Shakespeare where children a little older are plotted against and slaughtered on the orders of a tyrant. The young princes in *Richard III* are victims of Richard's ruthless ambition, and Young Macduff is stabbed on stage by murderers sent by Macbeth. In each case the tyrant is seen plotting their deaths. Richard, who has already disposed of his brother Clarence and his children, now requires Buckingham to murder the princes: 'I wish the bastards dead' (IV. ii. 18). Buckingham cannot stomach this, and Tyrrel instead is summoned to hear Richard's whispered commands. The princes' mother, grandmother and aunt all fear for their lives when Richard seizes them from sanctuary, and holds them in the Tower. The mother can only pray for the safety of her 'babes', though they are by no means infants:

> Pity, you ancient stones, those tender babes,
> Whom envy hath immur'd within your walls—
> Rough cradle for such pretty little ones!
> Rude ragged nurse, old sullen playfellow
> For tender princes—use my babies well!

> (IV. i. 98–102)

The princes are killed offstage, the women cannot do battle with the killers, but, after Tyrrel reports their death, 'The most arch deed of piteous massacre', in a long pathetic speech, they hurl their curses at Richard's head (IV. iv.). According to Tyrrel, the murderers, Dighton and Forrest, once the smothering is done, are, like the two Coventry soldiers, filled with 'conscience and remorse' (IV. iii. 20), and speak of their victims as 'gentle babes' (9), glorifying their innocence, though, on another occasion, when they are hired to kill Clarence their speeches of brutal determination, quelling all conscience, recall other cycle play soldiers' grimly comic exchanges.

Those ugly taunts appear again momentarily in *Macbeth*, as the Murderers set about killing the Young Macduff: 'What, you egg! [*Stabbing him*] / Young fry of treachery' (IV. ii. 83–84). As in the cycle plays the tyrant has announced what is to be done, quite openly, no whispering here:

> The castle of Macduff I will surprise,
> Seize upon Fife, give to th' edge o' th' sword
> His wife, his babes, and all unfortunate souls
> That trace him in his line.

> (IV. i. 150–53)

The audience waits for it to happen. In this scene the absolute helplessness of the mother to protect her children, felt so powerfully in the cycle plays, and in *Richard III*, darkens the whole of the dialogue between Lady Macduff and her son before the Murderers appear, her fears becoming more intense as Ross and a messenger deliver their warnings and then leave her. Killed off stage, immediately after her son, she has no chance to mourn him, but the tragi-comic exchanges with her son about Macduff's treachery in abandoning them convey indirectly her sense of their vulnerability before Macbeth's cruelty.

What distinguishes these Shakespearean massacres of innocents is that the victims, the princes and Young Macduff, are old enough to play out their innocence, to speak their 'innocent' prate and, like Rutland, who appears with his Tutor in *3 Henry VI* I. iii. and is stabbed by Clifford, to make speeches pleading for their lives. The model in the cycle plays for this young eloquence in the face of adult cruelty is the figure of Isaac.

Versions of the story of Abraham and Isaac dramatize the *proposed* slaughter of an innocent. In the York version, Isaac is a grown man, but the other five surviving plays conceive the story as one of violence against a child. Although the Genesis story is to be seen, as the Chester Expositor explains, as prefiguring God's sacrifice of his son, its dramatic potentialities for the poignant interaction between the father and son are obvious. They are realized in a unique fashion in the York play where Abraham, following Genesis, tells the spectators that he is a hundred years old, and, 'following Peter Comestor and the exegetical tradition',[32] Isaac 'Thyrty 3ere and more somdele' (82). Isaac is an obedient son but when it comes to the binding, he fears that he will 'of kynde' resist his father, and if he does so he will succeed because he is younger and stronger:

> I knaw myselfe be cours of kynde,
> My flessche for dede will be dredande.
> I am ferde þat 3e sall fynde
> My force youre forward to withstande,
> Therefore is beste þat 3e me bynde
> In bandis faste, boothe fute and hande.

> (209–14)

In all versions except Towneley Isaac is bound, but in Brome and Chester[33] the binding is one of a number of incidents which delay the child's death and draw out the suspense. Indeed, of all the versions the Brome play is the most dedicated (or 'shameless'[34]) elaboration of the pathetic aspects of the situation. The father's affection for his 'swete son', 'Thys fayer swet chyld', is painfully felt: 'I lovyd neuer thyng soo mych in erde' (76).[35] The Northampton play alone includes Sarah, Isaac's mother, and the effect, as Tydeman suggests, is to dissipate 'something of the familial bond'.[36] Isaac in Brome is always a small child, trying to keep up with his father as they walk to the 'mount' of sacrifice:

> Gowe, my dere fader, as fast as I may
> To folow 3ow I am full fayn,
>   Allthow I be slendyr.

> (124–26)

The tension builds in the first part of the dialogue as Isaac asks one question after another, at first with a child's insistence, and then more and more fearfully, until the truth comes out. The dialogue then becomes more rapid, the speeches shorter, two lines only, and finally single lines:

> *Abr.* A! Ysaac, Ysaac! I must kyll the.
> *Isaac.* Kyll me, fader? alasse! wat haue I don?

(167–68)

When Abraham wrings his hands, struggling against God's command, Isaac now urges him not to displease God for his sake:

> For, be I onys ded and fro 3ow goo,
> I schall be sone owt of 3owre mynd.

(201–2)

He asks for his father's blessing, Abraham blesses him, and then kisses his 'fayere swete mowthe'. Then follow no less than one hundred lines in which the moment of death is delayed by requests, hesitations and expression of grief. Isaac asks his father to say farewell for him to his mother; Abraham begs him to 'speke no more'; Isaac urges his father to 'make an enddyng'. Abraham moves to bind Isaac only to have Isaac protest: 'A, mercy, fader! Wy schuld 3e do soo?': he will not 'let' his father (247), asking only that his eyes be bound with a 'kerche'. Abraham lays '*a cloth ouer Ysaacys face*' (s.d. 289), an action not in Genesis but found in several versions. With the child lying on the altar, the suspense is drawn out further. Isaac is still afraid to see the 'sharp sword', and asks 'torne downgward my face' (291), only for Abraham to declare that he cannot find it in his heart to kill 'thys 3owng innosent'. Isaac has to beg again that his father 'schorte [him] of [his] woo' before Abraham will strike. It would be hard to imagine a version that did more to heighten the pathos by its imaginative realization of the distress of father and son, and the play of their feelings on each other.

The carefully structured movements of the episode, 'sentimental developments' complains one editor, provide a striking parallel to the scene in Shakespeare's *King John* where Hubert, on orders whispered by the King, unheard by the audience, prepares to blind the young Prince Arthur. This is another scene condemned as too sentimental in the twentieth century.[37] In his edition, E. A. J. Honigmann, who does not find it sentimental, makes the link between the two: he suggests that 'Shakespeare probably remembered the pathos of the Abraham and Isaac plays while writing this scene.'[38] Like the murder of the princes in *Richard III*, and of Young Macduff, the scene recalls in general terms the situation and feeling of the massacre of the innocents. Moreover, this is an episode where not only does a secular tragic human situation parallel that in the religious play, but one where, as Emrys Jones argues at length in *The Origins of Shakespeare* in the case of sequences of scenes in Shakespeare whose shape recalls the presentation of the Passion, the shape of the dramatic structure in which it is presented seems to be remembered from medieval play treatments of an analogous biblical story.

The scene in *King John,* like the episode of Abraham and Isaac, ends, on a human level, in a dramatic anticlimax: a man who loves a child prepares to perform an act of violence against the child but in the end does not do so. This is the curious, defining feature of these stories. It sets them apart from other classic tales of a father's sacrifice, such as that of Iphigenia, or those episodes of child sacrifice in George Peele's plays which seem to derive from his reading of one of Euripides' *Iphigenia* plays.[39] In *King John,* the pacing of the suspense relies on psychological causes of delay similar to those in the plays of Abraham and Isaac. Hubert is torn, like father Abraham, wanting to obey his king but reluctant to harm the 'young lad', the 'little prince'. Again, the child to be harmed has been made dramatically younger: Shakespeare's Arthur, 'a young warrior in Holinshed, becomes a helpless child in the play'.[40] Like Isaac, Arthur is a fair, loving child; he loves Hubert, and wishes Hubert were indeed his father. There is a sense of closeness between the two; they are companions, if not father and son. Arthur, again like Isaac, is quick to sense the man's mood: 'You are sad' (IV. i. 11). 'Are you sick, Hubert? You look pale to-day' (28). When he reads Hubert's warrant Arthur momentarily accepts his fate with an Isaac-like submission to divine will: 'If heav'n be pleased that you must use me ill / Why then you must' (55–56) but a moment later he cannot believe Hubert will harm him. Isaac is terrified at the sight of his father's 'sharp sword', Arthur not at seeing the instruments, but the executioners. Both victims resist being bound, and with the same promise. Arthur pleads:

> I will not struggle, I will stand stone-still.
> For heaven's sake, Hubert, let me not be bound!
> Nay, hear me, Hubert, drive these men away,
> And I will sit as quiet as a lamb.

$$\text{(IV. i. 76–79)}$$

Arthur's traditional simile, 'quiet as a lamb', is appropriate to this innocent, as it is more literally to Isaac, the sacrificial beast. In the earlier part of the scene Hubert is wary of the child's 'innocent prate' (25), fearful that Arthur may awaken his mercy, as Abraham is of the anguish that Isaac's words would inflict. He implores Isaac: 'Speak no more' (225). As Arthur pleads to be spared Hubert reminds him of his promise to sit 'quiet'. In reply Arthur, like Isaac, begs to be allowed to speak: 'Let me not hold my tongue, let me not, Hubert' (99). Hubert does let him speak, and he does spare him, at the intervention not of an angel, but of his mercy, awakened by the child's eloquent pleas.

The Brome play concludes with a speech by the Doctor pointing the moral; keep God's commandments, and without complaint. The effect of Shakespeare's scene of Hubert and Arthur is dramatic and thematic rather than moral. In contrast to Abraham's exemplary obedience, in the political world of *King John*, Hubert's refusal to obey his King is admirable. The dramatic function of the scene, the centre of the play in Honigmann's view, sets personal human values, manifest in Hubert's choice, and in the loving Arthur, against the dog-eat-dog ethos of the play. There are these obvious differences in function between the two episodes. Nevertheless, there are strong similarities between IV. i. of *King John* and Brome and other medieval plays of Abraham and Isaac, in situation and mood: a reluctant man must harm a loved child; the innocent child loves the man threatening him and pleads eloquently to him, and is finally spared. A further similarity is the pathetic conception of the noble-hearted, loving child. In both, horrific details set off the pathos: Abraham's sharp sword, the binding with cords, the executioners, the brazier and the heating of the irons. The instruments of torture are, as Foakes notes, brought on stage twice,[41] once before Arthur enters, perhaps for the audience's benefit, to heighten their anticipation. But, in terms of dramatic structure, the most striking similarity is the management of individual small movements in the action which draw out the suspense until the moment when Abraham's sword is poised to strike: '*and þe angell toke the sword in hys hond soddenly*' (s.d. 315), and when Hubert, moved by Arthur's four successive eloquent appeals, declares the boy's eyes are safe: 'Well, see to live; I will not touch thine eye / For all the treasure that thine uncle owes' (IV. i. 121–22).

It is now accepted that Shakespeare's audiences were more capable than us in the 'perception or recognition of arcane parallels or analogies':[42] Arthur may well have reminded them of Isaac. The wider structural resemblance suggested here depends on Shakespeare drawing on memories of old dramatic material, and grasping, perhaps unconsciously, how its shape might serve him. Memory feeds the creative process, as we all know, and this is what appears to be happening in the recreation of precedents offered by the English religious plays and their theatre of cruelty. Shakespeare made use of his secular English predecessors in the same way, as George Hunter notes in this comment on *King John*:

> *The Troublesome Reign* can be thought of as something like a pattern-maker's template for *King John*, for the structure, not only of the action in general but even of the progression of events inside each scene, is reproduced with remarkable fidelity though the language is completely different.[43]

In such a master of creative absorption, this was a usual practice.

Notes

1   Helen Cooper, 'Blood Running Down', review of *The Idolatrous Eye: Iconoclasm and Theatre in Early Modern England* by Michael O'Connell, *London Review of Books,* 9 August 2001, pp. 13–14.
2   'Characters of Dramatic Writers, Contemporary with Shakespeare', in *The Works in Prose and Verse of Charles and Mary Lamb*, ed. Thomas Hutchinson (Oxford: Oxford University Press, 1908), vol. 1, p. 65.
3   Three recent important essays which argue for Shakespearean connections are Michael O'Connell, 'Vital Cultural Practices: Shakespeare and the Mysteries', *Journal of Medieval and Early Modern Studies,* 29.1 (1999), 149–68, Peter Womack, 'Shakespeare and the Sea of Stories', *Journal of Medieval and Early Modern Studies* 29.1 (1999), 167–87, and Beatrice Groves, 'Hal as Self-styled Redeemer: The Harrowing of Hell and *Henry IV part I*', *Shakespeare Survey 57* (Cambridge: Cambridge University Press, 2004), pp. 236–48.
4   A. P. Rossiter, *Angel with Horns* (London: Longmans, 1961), pp. 282–84.
5   It is interesting to note that *The Cambridge Companion to Medieval English Theatre* follows this pattern; it has a chapter on modern productions, but does not contemplate possible continuity between medieval and early modern plays.
6   Glynne Wickham, *Early English Stages* (London: Routledge, 1963), vol. 2, p. 4.
7   R. J. P. Kuin, introduction to *A Letter* by Robert Langham (E. J. Brill: Leiden, 1983), p. 12.
8   A. C. Cawley, ed., *Everyman and Medieval Miracle Plays*, rev. edn (London: J. M. Dent, 1974), p. 235. For Kendal, see E. K. Chambers, *English Literature at the Close of the Middle Ages* (Oxford: Clarendon Press, 1945), p. 18.
9   R. W. Ingram, ed., *Records of Early English Drama: Coventry* (Toronto: Toronto University Press, 1981), p. xix. The last performance of the Chester Whitsun plays was in 1575.
10 Ingram, p. xvii.
11 Stephen Greenblatt, *Will in the World: How Shakespeare became Shakespeare* (London: Pimlico, 2005), p. 37; Peter Ackroyd, *Shakespeare the Biography* (New York: Nan A. Telese, 2005), p. 50.
12 Another enthusiast was Captain Cox, the Coventry mason, actor and collector of printed romances and other works, who features in Langham's *Letter* (Kuin, p. 54 and Appendix G).
13 Sir Philip Sidney, *An Apology for Poetry*, third edn, ed. Geoffrey Shepherd (Manchester: Manchester University Press, 2002), pp. 112, 110.
14 For relations between stage images and church iconography, see the discussion and illustrations in Sophie Oosterwijk, '"Long Lullynge haue I lorn"': The Massacre of the Innocents in Word and Image', *Medieval English Theatre*, 25 (2003), 12–36.
15 All quotations from Shakespeare follow *The Riverside Shakespeare*, second edn, general and textual ed. G. Blakemore Evans, with the assistance of J. J. M. Tobin (Boston: Houghton Mifflin, 1997).

16 See note to IV. i. 169 in William Shakespeare, *Richard II*, ed. Andrew Gurr, The New Cambridge Shakespeare (Cambridge: Cambridge University Press, 1984). Gurr finds a parallel in York and Chester; in the Chester Bakers' Play, Peter's 'All Hayle' is directed not to Christ but to the man with the water pot (p. 37).

17 Ackroyd, p. 51, points out that Shakespeare uses the phrase 'All Hail' with 'unhappy connotations' in *Macbeth* (as well as in *Richard II*, see note 16) following the cycle plays rather than the Gospels where Christ uses the phrase as a 'blessing'.

18 The full title is *The Medieval Theater of Cruelty: Rhetoric, Memory, Violence* (Ithaca: Cornell University Press, 1999). It is worth remembering that some 'medieval' cycle plays survive in sixteenth-century manuscripts, and that there was much revision, some datable to the sixteenth century.

19 Richard Fly, 'Shakespeare, Artaud, and the Representation of Violence', *Essays in Literature* 16.1 (1989), p. 3.

20 William Tydeman, 'An introduction to medieval English theatre', in *The Cambridge Companion to Medieval English Theatre*, ed. Richard Beadle (Cambridge: Cambridge University Press, 1994), p. 29.

21 A. P. Rossiter, *English Drama from Early Times to the Elizabethans* (London: Hutchinson, 1950), p. 69.

22 G. Wilson Knight, *The Wheel of Fire* (London: Methuen, 1930).

23 T. W. Craik, 'Violence in the English Miracle Plays', in *Medieval Drama*, ed. Neville Denny, Stratford-upon-Avon Studies 16 (London: Edward Arnold, 1973), p. 195.

24 'The Massacre of the Innocents', *The Chester Mystery Cycle*, ed. R. M. Lumiansky and David Mills, 2 vols, EETS, SS 3 & 9 (Oxford: Oxford University Press, 1974). Subsequent quotations from this cycle follow this edition.

25 'Herod the Great', *The Towneley Plays*, 2 vols, ed. Martin Stevens and A. C. Cawley, EETS, SS 13 & 14 (Oxford: Oxford University Press, 1994).

26 *The N-Town play: Cotton MS Vespasian D. 8*, 2 vols, ed. Stephen Spector EETS, SS 11 & 12 (Oxford: Oxford University Press, 1991). Subsequent quotations from this cycle follow this edition.

27 M. A. Anderson, *Drama and Imagery in English Medieval Churches* (Cambridge: Cambridge University Press, 1963), pp. 136–37.

28 See for instance the window at St Peter Mancroft, Norwich, reproduced in Anderson, illustration 22b, and also in Oosterwijk, p. 31, along with other examples.

29 Richard Beadle, ed., *The York Plays* (London: Edward Arnold, 1982). Subsequent quotations from this cycle follow this edition.

30 Emrys Jones, *The Origins of Shakespeare* (Oxford: Clarendon Press, 1977), pp. 82–83. Glynne Wickham had earlier dismissed this idea, primarily on the grounds of the appearance of Mors being unique in the N-Town cycle, in *Shakespeare's Dramatic Heritage* (London: Routledge and Kegan Paul, 1969), p. 231, n. 1.

31 'The Shearmen and Taylors' Pagent', *Two Coventry Corpus Christi Plays*, second edn, ed. Hardin Craig, EETS, ES 87 (Oxford: Oxford University Press, 1957). Subsequent quotations follow this edition.

32 Clifford Davidson, 'The Sacrifice of Isaac in Medieval English Drama', *Papers on Language & Literature*, 35.1 (1999), *Expanded Academic ASAP* via http://www.Gale.com.

33 The Chester *Abraham and Isaac* is, in a way yet to be explained, closely related to Brome.

34 John. C. Coldewey, 'The non-cycle plays and the East Anglian Tradition', in *Cambridge Companion to Medieval English Theatre*, p. 207.

35 'Abraham and Isaac', *Non-Cycle Plays and Fragments,* ed. Norman Davis, EETS. SS 1 (Oxford University Press, 1970). Subsequent quotations follow this edition.

36 Tydeman, p. 29.

37 For this attitude, see Ann Blake, 'Shakespeare's Roles for Children: a Stage History', *Theatre Notebook*, 48.2 (1994), 126–32.

38 E. A. J. Honigmann, introduction to William Shakespeare, *King John*, The Arden Shakespeare (London: Methuen, 1965), p. lxvii, n. 1.

39 See Brian Boyd, 'Mutius: An Obstacle Removed in *Titus Andronicus*', *RES,* New Series, 55.219 (2004), p. 203, for Peele's fondness for this motif, which Boyd attributes to his translating one of Euripides' Iphigenia plays, and then to his habit of repetition.

40 Honigmann, p. lxiv.

41 R. A. Foakes, *Shakespeare and Violence* (Cambridge: Cambridge University Press, 2003), p. 87.

42 Jones, p. 65.

43 George Hunter, *English Drama 1586–1642, The Age of Shakespeare* (Oxford: Clarendon Press, 1997), p. 223.

Magnificent Money:
Wealth and Nobility in *Magnificence* and *Gentleness and Nobility*

Karina Welna

Tudor interludes, performed for and often sponsored by the aristocracy of England, offer us a unique insight into how the elite discussed and viewed the changing face of their country.[1] Through the texts of John Skelton's drama *Magnificence* and the Rastell and Heywood collaboration *Gentleness and Nobility* this essay will examine the debates that surrounded the use of wealth and the definition of nobility, and how these topics were discussed before royalty and the elite. Although most probably written within a couple of decades of each other, between the end of the fifteenth century and beginning of the sixteenth, *Magnificence* and *Gentleness* show that opinion was hardly monolithic at the time. Within the plays an air of anxiety surrounds the prominent new wealth of the middle classes as well as their aspirations to rise both in power and status. *Magnificence* most obviously reveals a deep seated anxiety over the changing social and economic world of England. This drama sees the upward social mobility and rising economic affluence of the commonality as a result of sinful and ambitious behaviour, bound to destabilize the commonwealth and destroy the status of the nobility. In *Magnificence* nobleness can only be achieved by those who are born to the elite; 'commoners' are simply seen as incapable of nurturing and understanding this virtue regardless of the wealth they may have acquired. *Gentleness* has none of this ambivalence about the rising influence of the economically fortunate. Instead, it sees many similarities in the goals and beliefs of the affluent middling class and the established nobility. In fact, for *Gentleness,* it is this very similarity which can be the bar to both elite and 'common' people fully understanding what nobleness is and how wealth should be used. Together these plays reveal the breadth of opinion that existed over nobility and wealth and the anxieties and tensions that social and economic change could cause for the elite.

Magnificence was written by John Skelton, a poet laureate and satirist, the sometime tutor of Prince Henry (later King Henry VIII).[2] Written in the late fifteenth or the early sixteenth century[3] the play focuses on the financial, political and social responsibilities of a sovereign, particularly the relationship between wealth and nobleness. The close focus on monarchical matters results in only passing mention of the rising social and financial fortunes of many 'commoners', but what mention is made is derogatory, revealing an anxiety over and general dislike of such changes. *Magnificence* is a highly conservative work which seeks to reaffirm the status quo and the established social hierarchy, resisting all temptation to validate change of any nature that does not fit into its neat 'traditional' framework of what English society is, or rather, should be.

Gentleness and Nobility was first published in 1525, and was probably written only a few years before this date.[4] While no mention is made of John Heywood's authorship in the text, modern scholarship has shown a strong case for Heywood being the author of the bulk of the piece, Rastell only contributing the Philosopher's epilogue at the end.[5] Heywood has a connection to the court revels at this time, so it is not inconceivable that this drama may have been presented before royalty.[6] Unlike *Magnificence, Gentleness* openly acknowledges social changes apparent in contemporary England. Heywood's play features only three characters, a Knight, Merchant and Plowman, and their discussion focuses squarely on the relationship between wealth, power and status, and the true definition of nobility. The fact that a merchant is one of the central characters points directly to the rising prominence of this group as '[t]he rapid growth of a well-educated and wealthy middle class towards the end of the fifteenth century eclipsed the importance of "clergy" in social thinking and challenged the "gentle" class.'[7] During the fifteenth and sixteenth century men of non-noble origins, such as Thomas Wolsey[8] and Thomas More,[9] took prominent roles in the political sphere of England.[10] The exalted achievements of these 'new men' were made possible through the self-made wealth of their families as well as their own personal ambition. As a character, the Merchant represents not just persons of a mercantile background but also broadly those who have risen in rank and status through their own efforts. Within the play, this middling class character is given a role that allows him to be seen as a valued and important member of society, not prone to sinfulness or illicit activity any more than his counterpart, the Knight. In effect he is given dramatic equality with his social superior—the same amount of time on stage and the same validity attached to his arguments. Coupled with this acknowledgement of the changing social world of England is a strong emphasis on humanist values and beliefs, which probably sat well with the affluent rising middling classes. Colin Burrow notes, 'English humanism was in part a systematic programme for the self-advancement of low-born, highly educated and ambitious men.'[11] The influence of humanist learning is ever present in the dialogue of the characters.[12] Cameron's indispensable work on the background and sources of the play has shown that the playwright was drawing on the work of some very prominent humanists, such as More and Erasmus, to further his argument.[13] Analogues to the play can also be found in the work of prominent medieval writers, such as Chaucer and Christine de

Pizan, as well as anonymous works.[14] The reason the sources can be so broad for this drama is simply that the argument presented was in itself not new; what is unique is the way in which the play systematically refuses to believe that nobility in virtue could *only* be limited to the elite. Despite its progressive appearance, *Gentleness* is far from a simple endorsement of the newly rich and humanist philosophies; instead it is a thorough interrogation of both wealth and nobility according to the precepts of the new learning, revealing the problems of applying humanism to established definitions and understandings.

Magnificence is an allegorical work in the style of a morality play. Drawing on Aristotelian and Horatian influences Skelton constantly harks back to the classics by either direct reference to the works of the ancients or in the names of the characters that inhabit his play. Felicity, who is personified on Skelton's stage, features greatly in Aristotle's work *Politics,* as a common goal for a society to have for its citizens.[15] The very name Magnificence is a direct reference to Aristole's *Ethics* in which it is a central characteristic and virtue of leading a good life.[16] Magnificence is characterized by liberality and generosity, particularly in public spending, and a willingness to help others in any way possible. Coupled with many of the other Aristotelian virtues such as courage, temperance, high-mindedness, ambition and good temper, to name a few, it is clear that the person who is magnificent will never do anything solely for personal benefit; while great honours may come his way he would never indulge in vanity or seek to be glorified. Such a person realizes the importance of social bonds, is generous, gentle in disposition and a shining example of virtue. In a play that seeks to show the ideal character for a prince, magnificence, with its association of public spending and largesse, is an ideal worth espousing.

A similar case can be made for the central importance of the character of Measure within the play, since the idea of moderation is of vital importance to much of Aristotle's work on ethics. Some critics have also noted the influence of other classical authors, particularly Horace. In fact, William O. Harris makes a convincing case that the main classical influence behind the play is Horace, not Aristotle.[17] Ramsay (whose foundation work still influences many readings of the play) was the strongest voice to posit that Aristotle was the main classical reference behind the drama. While his case is strong, Ramsay is sometimes forced to claim that Skelton has misread or misunderstood the ancient author in order to strengthen his own argument. It is important to remember that the only classical author that Skelton directly refers to in the play is Horace, saying 'Oracius to record in his volymys olde, / With euery condycyon Measure must be sougth.' (114–15) In many respects Measure within the play is far more consistent with Horace's odes than it is with Aristotle's *Ethics.* Measure for Aristotle is a way to divide one's possessions in a fair minded way with liberality at its heart, while for Horace measure is more an outlook on life; a way to deal with adversity and prosperity in a level headed way.[18] The term 'magnificence' was also often used to refer to the cardinal virtue Fortitude.[19] This seems particularly appropriate for this drama since much of Magnificence's problem is his *lack* of fortitude in adversity. Harris has also shown that Skelton may also have been relying on the cardinal virtue tradition through the work of Thomas Aquinas.[20] It is likely that both scholars are correct to some extent, since the relationship between Aristotle and Thomas Aquinas is well documented, and Horace's work was also appropriated by various Christian scholars during the Middle Ages to espouse the cardinal virtue tradition.[21] Whatever the classical influences, they would all have come through the filter of the Christian school, thus the overriding moral philosophy is religious. While *Magnificence* may not be exactly like previous morality plays, in that it is not only concerned with the soul of its main character but also attempts to advise the audience on more earthly matters, any message it espouses is in the end a conservative religious one. Regardless of the dispute about the actual classical source, the influence of the ancients through the filter of religion is strong in the moral message of the play. The drama is constantly seeking to make its audience realize the role wealth plays in moulding the character of a person, particularly a noble, with regard to contemporary religious teaching rather than solely classical scholarship.

The play opens with the character of Felicity declaring that wealth is much abused despite the fact that it can easily be put to good purposes if men are reasonable and measurable in their use of it. Liberty is next to appear on stage and he laments the notion that he should be restrained declaring 'there is no Welthe where as Lyberte is subdude'(73).[22] Felicity continues that while Liberty is necessary it must be controlled in order to be useful and profitable. Measure enters and breaks up the fight between the two, asserting that he must be in charge for 'Welthe without Measure wolde bere hymselfe to bolde; / Lyberte without Measure proue a thynge of nought'(116–17). Magnificence appears on stage and ratifies Measure's organization of Liberty and Felicity, putting Measure in charge of all his affairs. All seems well until the prince's wits are put to the test with the entrance of the first vice, Fancy. Fancy enters proclaiming he is Largesse and, through his wiles and Magnificence's own foolhardiness, manages to snare the unwitting prince into his grasp. Having succeeded in making the sovereign accept him, Fancy opens the door for other undesirables to impact upon Magnificence's life and conduct. All the vice characters slowly introduce themselves to the audience through dramatic activity with each other and individual monologue, revealing their motivations and dispositions. Each vice expresses a wish to join the retinue of the monarch. In order to do this each assumes an alternate name; thus Counterfeit Countenance, the ring leader of the group masquerades as Good Demeanance, Crafty Conveyance calls himself Sure Surveyance, Cloaked Collusion: Sober Sadness, Courtly Abusing: Lusty Pleasure and Foly: Conceit. These advisors lead Magnificence to renounce Measure and live a courtly life filled to excess which eventually leads to the prince losing all his wealth. The sovereign is then visited by Adversity and Poverty, who inform him that God can restore all to him but he must learn to not trust so much in worldly things. Seeing himself in such a state, betrayed by those he held most dear, Magnificence falls into Despair's hands and is ready to kill himself. At this point Good Hope enters and saves him from damnation. Having repented his wrongful ways Magnificence is visited by Redress who will help him get back what he has lost. The play ends with Redress giving the final sober advice on how a nobleman should act with regard to his wealth.

Magnificence's obvious concern with Royal matters has led many critics to attempt to link it directly to a particular event or political position. Greg Walker and others posit that the play deals with expulsion of the minions,[23] Ramsay that it is Skelton's personal tirade against Cardinal Wolsey[24] and John Watkins that it is a stand against the 'new men' who often profited from Henry VIII's style of absolutist rule.[25] While such exercises are always interesting I have chosen to instead look at the drama outside of any specific event or political position. In my analysis I attempt to show that the concerns of *Magnificence* were general, and not specific, qualms about nobility and its relationship to wealth at the time. While Skelton's play can be seen to apply to Henry VIII, it also offers advice for any monarch ruling in the medieval and early modern period. Much like Scattergood, I see the drama as being deeply concerned with the financial dealings of a monarch, particularly the running of his household, and how this will inevitably affect his realm.[26] I also agree with Greg Walker's position that the Aristotelian influence cannot be denied and that its focus on measure can also be found in the protocols and organization of the royal household, as he notes: 'When Edward IV and his council attempted to reform the royal household in 1478, it was in the language of the Aristotelian mean and of personal virtue that they expressed their political desires.'[27] Throughout the period people constantly mixed philosophy with daily life, so it is not surprising that the organization of the nobility and royalty would often refer to and rely upon the classical philosophers. I believe Skelton, by using classically referential language in his play, seeks to make it part of an understood royal discourse that is already entrenched in the psyche of the ruling elite; thus his advice can be seen as both timeless and timely. While Skelton may have often written for or about an 'occasion', it is not always necessary to know what this event was to make some insightful discoveries about the playwright's time.[28]

From the first line of the play a clear relationship is asserted between wealth, happiness and nobility. Wealth and happiness are melded together into the character of Felicity, and throughout his opening monologue Felicity clearly links the prosperity of the realm to the character of the ruling sovereign. It is telling that within Felicity's opening it is already declared that wealth can be used well and to the benefit of the individual but only if 'noblenesse' is capable of nurturing the necessary skills and traits needed to use wealth in a good way,

> But yf Prudence be proued with Sad Cyrcumspeccyon,
> Welth might be wonne and made to lure,
> Yf Noblenesse were aquayntyd with Sober Dyreccyon.
>
> (17–19)

While both *Magnificence* and *Gentleness and Nobility* assert that nobility is an inner virtue, Skelton's work clearly does not acknowledge that a common person can be noble in any shape, way or form. Within the text of *Magnificence* nobility is a virtue that is inextricably linked to status and therefore can only be attached to those of the elite class. Only Magnificence is capable of cultivating nobility and carrying out its hallmark practices. Such a viewpoint is traditionally medieval:

> The frequency with which virtue is mentioned as a necessary qualification of the gentleman through the middle ages and the renaissance is misleading unless due attention is paid to current general definitions of nobility and explanations of the value of gentle birth. True nobility is almost always defined as that of race and virtue, and much of the insistence on virtue is intended not to comfort the lowly born but to admonish the well born who seem generally to have prided themselves on birth to the neglect of virtue.[29]

Whenever the text mentions those 'commoners' who have risen through the ranks to gain both riches and power it always insinuates that these people have either attained their positions and affluence illicitly, or, that they are simply incapable of carrying out and maintaining their offices in a proper manner. Lacking 'noblenesse' such people, once in possession of wealth, are often wasteful and extravagant in their use of it. Counterfeit Countenance, whose very name implies deception through appearance and demeanour, explicitly refers to the ambitious ways of many people in society. He notes that by striving to appear greater in status then they really are, these 'upstarts' only manage to act foolishly, squander what wealth they have, get into debt and pay the ultimate price for their wasteful ways. Through employing the services of Counterfeit Countenance,

> A knaue wyll counterfet nowe a knyght,
> A lurdayne lyke a lorde to syght,
> ...
> Thus make I them wyth thryft to fyght;
> Thus at the laste I brynge hym ryght
> To Tyburne, where they hange on hyght.
>
> (417–20)

Another character that similarly comments on the habits of some 'common' people is Courtly Abusyon, who notes that they will 'Spare for no coste'(891) to dress fashionably and in an excessive manner. Such wasteful behaviour results only in a sticky end, 'A Tyborne checke / Shall breke his necke' (910–11). Like Counterfeit Countenance Courtly Abusyon tells of the dire, virtually inevitable, results of living above ones means and station simply to satisfy status seeking behaviour.

In *Magnificence* there is not one example of a 'commoner' that has done well and used his affluence in a manner beneficial to himself and society. To further the sense that people of non-noble birth are simply not able to nurture truly noble behaviour Foly takes great glee in explaining how he humiliates those who have 'come vp of nought' (1241) and 'be set in auctorite' (1244). He makes them to be so proud and haughty that 'All that he dothe must be alowde'(1248) and thus 'maketh hym besy where is no nede'(1250) which leads to the person being ridiculed by all. While even the nobility can fall into such excessive and wasteful behaviours, and Magnificence does, it cannot be disguised that within the play there is a clear dislike of social changes which manifests itself by ridiculing the hallmark features of the rising 'commons': conspicuous affluence and powerful office. The drama continuously characterizes their activities as excessive, wasteful and possibly illegal. Magnificence is able to redeem himself through his noble faculty, something that 'commoners' are simply not seen to be in possession of.

Using wealth as a noble presents its own unique set of dilemmas, particularly in a modern world full of deception. It is telling that Magnificence's fall is inaugurated by the appearance of a vice, Fancy, who masquerades as Largesse. Fancy or in its original spelling *fansy* is, as Spinard reminds us, a variation on the word fantasy and in Skelton's age it meant a delusional mindset.[30] Fancy, therefore, is representative of a delusional and false version of largesse. The noble practice of gift exchange in itself is not criticized. Felicity notes that largesse should reside with Magnificence for it is 'encrease of noble fame'(271) and 'Largesse is laudable, so it be in Measure' (78). As long as Magnificence can be liberal in moderation it can only serve his nobility well; problems only arise when the purpose behind this generosity is misunderstood as extravagant, prideful display and a show of excessive expenditure.

Largesse, as the *Middle English Dictionary* defines it, is a 'Willingness to give or spend freely; liberality, generosity, munificence' and the 'Liberal bestowal of gifts, grace, etc.; free spending.'[31] Its purpose for the nobility was to facilitate the growth of a good reputation among subjects and allies and reinforce good social bonds.[32] This great generosity was both a public and private affair with social, political and economic goals; it was not meant to be an excuse to spend vast sums of wealth without reason on favourites and others. Fancy only revels in the material side of the gift exchange and misunderstands its broader, deeper social use, as he says, 'without Largesse Worshyp hath no place, / For Largesse is a purchaser of pardon and of grace' (267–68). Initially this statement may look quite right, but the use of the term 'purchaser' is a clue to how Fancy misunderstands this noble practice. Largesse is never meant as payment for a service or good but as an expression of favour and generosity that should be returned in turn with loyalty and goodwill. The material aspect is simply part of that expression. Further clues to how Fancy truly views noble generosity are shown in a story he tells Magnificence about how he came to have a letter of recommendation, supposedly from the virtuous Sad Circumspection. The vice tells how the guard at Pontoise thought he was a spy and wished to harm him physically. Fancy attributes his ability to get out of this situation to his use of largesse, as he says, 'Had I not opened my purse wyde, / I trow, by Our Lady, I had ben slayne', (347–48) and

> By my trouthe, had I not payde and prayde,
> And made Largesse, as I hyght,
> I had not ben here with you this nyght.
> But surely Largesse saved my lyfe;
> For Largesse stynteth all maner of stryfe.
>
> (363–67)

From Fancy's little tale it seems clear that he equates noble munificence with bribery, a far less exalted activity. As Fancy continues it becomes clear that he is completely uninterested in, or perhaps simply unable to comprehend, largesse's more subtle noble uses. To capture Magnificence he first plays on the prince's pride saying that,

> Syr, I here men talke—
> By the way as I ryde and walke,—
> Say howe you excede in Noblenesse,
> If you had with you Largesse
>
> (374–77)

and ridicules Measure's authority by saying that 'measure is mete for a marchauntes hall, / But Largesse becometh a state ryall' (382–83), finally telling Magnificence that '"A lorde a negarde, it is a shame"; / But Largesse may amende your name' (388–89). By appealing to the prince's pride and linking his solely materialistic definition of largesse to supposedly being capable of not only increasing but also fixing the apparently marred name of Magnificence, Fancy manages to join the royal retinue and thus starts the prince's slippery slide to ruin. The message is clear: by simply misunderstanding what the purpose of noble liberality really is, wealth will be lost and with it nobility—perhaps the playwright had in mind the sticky end that both Edward II and Richard II met in part because of their apparent misuse of royal favour. The great importance of wealth to nobility is shown in the final segment of the play, when Magnificence loses everything because he failed to understand the importance of moderation in his royal lifestyle.

By rejecting true largesse and instead engaging in reckless favouritism, spending all his wealth to appease the tastes and wishes of his vice-filled entourage, Magnificence fails to build a supportive network around himself. The lack of loyalty in the vices is illustrated amply when Magnificence comes begging while they revel in their successful ruination of him. Not only do they boast that 'we haue ryfled hym metely well'(*Magnificence*, 2170) but they also refuse to help poor Magnificence and instead taunt him. Wealth is a necessary and integral facet of nobility and its practices. As soon as Magnificence's fortune is squandered by his ill chosen companions he loses not only his comfortable life but his status and power and is reduced to the station of a humble beggar. As a noble Magnificence's God-given position in the play is that of a person with great power and wealth, to fulfil his role in God's plan he must come to terms with earthly wealth and learn to use it to his own and society's betterment. Nobility and wealth go hand in hand, Magnificence notes himself that without wealth his nobility is diminished and gone, 'Where is now my kynne, my frendys, and my noble blood?' (2060). For those of royal or even noble status, there is no happiness or nobility without wealth.

By the conclusion of the play the audience would have witnessed the importance of using wealth wisely to the maintenance of the noble estate. Furthermore the playwright has methodically defended nobility as both a quality and status, that cannot be achieved or earned by those not born to the high estate. But, while 'commoners' may not be able to be fully noble, the nobility can most definitely descend to the level of a 'commoner'. In order to rise to the demands of the noble status that one is born to, a member of the elite must use his 'noblenesse' to rule with reason and spend in moderation. Such behaviour will not be at the expense of the expressions of nobility, such as largesse and good dress, but rather to its exaltation, praise and longevity.

Where *Magnificence* shows a careful defence of noble wealth, noble practices and a deep suspicion of new wealth and social change, *Gentleness and Nobility* instead reveals an open willingness to explore the commonalities between nobles and commons, as well as interrogate the definition of nobility and its relationship to wealth. Throughout, the play uses humanist philosophies to support its overall belief that true nobility rests in the moral character of the individual, not his birth. Unlike in *Magnificence*, in which nobility is so intertwined with wealth that it ceases to exist when affluence disappears, *Gentleness* shows that nobility can be attained by even the lowest and poorest of men although it is also fully aware that such a position can be very problematic and unpalatable for some. This play lacks any plot; instead it is an extended dialogue between a Knight, a Merchant and a Plowman, each representing an estate in English society. At the conclusion of the play a Philosopher appears on stage to deliver a monologue that seeks to encapsulate, correct and emphasize the message of the drama. During their time on stage the three main characters discuss extensively how nobility should be defined and what role, if any, wealth plays in influencing a person's ability to develop nobleness.

The Plowman character is far from a realistic plowman; instead he is an amalgamation of a far reaching literary tradition,

> Behind him stands a Christian tradition of satirical *complaint*, in particular, of course, *Piers the Plowman* and its progeny: *Pierce the Ploughman's Crede*, the pseudo-Chaucerian *Plowman's Tale* [and] *Jack Upland*. The honest plowman was a touchstone against pretension, a licensed spokesman against exploitation by landlords, clergy, and the 'kyngis purviours'.[33]

Within *Gentleness* the Plowman's role is to spice up and enlighten what could have easily been a rather predictable and dull debate, as Axton notes: 'Insistence that true nobility depends on inner virtue and active merit became commonplace in humanist writing.'[34] The Plowman becomes a devil's advocate of sorts, more than willing to expose the flaws and assumptions of the other protagonists as well as add his own voice and opinion to the argument.

At the start of the play the Knight and the Merchant are both shown to have a rather limited perception of what makes a nobleman. The knight defines nobleness or *gentilnesse* in terms that are favourable to him saying, 'Mary, I call them gentylmen that be/ Born to grete landys by inherytaunce'[35] (I.30–31), while the Merchant offers a slightly different definition,

> For I call hym a gentylman that gentilly
> Doth gyf unto other men lovingly
> Such thing as he hath of hys own proper.
>
> (I.45–47)

Neither of the definitions is satisfactory because both fail to look at the inner characteristics and virtues of an individual. Remarkably the Merchant in his faulted definition actually seems to be referring to the practice of largesse, which, as *Magnificence* has shown, is a facet of the noble estate. This may reflect the simple fact that most merchant families actually aspired to join the established ruling class, often hoping to marry up into the nobility or gentry.[36] Merchants rarely hoped to stay as such. Astonishingly it seems that both the Merchant and the Knight, despite seeing themselves as opponents, are actually arguing for a defence of the same noble estate since both their definitions rely on seeing nobility more as status than virtue; perhaps the playwright is subtly suggesting that the 'rising' classes are not threats at all but instead strengthening supports to the traditional organization of society. During their arguments the Knight and the Merchant do show that they actually attach some internal qualities to their understandings of nobility, such as wisdom and intelligence, but they rarely seek to interrogate their own personal moral character; preferring instead to focus on the material and temporal achievements of their ancestors. Such a line of argument resists humanist understandings because it rests on asserting that nobleness is innate to a person and can be passed on through inheritance, rather than a virtue that is developed through environment, spiritual knowledge and education.[37]

It is the Plowman who is the first to attempt to turn the argument away from earthly or materialist scales of nobleness which see it mostly as a status or dependent on ancestral pedigree and instead focus it on the character of the individual. Up until the Plowman's entrance the Knight and the Merchant succeeded in reducing their debate into a contest of whose ancestors were better, a dispute that seemed to have no conclusion or victor. The reason for the focus on ancestral achievements is largely due to the Knight's strong belief in his nobleness resting in his ancestral blood which he attempts to prove is superior to the Merchant's ancestry. The fact that this line of argument does not prove the Knight's superiority easily shows already the fallacy of his belief, and necessitates a change in the debate. His line of argument, which in the medieval period was taken for granted, is denied its air of superiority and is now forced to defend itself.[38] Soon after his entrance, the Plowman tells the two that their arguments 'be not worth a fly'(I. 210), because they have falsely based their argument on the accomplishments of their ancestors and not on their own acts or personal qualities,

> Ther is nother of you both dyd prove or lay
> Ony of your actys, wherby that ye
> Shulde in reason prove you noble to be,
> Or therby deserve any maner praysyng.

> (I.212–16)

Through the Plowman's direction the debate between the Knight and the Merchant is transformed into a fuller and more developed argument. Forced to focus on their own personal qualities the Knight and the Merchant attempt to prove their superior nobleness through their own acts. Curiously, their debate results in their proving to the audience that they both provide necessary and integral services to the nation; the Knight through military and political leadership and the Merchant through ensuring economic growth and good trade relations. Clearly their argument will not be resolved if they only focus on the more material aspects of nobleness and character, so the Plowman adds another dimension to the definition of nobility, the spiritual or moral element, as he says,

Man is most noble of creaturys lyvyng,
Not by hys body, for that is impotent,
But by hys soule, beyng so excellent.

(1.376–78)

Through his soul man has reason and intellect which allow him to govern the earth, provide for himself and also to improve his character in a spiritual manner. While ethically both men may seem to or at least know how to behave correctly with reference to their station, on a personal spiritual level they seem lacking.

It is when looking at the personal spiritual aspects of nobility that both the Merchant and the Knight find it hardest to make themselves seem noble. Using the seven deadly sins as a measuring stick of sinfulness and lack of virtue, the Plowman systematically asserts and shows his own inner nobleness, while also revealing the many sinful activities of the estates that the other characters represent. The Plowman shows through examples that he is relatively free of lust, avarice, pride, envy, wrath, sloth and gluttony. He says he is content with his plain wife 'blak Maud' (II.925), and does not care for 'vanytese worldy' (II.944). The Plowman also lives in his simple cottage, dresses plainly, is not envious or prone to anger, works hard for his living and has a simple and basic diet. In contrast, he notes the apparent sinfulness of the Merchant and the Knight. The vicious activities and behaviours that the Plowman lists cannot be based on a personal assessment of either of the other characters simply because he does not know the Knight or the Merchant so intimately. Instead the sins that he attributes to the other protagonists refer to the commonplace and stereotypical practices and habits of the estates they embody. He cites the fine array of his dramatic companions as proof of their pride,

Furst, for pryde, your rayment shewyth what ye be,
For ye wyll never be content except that ye
Have the fynest cloth and sylke for to were.

(II.894–96)

The Plowman also assumes they are covetous because they 'covet evermore goodis, landis, and rent; / What so ever ye get, yet never content'(II.900–1). In addition they are probably wrathful and envious of every man. Their 'beddys so pleasaunt and soft'(II.910) make them slothful, their fine diet filled 'Wyth flesh and fysh most dylycate and fat, / All frutis and spyces that can be gat'(II.916–17) makes them indulge in gluttony and finally their lustfulness is also noted,

To aswage your carnall insurreccyons
What so ever she be—wyfe wedow or mayde—
If she come in the way, she shalbe assayd.

(II.919–20)

Undoubtedly the Plowman's opinion of himself and the other characters has some truth and also some fiction in it. Perhaps the most easily recognizable points that seem questionable are his claims to being slow to anger and non-violent. Only 200 lines previously the Plowman whipped the Knight in his indignation. Just like the Knight and the Merchant he also is an imperfect character, prone to seeing himself as better than he really is. The Knight, who holds himself to have the best of breeding, often resorts to name calling and insults when he feels too much opposition, calling the Plowman 'stark knave' (706) and even a 'swyne' (II.932). It was this sort of behaviour that earned him a beating. The Merchant also often engages in similar behaviour, calling the Plowman a 'sklanderours chorle' (II.922). Regardless of how much the Plowman may have exaggerated his goodness or the sinfulness of his companions, there is much truth in what he says and his reasoning. Nobleness can be found in a plowman, and the opposite in persons from higher estates.

It is interesting that much of the sinful behaviour of the Knight and the Merchant is linked to their affluence. Wealth is also much commented upon in the play, particularly on how it relates to virtue. The Plowman makes clear that wealth does not help cultivate good virtuousness,

> grete possessions
> Make no gentylmen but gentyl condycyons.
> That is the cause and best reason why
> One should be callyd a gentylman truly.

(491–92)

Wealth is a troublesome entity, as the Plowman notes, an obsession with maintaining wealth can lead to covetousness and wrong behaviour as well as too much pride in one's birth. It can also cause much suffering for the poor honest folk that he represents,

> Some wyll suffer hys dettis unpayd to be
> And dye and jeopard hys soule, rather than he
> Wyll any of hys landys mynysh and empayre,
> That shuld after hys deth come to hys heyre.
> And some of them so proud be of theyre blod
> And use small vertew and doo lytyll good,
> But gyfe all theyre myndys and theyre study
> To opprese the pore people by tyrrany.
> And some of them thynk thys for a surete,
> It is the most honour to them that can be
> To be able for to doo extorcyon
> And to mayntayn it wythout punycyon.

(695–706)

Leaning on the tradition of honest complaint that the Plowman character descends from there can be no denying the truth of his words. Those who have much will always be more likely to engage in worldly conceits, as Felicity in the opening of *Magnificence* reminds us. Regardless of his uneasy opinion of wealth and its effect on virtuousness, the Plowman is aware that affluence and wealth are necessary for people of high office, as long as such powerful positions are awarded on the grounds of true noble character:

> And such people of vertuouse condycyons
> And no nother shuld be chosyn governours,
> And thei shuld have landys to maintain their honours.

> (II.776–78)

What the Plowman argues is that virtuousness should be rewarded and be the source of power rather than wealth and birth; only in this way can the people be sure of having good men in office to lead the country. Wealth and power are only safe in the hands of those who are already virtuous. This argument, undeniably underpinned by humanist ideals and understandings, is completely in line with the 'humanist slogan (adapted from chivalric sources) that virtue, not birth, was the true nobility.'[39] Thomas Starkey's *Dialogue between Reginald Pole and Thomas Lupset* was even so radical as to suggest that monarchy should be decided on personal merit rather than birth; understandably this work remained in manuscript form.[40] While most works were not as radical as Starkey's, there is an innate belief in many humanist works that merit should be the primary way in which offices are bestowed. In a less radical but still revolutionary work, More's Utopians divide wealth equally; 'Among them virtue has its reward, yet everything is shared equally, and all men live in plenty.'[41] Furthermore their prince is elected by representatives of the Utopians.[42]

The Plowman's position on virtue, wealth and power, although sound and reasonable, is met with vehement opposition. Both the Knight and the Merchant refuse to accept that their wealth or birth does not entitle them to power or make them more likely to be virtuous.

By the end of the play, the Plowman, through his clever argument, has shown that virtuous and noble behaviour can be found even in the most lowly of men, and the opposite in the highest. Wealth and birth guarantee nothing about true nobility. This proves too much for his two companions, who decide to withdraw from this debate in annoyance rather than see who is the victor. The withdrawal of the Knight and the Merchant from the debate shows the difficulties in trying to convince others of the value of humanist philosophies. In his parting monologue the Plowman takes the attitude that if a man is set in his beliefs then no amount of talking will change them, 'In effect it shall no more avayle / Than wyth a whyp to dryfe forth a snayle' (II.992–93). The Knight and the Merchant are not interested in a philosophy that would not easily show them to be noble. Unable to argue with the Plowman's superior reasoning, they retreat. Having excluded the Plowman, the Knight and the Merchant simply reaffirm their previous positions on all accounts. The Knight declares 'That gentylmen borne to land must nedys be / For suffycyency of most noble'(ll. 1076–77) and the Merchant affirms 'He that hath grete haboundaunce of ryches / May use lyberalyte and gentylnes' (1090–91). The only effect of the debate seems to have been that the Knight and the Merchant have realized that they share much more in common than they once believed for, at the end of the play, these enemies are now good friends—perhaps a social comment on the period where men of lowly birth were beginning to rub shoulders with the elite.

The Philosopher's epilogue serves to reaffirm the value of the humanist reasoning and argument that has been represented within the play; primarily that virtue is the only real decider of nobility. The very need for this epilogue seems to belie the problems of applying a newer way of thinking to established value systems. While the philosopher reaffirms that nobility is an inner virtue, unrelated to class or status, and wealth and birth guarantee nothing in terms of moral character, the entire play shows that however correct or good such reasoning is, it may meet much resistance. Effecting change may take more than a good argument. Much as Thomas More's *Utopia* reveals, customs can often halt development and change.[43] *Gentleness and Nobility* shows a clear awareness of the difficulties inherent in effecting change. Just as *Magnificence* laments the lack of reason in the conduct of life, *Gentleness* shows a similar frustration—reason is not always easy to accept however right it may be.

Through their texts the Tudor dramas sought to discuss contemporary issues before the elite of England. These plays show that despite the rising influence of humanist beliefs and the easy prominence of 'commoners' in high office, neither of these developments was taken as self-evidently right or good. Both *Magnificence* and *Gentleness and Nobility* interrogate the social, economic and political changes that were occurring in contemporary England. While thinking differently about the value of such changes, they do agree on some fundamental points—both see nobility as, at least in part, an inner virtue and they agree that wealth should be used in a moderate way that only serves to enhance the individual and society. Such similarities reveal the strength of traditional values and understandings for the English elite. The primary difference between the plays rests, surprisingly, not in their definitions of nobility or their theories on how wealth should be used, but in their faith in change. *Gentleness*' positive association with humanism, an intellectual trend associated with the rising middling classes, makes it accepting and accommodating of change, while *Magnificence* is the opposite. The result of this distinction between the plays is that *Gentleness* is tolerant of social mobility, the reorganization of power and intellectual development, while *Magnificence* is genuinely suspicious of ambitious individuals and refuses to allow them to be perceived as potentially noble in character. The divergent opinions and arguments of the plays show the willingness of the audience and the playwrights to explore the many viewpoints surrounding nobility and wealth. Yet, the fact that neither play can unproblematically incorporate its agenda and philosophy reveals the anxieties that change of any sort could elicit.

Notes

1   For a more detailed discussion on the link between Tudor drama, patrons and households see Suzanne Westfall, '"A Commonty a Christmas Gambold or a Tumbling Trick": Household Theater', in *A New History of Early English Drama*, eds John D. Cox and David Scott Kastan (New York: Columbia University Press, 1997).

2   H. L. R. Edwards, *Skelton: The Life and Times of an Early Poet* (London: Jonathan Cape, 1949), pp. 15–28.

3   For discussions on the dating of the play see Greg Walker, 'A Domestic Drama: John Skelton's 'Magnyfycence' and the Royal Household', in *Plays of Persuasion: Drama and Politics at the Court of Henry VIII* (Cambridge, New York: Cambridge University Press, 1991) and Leigh Winser, 'Skelton's Magnyfycence', *Renaissance Quarterly* 23:1 (1970).

4   Richard Axton, *European Drama of the Early Middle Ages* (London: Hutchinson, 1974), p. 20.

5   Axton, p. 20.

6   Greg Walker, *The Politics of Performance in Early Renaissance Drama* (Cambridge: Cambridge University Press, 1998), pp. 78–79.

7   Axton, p. 22.

8   Wolsey's first biographer, George Cavendish, wrote 'Trewethe it ys / Cardynall wolsey somtyme Archebisshope / of york / was an honest poore mans sonne born in Ipsewiche' (quoted from George Cavendish, *The Life and Death of Cardinal Wolsey*, ed. Richard S. Sylvester, *The Early English Text Society* (London, New York, Toronto: Oxford University Press, 1959), p. 4.

9   Thomas More was the son of a distinguished lawyer and judge, for more biographical information see Anthony Kenny, *Thomas More* (Oxford, New York: Oxford University Press, 1983), Louis L. Martz, *Thomas More: The Search for the Inner Man* (New Haven & London: Yale University, 1990) and Richard Marius, Thomas More (New York: Knopf, 1984).

10 David Bevington, *Tudor Drama and Politics* (Cambridge, Massachusetts: Harvard University Press, 1968), p. 44.

11 Colin Burrow, 'Literature and Politics under Henry VII and Henry VIII', in *The Cambridge History of Medieval English Literature*, ed. David Wallace (Cambridge: Cambridge University Press, 1999), p. 802.

12 For a detailed discussion of the sources and influences of *Gentleness and Nobility* see K.W. Cameron, *Authorship and Sources of 'Gentleness and Nobility'* (Raleigh, N.C.: Wilson and Partridge, 1941).

13 Cameron, p. 20.

14 Cameron, pp. 22–25.

15 See Trevor J. Saunders, ed., *Aristotle: The Politics, Penguin Classics* (London: Penguin, 1992).

16 See Book IV of Ernest Rhys, ed., *The Nicomachean Ethics of Aristotle* (London: Dent, 1955).

17 See William O. Harris, 'The Thematic Importance of Skelton's Allusion to Horace in Magnificence', *Studies in English Literature, 1500–1900* 3, no. 1. *The English Renaissance* (1963).

18 Harris, pp. 11–12.

19 Harris, p. 16.

20 Harris, pp. 11–12.

21 Martha Fletcher Bellinger, *A Short History of Drama* (New York: Henry Holt and Company, 1927), pp. 89–90.

22 All quotations for *Magnificence* taken from John Skelton, *Magnyfycence*, ed. Robert Lee Ramsay, Early English Text Society (Warwick Square: Oxford University Press, 1908 reprint, 2000).

23 See Walker, also Alistair Fox, *Politics and Literature in the Reign of Henry VII and VIII* (Cambridge: Blackwell, 1989), David Starkey et al., *The English Court: From the Wars of the Roses to the Civil War* (London: Longman, 1987), pp. 101–5.

24 See Skelton, 'Magnyfycence', pp. cvi–cxxviii.

25 See John Watkins, 'The Allegorical Theatre: Moralities, Interludes, and Protestant Drama', in *The Cambridge History of Medieval English Literature*, ed. David Wallace (Cambridge: Cambridge University Press, 1999).

26 John Scattergood, 'Skelton's Magnyfycence and the Tudor Royal Household', *Medieval English Theatre* 15 (1993).

27 Walker, p. 80.

28 Scattergood, pp. 21–22.

29 Ruth Kelso, 'Sixteenth Century Definitions of the Gentleman of England', *JEGP*, 24 (1925), as quoted in Cameron.

30 Phoebe Spinrad, '"Too Much Liberty": *Measure for Measure* and Skelton's *Magnyfycence*', *Modern Language Quarterly*, 60:4 (1999): 435.

31 *Middle English Dictionary, s.v.* 'largesse'.

32 Britton J. Harwood, 'Gawain and the Gift', *PMLA* 106:3 (1991): 484–85.

33 Axton, p. 23.

34 Axton, p. 22.

35 All quotations taken from John Rastell, 'Gentleness and Nobility', in *Three Rastell Plays,* ed. Richard Axton (Ipswich: Brewer, 1979).

36 Alison Hanham, *The Celys and Their World: An English Merchant Family of the Fifteenth Century* (Cambridge: Cambridge University Press, 1985), p. 3.

37 Erasmus' *Institutio Christiani Principis* and *Declamatio de Pueris Statim ac Liberaliter Instituendis* both see education, not birth, as vital to cultivating virtue and goodness. Chapter VIII of *Pueris* advocates that the rich should help the poor in any way possible to gain an education.

38 See Kelso.

39 Burrow, p. 802.

40 Burrow, p. 802.

41 George M. Logan and Robert M. Adams eds, *More: Utopia, Cambridge Texts in the History of Political Thought* (Cambridge: Cambridge University Press, 1989), p. 38.
42 *Utopia*, pp. 48–49.
43 Burrow, p. 804.

Cosmos and History:
Shakespeare's Representation of Nature
and Rebellion in *Henry IV Part One*

Alicia Marchant

'Diseased nature oftentimes breaks forth
In strange eruptions; ...'

(*Henry IV Part One*, III.i.27–31)

In *Henry IV Part One* kingship and rebellion are described via a complex spatial dichotomy of interior and exterior, of centre and periphery. The various central points of power in the play (King Henry, his kingship and Jerusalem) are all depicted as under threat from peripheral forces. In addition, rebellion is represented as a disturbance not just of the political but of the natural order. Nature and natural order are central motifs in Shakespeare's *Henry IV Part One*, a play which tells of rebellion and disloyalty against an anointed (although arguably not legitimate) monarch. Strange weather and diabolical acts, events contrary to the laws of nature are recorded (and sometimes mocked) throughout the play, and culminate in the symbolic tripartite dissection of England's landscape on a map. The England of *Henry IV Part One* is a place where nature and the laws that govern it have been dislocated from their conceptual centre. Interestingly, this representation of the reign of Henry IV (1399–1413)[1] to some extent mirrors the picture of England presented by the authors of the so-called 'universal' chronicles[2] of the early fifteenth-century, who likewise interpreted contemporary events in the light of strange natural phenomena (such as comets and the migration of birds).

Thus one possible way of interpreting the 'strange eruptions' described in *Henry IV Part One* is as a remnant of the earlier universal history chronicle tradition whose use can be traced to Holinshed and Shakespeare; something which has not been sufficiently investigated. This article aims to place Shakespeare as at the end of a long tradition of historical writing, rather than to tie him to a particular chronicler. Beyond this I propose to explore connections between events recorded in Shakespeare's *Henry IV Part One* and the universal histories written in the early fifteenth century and the *mappae mundi* which frequently accompanied them; less in an attempt to determine the sources of Shakespeare's history plays than to chart the conceptual centre against which the strange eruptions of rebellion and nature are said to occur.

I. A Fine Balance: Nature, Rebellion and King Henry

'Things fall apart; the centre cannot hold;
Mere anarchy is loosed upon the world'

(William Butler Yeats, 'The Second Coming')

In *Henry IV Part One* rebellion is described as a series of tensions between the centre and the periphery. The imagery Henry uses to entice the rebelling Worcester back to the crown is a good example of this:

… Will you again unknit
This churlish knot of all-abhorred war
And move in that obedient orb again
Where you did give a fair and natural light,
And be no more an exhaled meteor,
A prodigy of fear and a portent
Of broached mischief to the unborn times?

(V.i.15–21)

Loyalty to the crown and legality are described as revolving around the centre, as natural, spherical in shape, centripetal,[3] static and regular. In contrast the rebel Worcester's position is peripheral; as an 'exhaled meteor', his activity is unnatural, centrifugal and disorganized. Rebellion is marked as disruptive and chaotic.

Henry and his kingship form one central point in *Henry IV Part One*, Jerusalem forms another. Henry himself acknowledges his centrality and encourages the use of this ideology. Henry states plainly that his accession has brought peace and stability to the nation, so that now 'England can march all one way and be no more opposed' (I.i.14–15). The 'England' of which he speaks is centred upon himself and his governance; the time is right, he says, for a crusade to Jerusalem. His belief rests on a notion of unity and stability which had previously not been achieved and one which allows him to plan to leave England with the (assumed) knowledge that the nation will hold strong in his absence. That Henry should see his position as king as spherical or as an 'orb' is significant within the context of legitimacy. The orb was a powerful symbol presented to the newly-crowned king at his coronation. Its shape was symbolic of the Earth itself, and represented the king's responsibility as a secular leader to protect humankind.

In *Henry IV Part One* there is a series of tensions constructed between the centre and the periphery, indicating a disturbance in the natural balance of the cosmos. Messages coming into Henry's court (the physical focal point of King Henry's nation) concerning Mortimer's revolt are described as 'loaden with heavy news' (I.i.37) and the Percies' failure to hand over Scottish prisoners is described by Westmoreland as the coming of 'uneven and unwelcome news' (I.i.50). The terminology used expresses a downward pulling movement and as we are told, King Henry himself believes Mortimer's attempts at fighting Owen Glendower were half-hearted and rebellious, to which Hotspur sharply replies, 'Revolted Mortimer! He never did fall off, my sovereign liege, / But by the chance of war' (I.iii.93–95). Movement downwards is not desirable, rather it is a trait of rebellion. It is difficult to get news to the centre from the periphery; it is burdened, 'loaden' and heavy, requiring a great deal of effort. Communications are not free and even. However it also raises the issue of the effectiveness of Henry as a centre; the news coming from the periphery to the centre is out of balance within the context of a centripetal universe, indicating that he too is out of balance, a point to which we will return in a moment.

In *Henry IV Part One* the king's weakened position due to rebellion is illustrated via a series of changes in nature; nature is out of balance, the scales are tipping, and this is expressed either through excesses in nature or through infertility. Henry describes England's landscape as damaged and parched by war, saying that 'No more the thirsty entrance of this soil / Shall daub her lips with her own children's blood' (I.i.5–6). In anger at Mortimer's defection, Henry is determined to let the rebel starve on barren mountains (I.iii.89). Mortimer has come to be associated with the barren mountain landscape, thereby establishing a contrast between the health and the fertility of the landscape and his rebellion. Owen Glendower's description of his own birth uses a similar image of the desolation and emptiness of the mountains, '… at my birth / The front of heaven was full of fiery shapes, / The goats ran from the mountains …' (III.i.35–37). Wasteland is connected to rebellion and to the rebel leaders particularly. Nature is vulnerable. There are several examples in *Henry IV Part One* of the landscape being changed through rebellion or acts of war by anthropogenic means. Hotspur's threat of building a series of canals to divert the river Trent would potentially distort the natural landscape. King Henry too describes the stability he believes his accession as king brings to England by saying, 'no more shall trenching war channel her fields' (I.i.6).

On the other hand there is an immense stimulation of nature brought on by rebellion and war and as Hotspur tells us, 'Diseased nature oftentimes breaks forth / In strange eruptions; …' (III.i.27–31). Owen Glendower tells us that at his birth there was what could be read as an earthquake: 'At my nativity / The front of heaven was full of fiery shapes. Of burning cressets; and at my birth / The frame and huge foundation of the earth / Shaked like a coward' (III.i.12–16). Indeed meteors and comets are referred to on several occasions in *Henry IV Part One*; Henry describes the civil war that has raged in England as 'like the meteors of a troubled heaven' (I.i.10); Worcester is referred to as a 'meteor' (V.i.19) that has been expelled from the central orb. Henry too desires to be wondered at like a comet (III.ii.47–49). Weather too is stimulated by rebellion, most particularly in Wales. Glendower tells us that 'Three times hath Henry Bolingbroke made head / Against my power; thrice from the banks of Wye / And sandy-bottomed Severn have I sent him / Bootless home and weather-beaten back' (III.i.62–65). Underlying this is the suggestion that Glendower defeated King Henry with the aid of weather, implying that he has the ability to contravene the laws of nature.

Wales is described as a diabolical and unbalanced space, a place of rebellion where nature has been transgressed. The Welsh rebel Owen Glendower's use of magic is a source of great discomfort for King Henry, and he refers to him as 'that great magician, damned Glendower' (I.iii.82). Likewise Falstaff refers to him as 'that devil Glendower' (II.iv.359–60).[4] Owen Glendower is introduced as 'irregular and wild Glendower' (I.i.40) which immediately describes his place in the periphery, away from the regular centre, a point which is frequently reinforced; we are told Owen Glendower has been marked as extraordinary and is 'not in the roll of common men' (III.i.41). In contrast, Hotspur's reading of Glendower's magical abilities is very different; he mocks Glendower and disregards his assertions as futile. While there are many layers of meaning to Hotspur's indifference to Glendower, one purpose may well be to emphasize the disorganization of the rebellion and to present the periphery in which rebellion sits as chaotic.

Likewise Owen Glendower's supporters carry out acts which are against nature, this time through the transformation of the body. Welsh women perform atrocities on the dead bodies of the English soldiers after the battle of Bryn Glas, in an act described as 'beastly, shameless transformation'. The whole passage reads:

> But yesternight, when all athwart there came
> A post from Wales, loaden with heavy news,
> Whose worst was that the noble Mortimer,
> Leading the men of Herefordshire to fight
> Against the irregular and wild Glendower
> Was by the rude hands of that Welshman taken
> A thousand of his people butchered
> Upon whose dead corpse there was such misuse,
> Such beastly shameless transformation
> By those Welshwomen done, as may not be
> Without much shame retold or spoken of.

(I.i.36–46)

In this scene the Welsh transgression is not merely a theory, but has been put into practice and has resulted in the transformation of English bodies. This highlights the complexity of imagery used to create the centre and periphery in *Henry IV Part One*. The Welsh women de-nature the bodies of the English soldiers and although we are not told exactly what occurred, Owen Glendower and his Welsh followers are set up as the direct opposite of Henry's central point; Glendower and his followers are not normal, but rather barbaric and 'rude', irregular and uncivilized, with the ability to metamorphose the human body, use magic and conjure up bad weather.[5] Glendower is centrifugal in intention and centripetal in effect; his disruption of weather and the atrocity perpetrated by the women is the cause of a great scurry homewards towards Henry. However Owen Glendower's actions result in the strengthening of Henry's centre, as the soldiers are drawn towards him. The rebellion as a whole is described as abnormal, oppositional, unbalanced and deviant from the central point or space.

II. *Henry IV Part One* and Universal Chronicles

Why then does Shakespeare use such specific constructions of rebellion as peripheral and chaotic? It is here that I would like to draw some parallels between the representation of rebellion and its connection to nature in *Henry IV Part One* and in universal chronicles of the reign of Henry IV.

It is possible to connect Shakespeare to these universal chronicles by mapping the historiography of Henry IV's reign between 1399 and 1598. It is well documented that Shakespeare utilized Ralph Holinshed's *Chronicle of Henry IV*,[6] published in 1577,[7] for the events of Henry IV's reign. However, modern scholars focus on the importance of Holinshed to the detriment of explorations of the earlier chroniclers' impact, in particular chronicles written contemporaneously with the events described in the play. Of particular note in this group of neglected chronicles is the work of Thomas Walsingham (d. 1422),[8] and the unknown writers of the *Continuatio Eulogii* completed c. 1413[9] and the *Historia Vitae et Regni Ricardi Secundi* (henceforth the *Historia Vitae*).[10] For instance, in his *Narrative and Dramatic Sources of Shakespeare*, Geoffrey Bullough does not mention this inheritance at all or its impact on the narrative of *Henry IV Part One*,[11] even though several scenes used by Shakespeare have come from these earlier chroniclers' works, in one instance unaltered, which we will look at in a moment. The historiography between Henry IV's reign and the composition of *Henry IV Part One* has not been sufficiently considered.

The influence of the chronicler Thomas Walsingham is illustrative; he was the most prominent and utilized of all the earlier sources for the reign of Henry IV; Walsingham's chronicles were used as authorities by contemporary writers such as the authors of the *Continuatio Eulogii* and the *Historia Vitae*.[12] Of the next generation of chroniclers, John Capgrave (d. 1464) relied heavily on Walsingham,[13] and after him the Tudor chroniclers Edward Hall (d. 1547)[14] and John Stow (d. 1605)[15] are known to have used Walsingham. Holinshed in turn drew on Hall and Stow, and Shakespeare used Holinshed.[16] This is a very linear case study, and does not take into account the wider influence of chroniclers who relied on Walsingham, thereby overlooking one branch of Walsingham's influence. And although one would be going too far in suggesting that Shakespeare read Walsingham, there is a tenable derivation from Walsingham in Shakespeare's *Henry IV Part One*.

It is possible to identify elements of Thomas Walsingham's influence, direct or indirect, in *Henry IV Part One*. Shakespeare's usage of the Welsh women performing atrocities on the bodies of the English soldiers is one such historical remnant which has been passed down from the earlier chroniclers. Describing the origins of Shakespeare's information for this passage, Terence Hawkes states that 'the source of this information is clearly Holinshed'.[17] In the most recent edition of *Henry IV Part I*, David Scott Kastan quotes from Holinshed in his commentary.[18] However, if we take it back further to the contemporary chroniclers of Henry IV's reign, it can be seen that the ultimate source was in fact Thomas Walsingham (d. 1422) who first recorded this incident at the Battle of Bryn Glas. Walsingham writes:

> When more than a thousand men had been killed from our countries, this crime had been perpetrated; unheard of in all the ages, for the women of the Welsh, after the conflict, cut off the genitalia of the slain. They placed the genitals, in the mouths of some slain ones. And they made the testicles hang down from the chin, and they pressed the noses into the bottoms of the same men; and they did not allow the bodies of the slain to be given their last rites without a great price.[19]

The image of the innocent soldier naked and helpless is an emotive one across the two different time periods. In his account Walsingham constructs this vivid image through a series of counterbalances, including perpetrators and victims, deceased and living, moral and corrupt and more immediately female and male, Welsh and English. The end result is the construction of the Welsh as harsh, cruel and uncivilized, particularly emphasized by the deeds of their womenfolk. Polydore Virgil and Edward Hall's descriptions of these events echo Walsingham. Likewise, Shakespeare uses this episode to construct the otherness of the Welsh, who we are told are 'rude' and their leader 'wild and irregular'. However, Shakespeare is not explicit in his re-telling of the incident but rather allows it to pass without the sordid detail, which acts to reinforce the civility of the narrator Westmoreland and his audience, the royal court of Henry.[20] It would be shameful to their ears to hear it. The Welsh women are, if you like, a spring-board from which to describe the civility of the English. Whilst the natural world around them may be unstable, English human nature is constant and consistent.

In the universal chronicle tradition rebellion against the body of the king or of the nation more generally is accompanied by a series of movements in nature.

Walsingham, the *Continuatio Eulogii*, and the *Historia Vitae* all record a ripple of magical activity and supernatural events occurring as a result of the Percy, Glendower and Mortimer rebellion. For example, from the initiation of the Welsh revolt in September 1400 to the death of Hotspur in 1403 the *Continuatio Eulogii* records a comet, storms and thunder, and an eclipse interspersed with the record of the revolt.[21] For the same time frame, Walsingham records a comet, an appearance of the devil in Danbury, Essex, and monsters of dark appearance in the woods near Bedford and Biggleswade.[22] Rebellion is depicted as against the laws of nature, and so movements in nature, and strange natural phenomena, are signs or evidence of a shift in the natural balance of the cosmos.

Nature responds to rebellion. Comets and meteorites are two examples of natural phenomena in *Henry IV Part One* which are used to establish Henry's centrality, as discussed earlier; Henry describes the civil disunity of England before his accession as 'like the meteors of a troubled heaven' (I.i.10); Worcester is referred to as an 'exhaled meteor' (V.i.19) that had been expelled from the central orb. Meteorites, comets and shooting stars had long been considered signs of impending war, famine and plague, and were read in primarily a metaphoric framework rather than a literal and scientific one;[23] they were signs of imbalance and disturbance in the natural equilibrium of the cosmos. Like Mortimer's 'falling off' from Henry's 'orb', meteors and falling stars too were considered to have a downward movement, falling towards the earth. They were irregular, came from the periphery of the cosmos and were considered to be movements in nature and signs of impending problems.[24] So when Worcester is likened to a meteor there is an interesting transferral: the disruption which Worcester embodies is likened to the natural sign that would normally signify that disruption.

It is significant and somewhat curious that there is no comet to signify the battle at Shrewsbury in *Henry IV Part One*, given the universal chronicle heritage. Shakespeare is re-writing a tradition; Thomas Walsingham records a comet in 1402, which he describes as signifying the shedding of blood in Wales and also in Northumbria,[25] most certainly a foreshadowing of the Northumbrian-based Percy rebellion. In the *Continuatio Eulogii* the unknown writer records two comets; one in 1402 and the other in 1403.[26] The first is described as being 'a horrible sight in the west, whose great flame rose on high'.[27] From the chronicler's position in England, the comet in the west would have pointed towards Wales. When a comet is mentioned in *Henry IV Part One* it is by King Henry telling his son Prince Hal of his desire to be recognized and celebrated in his youth, so that '… like a comet, I was wondered at / That men would tell their children "This is he!" / Others would say, "Where? Which is Bolingbroke?" (III.ii.47–49).' Henry desires to be an icon of change. Henry is a problematic centre; he tells us himself that he was not raised to be king. Henry deposes the anointed King Richard and in doing so creates a disturbance of the natural balance. Henry's questionable legitimacy is expressed though the alignment of himself with a comet, the very sign of cosmic disruption. His kingship is tenuous, he is not the central gazed-at figure that he ought to be, and this is primarily because of his stigma of non-legitimacy as king.

III. Jerusalem, Cartographic Space and Universal Chronicles

Jerusalem is a significant centre in *Henry IV Part One*; it is the idealized centre of Henry's world, and also of the cosmos as it was understood historically and geographically. Parts one and two of *Henry IV* are framed by the notion of Jerusalem as the object of Henry's desire. *Henry IV Part One* begins with the king's ambition to go on crusade to the Holy Land and at his death Henry asks to be moved to the Jerusalem Chamber at Westminster so that 'in Jerusalem shall Harry die' (*2 Henry IV*, IV.iii.370). Once more comparisons to universal history and to the *mappae mundi* which frequently accompany them are instructive in understanding the significance of Jerusalem in *Henry IV Part One*.

There is a strong connection between cartography and history in the Middle Ages; as Evelyn Edson has documented, there was a long tradition of cartography in medieval Western Europe and of universal chroniclers utilising maps. [28] Chroniclers such as Otto of Friesing (d. 1158), Matthew Paris (d. 1259), and Ranulf Higden (d. c. 1363; Figure 2) included *mappae mundi* in their historical texts, which served as visual accompaniments to the chronicle narrative. Further parallels can be drawn between the nature of the information that both of them contain: cartographic images represent visually (sometimes with labels) the more significant

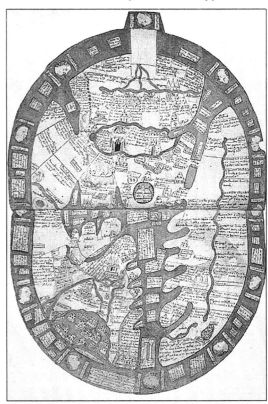

Figure 2: Ranulf Higden's Map. Higden's *Mappa Mundi* from his *Polychronicon*, B.M. MS. Royal 14.C.IX flv–F2

historical events which are documented in the universal chronicles. There are many references to events of history, both biblical and secular, on later maps such as Ranulf Higden's *mappa mundi*[29] of the fourteenth century. For example, Higden illustrates the Mount of Olives and Eden, Alexander the Great, and there is a gap in the Red Sea (literally coloured red) where Moses and the Israelites crossed.[30] Places of religious importance to Higden's contemporary era, such as Rome, are represented via pictures of large churches. In England monasteries too are depicted. Thus geography (as a visual representation of the natural cosmos) and history (as a chronological record of human endeavours) are interconnected. These events and places of human history are displayed within a cosmological framework in which nature and landscape features such as mountains, rivers and coastlines are depicted. Maps, such as Higden's, depict human history, their wars and rebellions as being inextricably linked to the landscape.

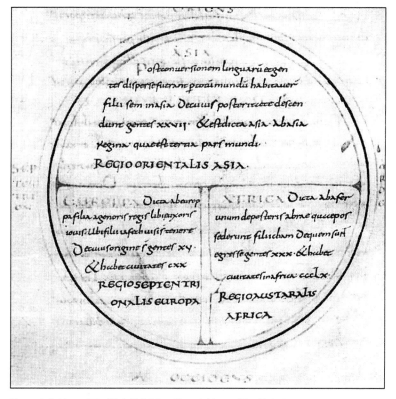

Figure 3: Isidore of Seville's T-O Map. From Isidore of Seville's *De Natura Rerum*, Burgerbibliothek Bern, cod. 417, f.88v Courtesy of the Burgerbibliothek, Bern.

Medieval maps were predominately spiritual, rather than having any practically geographical use.[31] Medieval cartography is oriented to emphasize the importance of the Holy Land. Isidore of Seville's T-O Map[32] (Figure 3) is oriented with Asia at the top, to emphasize the importance of that region for human history; it was here that the histories recorded in the Old and New Testaments were played out. Higden's *mappa mundi* depicts Jerusalem in the middle of the cosmos, and the city is emphasized by the use of bright colours. On Isidore's image there is recorded under each of the three continents (Asia, Europe and Africa) the name of one of Noah's sons, who were thought to have populated these three zones after the Great Flood in *Genesis* 10,[33] so for example Asia was populated by Sem, Europe by Japheth (spelt Jafeth on the map) and Africa by Cham.[34] While Isidore's map was produced long before that of Higden, for example, he was considered to be an authoritative source for later *mappae mundi*; Isidore's map exhibits clearly the structure of medieval cartography which underlies maps such as Ranulf Higden's. East is always at the top, Jerusalem is in or very near to the middle and away from the centre, in the peripheral regions are areas of unknown and undocumented lands, animals, and people, a point to which I will return in a moment.

Universal history and cartography construct strict boundaries of inclusion and exclusion.[35] What is displayed on the *mappae mundi*, and likewise included in universal chronicles is the collective history of Christian humankind; excluded are non-Christian histories and regions, other than some classical history, which have no relevance within the context of human salvation history. History has long been viewed as something which defines humans from brutes; Henry of Huntingdon (d. 1155) commented 'the knowledge of past events ... forms a main distinction between brutes and rational creatures.'[36] One of the purposes of historical composition in the Middle Ages was to document humanity's movement towards salvation, in the light of the fall of humankind in the Garden of Eden.[37]

The Holy Land was an important focal point for Christendom both spatially (it is in the middle of a defined world) and chronologically. The narrative of chronicle history was divided into sections or *aetates* (ages), most commonly into six ages; the first age was from Adam to Noah and the sixth age from the birth of Christ to the contemporary age.[38] While the life of Christ is not the mid-point of the history of the world (indeed it begins the last sixth of world history), it is figuratively central to salvation history and was used as a chronological marker; time is calculated from the birth of Christ in AD 1. Universal chronicles were structured in a strict chronological fashion and use referential dates in the margin. The year (*Anno Domini*) is consistently used at the start of each new year both in the text and in the margins, and is frequently scattered throughout also; thus documenting the distance between the life of Christ and the contemporary period. This chronological thread unites the narrative of history; by association the Holy Land and Jerusalem in particular as the main city in the Holy Land and as the place where Christ was tried and crucified, results in the construction of the Holy Land and Jerusalem as central loci of the narrative.

The king, like Jerusalem, is an important centre in universal history with regard to chronology. Given the massive undertaking that writing a universal history entails, it was inevitable that the composition of history would be reduced from a broad history of the whole known world to one which focused on particular nations or kingdoms *(regna)*.[39] Whilst maintaining the strict chronological sequence, it was typical for sections to be titled after a particular king and to refer to the years since the coronation of the king. For example, in the *Continuatio Eulogii*, the year 1402 begins with '[i]n the year of our lord 1402, and the third year of the king ...'.[40] The king, Jerusalem, and the history of the world are interconnected.

King Henry is drawn to Jerusalem; Henry's desire to go on crusade to Jerusalem is of a personal nature: he craves spiritual fulfilment and forgiveness. It is a penitential journey, we are told in *Richard II*, 'to wash this blood from my guilty hand' *(Richard II*, V.vi. 49–50). Henry's yearning for Jerusalem can be read as a desire for his own re-centring; Henry is unsatisfied and is incomplete and decentred. His past misdeeds have left him tainted and it is only through the freeing of Jerusalem from Muslims, or 'pagans' as Henry refers to them (I.i.24), that he can perform contrition, receive absolution and then restore his own spiritual balance.

While Henry is a problematic centre (he has a stigma of non-legitimacy) so too is the overrun Jerusalem, which can no longer function (in real and practical terms at least) as the centre of the Christian cosmos. In *Henry IV Part One* Jerusalem needs Henry and Henry needs Jerusalem and so it would appear that it is only through the meeting of the two central points that both can be re-centred, thereby restoring natural balance in the cosmos.[41] Henry's penitence is important for the whole of Christendom; it is through Henry's remorse, self-evaluation and self-reflection that the cosmic balance could conceivably be re-instated.

However, rebellion prevents Henry from going on crusade to free Jerusalem. On announcing his intention to go on crusade, Henry is at once diverted by 'heavy news' of Mortimer's defection to Owen Glendower. It is a dislocation of Henry's political and personal ambitions and reflects the de-centring effect of rebellion; Henry can no longer travel to Jerusalem and receive absolution for his part in Richard's demise, but must fight off a challenge to his legitimacy as king. The choice is entirely out of his control, and he is left ineffectual as king. It is significant that it is news of Mortimer's rebellion and not Glendower's or the Percies' revolt which prevents Henry from reaching the centre at Jerusalem; Mortimer's younger nephew, Edmund Mortimer, with whom he is commonly confused, had a solid claim to the throne.[42] Henry's position is revealed to be tenuous and his options for rectifying his predicament are severely limited. And while Henry does finally reach Jerusalem, it is only in death.

In being moved into the Jerusalem Chamber, Henry is able to die in an abstract or replacement Jerusalem, which is located at Westminster, the administrative heart of his nation, where the laws are enacted, thus bringing together the play's primary centres.

It is of considerable importance that the rebels plot their rebellion out on a map;[43] the scene makes an explicit connection between the cosmos, nature and rebellion. In the most significant and deliberate act of rebellion against Henry, the rebels Hotspur, Mortimer and Glendower divide England between themselves, formulating a tripartite division of England, reminiscent of the division of the world into three by earlier medieval cartographers like Isidore of Seville (Figure 3).[44] We are told:

> The Archdeacon hath divided it
> Into three limits very equally:
> England, from Trent and Severn hitherto,
> By south and east is to my part assigned;
> All westward, Wales beyond the Severn shore
> And all the fertile land within that bound,
> To Owen Glendower; and dear coz, to you
> The remnant northward laying off from Trent.

(III.i.70–77)

The natural world is dissected into three and through this action the periphery becomes central; England is re-oriented to reflect the rebels' ambitions, thereby removing Henry's sphere of influence. On the map England is both a nation and a natural landscape; attention is given to the natural features, rivers particularly, in placing the boundaries, and to fertility which is the cause of tensions between Hotspur and Glendower. Hotspur contends that the tripartite division 'cuts me from the best of all my land' (III.i.97), reiterating Mortimer's 'fertile' of line 75. A similar notion is evident in Hotspur's ideas of changing the landscape via a channel to alter the course of the River Trent and thus increase his territory to include the fertile lands of Nottinghamshire and Lincolnshire, 'I'll have the current in this place damm'd up / And here the smug and silver Trent shall run / In a new channel, fair and evenly' (III.i.99–101). Glendower is horrified at the thought. To alter the map and its newly constructed boundaries is one thing, but to change the landscape is quite another. Glendower recognizes the significance of altering the landscape and reiterates in three different ways 'I'll not have it altered' (III.i.113). For Glendower this is a sign of future problems that Hotspur could potentially bring to the tripartite alliance; Hotspur could rebel and disregard their plans, which he does end up doing and dying in the process, a point to which we will return.

IV. *Henry IV Part One*, Cosmos and History

The conventions of time and space with Jerusalem as centre point evident in Shakespeare's *Henry IV Part One* are parallel to a cartographical tradition which is earlier than Shakespeare's era. *Mappae mundi* were linked to universal history, or at least, concepts of a universal history. By Shakespeare's day cartography had become more accurate and technical. Making a case study of *Othello*, Christopher Wortham has argued that the re-orientation of cartography from its spiritual and conceptual framework (used by Isidore of Seville and Ranulf Higden) to a more scientific one for the purposes of travel led to anxieties and disorientation about the centrality of Jerusalem.[45] Jerusalem was no longer the centre point in these maps, nor were they oriented with east at the top.

Shakespeare clearly had in mind for *Henry IV Part One* a cosmological structure which was of the old and spiritual variety of cartography rather than the newer more geographically aware maps which broke with the conventions of the T-O map. In *Henry IV Part One* there is no anxiety about Jerusalem's centrality; it is undoubtedly a central point which draws Henry to it. Indeed Jerusalem is pivotal to Henry's personal salvation and his legitimacy as monarch. Hotspur, Glendower and Mortimer too use the conventions of the T-O map when they dissect England and Wales between themselves in three, reminiscent of the tripartite world of Isidore of Seville (Figure Two). However it is here that tensions between the old and the new cartography can be seen. The archbishop, we are told, divides England so that the largest and most dominant third (Hotspur's Northumberland) is at the top of the map, just was it is in Isidore's *mappa mundi*. However there has been a re-orientation so that now north is in the place of east at the top of the map, just like the contemporary maps of Shakespeare's era.

Shakespeare too recognizes and uses the earlier spiritual *mappae mundi's* time-space devices. As David Read has argued, the tripartite map of Mortimer, Hotspur and Owen Glendower is used by Shakespeare to foreshadow future events; the course of the rebellion is played out and enacted upon it.[46] The map is concrete evidence of the future plans of the rebels; Hotspur's attempts at changing the map indicate his erratic nature. It is inevitable that Hotspur will try to alter the plans, just as he did the River Trent, and that he will be killed in the process. Subsequently Hotspur is killed at Shrewsbury when he disregards the plans, and Owen Glendower is unable to come to his aid. In this example the map represents a piece of history in the making. This is parallel to the representation of time on the *mappae mundi*. Time is collapsed and past and present events are represented in one visual image. As the *mappa mundi* of Ranulf Higden shows, maps contain events from different time periods. For example Noah from the Old Testament (whose ark is depicted on Mount Ararat to the left of Jerusalem) and in the lower part of the same image appear monasteries in England of much more recent foundation. Events of different eras are projected into one temporal reality.

The collapsed historical chronology of the *mappae mundi*, which places the distant past alongside the recent past and the contemporary in one visual image, results in a spatial articulation of centre and periphery based on notions of civility and rationality. While Jerusalem forms the centre and is a focal point of history and cosmology, the frontier regions of Christendom occupy the periphery and are allochronic, existing in another time and space. Pockets of strange beings are frequently represented on edges of maps, usually in the region of Africa. The Psalter map of c. 1250 and the Hereford *Mappa Mundi* of c. 1290 are good illustrations of this.[47] Dragons, giants and blemmyes (people with their faces on their chests and no heads) are illustrated in the peripheral regions; they are deviant human forms, not made in God's image, which was considered important within the context of human salvation.[48]

Shakespeare draws on this very specific spatial articulation of civility in *Henry IV Part One* to construct the alterity of the Welsh, and most particularly the Welsh women.[49] Wales occupies the peripheral space within Britain, it is distant from the centre point of Henry's nation, based around Westminster, and is farther west from Jerusalem than England; Shakespeare's Wales is a place of magic and strange weather and the inhabitants of Wales personify their nation space. Collectively the Welsh in *Henry IV Part One* are constructed as barbaric, disorganized and rude, and while the bodily features of the Welsh are not deviant, they do transgress the limitations of individuals by transforming other people's bodies. Indeed to further emphasize the peripheral position of the Welsh, Hotspur mocks Owen Glendower's concept of history, saying to Mortimer:

> ... Sometime he angers me
> With telling me of the moldwarp and the ant,
> Of the dreamer Merlin and his prophecies,
> And of a dragon and a finless fish,
> A clip-winged griffin and a moulten raven
> A couching lion and a ramping cat,
> And such a deal of skimble-skamble stuff
> As puts me from my faith ...
>
>   (III.i.144–51)

In direct contrast Hotspur's historiography is centred on chronological progression and fact, rather than myth and legend; he desires his name to '... fill up chronicles in time to come' (I.iii.170). For Hotspur, Owen Glendower's historiography is unsuitable and unreliable, which is significant within the context of cartographic space and universal history, and its strategy of inclusion and exclusion. The Welsh women are constructed as the 'marginal' within the marginal Welsh community so to speak;

they remain unnamed and are certainly not given individual qualities.[50] Indeed they form a community which can be aligned with the discourse of witches; the Welsh women steal men's private parts, an act to which there is an entire chapter devoted in the *Malleus Maleficarum*.[51] The Welsh women have transgressed the norms of social behaviour. They are associated with strange weather occurrences, thus formulating a link between rebellion, witches and the weather.[52] The Welsh women serve to highlight the barbarity of the Welsh whilst simultaneously constructing the centrality and civility of the English.

V. Conclusion

The representation of rebellion and kingship in *Henry IV Part One* is constructed in part through a system of spatial and conceptual oppositions between various centres (King Henry, his kingship and Jerusalem) and a wild and unpredictable periphery. Through analysis of the devices of universal history and cartography it is possible to see clearly that the major tensions of *Henry IV Part One* are articulated through spatial patterns which are derived from this very tradition. Similarly adopted from the chronicle tradition are the images of disordered nature and the disordering of the human body, though this last is only alluded to in Shakespeare's play. These sorts of comparisons are not an end in themselves, but serve to elucidate the creative selections of materials which Shakespeare makes. While analysing texts in terms of centre and periphery is not new, it can be revealing to consider how these spatial relationships develop from similar relationships in universal history and *mappae mundi*. Analysing these creative selections encourages us to look beyond Holinshed for Shakespeare's sources and inspirations and to see the creative and dramatic uses to which Shakespeare puts them.

Notes

My thanks to the anonymous reader of this article; the editors of this collection; and to R. S. White, Philippa Maddern and Susan Broomhall who made numerous helpful suggestions as to how this article might be improved.

1   Throughout this essay I use 'Henry' to denote the character in *Henry IV Part One* and 'Henry IV' to denote the historical figure.
2   Universal chronicles were a genre of medieval historiography considered to be temporally and geographically universal; covering the history of the known world. Universal history starts with the creation of the world in Genesis and proceeds to the contemporary age of the chronicler. For further discussion see Michael I. Allen 'Universal History 300–1000: Origins and Western Developments', in Deborah Mauskopf Deliyannis, ed., *Historiography in the Middle Ages* (Leiden, The Netherlands: Brill, 2003), pp. 17–42;

Rolf Sprandel 'World Historiography in the Late Middle Ages' in Mauskopf Deliyannis, ed. *Historiography in the Middle Ages*, pp. 157–80; also see below note 40.

3 For a definition of the terms centripetal and centrifugal in relation to language, see M. M. Bakhtin, *The Dialogic Imagination*, trans. C. Emerson and M. Holquist (Austin: University of Texas Press, 1981), pp. 272–73. I use these terms to refer not just to physical movement to and from a centre but rather to movement which also signifies support for or revolt from that centre as a position of power.

4 Little is revealed about Glendower other than a few details of his life and education: that he studied at an English court and can play the harp (III.i.119–20), the purpose of which may be to emphasize how far he has fallen from the centre.

5 I shall examine the nexus between weather, rebellion, witches, and changing of the male body by witches in Section IV: *Henry IV Part One*, Cosmos and History.

6 Ralph Holinshed, *Chronicles of England, Scotland and Ireland*, ed. Henry Ellis (London, 1807–08).

7 Available as *Shakespeare's Holinshed: the Chronicle and the Historical Plays Compared*, ed. W. G. Boswell-Stone (London: Chatto and Windus, 1907).

8 Thomas Walsingham's two main chronicles are the *Chronica Majora* which he began in 1376 which is printed in the Rolls Series under the title of *Annales Ricardi Secundi et Henrici Quarti, Regum Angliae, Chronica Monasterii S. Albani*, ed. Henry Thomas Riley, 3 vols (London: Rolls Series, 1866) and the *Historia Anglicana* printed as *Thomae Walsingham, Quondam Monachi S. Albani, Historia Anglicana*, ed. Henry Thomas Riley, 2 vols (London: Rolls Series, 1863).

9 This is printed in vol.3 of the *Eulogium (Historiarum sive Temporis): Chronicon ab Orbe Condito Usque ad Annum Domini M.CCC.LXVI., A Monacho Quodam Malmesburiensi Exaratum. Accedunt Continuationes duae, Quarum una ad annum M.CCCC.XIII. Altera ad Annum M.CCC.XC. Perducta Est*, ed. Frank Scott Haydon (London: Rolls Series, 1858), pp. 333–421.

10 Printed as *Historia Vitae et Regni Ricardi Secundi*, ed. George Stow (Pennsylvania: University of Pennsylvania Press, 1977).

11 Geoffrey Bullough, *Narrative and Dramatic Sources of Shakespeare, Volume IV Later English History Plays King John, Henry IV, Henry V, Henry VIII* (London: Routledge, 1962). For example, Bullough mentions in passing Thomas Walsingham on pp. 159 and 169, but goes no further than recording his name. The *Continuatio Eulogii* is not mentioned at all, nor is the *Historia Vitae.*

12 The writer of the *Continuatio Eulogii* lifts whole passages from Walsingham's *Chronica Majora*, particularly for the Welsh Rebellion of 1400 to c.1410. For the relationship between the *Historia Vitae* and Walsingham see Stow's commentary in his edition of 1977.

13 John Capgrave's *Liber de Illustribus Henricis*, ed. F.C. Hingeston (London: Rolls Series, 1858). Antonia Gransden notes that '[Capgrave's] chronicle [is] a compilation almost entirely from Walsingham', see *Historical Writing in England, Vol. II, c. 1007 to the Early Sixteenth Century* (London: Routledge & Kegan Paul, 1982), p. 390.

14 *Hall's Chronicle*, ed. Henry Ellis (London, 1809.) There are significant similarities between Hall's and Walsingham's descriptions of the battle of Shrewsbury in 1403. For example, Hall and Walsingham are similar in describing Henry IV's praises to God after

Shrewsbury, and in Douglas injuring a testicle in the battle. Compare *Hall's Chronicle* pp. 30–31 with Walsingham's *Annales Ricardi Secundi et Henrici Quinti*, vol. II, pp. 362–68. See also a useful discussion by W. Gordon Zeeveld, 'The Influence of Hall on Shakespeare's History Plays', *ELH*, 3: 4 (1936), 317–53.

15 John Stow, *Chronicles of England*, London, 1580 and his *Summary of English Chronicles*, London, 1565. See also Gransden, *Historical Writing in England, Vol. II.*, p. 477.

16 C. L. Kingsford, *English Historical Literature in the Fifteenth Century* (New York: Burt Franklin, 1913), p. 272.

17 Terence Hawkes, 'Bryn Glas', *Post-Colonial Shakespeares*, eds Ania Loomba and Martin Orkin (London: Routledge, 1998), p. 121.

18 *King Henry IV, Part One*, ed. David Scott Kastan (London: Arden Shakespeare, 2002), p. 144, n. 44. In his Appendix on the 'Sources of *1 Henry IV*', Kastan mentions Walsingham only once (and this is only in passing) regarding Walsingham's portrayal of Prince Hal as a prodigal son, which would have been circulating during Prince Hal's (later Henry V) lifetime.

19 My translation. Thomas Walsingham, *Historia Anglicana*, p. 250.

20 For further discussion of the significance of the battle of Bryn Glas, see Terence Hawkes, 'Bryn Glas', pp. 117–40.

21 *Continuatio Eulogii*: comet p. 389; storms and thunder p. 392; eclipse p. 397.

22 Walsingham, *Historia Anglicana*: comet p. 248; devil p. 249; monsters p. 254

23 For example, in his Seventh Century text *De Natura Rerum* or *On the Nature of Things*, Isidore of Seville (d. 636) in Chapter 71 'On the names of Stars' gives the correct Greek etymology that 'a comet is so called because it spreads light from itself as if it were hair. And when this kind of star appears it indicates pestilence, famine or war.' From Edward Grant ed., *A Source Book in Medieval Science* (Cambridge, Mass.: Harvard University Press, 1974), p. 16.

24 Comets, meteorites, shooting stars and the like were considered to be natural phenomena that were in the wrong place, as is described in the chapter on 'Of the fyre and of the sterres that seme to falle' (Chapter 30) in *Caxton's Mirrour of the World*, ed. Oliver H. Prior (London: Early English Text Society, 1913), p. 122. For further discussion of cosmology in Shakespeare's era, see E.M.W. Tillyard, *The Elizabethan World Picture* (Harmondsworth: Penguin, 1943).

25 Thomas Walsingham, *Historia Anglicana*, vol. 2, p. 248.

26 *Continuatio Eulogii*, p. 389.

27 *Continuatio Eulogii*, p. 398.

28 Evelyn Edson, *Mapping Time and Space: How Medieval Mapmakers Viewed their World* (London: The British Library, 1999), especially her chapter on 'Maps in Medieval Histories', pp. 97–131.

29 Higden deserves special mention as both a cartographer and a chronicler. Higden's *Polychronicon* was extremely popular throughout his own lifetime and well into the fifteenth and sixteenth centuries. Antonia Gransden records that 'over 120 manuscripts survive, dating from the fourteenth and fifteenth centuries, and the early date of some shows that the fame of the work spread during Higden's lifetime', Gransden, *Historical Writing in England, Vol. II*, p. 43. It is known that King Henry VIII had two copies, one from which the *mappa mundi* in Figure One has been taken. Higden's influence in

historiography should be noted; his influence on the chroniclers of Henry IV's reign is significant, the *Continuatio Eulogii* and Thomas Walsingham's *Annales Ricardi Secundi et Henrici Quarti* both profess to be continuations of the *Polychronicon* and both start their history at the date at which Higden stops. See A. S. G. Edwards, 'The Influence and Audience of the *Polychronicon*: some observations', *Proceedings of the Leeds Philosophical and Literary Society*, 17:6 (1980), 113–15.

30 For a further discussion of Higden's map, see John Taylor, *The Universal Chronicle of Ranulf Higden* (Oxford: Clarendon Press, 1966) esp. pp. 63–71.

31 For further discussion of medieval maps and cartographic space see Berthold Kupisch, 'Medieval World Maps: Embedded images, Interpretive Frames', *Word and Image*, 10 (1994), 262–88; Margriet Hoogvliet, '*Mappae Mundi* and the Medieval Hermeneutics of Cartographical Space', in Peter Ainsworth and Tom Scott eds, *Regions and Landscapes: Reality and Imagination in Late Medieval and Early Modern Europe* (Oxford: Peter Lang, 1998), pp. 25–46; David Woodward, 'Reality, Symbolism, Time and Space in Medieval World Maps', *Annals of the Association of American Geographers*, 75: 4 (1985), 510–21.

32 This map of Isidore is from his *De Natura Rerum*, and is a copy from the late ninth Century. Unfortunately none of Isidore's original T-O maps have survived to this day.

33 My thanks go to Professor Christopher Wortham for his comments and suggestions on this subject. Professor Wortham presented a thought-provoking talk on 'Cartography and Shakespeare' to the English and Communication Studies work in progress seminar series in April 2005 at the University of Western Australia.

34 On Isidore's map the texts reads, as an example 'Asia. Post conuersionem linguarum et gentes disperse fuerant per totum mundi habitauerant filii Sem in Asia. De cuius posteritate descendunt gentes xxvii. & est dicta Asia ab Asia regina. quae est tertia pars mundi. Regio Orientalis Asia.'

35 This will be further discussed below in Part IV: *Henry IV Part One*, Cosmos and History.

36 Henry of Huntingdon, 'Prologue Addressed to Alexander, Bishop of Lincoln', *Historia Anglorum*, ed. and trans. Diana Greenway (Oxford: Clarendon Press, 1996).

37 For further discussion of this see Marjorie Reeves, 'The Originality and Influence of Joachim of Fiore', *Traditio: Studies in Ancient and Medieval History, Thought and Religion*, 36 (1980), 269–316.

38 St Augustine (d. 430) and the Venerable Bede (d. 735) record that the first age is from Adam to Noah, second is from Noah to Abraham; third is from Abraham to David; fourth is from David to the Babylonian captivity; fifth is from the Babylonian captivity to the birth of Christ and finally the sixth age is from the birth of Christ to the present. For further discussion of the epochs of universal history see Edson, *Mapping Time and Space*, pp. 97–102.

39 For a case study of the geographical scope of Otto of Freising's (d. 1158) work of universal history see Hans-Werner Goetz, 'On the Universality of Universal History', in Jean-Philippe Genet ed. *L'historiographie Médiévale en Europe: Acte du colleque organisé par la fondation Européenne de la science au Centre de Recherches Historiques et Juridiques de l'Université Paris I du 29 Mars au 1er avril 1989* (Paris: Editions du Centre National de la Recherche Scientifique, 1991), pp. 247–61.

40 *Continuatio Eulogii*, 389: 'Anno Domini 1402, et anno hujus Regis 3...'.

41 The link between Henry, Jerusalem, and the cosmos in *Henry IV Part One* is further illustrated by several pieces of imagery: Henry's 'obedient orb' can be read as a reference to the spherical cosmos; the representation of rebellion as a disturbance of the natural order which is implicit in portents and in the imagery of Worcester as meteor; and the parallel threatened centres of Henry and Jerusalem.

42 Edmund Mortimer (d. 1409) was the protector and uncle of the young Earl of March, whose name was also Edmund Mortimer (d. 1425).

43 This is not the only map referred to in Shakespeare's plays. Maps are found most notably in *Henry V*: 'if you look in the maps of the world' (IV.vii.22); *King Lear* in which England is divided in three: 'Give me the map there. Know that we have divided/ In three our kingdom' (I.i.37–38). There are also references to maps in *The Tempest*, *Twelfth Night* and others. For a discussion of this see John Gillies, *Shakespeare and the Geography of Difference* (Cambridge: Cambridge University Press, 1994), pp. 45–69.

44 It is interesting to note that like the three sons of Noah, the three rebels too are related. Mortimer and Hotspur are brothers-in-law, and Mortimer and Glendower are son and father-in-law.

45 Christopher Wortham, 'Disorientation: The Case of *Othello*', in *The Touch of the Real: Essays in Early Modern Culture*, ed. Philippa Kelly (Perth: University of Western Australia Press, 2002), pp. 177–201.

46 David Read, 'Losing the Map: Topographical Understanding in the *Henriad*', *Modern Philology*, 94 (1996–7), 475–495 (478).

47 For further discussion on the Psalter and the Hereford maps, see Naomi Reed Kline, *Maps of Medieval Thought: The Hereford Paradigm* (Suffolk: Boydell Press, 2001).

48 Men and women are made in God's image in Genesis 1: 26–27.

49 John Gillies has examined the connection between cartographic discourse and the construction of otherness in Shakespearean drama in his *Shakespeare and the Geography of Difference* in relation to such texts as *Antony and Cleopatra*, *Titus Andronicus*, the *Merchant of Venice* and others. See John Gillies, *Shakespeare and the Geography of Difference*, esp. Chapter Four: '"The Open Worlde": the Exotic in Shakespeare', pp. 99–155.

50 For further discussion of the significance of the Welsh women, see Jean E. Howard and Phyllis Rackin, *Engendering a Nation: A Feminist Account of Shakespeare's English Histories* (London: Routledge, 1997).

51 *Malleus Maleficarum*, ed. Montague Summers (London: John Rodker, 1928). Part 2 Chapter VII is entitled 'How, as it were, they Deprive Man of his Virile Member' and tells of witches who 'sometimes collect male organs in great numbers, as many as twenty or thirty members together, and put them in a bird's nest, or shut them up in a box'(p. 121). For further discussion see Moira Smith, 'The Flying Phallus and the Laughing Inquisitor: Penis Theft in the *Malleus Maleficarum*', *Journal of Folklore Research*, 39:11 (January 2002), 85–117; Lyndal Roper, 'Witchcraft and the Western Imagination', *Transactions of the Royal Historical Society*, 16 (2006), 117–41.

52 For further discussion of this see Philippa Maddern, 'Weather, War and Witches: Sign and Cause in Fifteenth-Century English Vernacular Chronicles', *A World Explored: Essays in Honour of Laurie Gardiner* (Melbourne: History Department, University of Melbourne, 1993), pp. 77–98.

The Plague of Christendom: Discord and Chastity in *Othello*

Helen Vella Bonavita

It is possible to consider *Othello*, for all its murder and betrayal, as a play about events which never happen but which nonetheless have a critical impact on the narrative. One example of such a 'non-event' is Brabantio's claim that his daughter Desdemona has been seduced by witchcraft by the Moorish General, a claim successfully disproven by Othello. Another, more significant, is the failed attack which prompts Othello's journey, accompanied by his wife, his lieutenant Cassio, ensign Iago, and Desdemona's lady-in-waiting Emilia. Othello is dispatched by the Doge of Venice to defend their outpost Cyprus against an attack by the Ottoman fleet which never happens, a threat which, by the time they reach the island, has been dispersed by storms. Desdemona is finally murdered for adultery, a crime that she has not committed. It is a play with a vacuum at its centre. Deprived of the immediate external threat posed by the Ottoman forces, the small Christian community on Cyprus loses its sense of cohesion and collapses upon itself in murderous fashion, victim to the internal threat of dissension embodied by the figure of Iago.

Even though the literal threat of the Ottoman fleet is dispelled by the beginning of Act 2, they remain an ominous presence for the rest of the play, both in terms of actual political and military threat and, more generally, as an emblem of spiritual and physical destruction. Othello's cry to his brawling soldiers, 'Are we turned Turks, and to ourselves do that / Which heaven has forbid the Ottomites?' (II.iii.164–65) foreshadows the discord and murderous climax of the play, while Othello's increasing obsession with Desdemona's supposed adultery along with Iago's seemingly causeless and insatiable appetite for destruction have led some critics to view the play as one in which precisely this happens: that Iago, in particular, *has* 'turned Turk' and as a result is seeking to destroy Christian society from within when that destruction cannot be brought about externally.[1]

Daniel Vitkus, in 'Turning Turk in *Othello*: The Conversion and Damnation of the Moor', discusses the play in terms of the concern over Christian renegades that was an anxiety of the early seventeenth century.[2] With the growth of trading links with Ottoman and Islamic nations, and a decreased threat of invasion, the number of Christians voluntarily renouncing their religion in favour of Islam was growing substantially in the early seventeenth century.[3] After all, compared to early seventeenth-century England and indeed Europe, the Ottoman world was a meritocracy, one in which men could, and did, rise to the peak of society by dint of their own efforts rather than accident of birth. Nabil Matar notes that by 1612 the problem was so widespread that a whole play had been written on the subject by Robert Daborn, *A Christian Turn'd Turke, or The Tragicall Lives and Deaths of the two Famous Pyrates, Ward and Danisker*, and a special service for the re-baptism of those who had briefly embraced Islam had been composed.[4] Where Christendom had previously feared destruction by military conquest, it now feared an even worse threat: defection. In this context, it could be argued that Iago, having himself apostatized, brings about Othello's own conversion and 'turning' towards 'a bestial, sex-obsessed condition'.[5] By repeatedly emphasizing Othello's racial and moral *difference*—thick lips, erring barbarian, lustful Moor—Iago creates a personality for Othello, one that corresponds exactly to the European image of the Turk. Thus, Othello's eventual murder of Desdemona becomes a microcosm of the wider threat besetting Europe at the time: Desdemona the figure of Christendom violated by those who should be protecting her.

While it seems impossible *not* to view Desdemona as being on one level a personification of suffering Christendom, I shall argue that although a reading of the play which considers Othello, or even Iago, as having 'turned Turk' and rejected Christianity completely is entirely feasible, it is not the only possible interpretation of the play which takes into account contemporary Ottoman affairs. The fear of religious instability, of betrayal from within which was symbolized by the Christian renegade, is founded on an earlier Christian anxiety, one which identified Christian disunity as the chief cause and facilitator of Turkish advances. From the fall of Constantinople in 1483 onwards, the Ottoman empire had been steadily increasing its boundaries. In the first half of the sixteenth century Ottoman forces occupied Bulgaria, Serbia, the final existing fragments of Byzantium and the Kingdom of Hungary in rapid succession, and they appeared to have no intention of stopping. The duty of all Muslims to extend the Domain of Peace—the areas where Islam reigned supreme—into the Domain of War—the areas where it did not—coupled with a succession of warlike and efficient Sultans formed a threat that menaced Europe from along the coast of Africa and also in Eastern Europe. Cyprus itself in the sixteenth century was on the borderline, held by the Venetians in Ottoman-dominated waters; battle for its possession was permanently in the offing.

The seemingly unstoppable Turkish advance was, furthermore, assisted by the fragmented state of European politics. Latin Christendom had been split by the Reformation, the two major Catholic powers of France and the Hapsburgs were too caught up in their own conflict to pose any great challenge to the Turkish advance and France, at least, was quietly pursuing its own alliances with the Ottomans.[6] Contemporary writers recognized and lamented the destructive potential of disunity;

as Richard Knolles in his *Generall Historie of the Turks* expressed it: 'By ciuile discord the noble countrey of Græcia perished, when as the father rising against the sonne, and the sonne against the father, and brother against brother, they to the mutuall destruction of themselues, called in the Turke, who like a greedie lyon lurking in his den, lay in wayt for them all.'[7] Catholics and Protestants alike could agree on the reality of the Turkish menace while remaining divided on its origin and function in the Divine Plan. Luther began by counselling acceptance of Turkish depredations as being a punishment deservedly inflicted by God, although admittedly this was in 1521 when the Turks constituted no immediate danger.[8] In 1529 when the Ottoman army led by Suleiman I was approaching Vienna he reconsidered his position.[9] Protestant polemicists argued that the Turks were God's punishment for the flagrant immoralities of the Catholic Church; Catholics retorted that the Devil supported the Turks through stirring up division and heresy within the One True Faith.[10]

The 'greedie lyon' was an object both of fear and fascination. Treatises such as that of Bartholomaeus Georgievits (translated into English by Hughe Goughe in 1553) combine condemnation of the Ottoman religion and culture with intrigued interest in those very aspects of their society.[11] Encounters with Ottoman military forces offered an opportunity for political or religious polemic and a view into an exotic culture, not to mention a dramatic narrative, but on one point all were agreed: the Turks posed a devastating threat to Christendom, and Christendom's own lack of ability to maintain the true Christian faith (whatever that might be) was further enabling Turkish success.

Within the babel of voices blaming each other for the invasion of the infidel, a third party had been heard for some time, calling for unity among Christian princes:

> Discord was the vtter vndooyng and defacyng of the *Sarracens* Empire, as in this history it shall playnly appeare: and the same plague doth at this day so infest and trouble all Christendome that I feare (and I beseech God my feare may be without effect) least wee shall to late rue and lament either the utter subuersion or at least, the miserable oppression thereof.[12]

So wrote Thomas Newton in his *Notable History of the Sarracens*, a book which unlike the semi-prurient descriptions of circumcision procedures, fratricide and concubinage that characterize much of English literature concerning the Turks at this time, focuses almost exclusively on the territorial ambitions of the Saracen Empire and those of its successors, the Ottomans. The book is explicit in its intent: the dangers of internecine discord among the Christian princes is repeatedly shown to bring about Saracen, and later Ottoman, victory. One key episode which lends itself well to discussion of *Othello* deals with the fall of Spain itself to the Saracens.

Rodericke Visigotte, King of Spain, is smitten with an unholy lust for the

daughter of one of his men, Julian Earl of Cepta (now Ceuta), a Spanish outpost on
the African coastline. The Earl is a prominent figure in the kingdom, not only for
his large landholdings (including the island of Viridis) but for his 'whole charge, to
defende Spayne on that side from the inuasions of the Saracenes, and to kepe the
narow Seas'.[13] The daughter, Caba, is 'by force or fraud' deprived of her virginity
by Rodericke, and as soon as she is able complains of this 'unprincely trick' to
her father. Whether, like Lucrece, she later expiates her shame in her own blood
is not stated. In revenge, Julian gathers his friends and relatives, retreats to Cepta,
and makes alliance with the Saracens to overthrow Rodericke (although he himself
does not convert to Islam). The consequent bloodbath results in Spain being wholly
conquered by the Saracens, and Rodericke himself retreating to the desert where he
speedily dies in shame and misery. The following epitaph adorns his grave:

> Here lyes the Corps of *Roderick*, late King
> Of Gothes, accurst and fraughte with furie dire:
> Whose sensuall raigne brought dule and deadly sting
> To *Spanish* soyle: because of *Julians* yre,
> Which would not be appeasde till he had wrought
> The Toyle of strife, and brought all thinges to nought.
>
> All mad with rage and spightfull rancours moode
> By devilish fate incensde, *Gods* heastes despisde,
> His faith renounced, religion eke withstoode,
> A foe to frindes, his Countries wracke devisde:
> Unto his Lorde an arrant traytrous Elfe,
> A murthrous wight, and cruell toward hymselfe.
>
> Embrued with guylt, for sheading Christen bloud
> Which by his driftes were brought to fatall end,
> An Homycide, of mangling Butchers broode
> Did ruyne to his native soyle pretend.
> His memorie shall dye with men for aye.
> His name shall rotte, as doth his Corps in clay.[14]

Setting aside the quality of the verse, the epitaph is interesting for two reasons.
Firstly, the attribution to sensuality of Rodericke's catastrophic demise and secondly,
the fact that the bulk of the poem castigates Julian, in some sense the victim of
Rodericke's sensuality, rather than Rodericke himself. (Caba, the victim, does
not rate a mention.) Structurally it is interesting that Julian of Ceuta, like Othello,
has the task of defending the border from the Saracens, and that it is a figure from
the Christian mainland who has deprived him of his female possession—be that
possession wife or daughter. Sexual discord within the Christian forces leads to

betrayal and finally external disaster, and the figure of the victim, Caba, implicitly embodies the concept of Christendom, despoiled by those who should protect her and hence laid open to assault by an external enemy. In similar vein, we may see Desdemona's murder at the hands of Othello as being emblematic of Christendom despoiled by the Saracens—but only, crucially, after her initial betrayal by those who should have protected her: in Caba's case, the King Roderick, but in Desdemona's case, Venetian society as symbolized by its representatives: Emilia, Cassio, Iago and Othello himself, Venice's appointed protector. Just as the story of Caba ends with the downfall of Spain, the play *Othello* ends with Desdemona murdered, her husband dead and Cassio 'rules in Cyprus'. But for how long? As Shakespeare's audience would have been aware, Cyprus was ceded to the Ottomans in 1573, collapsing almost without a struggle. The moral seems clear: Christian dissention is the cause of, or enables, Turkish success, and in his representation of that disunity in images of sexual violation or corruption Shakespeare is building not only on Cinthio's original story of lust and jealousy but also on the century-long accretion of polemic calling for Christian unity in the face of Muslim aggression, and exemplary histories which dramatized disunity in terms of sexual promiscuity.

Vitkus demonstrates conclusively that the Islamic religion was characterized by Europeans as being lustful and vicious, and that therefore the explosion of murderous lust and jealousy in *Othello* could be read as signs of Islam, whether Othello is conscious or unconscious of his 'conversion'. While this argument is convincing, *Othello* lends itself with equal readiness to a reading that focusses on the earlier fear, that of discord resulting in invasion rather than fear of the renegade. In this context, it is not necessary to see Othello as turning Turk himself, nor yet to see Iago as being a Christian renegade. Instead, the play demonstrates the catastrophic effects of Christian disunity and does so in terms that polemicists throughout the sixteenth century would have recognized, disunity symbolized by sexual licence, and in *Othello* it is a sexual licence which pervades the play, not something that exists only in Iago's insinuations.

The concern over sexual misconduct in *Othello* begins in act one when Othello is called upon to justify his behaviour in marrying Desdemona without Brabantio's parental consent. Here, Othello's blackness takes second place to the charges of deceit, betrayal and seduction. Brabantio's outrage over Desdemona's defection is certainly augmented by the colour bar that she has crossed, but it is the deception of her father as much as anything else that appears to be the cause of his fury.

O heaven! How got she out? O treason of the blood!
Fathers, from hence trust not your daughters' minds
By what you see them act

(I.i.170–73)

'Treason of the blood' may refer to Desdemona's filial duty, which she has abandoned, or to her Venetian blood that will now be contaminated by Othello's blackness; the Duchess of Malfi's brother Ferdinand speaks of the 'royal blood of Aragon and Castile' which has been 'attainted' by his sister's sexual activity (II.v.21–22). It can also mean that the sensuality that is an intrinsic part of her nature has found an outlet; she has been betrayed by the 'hot blood' of youth and more specifically, of Christian youth, the 'excess of venery' as Robert Burton's *Anatomy of Melancholy* puts it, and as Othello himself will later assert, the 'young and sweating devil' (III.iv.38).[15] Othello defends himself against a charge of seduction, not of miscegenation. The crime of which he is accused could be imputed to any Venetian with equal weight and danger as the Duke's words show:

> Whoe'er he be that in this foul proceeding
> Hath thus beguiled your daughter of herself
> And you of her, the bloody book of law
> You shall yourself read in the bitter letter
> After your own sense, yea, though our proper son
> Stood in your action.

(I.iii.65–70)

The charge is certainly serious, but it is also one which could be levelled against any Christian; Othello's 'Moorishness' does not, at this stage, appear to contribute to the accusations. It is deceit, and more importantly sexual deceit, that is the cause of the trouble. The Duke's final comments on the subject, 'If virtue no delighted beauty lack, Your son-in-law is far more fair than black', and that of his senator: 'Adieu, brave Moor: use Desdemona well' (I.iii.286–88), appear to confirm this while Brabantio's ominous farewell: 'Look to her, Moor, if thou hast eyes to see. / She has deceived her father, and may thee' (I.iii.289–90) emphasizes the propensity for deceit, and hence for sexual infidelity, which in this play at least appears to be a major element of the Venetian mentality. By the turn of the seventeenth century the glory of Venice was tarnished. Its trading monopolies were monopolies no longer, social inequities were great and growing greater, and its negative elements were overshadowing its redeeming features of culture, welfare and equity.[16] These negative elements included 'sexual tyranny in private life combined with a cold licentiousness in public', and Shakespeare's depiction of the matter-of-fact acceptance of adultery and fornication as a part of life by Emilia, Roderigo, Iago and Cassio in their different ways emphasizes this aspect of Venice in the play.[17]

The plot as it unfolds continues to depend on deceit leading to sexual transgression, real or imagined, but the deceit, and the moral licence, are placed firmly in the Venetian camp rather than in the Moorish one. In this point the play diverges sharply from one of the standard elements of the Turkish or Moorish character as it was known on the Elizabethan stage: its lustfulness. Plays such as *The Fair Maid of the West* depend for much of their plot on the voracious sexual appetite of the Moor, particularly where Westerners are concerned; a further example is Kyd's *Soliman and Perseda* (1592), where the Sultan's lust for Christian Perseda leads him to treachery and murder. The lecherous appetite of the Turk, particularly when confronted with Western beauty, was considered to be beyond measure:

> And a most lamentable howlynge and wepynge is heard throughe the darke of youthelye wightes of both kinds susteining violence, neyther maye the age of sixe of seven yeares defende the miserable wretches from suche filthines, the malicious nation is so fearce and fervent, bothe against and beside all course of nature in libidinous lecherye.[18]

In this play, however, it is the Venetians rather than the Turks who are noteworthy for their lechery. Even Desdemona complains that should she be left behind she will be deprived of 'the rites' for which she loves her husband. While in its context this may mean the soldierly occupations for which Desdemona first loved Othello, we may assume that the phrase includes a reference to the conjugal rites to which she is also entitled. Othello, on the other hand, stands out among the highly sexed Venetians for his restraint. He is prepared to leave his wife behind as he sails for war in Cyprus, and when he does agree to take her, he insists that he is not doing so to 'comply with heat'. It is, as Iago shows us, the sexual desires and licence that the Venetians carry with them which prove their undoing and that lay them open to Turkish invasion.

It would be reductive to ascribe Iago's malice simply to sexual jealousy. He can be read as Machiavellian villain, Vice figure, malcontent or plain embodiment of evil. As Vitkus and Matar have suggested, Shakespeare may have drawn inspiration for his character from the figure of the Christian renegade, far more dangerous than the simple Turk in his apostasy. Certainly, Thomas More's comment in his *Dialogue of Comfort against Tribulation* that the Christian turned Turk is infinitely more cruel to his faithful victims than the Turk himself is applicable to Iago. Iago's *own* explanation of his malice, however, is based primarily on his suspicions of his wife, with Othello and with Cassio. Setting aside for the moment the fact that not Cassio, nor Othello, nor for that matter Emilia give the smallest sign of having deserved this *particular* suspicion, Iago's ready assumption of sexual infidelity, and for that matter, Emilia's cynical views on adultery coupled with Cassio's own affair with Bianca, provide further evidence of the seamier side of Venetian life. Thus, Iago's mistrust of his fellow men—and women—is not entirely unfounded; it could even be argued that he is a clear-sighted chronicler of Christendom's faults as well as being himself, in his own ready suspicions and ceaseless envy, the logical result of those failings.

In fact, the Christian outpost against the Turks gives the strong impression of being rotten from within. Cassio, despite the 'daily beauty in his life' for which Iago loathes him, is the unwitting lynchpin to Iago's plots. His expostulation that Othello's suspicions were groundless, 'Dear General, I never gave you cause', appear poignantly true, but are they? It is Cassio's relationship with Bianca the courtesan that gives Iago the chance to work poison on Othello. Cassio's laughing, contemptuous dismissal of Bianca's love for him and the possibility of marriage lend further weight to the image of Venice as a centre of luxury and licence rather than the Christian frontier against a Turkish assault (IV.i.116–30). Iago's ready jealousy of Othello and intention to become 'evened with him, wife for wife' (II.i.290) become more comprehensible when set against a society where infidelity is the rule rather than the exception. Iago does not need to 'turn Turk' for his evil to bring about Christian ruin. It is Christian frailty and Christian sensuality that provide the medium for Iago's ill-will.[19] As Robert Burton puts it in his *Anatomy of Melancholy*:

> The greatest enimie to man, is man, who by the Divels instigation, is still ready to doe mischiefe, his own executioner … We are all brethren in Christ, or at least should be, members of one body, servants of one Lord, and yet no feind can so torment, insult over, tyrannize, vexe, as one man doth another.[20]

By 1604 the possibility of Turkish invasion of Europe had faded, the professed enemy had been kept from the gate but it was still present. *Othello* appears to represent that situation admirably, with Turkish wolves shadowing the sidelines, waiting for Christian frailty to undo itself and enable entrance. The sense of danger from Turkish invasion is summed up admirably in Newton's conclusion to his *History*:

> Uppon the Seas about *Tunyce* were seene 350 Saile of the Turkes, whose intent and meaning was … to recover and wynne the new Fort … together with *Goletta* and other Peeces there. With whom also a mighty rablement of traiterous Moores … joined side: which dispossessed thence the Spanish garrisons, to the great furtherance of their develish purposes and to the lamentable griefe of all Christendome, considering what a small way they have from thence into Spaine and so into the rest of other Christian Realmes, unlesse the good and gracious providence of our God qualefie and as with a Snaffle reine this raging Beaste and bloudy Tyraunt, the common robber of all the world from further invasion, which he graciously graunt for his mercye sake through the mediation of his Sonne Christ our Lord and onely Saviour Amen.[21]

Like Julian, whose revenge for his daughter brought about the fall of Spain, Othello's murderous actions are in revenge—although in his case the revenge is unjustified— for an initial wrong that stems from the Christian, not the Turkish forces. Like Julian, in bringing about his revenge, his own name is made a by-word of infamy. Before he kills himself Othello is to be kept 'close prisoner'; the honour and reputation that he has previously earned are irreparably smirched. And finally, like Julian, Othello's revenge brings about a collapse in the society that he was sworn to protect. But I do not think we need to view Othello as having 'turned Turk', backsliding from Christian redemption into his original Moorish nature. If, instead, the play is read with a focus on the need for Christian integrity in all senses of the word and the catastrophic effects of its lack, then Othello himself is not the focus of condemnation. Rather, it is the society from which Desdemona comes which brings about her murder. Roderigo's reliance on jewels that 'would half have corrupted a votarist' (IV.ii.187), Emilia's assurance that it is 'a small vice' (IV.iii.65), Cassio's laughter at the idea of marrying Bianca: 'I marry her! What! A customer!' (IV.i.20) all speak of a society where the concept of chastity has been thoroughly compromised, and in that failing lies its downfall. Waiting anxiously in Cyprus for Othello to arrive, Cassio prays for a safe journey:

> Great Jove, Othello guard,
> And swell his sail with thine own powerful breath,
> That he may bless this bay with his tall ship,
> Make love's quick pants in Desdemona's arms,
> Give renewed fire to our extincted spirits,
> And bring all Cyprus comfort.
>
> (II.i.76–81)

There is nothing particularly new in pointing out the conflation of sexual strength and military valour expressed in these lines; it is, perhaps, worth pointing out that it is sexual strength in a specifically *marital* context. Vitkus notes that throughout the sixteenth century 'the traditional notion of a marriage between Venice and the sea led to jokes about the Turk cuckolding the impotent Venetian patriarchs or raping the Venetian virgin'.[22] Cassio, in the lines quoted above, evokes this marriage; Othello's conjugal embrace will renew the strength of the Venetians in Cyprus and protect Venice from her enemies. But Cassio, like his compatriots, will prove himself to be unworthy of the alliance offered him. If Venice needs a strong (male) power to preserve her then a chaste, exclusive relationship is required, one which may be epitomized in the figures of Desdemona and Othello, but one which is also affected by the actions of those around them. In this case, Venice has failed to keep her side of the 'marital' bargain and although Desdemona herself may be innocent, the city and society, the Venetian virgin that she represents, is not.

In this context, Desdemona stands alone. She is in the world of Venice but not of it. R. S. White likens her to Spenser's Una in Book 1 of the *Faerie Queene*; Desdemona stands for the true Church, and her marriage to Othello is the ideal union of innocence and strength. In herself the epitome of virtue, she is nonetheless incapable of active self-defence and must rely on others for her protection. And it is those others that fail her. Christendom, in the body of Desdemona, is undone by the failings of her own side, not by external evil. Her answer to the question of who has murdered her: 'Nobody—I myself' takes on a further resonance in this context, and so does Othello's own self-mutilation. Othello is not killing the Turk in himself; he is enacting the fact that the forces of Christendom have destroyed themselves. R. S. White notes that 'the worst thing about Iago is that he *survives*' and goes on to liken him to the Blatant Beast of slander in books 5 and 6 of *The Faerie Queene* who, like Iago, is still loose in society at the ending of the poem.[23] Like the Blatant Beast, Iago is a domestic product. We do not need to look to the Turks for an explanation of his malice; Iago's evil is bred in a Christian society and takes full advantage of that society's shortcomings. As he never tires of reminding Othello, Othello has no notion of how Christians truly behave—and Iago does:

> I know our country disposition well:
> In Venice they do let God see the pranks
> They dare not show their husbands; their best conscience
> Is not to leave't undone, but keep't unknown.

(III.iii.199–202)

Emilia's flippant comment that, although she would not commit adultery in the heavenly light, she might do so in the dark, seems to bear out Iago's assertion; while his suspicions of his wife with Othello may not be specifically true, they are true in general. The final speeches of the play seem anticlimactic as Othello's possessions are distributed to the next of kin, Iago is dispatched to torments that seem somewhat futile now that the damage has been done, and 'Cassio rules in Cyprus' (V.ii.328). It is interesting that aside from the reference to rulership, the question of who will now defend the Venetians against their enemy is left unanswered. Cassio, as a representative of the feminine Venice and having proved himself flawed both in terms of his responsibilities as a soldier and his relationship with Bianca, does not fill us with confidence in his abilities as the new governor of the island and in fact, Cyprus was ceded to the Turks by the Venetians in 1573. It is tempting to view the deaths of Desdemona and Othello as representative of the moral and military vacuum that permitted this. At any rate, the Turks have maintained a shadowy presence throughout the play, and the way is now left open to them by the death of Othello, the strong power that could and should have protected the figure of Christendom.

The claustrophobic medley of emotions and ideologies in *Othello* render the task of identifying one individual strand problematic. In the light of this discussion however, the play may be perceived to be drawing heavily not so much on the danger of 'turning Turk'—the later concern—as on the older fear of Christian disunity enabling Turkish victory, a fear that was incorporated into the newer danger, but that never quite vanished. Like the unfortunate Caba, Desdemona becomes a figure of Christendom violated by itself and left a prey to further invasion, and Othello's self-mutilation equally embodies the image of a society turned against itself, that 'to ourselves [does] that / Which heaven hath forbid the Ottomites' (II.iii.165). Destroyed by its own lack of integrity, Cyprus, Venice and by extension Christendom, can only await further invasion.

Notes

1   William Shakespeare, *Othello*, ed. Kenneth Muir (London: Penguin, 1996). All later references are to this edition.

2   Daniel Vitkus, 'Turning Turk in *Othello*: the Conversion and Damnation of the Moor', *Shakespeare Quarterly* 48 (1997): 145–76. See also J. D'Amico, *The Moor in English Renaissance Drama* (Tampa: University of South Florida Press, 1991) and N. Matar, *Islam in Britain 1558–1685* (Cambridge: Cambridge University Press, 1998).

3   Nabil Matar, 'The Renegade in English Seventeenth-Century Imagination', *Studies in English Literature*, 33 (1993): 489–505.

4   Matar, p. 492.

5   Vitkus, 'Turning Turk in *Othello*', p. 156.

6   See Stephen A. Fischer-Galati, *Ottoman Imperialism and German Protestantism 1521–1555* (Cambridge, Mass.: Harvard University Press, 1959). See also Kenneth Setton, *The Papacy and the Levant (1204–1571)* vol. IV: *The Sixteenth Century from Julius III to Pius V* (Philadelphia: the American Philosophical Society, 1984).

7   Richard Knolles, *The Generall History of the Turkes* ([London]: Adam Islip, 1610), fol. A^v.

8   Brandon Beck, *From the Rising of the Sun: English Images of the Ottoman Empire to 1715*, American University Studies Series IX (History) vol. 20 (New York: Peter Lang, 1987), p. 19.

9   Samuel Chew, *The Crescent and the Rose* (New York: Octagon Books, 1965), p. 102.

10   Chew, p. 101.

11   For a more detailed discussion of this area see Nabil Matar, 'English Accounts of Captivity in North Africa and the Middle East: 1557–1625', *Renaissance Quarterly*, 54 (Summer 2001), 553–72.

12   Augustine Curio, *Sarracenicae Historia Libri III*, translated by Thomas Newton as *A Notable History of the Saracens* (London, William How 1575), fol. Biiii^r. All further references are to this translation and edition.

13   Newton, fol. 27^r.

14   Newton, fol. 30^v.

15   Burton, *Anatomy of Melancholy*, ed. T. Faulkner, N. Kiessling and R. Blair (Oxford: Clarendon Press, 1994), vol. 3, p. 55. All further references are from this edition.

16   John Hale, *England and the Italian Renaissance* (London: Fontana Press, 1996), pp. 20–23. See also Maurice Hunt, 'Shakespeare's Venetian Paradigm: Stereotyping and

Sadism in the *Merchant of Venice* and *Othello'*, *Papers on Language and Literature*, 39 (2003), 162–85.

17   J. R. Mulryne and Margaret Shewring, eds, *Theatre of the English and Italian* Renaissance (London: MacMillan, 1991), p. 107. See also E. Honigmann, ed., *Othello*, The Arden Shakespeare 3rd edn (London: Thomas Nelson, 1997), pp. 10, 11.

18   Bartholomaeus Georgivitz, *The Ofspring of the House of Ottomano, and officers pertaining to the greate Turkes Court. Whereunto is added Bartholomaeus Georgeviz Epitome, of the customes Rytes, Ceremonies, and Religion of the Turkes; with the miserable afflictions of those Christians, which live under their captivitie and bondage* (London: 1553), fols. Hiᵛ, Hiiʳ.

19   In a different context, Michael Murrin makes a similar point with regard to earlier villains: '… fraud breeds fraud … Malory associates fraud with Gawain and his brothers, and Mordred comes from that family … Mordred, and not the barons, Romans, or Saxons, brought down Arthur's kingdom', *History and Warfare in the Renaissance Epic* (Chicago and London: University of Chicago Press, 1994), p. 132.

20   Burton, 1:1; 126.

21   Newton, fol. 145ʳ.

22   Vitkus, p. 163.

23   R. S. White, *Innocent Victims: Poetic Injustice in Shakespearean Tragedy* (Newcastle Upon Tyne: Tyneside Free Press, 1982), p. 76.

Othello's Exsufflations

Graham Bradshaw

I. Making things out, and making them up

Iago's basic tactic, when he is persuading others to believe what cannot be proved because it is not true, might be described as a presciently Freudian variation on Nietzsche's famous and vigorously healthy maxim that belief is a form of not wanting to know. As Wittgenstein remarked, Freud's method of argument usually involved persuasion, not evidence; his patients and readers were persuaded that what they didn't want to know, or thought unthinkable, was likely to be what they needed to know—or rather, believe.[1] A. D. Nuttall recalls how the philosopher Sidney Hook kept asking Freudians what would count as evidence that a child did *not* suffer from the so-called Oedipus complex, and never received an answer.[2] In *Othello*, the first success of Iago's Freudian method comes when Brabantio suddenly feels driven to admit,

> This accident is not unlike my dream;
> Belief of it oppresses me already.[3]

When he says this Brabantio has not been confronted with, let alone convinced by, anything that could be called evidence. He has not even checked whether Desdemona is still at home. Instead, he has been persuaded by what is, to use his own significant phrase, 'palpable to thinking' (I.2.76). The hitherto 'grave and reverend Signior' whose judgment was so valued in the Senate, and who had eagerly welcomed Othello into his home, is soon babbling about witchcraft in a bigoted way. Of course Desdemona is no victim of 'witchcraft'; but her father is, in a figurative sense that has to do with Iago's genius for showing what his victims have it in them to become.

In this respect Iago and his creator are complicit, since this play so fiercely exposes and opposes its characters' conventional ways of thinking about the 'Self'. Any English speaker at any time might be struck by the sheer oddity of seemingly simple utterances like 'I am by myself', or 'I let myself down'. Or, to take a complex case that traditional linguists and philosophers cannot readily explain because it involves different ways of splitting the 'Self', we somehow understand the profound difference between 'If I were you, I'd hate myself' and 'If I were you, I'd hate me'. Cognitive linguistics has shown how our ways of conceptualizing the 'Self' are always metaphorical, and always involve a Subject and one or more Selves.[4]

But in *Othello* the play's characters repeatedly subscribe to the folk belief in some real or essential Self, which they then speak of as something that can be seen—or made out, not made up. And so do stellar critics like Bradley and Leavis or, far more unexpectedly, Stephen Greenblatt and Ania Loomba, when they write about Othello's Self as though it were fixed, autonomous and stable.[5]

When the lovingly confident Desdemona affirms, 'I saw Othello's visage in his mind' (I.3.250), this tells us less about Othello than about her; clearly, she can't 'see' the mind of her murderer. When the Duke tells Brabantio, 'If virtue no delighted beauty lack, / Your son-in-law is far more fair than black' (I.3.287–88), he confidently brushes past what may be non-predictive in that little but huge word, 'If'. When Othello sees Desdemona as externally fair but internally foul, he calls her a 'fair devil' (III.3.479); when Emilia sees the black Othello as externally foul and internally worse, she calls him 'the blacker devil' (V.2.134). Like the 'Dark Lady' sonnets, this play seems obsessed by the difference between external and internal senses of words like *black* and *fair*. We might then say that this play's characters are all too confident about what can be read off, and keep mistaking the relation between external signs and some inner reality. But to say that would still imply that what is within is static and fixed, whereas *Othello*, like *Measure for Measure* and the Sermon on the Mount, projects a view of the 'Self' as a matrix of possible selves, that includes everything that Iago's various victims, or Angelo and Isabella in the earlier play, have it *in* them to become. To say this is not to claim that Roderigo has it in him to become an Iago or Othello: the idea of a coherent 'core' Self is not self-evidently absurd, and many would think it more absurd to reject that idea. But, if it is more than notional, the coherence in question will still not allow for confident predictions or claims about what can be 'seen' when the matrix in question is dynamic, and terrifyingly unstable.

In Act Two's harbour scene, when Iago and Roderigo observe the gallant Cassio kissing Desdemona as he tries to calm her, Iago knows perfectly well that Cassio is not Desdemona's lover; so does Roderigo, and so do we. But Iago can see how what he and Roderigo have seen could submit to that different interpretation, which he immediately tries out on Roderigo—as the kind of experiment that makes *Othello* a cognitive tragicomedy in which seeing is not knowing. Roderigo immediately, and rightly, dismisses Iago's interpretation; yet the very confidence of this rejection exposes him to Iago's Freudian variation on another admirable Nietzschean maxim, that we should always doubt what we most *want* to believe. Iago eagerly goes to work, not by presenting evidence but by undermining Roderigo's confidence that he can read the signs. Like Brabantio, Roderigo quickly collapses. Such examples suggest how Iago also resembles literary critics who thrive on new interpretations, like the new interpretation this paper will offer. Iago describes himself as 'nothing if not critical' (II.1.119) and speaks, hauntingly, of what is 'probal to thinking'

(II.3.325). As Arrigo Boito, who wrote the libretti for Verdi's *Otello* and *Falstaff*, explained in his character sketch of Iago: 'Jago is Envy. Jago is a scoundrel. Jago is a critic.'[6] More specifically, Iago is Shakespeare's most powerful exponent of what Harold Bloom calls strong readings.

Later in the second act, when Iago goes to work on Cassio, the real challenge is not that of engineering Cassio's drunken, murderous assault on ex-governor Montano. The real challenge comes when Cassio is devastated by shame at what he has done. In emphasizing shame, rather than guilt, I am following the lead given by philosophers like Bernard Williams and by Ewan Fernie's original exploration of *Shame in Shakespeare*.[7] As Fernie observes, guilt is a predominantly legalistic conception that is directed towards the need for 'negotiation with the party offended, usually by accepting punishment from it or offering some other compensation', whereas 'shame is a function of being', not of 'doing or interacting', and 'requires renegotiation of the subject's relationship with itself' (14). When I am deeply shamed by something I have done or not done, what hurts so much is my sense of what I *am*. Because such agonies of moral shame are so inward and radical they often seem to be, or just are, terminal. To understand is not necessarily to forgive; after some kinds of knowledge there is no forgiveness, and what Fernie calls 'renegotiation' between the Subject and Self becomes impossible. The Subject may then judge and kill the Self, like Othello in the final scene, or Anna Karenina. When Cassio is so shattered by his discovery of what he had it in him to become he can be of no further use to Iago, unless he can be persuaded to 'negotiate' on his own behalf. Iago must go to work, again. This time he persuades Cassio that, although his capacity for self-criticism is one of his most attractive features, he is 'too severe a moraler' (II.3.288) and owes it to himself to see that his actions were not the result of something in him, but the result of the devil in drink. Of course we don't want Cassio to commit suicide, but seeing how readily he responds to Iago's invitations to slip into something more comfortable is theatrically riveting and morally dreadful.

The worst moral terrors are still to come, since Iago doesn't go to work on his main target until III.3. By then what is traditionally regarded as *the* play about 'jealousy' is almost half over, before it has begun to be a play about sexual jealousy. In III.3 Iago once again works through hints, mumbling game he dare not bite and carefully avoiding any claim that depends on evidence and might then be refuted, with dangerous or fatal consequences for Iago. Othello sees—up to a point—what Iago is doing, and angrily accuses him of speaking 'As if there were some monster in thy thought / Too hideous to be shown', and 'As if thou then hadst shut up in thy brain / Some horrible conceit' (III.3.110–11, 117–18). Yet Othello cannot see how his mind has been impregnated, so that he is already labouring to conceive whatever 'Monster' is in Iago's mind. The result of his struggle to make out what Iago is actually making up is a terrible triumph of what is 'probal' or 'palpable to thinking':

his own mind gives birth to, and is soon possessed by, the monstrous thing. Another very important result of the Iago tactic is that even when Othello resists it he finds himself boxing with shadows because he is fighting his own interpretation of what Iago may have meant but did not say. So, when Iago suddenly warns Othello *not* to be jealous, Othello makes out the implication that he should be jealous, and immediately rejects his own reading of Iago's implication in the long speech that includes these lines:

> Exchange me for a Goat,
> When I shall turne the businesse of my Soule
> To such exufflicate, and blow'd Surmises,
> Matching thy inference.

(III.3.182–84)

Or that is what Othello says in the First Folio; in the Quarto he speaks of 'exufflicate and *blown* surmises'. Both the Folio and Quarto read *exufflicate*, which most editors (following Malone) emend to *exsufflicate*. As Michael Neill observes in his new Oxford edition of *Othello*, *exsufflicate* is 'glossed by OED (citing only this example, and conjecturing an arbitrary formation from *exsufflate* = blow out, blow away) as "puffed up, inflated, windy". Since the word appears to form a doublet with *blown*, this is not impossible, but the etymology seems strained.'[8]

I must now admit that this paper is concerned with what *exsufflicate* might mean. My subject—Shakespeare's one and only use of a word that no other writer has used—might seem somewhat narrow, and this paper would doubtless seem altogether pointless if it were not proposing a better way of understanding what *exsufflicate* means. However, as I struggled with what I feared might be my own exsufflicate and blown surmises I became ever more concerned with what prompts Shakespeare to invent such a word and with the ways in which we go about deciding what counts as a possible meaning. My ostensibly tiny subject was opening out.

II. 'Across the fulcrum of that "and"'

When Macbeth describes life as 'a tale told by an idiot, full of sound and fury, / Signifying nothing', *sound* and *fury* are linked by the little word *and* but are also strangely disconnected from each other. *Sound* and *fury* are not synonyms, and are not obviously related like *sight* and *sound*. The elusive, disagreeable effect of not being able to see just how they are related resembles the queasiness we feel when we can't bring something into focus. In an odd way, this contributes to our sense of Macbeth's disconnection from life; to describe life as full of *sounding fury*, or *furious sounds*, would not produce this effect because it would signify something.

The syntactic 'A *and* B' structure is of course very common and usually simple, but not in this case—and not when, in one short speech to the Venetian Senate

(I.3.255–72), Othello refers to the Senate's 'serious, and great business', links his own 'defunct, and proper satisfaction' to his wish to be 'free, and bounteous' to Desdemona's mind, and speaks of his 'speculative, and offic'd Instrument'. (These last quotations are from the First Folio, which prints the 'A *and* B' structure as 'A, *and* B' with a comma to mark some pause or emphasis.) Generally, there is a sense in which the 'A *and* B' formula promises to be simple by setting A and B in a syntactic, grammatically parallel relationship that leads us to expect that the logical and semantic relationship between A and B will be correspondingly straightforward. But that does not happen in these Shakespearean examples.

The classic, pioneering discussion of this strange use of the 'A *and* B' figure is George T. Wright's essay on 'Hendiadys and *Hamlet*'.[9] Wright shows how this figurative device is not only peculiar in itself, so that the few classical and Elizabethan rhetoricians who discussed it were sometimes confused about what hendiadys means or involves, but is also so peculiarly Shakespearean that it becomes a distinctive, characterising feature of 'Shakespeare's style' – which, Wright remarks, has 'never been adequately explored' (10). In his meticulously documented essay and appendices, Wright's account of the increasing, startling importance of Shakespearean hendiadys admits and traces various early examples—like young Clifford's horror in *Henry VI, Part II* when he addresses his dead father, murdered 'in thy reverence and thy chair days'(V.2.48). Wright then shows how Shakespeare only began 'to use the device with some frequency' in 1599, when writing *Henry V*, then used it frequently in the ten 'weighty' plays that followed (excluding *The Merry Wives of Windsor,* which includes no examples of hendiadys), and used it most frequently—'more than twice as often as in any other play'—in *Hamlet.* After *Hamlet*, the play that most abounds in examples of this perplexing figure is *Othello* (12). The classic status of Wright's profoundly original essay follows from the way in which it demonstrates something startling that, once seen, cannot be unseen.

Wright is keenly alert to the ways in which hendiadys is usually disagreeable. As he observes, the figure's effect is usually 'of some meaning blurred, or of a relationship inaccurately represented, and represented as more straightforward, more dignified, more grand than it actually is' (174): it 'makes us do a double take' (175). After observing that Virgil found hendiadys congenial whereas other Roman poets did not, Wright directs attention to the way in which Shakespeare also found this 'perplexing figure' congenial, whereas later English writers, including writers who revered Shakespeare, did not. They avoided the figure, Wright suggests, because it is 'too confusing, too disorderly' (10) and 'has always struck English-speaking people as a disturbing and foreign device' (7). And yet, Wright argues, this figure, which 'reminds us, in comic as in tragic moments, how uncertain and treacherous language and behaviour can be' (17) is especially appropriate to *Hamlet*, with its 'themes of anxiety, bafflement, disjunction and the falsity of appearances' (20). Wright's comment on Macbeth's 'a tale / Told by an idiot, full of sound and fury' is too good not to quote: 'the fury has been separated from the sound; nothing is compact, normal unions are disassembled' (15).

Nonetheless, Wright's magisterial essay raises an important question—actually, two questions—about what should be attributed to the author or to the character. In his brief but precious comments on *Othello* Wright criticizes Shakespeare's Moor for the occasions when he 'falls into hendiadys' and reveals his 'carelessness about the precise relations between entities': Othello 'rewords for effect, though the second term is sometimes anticlimactic'; he is 'excessively disposed to use the doublet theatrically'; in his case, as in that of Polonius, 'the use of hendiadys may betray a tendency to orotundity' (16). Maybe so, yet Wright is also showing how hendiadys became an important, characterizing feature of Shakespeare's—not just Othello's— style. Since hendiadys always produces some sense of strain and is 'one strand of the verbal web that made Shakespeare's work seem to its early critics undisciplined and rough' (10–11), its prominence in the mature tragedies may help to explain Dr Johnson's ultimate preference for the comedies, in which he thought Shakespeare less 'strained' and more 'natural', or Ben Jonson's earlier judgment that Shakespeare was the equal of the ancients in his tragedies, but surpasses them in his comedies.

The other question about what is to be attributed to the author, not the character, concerns the way in which new, potentially difficult words and uniquely Shakespearean words like Othello's *exsufflicate* or Macbeth's *incarnardine* flood into the plays written in this period.[10] When confronted with such words, modern actors who have been trained in, or simply grown up with, the kind of naturalistic 'inside-out' method associated with Stanislavky, and the later American 'Method' school of acting, all too frequently resort to what I have elsewhere described as the 'Eureka! effect'.[11] Gazing with horror at his bloody hands and thinking that a little water or even an awful lot of water will not be enough to wash away this deed, the modern Macbeth says that the blood would the 'multitudinous seas'—but then pauses, mangling the verse line as he is casting about for a suitably stupendous word, which he discovers and then shouts: 'incarnadine!' Not only is this savage warrior a secret reader who can coin new words, he is unexpectedly courteous, and provides the groundlings with an immediate gloss: 'making the green one red'.[12] Like Macbeth, Othello is also a warrior, or a very successful mercenary, who knows no Latin and is, as Iago sneers, 'unbookish' (IV.1.101); but unlike Macbeth, the Moor is bilingual, and speaks excellent Venetian English. However, in his case as in Joseph Conrad's, foreignness sometimes peeps through; he comes up with strange words like 'exsufflicate' and 'provulgate', and he frequently 'falls into hendiadys', choosing two words where one would do, and do better. Do you believe all this? I hope not! That would be like believing that Macbeth is a poet, or believing that Othello chooses to speak prose in the eavesdropping scene. The modern Western actor and director would do better to ponder the great Japanese director Tadashi Suzuki's remark that many of Shakespeare's characters would be unable to understand their own speeches.[13]

III. Searching for doublets

We speak of cleaving a log when we have almost, but not quite, split it; we also speak of a child cleaving to its mother when the child seems reluctant to separate and 'grow up'. In cases where A and B are yoked together but pull apart, like 'sound and fury', Wright speaks of 'full hendiadys', which acknowledges the existence of less than 'full', moot or marginal cases. Since the figure equivocates, we should not be surprised that there are so many equivocal instances. When Othello is described as an 'extravagant and wheeling stranger'(I.1.133), or when he speaks of 'the very head and front of my offending' (1.3.80), the A and B seem heterogeneous but can be pulled together, with a little effort. Similarly, when Othello says that if he did not love Desdemona he would not put his 'unhoused free condition' into 'circumscription and confine' (I.2.26–27) we can drag the A and B together, while perhaps feeling that Othello is putting it on, like Pistol when he refers to 'base durance and contagious prison' (*H5*, V.5.36). When, in one speech of just eleven lines, Othello refers to 'the flinty and steel couch of war' (I.3.231), 'place and exhibition' (238), 'accommodation and besort' (239), and 'worldly matters and direction' (300), we can consider whether these are examples of 'full' or marginal hendiadys, but we might also catch ourselves blinking and thinking, 'Not another A and B!'

Still, this is how the mind works, when confronted with this syntactic structure: if the A and B seem to pull apart we always try to figure out some way in which they are not just yoked together but might belong together. This natural impulse sometimes has a logically curious result, that can be traced through several editorial glosses on *exsufflicate, and blown Surmises*. Suppose, for argument's sake, that *exsufflicate* had only two meanings, that it might mean 'inflated' but could also mean 'spat-out'; and suppose that *blown* had only two meanings, that it might also mean 'inflated' but might mean 'fly-blown'. This very limited range of alternative meanings would then allow a correspondingly limited number of combinations. Logically, these combinations would include 'spat-out and inflated' and 'inflated and fly-blown'. I am not recommending these combinations as readings, but I am asking you to notice how they are silently ruled out by the editors of the 1958 New Arden edition, the1968 Penguin edition, the 1997 Norton Shakespeare, and the 2005 Norton Critical Edition:

> *Exsufflicate*: *O.E.D.* records no other example; it is clearly a term of contempt, and if 'blown' means, as it probably does, 'fly-blown', then *exsufflicate* presumably means something the same. (New Arden, p. 104)

Inflated and blown up (but some think the words mean 'spat out and fly-blown').
(Penguin, p. 177)

Both adjectives may mean 'blown-up, inflated,' or the phrase may mean 'spat-out and
fly-blown'. (Norton Shakespeare, p. 1270)

(1) spat out and flyblown (i.e., disgusting) speculations, (2) inflated and blown abroad
(rumoured) notions. (Norton Critical Edition, p. 59)

In each case the editors are looking for doublets, for synonymous or related
meanings: if A means this, then B 'presumably' means that—although hendiadys is
so prominent in *Othello*.

We see the same thing happening in an almost comical way when the editor of
the 1957 Folger edition glosses *exsufflation* by providing an unexpectedly arbitrary
(that is, unexplained though not inexplicable) account of what the Latin *exsufflare*
means, and then insists—no less arbitrarily, while using the word 'literally' in a way
that is untruthful and subliterate—that the desired synonymity is still within reach:

> *Exsufflicate*: Presumably Shakespeare formed the word from *exsufflare*, 'to contemn,
> despise,' and the meaning is 'odious, contemptible'; *blown* means literally 'fly-blown'
> and is therefore synonymous. (p. 64)

John Porter Houston is clearly in another class; his 1988 study *Shakespearean
Sentences: A Study in Style and Syntax* contains the best discussion of adjectival
hendiadys that I know, and he is vigilantly concerned with what he calls 'heterogeneous
doublets'. Yet Houston's comment on 'exsufflicate, and blown Surmises' proposes
that the doublet we have is the doublet we want, since A and B are synonymous, not
heterogenous:

> Obviously 'exsufflicate and blown surmises' (*Othello*, III, iii, 182) constitutes Latin
> and Germanic synonymity.[14]

Certainly, there are many cases where, as Ted Hughes puts it, Shakespeare 'requisitions'
the 'A *and* B' formula so that B 'translates' A, and 'and' means 'means'.[15] Our
problems are then at an end—so long as we know what A or B means.

The introduction of a possible new meaning for A sets up what cognitive linguists
call a *mental space*,[16] and we start trying to see whether and how B fits into the new
mental space. Trying to see that typically involves a rapid flurry of cognitive activity,
of which scarcely a trace will survive in an editorial gloss. Consider the excellent,
editorially original gloss on *blown* in the 1984 New Cambridge edition:

Usually taken in one of two senses: (1) flyblown (as in *WT* 4.4.791); (2) swollen, inflated (as in *Lear* 4.4.27). However, the meaning is surely 'bandied about, rumoured' as in *2H4* Induction 15–16, where it is used in conjunction with precisely the same vocabulary as Othello is using here: 'Rumour is a pipe / Blown by surmises, jealousies, conjectures.' (121)

This is so convincing that we immediately want to see whether and how *exsufflicate* fits into the new mental space. The expert New Cambridge editor must have tried but failed to see that, since his gloss on *exsufflicate* rounds up the usual two suspects:

This is the only occurrence of this word in the language and presumably means 'puffed up, inflated', although some editors take it to mean 'spat out'.

In his new edition of *Othello*, which has appeared in the very week that I am writing this, Michael Neill proposes a more drastic solution:

Exsuffilate, the reading proposed here, would mean 'hissed, whispered'. Hanmer first suggested a possible coinage from Italian *suffolare* (=whistle, hiss), which Florio lists in the form *suffilare*. If this conjecture is correct, then *blown* would mean either 'whispered' or 'rumoured'.

James Boswell the Younger considered and rejected Hanmer's reading in his 1821 revision of Malone's edition of Shakespeare. But Boswell was suggesting another way of understanding *exsufflicate*:

It seems to me that all the criticks have overlooked the meaning of the passage. *Exsufflicate* may be traced to the low Latin, *exsufflare*, to spit down upon, an ancient form of exorcising; and figuratively, to spit out in abhorrence or contempt. *Exsufflicate* may thus signify *despicable*.[17]

Such customs were indeed 'ancient': people were blowing away or spitting at *daemones* before Christians gave this custom a new twist by claiming that the demons they were exorcizing included other people's divinities. But Boswell appears not to know that the 'ancient' customs he describes continued in the Roman Catholic sacrament of baptism.

Charles Richardson clearly did know that, when he developed Boswell's gloss in his fascinating *A Dictionary of the English Language, Combining Explanation with Etymology* (1844):

The first folio of *Shakespeare* reads *Exsufflicate*. (See *Shakespeare*, by Boswell.) *Exsufflare*, it is true, is explained by Du Cange (consequentially) to signify *contemnere*, *despuere, rejicere*; arising from the custom in the Romish administration of baptism, of renouncing the devil and all his works, *exsufflando et despuendo*, by blowing and spitting him away. Hence also, the application of *exsufflare* and *exsufflatio* (common words among early Latin ecclesiastical writers,) to a species of exorcism ...

> *Exsufflicate*, in *Shakespeare*, is not improbably a misprint for *Exsufflate*, i.e. *efflate* or *efflated*, puffed out, and consequently, exaggerated, extravagant—to which *blow'd* is added, not so much for the sake of a second epithet, with a new meaning, as of giving emphasis to the first.[18]

This explains why modern editors suggest that 'exsufflicate' may mean 'spat out'. It also brings us much closer to what I take to be the best way of understanding the Folio's 'exufflicate, and blow'd Surmises'. What is disconcerting is that all modern editors of *Othello* have consulted Furness's Variorum edition, which includes extracts from Boswell and Richardson; and of course they all consult the *OED*, which suggests that *exsufflicate* is 'an arbitrary formation on EXSUFFLATE' but records no usage of words like *exsufflate*, *exsuffle* or *exsufflation* that predates *Othello*—with one exception, which was current through the sixteenth century. Citing examples from Wynken de Worde (1502) and Reginald Scot's *The Discoverie of Witchcraft* (1584), a book with considerable interest for the author of *Macbeth*, the OED records that *exsufflation*, in its *ecclesiastical* sense, was 'the action of blowing, performed by the priest upon a child or grown person at baptism, by way of exorcising the devil, or by the person baptized in token of renouncing the devil'. Once again this brings us close to what I take to be the best reading, and yet every modern editor has presumably considered and then dismissed that possibility. I suggest that we need to look more closely at what Augustine called the 'sacrament of exorcism', while giving more weight to the way in which Shakespeare deliberately departed from his sources by making his Moor a Christian convert.

IV. *Exsufflando et despuendo*

As George Orwell once remarked, there must have been one day in the eighteenth century when the majority of English men and women ceased to be Christian. That change undoubtedly took place, but since we don't know the day in question we can't celebrate it. In 1679, when Timothy Puller's contented book on *The Moderation of the Church of England* was published, the great majority of English men and women were still Christian, but would not have been familiar with the practice of exsufflation. Puller's book took stock of the wonderful ways in which 'Our Church doeth wisely distinguish between what is necessary for Salvation, and what is not' and 'requires our consent in nothing contrary to sense of reason'.[19] In Chapter X, 'Of the Moderation of the Church in reference to the Holy Sacraments', Puller praises the Church of England for offering the 'right administration' of the sacrament of baptism, 'without that wondrous number of Ceremonies (in Exorcism, *Exsufflation*, use of salt, spittle, inunction, &c.) in the Church of Rome required' (282).

In fact, the 'Ceremonies' that Puller was so heartily glad his own Church had abandoned were still set out in the first, 1549 edition of the English Prayer Book. The ceremonies were North African in origin; Tertullian and especially Augustine, who were of course both African, attached great importance to them. The various texts quoted in the first volume of J. D. C. Fisher's *Christian Initiation,*[20] confirm that the 'Ceremonies' in question all involved exorcism. 'Exsufflation' referred to the practice of blowing three times under the eyes of the infant—or of an adult convert like Othello—to blow away the demons ('Depart thou unclean spirit'), and spittle also figured in the *Effleta*. The tablet of salt had to be blessed or exorcized ('I exorcize thee, creature of salt') before being placed in the child's or adult convert's mouth. When adjuring and ejecting demons it was also important to be facing West— as Reginald Scot noted in *The Discoverie of Witchcraft* when, with his determined indifference to good theatre, he dryly *itemized* the richly dramatic procedures for rebaptizing those who had been possessed:

> The right order of exorcism in rebaptisme of a person possessed or bewitched, requireth that exsufflation and abrenunciation be done toward the west. *Item*, there must be erection of hands, confession, profession, oration, benediction, imposition of hands, denudation and unction, with holie oile after baptisme, communion, and inundation of the surplis.'[21]

The 1549 English Prayer Book was already in the process of publication when the Protestant reformer Martin Bucer took up Thomas Cranmer's invitation to come to England, and became Regius Professor of Divinity at the University of Cambridge. However, Cranmer also invited Bucer to comment on the first English Prayer Book, and in 1551, the last year of his life, Bucer published his *Censura*, or Judgment. One of his recommendations was that 'the words of exorcism and adjuration against evil spirits require to be changed to words of prayer.'[22] Bucer explained that he recommended this change—which was then made in the 1552 edition—because 'for some time we have seen the effects produced by the Romish Antichrists and by the impiety innate in all men by which they continually turn sacred ceremonies for the worship of God into various wicked shows' (Fisher 1970, p. 99). He allowed that the practice of exorcizing those who are to be baptized was 'very ancient', but argued that

> nothing is to be preferred to that which is taught by scripture, the word of God, than which nothing is older. For there only those to whom has been given the gift of power are ordered to adjure demons, and these are ordered to expel demons not from any men but only from demoniacs: and, thanks be to God, such are not all men, nor indeed many of those who are brought or come to baptism. (101)

The 'sacrament of exorcism' seemed all the more important to Augustine because he was so concerned with questions that Timothy Puller would have scorned. For example, what kind of body did a demon have? In *The City of God*, Augustine followed the North African pagan Apuleius in supposing that demons have animal natures but aetherial bodies; but other questions were then very pressing for a North African Christian. If hellfire is material, how could it hurt aetherial bodies? How can a spiritual being occupy a physical space? And, if no two bodies can occupy the same space at the same time, how could Christ enter a body that was already possessed by a demon? As Augustine explained in his *De Symbolo ad Catechumenos* (On the Creed: A Sermon to the Catechumens), it was vitally important that 'even little children undergo exsufflation, exorcism; to drive away from them the power of the devil their enemy' so that Christ can enter.[23] So, on the vigil of Easter Sunday the *competentes* or candidates for baptism were exorcized before being baptized and subsequently confirmed. When infants were baptized their godparents delivered the responses, but adult converts like Othello would respond for themselves. In his Easter Sunday sermons Augustine was fond of deploying a bakery metaphor. In one such sermon he explained:

> When as catechumens you were being temporarily deferred, you were under observation in the granary. Then you were enrolled; the grinding process, achieved by fastings and exorcisms, began.[24]

In another sermon he observed:

> For, unless the grain is ground and moistened with water, it cannot arrive at that form which is called bread. So, too, you were previously ground, as it were, by the humiliation of your fasting and by the sacrament of exorcism.[25]

For Augustine, 'exorcism' and 'exsufflation' are almost interchangeable, and at this point a nineteenth-century critic who thought this provided the best way of understanding 'exsufflicate' might have suggested that Othello, as an adult North African convert, was remembering his own sacrament of baptism. I have already admitted my squeamishness, in thinking that this kind or line of argument sooner or later raises doubts about what is to be attributed to the character or to the author. The cognitive concern with mental spaces or frames seems to me more helpful.

V. Mental spaces: conversion and perversion

Why did Shakespeare depart from his sources in making his Moor an adult convert to Roman Catholicism? We can only judge Shakespeare's intentions from consequences, but one consequence seems obvious: no other Shakespearean protagonist refers so frequently to 'Heaven' and his 'Soul' as Othello in the first half of this play. Of course Othello is doing that again when he refers to his 'soul' in rejecting Iago's devilish 'surmises':

> Exchange me for a goat
> When I shall turn the business of my soul
> To such exufflicate and blowed surmises,
> Matching thy inference.

'Exchange me for a goat' is Othello's version of 'when pigs fly': Othello-the-Subject is re-affirming his sense of the Self that he regards as the Real Me—selecting one Self from the dynamic, unstable matrix of Selves that he has it in him to become. When the play begins this Moor is a triumphant, stunning example of what Greenblatt calls 'self-fashioning': this runaway slave and successful mercenary has indeed *made*, or fashioned, a new Self by committing himself to Venice, to Christianity, and to his love for Desdemona. In the play's second half we watch that Self being un-made.

Whether we attribute it to the character or the author, the reference to exsufflation builds a mental space, or frame, in which the doublet we have is, after all, the doublet we want, since *exufflicate* (F, Q) suggests how to understand *blow'd* (F) or *blown* (Q). The frame in which demons are blown away then resurfaces later, at crucial moments when Othello believes there is a demon in Desdemona, not just in her name.

Soon after Othello's rejection of Iago's devilish 'inferences' Desdemona enters, and the Christian convert exclaims to himself:

> If she be false, heaven mocked it selfe:
> I'll not believe't.

> (III.3.280–81)

Not believe what? The 'heavenly' Desdemona and 'heaven' are curiously entangled, as though losing faith in the one would destroy faith in the other. Which is what happens a few minutes later in the same scene, when Othello tells Iago to watch his stagily ritualistic perversion of exsufflation—and then, at the very moment when this Christian convert ceremoniously blows away his love for the 'fair devil', he reverts to earlier dark gods:

> Now do I see 'tis true. Look here, Iago:
> All my fond love thus do I blow to heaven.
> 'Tis gone.
> Arise black vengeance, from the hollow hell!

> (III.3.444–47)

The Christian heaven has vanished from Othello's mind when he invokes 'yond marble heaven, / In the due reverence of a sacred vow' to kill the 'fair devil'—'O, damn her! damn her!'—and instructs Iago to murder Cassio (III.3.460–61, 475). 'Now art thou my Lieutenant', he tells Iago, who replies, 'I am your owne for ever'.

In the final scene the exorcistic scenario or frame reappears in two ways. Firstly, the final scene includes two crucial stage props: a *bed*, with Desdemona in it, occupies the space where the throne would be in the history plays, and Othello is holding a *light* when he enters. If the light is a candle the actor would be shielding it, because candles are treacherous props. They are easily blown out, just as lives are easily blown away, or snuffed. That frightening connection is there, visually, even before Othello makes it explicit by saying that he could relight the 'light' but not Desdemona's life:

> Put out the light, and then put out the light.
> If I quench thee, thou flaming minister,
> I can again thy former light restore,
> Should I repent me. But once put out thy light,
> Thou cunning'st pattern of excelling nature,
> I know not where is that Promethean heat
> That can thy light relume.

(V.2.7–13)

Secondly, the beginning of the same speech shows how Othello's mind is now possessed by another, viciously perverted version of the exorcistic frame or mental space, in which he is ridding the world of a demon as a terrible duty. He says, 'It is the cause, it is the cause, my soule', while refusing to 'name it' (1–2); what he means becomes clearer when he says, 'Yet she must die, else she'll betray more men' (6). The lines about putting out the light then follow, before Othello starts smelling and kissing Desdemona, and then exclaims, 'This sorrow's heavenly, / It strikes, where it doth love' (21–22). When she wakes he tells her to pray to 'heaven and grace' (another peculiarly jarring example of hendiadys), since

> I would not kill thy unprepared spirit,
> No, heavens forefend! I would not kill thy soul.

(31–32)

But then, when she enrages Othello by protesting her innocence, Othello finds his rage still more infuriatingly at odds with his deranged fantasy that he is engaged in some necessarily severe yet just, quasi-priestly 'sacrifice'. Of course he blames Desdemona for that as well, like any wife-beating husband who asks, as his blows rain down, 'Why do you *make me* do this?'—

O perjured woman! thou dost stone my heart,
And makes me call what I intend to do
A murder, which I thought a sacrifice.

(64–67)

Of course in Christian terms this is atrociously confused as well as murderous. In the 'sacrament of exorcism' or exsufflation the priest blows demons away so that Christ can enter the newly born body; he does not kill or 'sacrifice' the catechumen to rid the world of a demon.

Notes

1   Wittgenstein observes that the 'attraction' of a Freudian 'explanation' is in itself 'an extremely interesting phenomenon' since it is 'not a matter of discovery, but persuasion' and 'It may be the fact that the explanation is extremely repellent that drives you to adopt it.' Ludwig Wittgenstein, *Lectures & Conversations on Aesthetics, Psychology, and Religious Belief* (Oxford: Basil Blackwell, 1983 reprint), pp. 23–27.

2   A. D. Nuttall, 'Freud and Shakespeare: *Hamlet*', in John Batchelor, Tom Cain and Claire Lamont, eds, *Shakespearean Continuities: Essays in Honour of E. A. J. Honigmann* (London: Macmillan, and New York: St. Martin's Press, 1997), p. 128.

3   *Othello*, 1.1.139–40. Unless otherwise specified, the quotations from *Othello* in this essay are taken from the modernized text in Edward Pechter's Norton Critical Edition (New York: W. W. Norton, 2004.)

4   For a rich account of counterfactuals involving the Self, see George Lakoff, 'Sorry, I'm Not Myself Today: The Metaphor System for Conceptualizing the Self', in Gilles Fauconnier and Eve Sweetser, eds, *Spaces, Worlds and Grammar* (Chicago and London: University of Chicago Press, 1996), pp. 91–123.

5   See Edward Pechter, *'Othello' and Interpretive Traditions* (Iowa: University of Iowa Press, 1999), pp. 185–86: 'Most remarkable of all', Pechter notes, before considering the readings of Stephen Greenblatt and Ania Loomba, 'is the persistence of a character-based commentary on *Othello* even now, and even among those critics most passionately wed to the theoretical claims by which such a commentary has been explicitly disavowed.'

6   Hans Busch, ed. and trans., *Verdi's 'Otello' and 'Simon Boccanegra' (revised version) in Letters and Documents*, 2 vols. (Oxford: Clarendon Press, 1988), vol. 2, p. 485.

7   Bernard Williams, *Shame and Necessity* (Berkeley: University of California Press, 1993), and Ewan Fernie, *Shame in Shakespeare* (London: Routledge, 2002).

8   Michael Neill, ed., *Othello* (Oxford: Oxford University Press, 2006).

9   G. T. Wright's frequently reprinted essay 'Hendiadys and Hamlet' first appeared in *PMLA*, vol. xcvi (March 1981), pp. 168–93, and later became the first chapter of Wright's fine collection, *Hearing the Measures: Shakespearean and Other Inflections* (Madison: University of Wisconsin Press, 2002), from which my quotations are taken.

10 The newness of a word does not make for difficulty if the new word builds on another,
    already familiar word. The word *exufflicate* (Q and F) baffles the modern reader, whereas
    the words *blow'd* (F) or *blown* (Q) seem familiar. But if Shakespeare's contemporaries
    related the uniquely Shakespearean word *exsufflicate* to the practice of exsufflation, that
    would have directed their sense of how to understand *blow'd* or *blown*. In this case the
    seemingly familiar word is the more problematic word, because it has so many different
    meanings.

11 Graham Bradshaw, '*Othello* in the Age of Cognitive Science', in *Shakespeare Studies*, 38
    (Tokyo, 2001), pp. 17–38.

12 In this case B doesn't fully 'translate' A, since *carno*, the Latin root for 'incarnadine'
    and words like 'incarnation', means 'flesh', not 'blood'. The frightening idea of water
    becoming fleshlike is not present in 'making the green one red'. Later, when the Caroline
    poets Thomas Carew and Richard Lovelace borrowed the word 'incarnardine', they were
    describing feminine cheeks or complexions, which would not have won these poets'
    praise if they were 'one red'.

13 'Interview with Suzuki Tadashi', *Performing Shakespeare in Japan*, edited by Minami
    Ryuta, Ian Carruthers and John Gillies (Cambridge: Cambridge University Press, 2001),
    pp. 196–207. Suzuki's comments are further discussed in Tetsuo Kishi and Graham
    Bradshaw, *Shakespeare in Japan* (London: Continuum Press, 2005), pp. 90–91.

14 John Porter Houston, *Shakespearean Sentences: A Study in Style and Syntax* (Baton
    Rouge: Louisiana State University Press, 1988), p. 66.

15 Ted Hughes, *Shakespeare and the Goddess of Complete Being* (London: Faber and Faber,
    1992), p. 141. The heading for this section of my essay, 'Across the fulcrum of that
    "and"', is taken from Hughes, p. 134.

16 The theory of 'mental spaces' was first developed by Gilles Fauconnier in 1985; the best,
    most up-to-date account of it is in Barbara Dancygier and Eve Sweetser's brilliant new
    book *Mental Spaces in Grammar: Conditional Constructions* (Cambridge: Cambridge
    University Press, 2005).

17 See Boswell's 1821 revision of Edmond Malone's *Plays and Poems of William
    Shakespeare* (London: R. C. and J. Rivington, 1821), vol. 9, p. 365.

18 See the entry for *exsufflicate* in Charles Richardson, *A Dictionary of the English Language,
    Combining Explanation with Etymology* (London: William Pickering, 1844).

19 Timothy Puller, *The Moderation of the Church of England* (London: Richard Chiswell,
    1679), p. 114.

20 J. D. C. Fisher, *Christian Initiation: Baptism in the Medieval West: A Study in the
    Disintegration of the Primitive Rite of Initiation* (London: SPCK, 1965).

21 Reginald Scot, *The Discoverie of Witchcraft*, Book 15, Chapter 24 (London: William
    Brome, 1584), p. 440. Scot's discussion of the 'manner of conjuring salt' follows on p.
    445.

22 Quoted in J. D. C. Fisher's second volume: *Christian Initiation: The Reformation Period:
    Some Early Reformed Rites on Baptism and Confirmation and other contemporary
    documents* (London: SPCK, 1970), p. 102.

23 Quoted from the translation by C. L. Cornish on the internet: www.ccel.org/fathers.

24 Sermon 229, in *St. Augustine: Commentary on the Lord's Sermon on the Mount with Seventeen Related Sermons*, tr. Danis J. Kavanagh (Washington, DC: Catholic University of America Press, 1951), p. 201.

25 Sermon 227, in *St Augustine: Sermons on the Liturgical Seasons*, trans. Sister Mary Sarah MulDowney (New York: Fathers of the Church, Inc., 1959), p. 196.

'What are these faces?'
Interpreting Bearded Women in *Macbeth*

Brett D. Hirsch

On the 16th of February 1631, Magdalena Ventura stands next to her husband while her infant son suckles on her exposed breast. As fate would have it, this scene has been masterfully captured on canvas by Jusepe de Ribera, under instructions to do so by Ferdinand II, Third Duke of Alcalá. The purpose of the painting (Figure 4) is announced to the viewer in large, capital letters on a stone plinth positioned next to Magdalena: 'EN MAGNVM NATVRAE MIRACVLVM'. At first glance, there seems little to indicate that Ribera has portrayed a 'great wonder of nature'. That is, until the viewer realizes that there are two bearded figures in the painting: and the woman breast-feeding her child is one of them. The viewer—perhaps experiencing shock, awe, revulsion, or any combination of these—then turns to the rest of the superimposed inscription on the plinth to read that Magdalena was aged thirty-seven when she began to become hairy and grew a beard, so long and thick that it seemed more like that of a gentleman than that of a mother who had borne three sons by her husband.[1] For good measure, the gender ambiguity that pervades the scene is reinforced iconographically by the inclusion of a spindle of wool and a snail on top of the plinth: the former a symbol of feminine domesticity, the latter of the hermaphrodite.

According to the earliest text of

Figure 4: Jusepe de Ribera, *Magdalena Ventura with Her Husband and Son*. 1631. Oil on canvas. By permission of the Fundación Casa Ducal de Medinaceli, Seville.

Shakespeare's *Macbeth* available to us—the First Folio of 1623—audiences of early performances of the play in Jacobean London presumably experienced a similar spectacle on the stage, as Macbeth and Banquo first approach the weyward Sisters:

> *Banquo.* How farre is't call'd to Soris? What are these,
> So wither'd, and so wilde in their attyre,
> That looke not like th' Inhabitants o'th' Earth,
> And yet are on't? Liue you, or are you aught
> That man may question? you seeme to vnderstand me,
> By each at once her choppie finger laying
> Vpon her skinnie Lips: you should be Women,
> And yet your Beards forbid me to interprete
> That you are so.

$$(138-46; 1.\ 3.\ 37-45)^2$$

Critical assessment of Banquo's comment in this early scene—that the presence of beards prohibits his identifying the Sisters as women—have ranged between regarding the line as 'an act of genius or a happy accident',[3] through to the more serious accusations of 'unbridled sensationalism' on Shakespeare's part, since such representations 'refuse any serious engagement with witchcraft' in favour of 'a low-budget, frankly exploitative collage of randomly chosen bits of witch-lore',[4] ultimately suppressing the voices and concerns of those who have witnessed or experienced the reality of witchcraft persecutions.

This essay seeks to reconstruct how an individual in the audience of an early performance of *Macbeth* might, like Banquo, have interpreted these bearded women, drawing on contemporary accounts of witches, pamphlet literature on fashion, medical treatises, the lives of saints, popular ballads, ethnographic reports, and travel literature. In light of these different cognitive strands, it is the argument of this chapter that regardless of whether Shakespeare's deviation from his source is deliberate or not, or even his own, that the variety of possible audience responses to the bearded women on display onstage are all significant, and that they enrich our understanding of both the play itself, and the culture that produced and consumed it.

It is worth noting at the outset that this essay relies on the assumption that the weyward Sisters were staged as bearded.[5] This is an important assumption, since it undermines the only available account of an early performance of *Macbeth* available to us: that of Simon Forman. Forman's account of the production he attended in 1611 makes no reference to the Sisters as having beards, describing them as '3 women feiries or Nymphes'.[6] This has led some critics to conclude that the beards were only incorporated into the play later in a revision by Middleton to allow for the increasing number of parts for boy actors,[7] or that the account is evidence of a 'lost text' of the play.[8]

While it is certainly possible that the beards are a later revision, it is just as likely that they were present in earlier performances of the play. As countless scholars have noted, Forman's account of the play deviates markedly from the playtext, leaving out entire scenes and introducing others that are not present in the Folio.[9] That his account of the play does not describe the Sisters as bearded does not of itself prove that this was the case, since it appears that Forman's account of the performance has been corrupted by his recollection of Shakespeare's sources, in particular the *Chronicles* of Raphael Holinshed, in which the Sisters are described as 'Goddesses of destinie, or els some Nimphes or Feiries',[10] with an accompanying woodcut (Figure 5) depicting the Sisters as 'young and attractive females, well coiffed and richly dressed',[11] with apparently little correlation to the narrative in which it appears.

Figure 5: Woodcut from Raphael Holinshed, *The Chronicles of England, Scotlande, and Irelande.* London, 1577. Courtesy of the Rare Book and Manuscript Library, University of Pennsylvania.

Further, textual scholarship has yet to establish with any certainty the exact nature of Middleton's relationship to the text of *Macbeth* as we know it. While it seems clear that his hand was present at least in the additional songs and witch scenes later in the play, there seems little to suggest that Banquo's description of the Sisters as bearded was one of these later revisions. Finally, while Forman's account omits references to the Sisters as bearded—since one assumes that Forman understood nymphs and fairies as we tend to, that is, without beards—there is little evidence to suggest that they were not presented as such. The false beard was an important prop in the early modern theatre, with a variety of colours and shapes available to suit every need.[12]

The use of prosthetic beards on stage was evidently popular enough to merit satire and dramatization, such as Bottom's quibble in *A Midsummer Night's Dream* over which beard he should wear (351–58; I. 2. 83–89), or the postponement of the play in *The Book of Sir Thomas More* by one of the players while he sends 'for a long beard' to borrow for the performance.[13] While it is possible that Forman's account is accurate—that the Sisters were not staged as bearded women—the prevalence of using false beards in the Jacobean theatre coupled with the problems with Forman's account itself suggests that it is more likely that an audience actually saw what Banquo described.

I. Bearded Witches

Jacobean audiences, much like audiences today, would have immediately recognized the bearded Sisters as witches. Although the pamphlet literature on witchcraft and witchcraft trials is silent on the presence of beards,[14] the link between bearded women and witchcraft seems to be firmly embedded into the cultural consciousness of early modern England. Perhaps there are no explicit references to beards in the records simply because it went without saying: to borrow from Mark Twain, 'deformity and female beards' may have been 'too common' in these cases 'to attract attention'.[15]

Whatever the reason for this silence in the archives, the association is frequently made on stage. When Falstaff disguises himself as a woman in *The Merry Wives of Windsor*, the reaction he receives from Evans is to be taunted as 'a witch indeede' since he appears to be a woman with 'a great peard' (2076–77; IV. 2. 179–80). Similarly, in Beaumont and Fletcher's *The Honest Man's Fortune,* Longavile describes women turning to witchcraft for revenge:

> Thus the bauds would all turn witches to revenge
> Themselves upon us and the women that
> Come to us, for disguises must wear beards,
> And that's they say, a token of a witch.[16]

The same reasoning occurs in the first part of Thomas Dekker's *The Honest Whore*, where the servant does not admit a messenger with 'haires at his mouth, for feare he should be a woman', on the basis that 'some women haue beardes' and that 'mary they are halfe witches' (sig. G3R). While it seems that the association of bearded women with witchcraft is more prevalent in works of comedy, it does occur outside the genre as well: in *King Lear* Goneril is described as 'with a white beard' (2543; IV. 5. 96), and Leontes's description of Paulina as a 'mankind Witch' (981; II. 3. 68) and 'a grosse Hagge' (1031; II. 3. 108) are all suggestive of the connection between witchcraft and bearded women.

The beard as a token of a witch forms part of a wider association of monstrosity with diabolism and the supernatural.[17] According to both popular superstition and 'learned' witchcraft treatises, the body of the witch was supposed to be physically deformed, as an outward manifestation of inward, moral aberration, or branded by the Devil. As Reginald Scot reports, 'one sort of such as are said to bee witches, are women which be commonly old, lame, bleare-eied, pale, fowle, and full of wrinkles', or 'miserable wretches', 'odious vnto all their neighbors'.[18] For example, in *The Faerie Queene*, Spenser's lengthy description of the deformed witch Duessa concludes by stating that she is 'more vgly [in] shape yet neuer liuing creature saw'.[19] Elizabeth Sawyer, the title role in *The Witch of Edmonton*, is taken for a witch since she is 'poor, deform'd and ignorant', and has only one eye.[20] In light of the popular perceptions of witches as physically deformed, and the common assessment of bearded women as witches on stage, it is clear that many members of the Jacobean audience watching *Macbeth* would have interpreted the bearded Sisters, 'so wither'd, and so wilde in their attyre' (139; I. 3. 38), as witches.

II. Bearded Saints

A young woman is pledged to marry a pagan king by her father. To preserve her vows of chastity and desire to live a pious life, she prays to God for deliverance. The morning of the wedding it becomes apparent to all that her prayers have been answered: overnight she has sprouted a beard so lavish that her veil cannot conceal it from the now (understandably) upset groom, who refuses to go through with the marriage. Her father, furious at this miraculous turn of events, has her crucified.

This is the legend of the virgin and martyred Saint Uncumber, known also as Wilgefortis and by many other names throughout Europe, whose popularity continued throughout the late medieval period and into the early modern. It is now believed that the Uncumber legend is the result of a case of mistaken identity, attached to the statue of the Volto Santo in Italy:

> Lead badges of the statue were brought home by pilgrims on their hats and tunics, and other equally crudely made small copies circulated widely, rather like models of the Eiffel Tower or the Leaning Tower of Pisa bought by tourists today. Now these seemed very strange to people who had never seen either the Volto Santo or a crucified Christ clothed in a long robe. They were soon taken to be figures of a woman, a fully dressed bearded woman stretched out on the cross. But why would a bearded woman be crucified? A legend was constructed to give a rational basis for this figment of pious popular imagination.[21]

Regardless of how the legend began,[22] Uncumber became a venerated and popular saint in England. Her statue still stands in the Henry VII Chapel of Westminster Abbey (Figure 6), and 'numerous tapestries and murals of this girl dating from the fifteenth and sixteenth centuries' are to be found in 'churches throughout the southern counties' of England.[23] Her story struck a particular resonance with unhappy wives,

since it was said that for 'a pek of otys
she wyll not fayle to vncumber them of
theyr husbondis'.[24]
    Uncumber was not the only saint
to be blessed with a beard to safeguard
her virginity. Others, including the
bearded Paula of Avila and Saint
Galla, form part of the tradition of
virginitas deformitate defensa, where
some form of virginal disfigurement
(including leprosy, struma, blindness,
and insanity) 'stressing heroic actions
or strategies of affliction which are
condoned by the Church as necessary
for the maintenance of chastity'.[25]
    It is certainly possible that an
audience member watching *Macbeth*
in Jacobean London may, at that
cultural moment, have linked the visual
representation of bearded women on
stage with memories of the stories of
bearded virgin martyrs, or even with
the images of the saints themselves.
How, then, would such a cognitive
association affect an interpretation of the play?

Figure 6: Statue of Saint Uncumber. Henry VII
Chapel, Westminster Abbey, London. By permission
of the Courtauld Institute of Art.

    The presence of beards on both the weyward Sisters and the saints operate as an
indication of their relationship with the supernatural, whether diabolical or divine.
Both the superstitious beliefs surrounding Saint Uncumber and the tale reported
by one of the Sisters contain the connected elements of dispatching husbands and
food. The witch recounts an incident with a 'Saylors Wife' who refused to share
the 'Chestnuts in her Lappe' (101; I. 3. 3). As a result of being turned away, the
witch confides that she will sneak 'like a Rat without a tayle' (107; I. 3. 8) aboard
the sailor's ship to exact her revenge.[26] Alternatively, for those wives who 'can not
slepe but slumber', to 'giue oates unto saynt Uncumber' meant the hope of divine
assistance in un-encumbering themselves of their husbands, who presumably
impaired their sleep by snoring.[27] The association between food (offered or rejected)
and removing husbands (intentionally or inflicted), while shared by both the stories
of the witch and Saint Uncumber, is perhaps a tenuous link at best, but it is certainly
one that an audience was able to make during the early performances of *Macbeth* in
Jacobean London.

III. Bearded Bodies

Standing alongside St Thomas's Hospital, the Globe Theatre certainly played to audiences that counted among them doctors, physicians, surgeons, and barber-surgeons. However, these professionals were not the only members of the Jacobean audience to possess some medical knowledge: aside from religious tracts, the printing presses teemed with books on medicine, anatomy, surgery, herbals, and compilations of diverse ways to stay the plague, prolong life, and assuage illness of all kinds. One such publication was *The Historie of Man*, compiled by the physician John Banister in 1578, in which we find the following account:

> It is straunge to vs that women haue beardes, albeit not so euery where: for in Caria it is a thyng familiar: whereas some of them beyng a while frutefull, but after widowes, and for that suppressed of naturall course, put on virilitie, being then bearded, hoarie, and chaunged in voice.[28]

Banister is referring to a tale found in Hippocrates' *Epidemics* in which Phaetousa, the wife of Pytheas and mother to his children, 'stopped menstruating for a long time' after her husband was exiled from their home in Abdera. As a result, 'her body was masculinized and grew hairy all over', she 'grew a beard' and 'her voice became harsh' like that of a man. Hippocrates goes on to report that the physicians attending to her agreed that there was only 'one hope of feminizing her', that is, 'if normal menstruation occurred', but all their attempts to 'bring forth [her] menses' were in vain, and she died shortly afterwards.[29]

There were many other narrative accounts of women who grew beards in the printed literature available to readers in early modern England. These contemporary accounts, found mostly in continental treatises in translation, include the argument that 'should a beard grow on her chin, and her floures surcease' a woman should 'become as perfect a man, as nature could produce'.[30] Others observed that the production of a beard was a significant indication that a change in sex had occurred. For example, Tomaso Garzoni relates the tale of a woman who 'married her-selfe to a man, and the day of her marriage became male, sprowting foorth a bearde, with members genitall'. This same individual later 'tooke a wife, being thus (as hee saith) for euer conuerted into a man'.[31] The same is repeated in Antonio de Torquemada's *The Spanish Mandeuile of Miracles*, who includes stories of this 'wonderful nouelty' culled from both classical and contemporary sources.[32] In these reports, it seems to be taken for granted that the transformation of women into men involves growing a beard, since Torquemada feels the need to stress the lack of a beard in one particular case reported by a Portuguese doctor of a woman who

> [A]t such age as by the course of nature her flowers should haue come downe, in sted thereof, as though it had before lyen hidden in her belly, there issued forth a

perfect and able member masculine, so that of a woman shee became a man, and was presently clothed in mans habite and apparrell, and her name changed from Marie to Manuell Pacheco ... she shortly afterward married a Gentlewoman of a very Noble house, by whom whether she had any children or no, he writeth not: but onely that she neuer came to haue any beard, retayning alwayes a womanly face & countenance.[33]

Perhaps the most famous of these accounts is that given by Montaigne in his essay, 'Of the force of Imagination', which was translated into English by John Florio in 1603. The essay describes a man, who up until the age of twenty-two was 'both knowne and seene to be a woman-childe' named Marie. Apparently this all came to change when straining to leap over something, Marie found that 'where before [s] he was a woman, [s]he sodainly felt the instruments of a man to come out of h[er]'. Adopting her new sex and a new name, the 'woman-childe' Marie became the man Germane, who would in later years grow 'a longe bearde'. The event became the subject of a new song for young girls 'to warne one an other' that 'when they are leaping, not to straine themselves overmuch' and not to 'open their legs too wide, for feare they should be turned to boyes, as *Marie Germane* was'.[34]

For both physicians and laypersons with an interest in medicine, accounts such as these stood as authoritative testimony that the event of a woman growing a beard, however marvellous a sight, was one that occurred naturally. Indeed, even those authorities that could usually be counted on to assign supernatural causes for such phenomena, namely, the demonologists, conceded that women that produced beards (or even went so far as to *become* men) did so 'not, however, by witchcraft but naturally'.[35] How, then, were such transformations explained?

According to the accepted medical knowledge of the age—the Galenic or humoral model of the body—the central constitutional difference between the sexes was that of heat, with male bodies being hotter (and therefore more efficient) than female bodies. Essentially this results in a different 'degree to which [the sexes] refine their superfluities, and also in the way they dispose of them'; thus, 'women lack the special pores through which men produce sweat and beards', since 'they give off their residues through menstruation'.[36] For example, Thomas Hill's *The Contemplation of Mankinde* describes the production of the beard using the analogy of an oven:

[M]uch lyke to the smoke of an Ouen heated, that passeth so long through the chinks of the same, untill those passages, through the heate are wholy stopped, that no more smoke can after passe through them. Euen the like, doe the fumosities of man issue forth, into the maner of heares: which are properly named the heares of the Bearde.[37]

For Hill, the body operates like an oven, with superfluities likened to smoke and fumes. In male bodies, hairiness is evidence of the 'superior' male capacity to refine and purge superfluities through pores as sweat or as hair. Female bodies, on the other hand, apparently lack these mechanisms for expelling waste, and rely instead on menstruation to do the job. Thus cases of bearded women, such as those reported by Hippocrates or captured on canvas by Ribera, were interpreted as being the result of the female body lacking the ability to properly purge itself by menstruation.

Alternatively, bearded women were thought to have hotter bodies like those of men, which would explain their shared capacity for expelling superfluities in the form of sweat and hair:

> And therefore sometime women hot & moyst of complection haue beards, and in the wise men of colde and drye complection, haue lyttle beards, and therfore on men that be gelded, growe no beards: for they haue lost the hot members that should breed the hot humour & smoake, the matter of hayre.[38]

Thus, in the early modern mind, the presence of a beard on a woman was taken to be either a 'signe and token of [the] heate and of substantiall humour' usually found in male bodies,[39] or as the result of the cessation of menstruation. Further, the cessation of the 'monethlie melancholike flux or issue of bloud' in women was linked to 'weakenesse both of bodie and braine', occasioned with 'melancholike imaginations'.[40] In these cases of amenorrhea, 'the same blood not finding any passage, troubleth the braine' with 'idle fancies and fond conceipts', 'diverse imaginations of horrible spectres', and 'fearefull sights' that have been known to bring some sufferers 'to throwe and cast themselves into wells or pittes' or to otherwise 'destroy themselves by hanging, or some such miserable end'.[41]

It is at this point that the discourses of witchcraft and medicine intersect, since, as we have seen, women who were accused of witchcraft were often elderly and deformed. Likewise, melancholia was a 'disease that was most likely to affect the malnourished and the elderly', to which 'menopausal women', and those whose menstruation has otherwise ceased, 'were particularly susceptible'.[42] The authorities that sought to point out the credulity of witchcraft persecutions—including the figures of Reginald Scot and Johannes Weyer—raised this striking correspondence, arguing that witches were, for the most part, elderly women who either confessed to being such as a result of their melancholy delusions, or believed they were so on account of their troubled minds.

To those members of the audience armed with varying degrees of medical knowledge, watching the three bearded Sisters in *Macbeth* would have stirred up recollections of tales of women being suddenly transformed into men, or of descriptions of the reported side effects of menopause. Who are these bearded figures? Are they elderly women who have ceased to menstruate? Do they possess bodies that, like men, produce more heat? Are they in some stage of transformation into men?

Perhaps, if their beards are an indication that they have stopped menstruating, they are also suffering from melancholic delusions: this would certainly explain Lady Macbeth's tortured mind after she has sought to 'make thick [her] blood', to 'stop vp th'accesse, and passage to Remorse' (394–95; I. 5. 42–43) and (presumably) cease menstruating herself.

In this way, medicine works to demystify what would ordinarily appear to be supernatural: instead of being witches with diabolical powers, the Sisters become menopausal melancholics with symptoms like facial hair and troubled minds. Similarly, Lady Macbeth's later mental instability can be seen as a consequence of her amenorrhea.[43] In both cases medical knowledge offers those members of the audience sceptical of the reality of witchcraft a natural model for understanding the spectacles on display.

IV. Fashion and Travel: Beards at Home and Abroad

As Will Fisher has recently shown, 'sex was materialized through an array of features and prosthetic parts' (157), that is, that both genital and non-genital markers of sexual difference, such as beards, items of clothing, hair, and weapons, were constitutive elements of gendered identity in early modern culture. For Fisher, in the Renaissance 'the beard was one of the primary ways in which masculinity was materialized', and 'not simply a "secondary" sexual characteristic' (184), challenging the exclusively genital focus of the model of sexual difference posited by Thomas Laqueur.[44] Similarly, Mark Johnston has argued that the beard, 'as both a linguistic and physical entity', was 'the most important of all the visual social signifiers' on the early modern English stage, 'signifying in its absence as well as its presence and gesturing toward a complex interplay among masculinity, theatricality, and economics'.[45]

There is certainly a large body of English Renaissance literature to support both Fisher's and Johnston's assertions. In 1553, Piero Valeriano's defence of the growing of beards by ecclesiastical dignitaries, *Pro sacerdotum barbis,* was translated into English, which states 'that a beard is a token of manly nature, the thynge selfe dothe shewe more playne, than any man can declare', and

> It is openly knowen amongest all kyndes of men, that chyldren, women, gelded men, & those that are tender and delycat, are euer sene withoute beardis: and therby it may be easily understande, to whome those that are shauen, may be likened.[46]

This idea, that the beard is a token of manhood, is a common topos in the literature of the Renaissance, and is found variously in religious tracts, pamphlets on fashion, and ethnographic treatises. Thomas Hall, pastor of Kings Norton, wrote that a 'decent growth of the Beard is a signe of Manhood' that is 'given by God to distinguish the Male from the Female sex'.[47] As noted by Heinrich Cornelius Agrippa, 'every female beardles doth remaine', regardless of age: 'but old and yong her face is still the same'.[48] A popular ballad of the time, 'A Commendation and Censure of Beards', suggested that a 'beard is a thing / That commands in a King', and

> If it be such a thin
> Or femal chin,
>> To see a beard to sprout,
> What a Monster than
> May we call that man
>> Whose face is quite without?[49]

This sentiment rings true for John Bulwer, since he writes that 'shaving the Chin is justly to be accounted a note of Effeminancy', and that men who 'produce not a Beard, the signe of virility', are therefore 'not without cause' to be called 'women'.[50] For Bulwer, the absence of a beard, which is 'the naturall Ensigne of Manhood appearing about the mouth' (193), is the greatest evidence of effeminacy, and 'to be seen with a smooth skin like a woman' is 'a shameful metamorphosis' (199) for a man. Bulwer devotes entire pages on this 'piacular' and 'monstrous' habit of shaving, citing classical and biblical authorities to show that to shave the beard is 'an Act not only of indecency, but of injustice, and ingratitude against God and Nature' (199–200). At the same time, his attack on the practice of shaving participates in contemporary anxieties about the relationship between fashion and identity, fearing that those who shave their beards are on a slippery slope of effeminate behaviour and may proceed to 'go apparelled like women', and perhaps go so far as to 'not only counterfeit their speech', but 'also sit down and spin' (199). The anxiety that clothing could somehow transform the wearer's sexual identity was hardly new. Such attacks were usually directed at the theatres, since male actors had to don women's clothing to assume female roles.[51] Others were concerned about the growing trend of women wearing men's attire. Writing against this practice, the Puritan Philip Stubbes argued that:

> Our Apparell was giuen us as a signe distinctiue to discern betwixt sex and sex, & therfore one to weare the Apparel of another sex, is to participate with the same, and to adulterate the veritie of his owne kinde. Wherefore these Women may not improperly be called Hermaphroditi, that is, Monsters of bothe kindes, half women, half men.[52]

As the Puritans, religious zealots, and morally concerned citizens of England anguished over a fashion they believed to be unnatural, increased international trade with the old world and competition to discover and colonize new ones resulted in an improved awareness of other cultural practices. Following his extended attack on the practice of shaving, Bulwer proceeds to catalogue the fashions in facial hair found in different cultures. These include the Tartars who 'shave their upper Lips, and warre with the *Persians* for not doing so' (195), through to the men in 'the Kingdome of *Mancy* in great *India*' who 'have Beards as it were Cats' (205). Facial hair operated as a sign of cultural difference between the Europeans themselves, with 'the *Hungarians* [who] shave their Beards and leave nothing but the Mustachoes' (198) and the Germans, who are 'a little too indulgent' with their beard growth, 'insomuch as some of them have been seen to have had their Beards so long, that they would reach unto their feet' (210).

Before its encounter with the New World, the European mind identified the Jew and the Muslim as the foremost cultural Other, both 'widely imagined and graphically represented as being bearded'.[53] Elliott Horowitz has argued that a radical shift took place during the age of discovery, as the beard, now fashionable, became instead aligned with a Christian Europe that faced a new cultural Other: the beardless inhabitants of the New World. According to Bulwer, Horowitz's argument appears to be true: the 'Naturall Inhabitants of *Virginia*' wear 'halfe their Beards shaven' (201), while in 'the Province of *Mexico* the men are Beardless' (203), and those in '*Elizabeths* Island, toward the North of *Virginia*' have 'no Beards, but counterfeits' (205).

Reports of bearded natives were not exclusively of men. 'There is a Mountaine of *Ethiopia*', writes Bulwer, 'where women live with prolix beards' (215–16). Not to be outdone, the women in '*Brasile, Caneda*, and *Nova Francia*' are 'said to have some kind of Beard under their Chins' (216). Although Bulwer prefaces these reports with those of individual sightings of bearded women in Europe, and the explanation that women 'through discontinuance of the Company of men, and defect of their Courses, have grown Bearded', he maintains that 'Woman by Nature is smooth and delicate', and 'if she have many haires she is a Monster' (215).

What did this all mean to an audience watching *Macbeth* in Jacobean London? For some members of the audience, the spectacle of three bearded women may have fuelled anxieties about the relationship between costume and sexual identity. That male actors could present themselves so convincingly in female roles was threatening enough, since it raised the unnerving possibility that sexual identity might be merely a performance itself. To add costuming to the mix, as well as the beards—misplaced material signifiers of masculine identity—could only add to the possible anxiety and confusion. To borrow a phrase from David Scott Kastan, 'the cultural anxiety about the fluidity of social role and identity found shrill voice' in *Macbeth*'s bearded Sisters.[54]

It is also possible that members of the audience were familiar with tales of women that grew beards in foreign lands, and that this informed their interpretation of the weyward Sisters. Perhaps others were familiar with reports of bearded women closer to home than the New World and the dark parts of Africa: Gerald of Wales had, in his *Topography of Ireland*, described a woman 'that had a beard down to her waist', as well as a 'crest from her neck down along her spine'. This same woman, 'in spite of these two enormities was, nevertheless, not hermaphrodite' and 'was in other respects sufficiently feminine'.[55] On the Irish in general, Gerald wrote that 'their external characteristics of beard and dress', and their 'internal cultivation of the mind' are 'so barbarous that they cannot be said to have any culture' (101).

Descriptions of Irish barbarity extended to their language. As Patricia Palmer has shown, 'Irish was consistently equated with bestial utterance', and 'with the metaphorically beastly dialect of the ungodly: of heathens, witches, papists'.[56] Early modern English writers, such as Barnabe Rich, made the explicit link between the Irish and witchcraft and heathenism, likening the mourning of Irish women to the 'houling of dogges', the 'croaking of Rauens' and 'the shrieking of Owles', a practice 'fitter for Infidels and Barbarians', than 'to be in vse and custome among Christians'.[57]

Christopher Highley has recently posited that the English perception of the Irish as barbaric, both in culture and language, extended to the Gaelic Scots:

> The label of 'barbarian' that [King] James and like-minded Southerners routinely used for the Highlanders and Islanders of Northern Scotland had at least two etymologies in the Renaissance. In a fanciful folk etymology related by Gerald of Wales, 'barbarian' was derived from 'barbaros' or bearded, a meaning activated when Banquo exclaims upon first encountering the witches.[58]

Tracing a more authentic etymology of the word 'barbarian' to 'the Greek for a non-Greek speaker', Highley argues that '*Macbeth* exploits a similar mingling of cultural categories when the witches speak a bestial language' (62). As such, the witches can be interpreted as 'conjuring up the archetypal figure of the barbarian', one that is 'menacingly instantiated in the Gaelic Highlander at the time of *Macbeth*'s early performances' (63).

In light of English perceptions of the Irish, and the Gaelic language and reputation for barbarism they shared with the Highland Scots, coupled with the historical reports of bearded women hailing from the Celtic fringe, it is possible that members of the audience watching early performances of *Macbeth* may have interpreted the weyward Sisters, 'stubbled and stammering',[59] as originating from those uncivilized northern lands.

V. Aliens in their Midst

In his brilliant analysis of the monstrous races in medieval art and thought, John Friedman explains that, 'even the most bizarre, however, were not supernatural or infernal creatures, but varieties of men, whose chief distinction from the men of Europe was one of geography'.[60] For example, in his illustration of the 'Second

Figure 7 (left): Woodcut from Hartmann Schedel, *Liber Chronicarum*. Nuremberg, 1493. Courtesy of Special Collections and Archives, Leatherby Libraries, Chapman University.

Figure 8 (right): Detail of the bearded woman.

Age' of man—a fallen and degenerate world before the Flood—Hartmann Schedel's *Liber Chronicarum* (otherwise referred to as the Nuremberg Chronicle) includes woodcuts of a variety of grotesque figures, of which one is a bearded woman (Figures 7 and 8). We read on the recto side of the leaf (fol. XII) that these 'women with beards down to their chest but with bald heads, without hair' are from India.[61]

As the reports by the Nuremberg Chronicle make clear, the distance from the Rhine to the Ganges was more than simply a matter of geographic space, but of moral and spiritual distance. The cartographic imagination therefore operated in two dimensions, simultaneously mapping the bodies of land and water, as well as the increasingly deformed bodies of those that approached the extremities. This partially explains why in the Renaissance—an age of increased international contact and trade, of discovery and colonial enterprise—books like the *Liber Chronicarum* and *The Voyages and Trauailes of Sir John Maundeuile* and their tales of strange and wondrous peoples in far-off lands were immensely popular. Indeed, the cartographic imagination was a powerful cultural phenomenon: as Friedman has suggested, even 'as geographical knowledge grew, and the existence of many of these races began to appear unlikely', perceptions of monstrous difference persisted and 'were shifted to regions less well known—the Far North and ultimately the New World', rather than being dismissed outright as fictions.[62] In the early modern mind, like the medieval, longitude and latitude continued to measure both *distance* and *difference*, with the relationship between the two in constant negotiation as new knowledge prompted reassessment.

An audience watching *Macbeth* during an early performance in Jacobean London brought with them more than the coins to cover the cost of admission to see the performance. They brought with them an infinite number of individual experiences, as well as a shared cultural milieu, both of which took part in the construction of meaning they would glean from the play. Some patrons would have brought with them specialized knowledge, such as the physicians, surgeons, and divines. Others may have had access to this knowledge, due to the popularity of such topics at the printing presses and bookstalls.

It is this constellation of the possible available knowledge that an audience could employ to interpret the early performances of *Macbeth* that this essay has thus far sought to reconstruct. Regardless of whether Shakespeare's deviation from Holinshed was deliberate or not, or even his own, the variety of possible audience responses to the bearded women onstage—responses linking them to other witches, amenorrhea and melancholia, the lives of saints, or barbarians from the Celtic fringes—are all significant. Each of these possible cognitive strands forms part of a rich tapestry of potential meanings that enrich our own understanding of *Macbeth* and its cultural moment. But the central question still remains: why are there bearded women in *Macbeth*?

According to Christopher Wortham, 'since the accession of the new monarch' the 'mood in England was one of lingering hope mingled with growing misgivings', with the English having 'to accommodate themselves to more changes than they found easy to bear'. This is evident in Shakespeare, where 'the brilliant light of English nationalism' that he had 'both celebrated and interrogated in his plays of English history in the 1590s now burned but dimly', as the new king, 'a Scot, who spoke in a strange and thick accent not of England but of Great Britain as his realm',[63] seemed increasingly less likely to replace Elizabeth as 'an effective symbol of national aspirations'.[64] As R. Malcolm Smuts has pointed out, while 'the traditional portrait of a slovenly, homosexual king presiding over a debauched court is grossly exaggerated and one-sided', at the same time 'it does contain a significant core of truth':

> The lapses of decorum within the court, the presence there of unpopular Scottish and homosexual favorites, the mounting costs of the royal household, and James's own surliness in public all tarnished the monarchy's prestige, inhibiting spontaneous public support.[65]

Smuts is quick to note that 'these shortcomings did not mean that James was a bad king in any absolute sense', and that James 'had a number of political talents', but 'the ability to project a majestic and dignified image and to inspire reverence for himself and his entourage was not among them' (28). His bizarre behavior and unpopular changes at court—putting the old, English courtiers out to pasture and replacing them with Scottish drinking buddies and homosexual flatterers—understandably resulted in a growing anti-Scottish sentiment amongst the English, and the perception that the Scots were aliens in their midst.[66] In the minds of many English, this sort of behaviour only highlighted the cultural distance between England and Scotland: it is little wonder, then, that James's repeated attempts between 1604 and 1607 to unify both realms under the banner of 'Great Britain' were rejected.[67]

The importance of Jacobean court culture in understanding the complexities of *Macbeth* has long been recognized, although critics remain divided as to the precise nature of James's influence on the play.[68] For some, Shakespeare is seen as toeing the ideological line by engaging in topics close to his patron's heart: witchcraft, treason, the Stuart myth, and the divine right of kings.[69] Others assert more subversive readings, arguing that instead of promoting the Stuart ideology the play exposes it, stressing the unflattering picture painted by Shakespeare of a Scotland filled with blasted heaths, witches and spirits, barbaric savages, tyrants and traitors, and, to top it all off, cannibalistic horses that 'eate each other' (946; II. 4. 18).[70] More recent studies adopt a more sensible approach, demonstrating that these issues are more problematic in *Macbeth,* and that to characterize the play as simply endorsing Stuart ideology on the one hand, or solely challenging it on the other, is reductive and ultimately a failure to acknowledge its complexities.[71] As Jean Howard suggests judiciously, 'the intertextual links between *Macbeth* and the more general 'matter of Scotland' are best understood as complex and associative, rather than direct and definite'.[72]

This tempered approach can be applied to the question of why there are bearded women in *Macbeth*. James was Shakespeare's patron—his troupe was not called the King's Men for nothing—and Shakespeare was certainly aware of James's interests in witchcraft and demonology, and as such it is easy to account for the presence of the bearded Sisters in the play. But Shakespeare did not only play for his royal patron, but to paying audiences of thousands, many of whom (as we have seen) were at the very least suspicious of the growing numbers of Scots in their midst and at court, not to mention the particularly unflattering individual at its centre. As Richard Helgerson has insightfully shown, English xenophobic attitudes rose during this period, due in large to the Elizabethan project of nationhood, which, in the course of defining what it meant to be 'English', demonized and alienated those who did not fit the paradigm.[73] As noted by a number of critics, these prejudiced views of aliens and outsiders often found their expression in popular culture, and were prominent in the drama of the age.[74] With this in mind, it is possible to read the bearded women in *Macbeth* as participating in this wider movement of English self-fashioning and its strategies of cultural estrangement: the weyward Sisters, 'stubbled and stammering',[75] would have not only been perceived as being 'Scottish', but quintessentially '*un*-English'. Thus, while his patron was fervently seeking to erode the perceived distinctions between his Scottish and English subjects, Shakespeare's *Macbeth* seems only to highlight their differences.

As we have seen, whether on a male or female body the beard operates as a site of physiological, supernatural, social, and cultural difference. In the case of men, as brilliantly examined by Will Fisher and Mark Johnston, the beard was not simply an object of fashion but an important signifier in discourses of national, class, gender, and sexual identity. On women, the presence of a beard was perceived as an aberration—the result of physiological excess, divine or demonic intervention—or as an index of cultural difference from the viewer. Shakespeare's construction of the bearded Sisters in *Macbeth* engages with all of these various meanings. Like Macbeth's first words, describing the day as 'foule and faire' (138; I. 3. 36), the bearded women are a contradiction: they 'looke not like th' Inhabitants o'th' Earth, / And yet are on'it', it is unclear whether they 'Liue' or are 'aught / That man may question', and while they 'should be Women', they are bearded like men (140–45; I. 3. 39–45). In the words of Jean Howard and Phyllis Rackin, their beards are the sign of the uncanny, associating 'sexual ambiguity with the dangers that lurk at the boundaries of the known, rationalized world of sexual difference and sexual exclusion constructed by patriarchal discourse'.[76] Their beards are also emblematic of their other-worldliness and supernatural powers, as the audience witnesses these bearded figures committing acts that were readily identifiable as witchcraft, acts that their new sovereign had recently reaffirmed as illegal by statute in 1604.[77] Finally, the bearded Sisters epitomize the sense of cultural difference that pervades the play, estranging the Scottish characters portrayed onstage from its (mostly) English audience. We have seen how a culture of ambivalence and unease characterized the early years of James's reign, as the English were confronted with the task of accommodating increasing numbers of Scots—peoples of a nation that many English were old enough to remember being at war with—as neighbours rather than as aliens. While it is unclear whether an audience would have interpreted the bearded women onstage as Scottish, or whether *Macbeth* was written to gratify or challenge a king, what is clear is the cultural meaning of the beard: difference.

Notes

1   The full inscription on the plinth reads: EN MAGNVM NATVRAE / MIRACVLVM / MAGDALENA VENTVRA EX / OPPIDO ACVMVULI APVD / SAMNITES VVLGO EL A / BRVZZO REGNI NEAPOLI / TANI ANNORVM 52 ET / QVOD INSOLENS EST CVM / ANNVM 37 AGERET COE / EXT VT POTIVS / ALICVIVS MAGISTRI BARBATI / ESSE VIDEATVR QVAM MV / LIERIS QVAE TRES FILIOS / ANTE AMISERIT QVOS EX / VIRO SVO FELICI DE AMICI / QVEM ADESSE VIDES HA

/ BVERAT. / IOSEPHVS DE RIBERA HIS / PANVS CHRISTI CRVCE / INSIGNITVS
SVI TEM– / PORIS ALTER APELLES / IVSSV FERDINANDI II / DVCIS III DE
ALCALA / NEAPOLI PROREGIS AD / VIVVM MIRE DEPINXIT / XIIIJ KALEN.
MART / ANNO MDCXXXI.

2   All quotations from Shakespeare are given in the original spelling of the First Folio with
     references to the through line numbers, followed bt references to the Oxford *Complete
     Works*, ed. Stanley Wells and Gary Taylor (New York: Oxford University Press, 1986).
     For other works of the period, I have retained the original spelling wherever possible,
     giving folio or signature references as more reliable than pagination. In all cases I have
     included standard reference numbers (abbreviated STC and Wing) from *The Short-Title
     Catalogue of Books...1475-1640*, ed. A. W. Pollard and G. R. Redgrave, 2nd ed. (London:
     Bibliographical Society, 1986), and *The Short-Title Catalogue of Books...1641-1700*, ed.
     Donald Wing, 2nd ed. (New York: Modern Languages Association, 1972).

3   James Schiffer, 'Macbeth and the Bearded Women', in *Another Country: Feminist
     Perspectives on Renaissance Drama*, ed. Dorothea Kehler and Susan Baker (Metuchen:
     Scarecrow Press, 1991), pp. 204–17, (206). Further citations are given parenthetically in
     the text.

4   Diane Purkiss, *The Witch in History: Early Modern and Twentieth-Century Representations*
     (New York: Routledge, 1996), p. 207. Further citations are given parenthetically in the
     text.

5   This is, of course, exactly what Lorraine Helms warns against as 'theatre history exceeds
     its brief if it tries to decide whether Forman (or any other spectator) saw what Banquo
     suggests he should have seen rather than what Forman himself describes', in 'The
     Weyward Sisters: Towards a Feminist Staging of *Macbeth*', *New Theatre Quarterly*, 8.30
     (1992): 167–77, (169).

6   The original of Simon Forman's manuscript is held in the Bodleian Library, Oxford (MS
     Ashmolean 208). The transcription supplied here is from Samuel Schoenbaum, *William
     Shakespeare: Records and Images* (London: Scolar Press, 1969), p. 7.

7   This is the argument made most recently by Gary Taylor, 'Shakespeare Plays on
     Renaissance Stages', in *The Cambridge Companion to Shakespeare on Stage*, ed. Stanley
     Wells and Sarah Stanton (Cambridge: Cambridge University Press, 2002), p. 18; and
     David Grote, *The Best Actors in the World: Shakespeare and His Acting Company*
     (Westport: Greenwood Press, 2002), p. 141.

8   Graham Holderness, '"To be Observed": Cue One *Macbeth*', in *Re-Visions of Shakespeare:
     Essays in Honor of Robert Ornstein*, ed. Evelyn Gajowski (Cranbury: Associated
     University Presses, 2004), pp. 169–75.

9   This has been asserted most recently by Stephen Orgel, 'Acting Scripts, Performing
     Texts', in *The Authentic Shakespeare, and Other Problems of the Early Modern Stage*
     (New York: Routledge, 2002), pp. 21–48 (33–34).

10   Raphael Holinshed, *The Chronicles of England, Scotlande, and Irelande* (London, 1577;
     STC 13568), 243 (sig. D2^R). The woodcut also appears on this page.

11   Frederick Kiefer, *Shakespeare's Visual Theatre: Staging the Personified Characters*
     (Cambridge: Cambridge University Press, 2003), p. 111.

12   The uses of the prosthetic beard, as well as evidence of its popularity, are discussed in
     detail by William Fisher in his article, 'The Renaissance Beard: Masculinity in Early

Modern England', *Renaissance Quarterly*, 54.1 (2001): 155–87, esp. 163–65. Further citations are given parenthetically in the text.

13   *The Book of Sir Thomas More*, ed. W. W. Greg (London: Malone Society Reprints, 1911), p. 34.

14   I have been unable to locate a single reference to accused witches sporting beards in the witchcraft pamphlets and trial accounts printed during Shakespeare's lifetime. It is possible that such references exist in trial records that were not printed or made publicly available.

15   Mark Twain, *The Innocents Abroad, or The New Pilgrim's Progress* (Hartford: American Publishing Company, 1869), p. 199. Twain is referring comically to the perception of Italian women as hirsute.

16   Francis Beaumont and John Fletcher, *The Honest Mans Fortune*, in *Comedies and Tragedies Written by Francis Beavmont and Iohn Fletcher* (London, 1647; Wing B1581), p. 154 (sig. 5T3^V).

17   For a detailed discussion of notions of monstrosity and wonder in the medieval and early modern periods, see: Dudley Wilson, *Signs and Portents: Monstrous Births from the Middle Ages to the Enlightenment* (New York: Routledge, 1993); Kathryn M. Brammall, 'Monstrous Metamorphosis: Nature, Morality, and the Rhetoric of Monstrosity in Tudor England', *Sixteenth Century Journal*, 27.1 (1996): 3–21; and Lorraine Daston and Katharine Park, *Wonders and the Order of Nature, 1150–1750* (New York: Zone, 1998).

18   Reginald Scot, *The Discouerie of Witchcraft* (London, 1584; STC 21864), 7 (sig. C4^R).

19   Edmund Spenser, *The Faerie Qveene* (London, 1590; STC 23081), sig. H4^V.

20   William Rowley, Thomas Dekker, and John Ford, *The Witch of Edmonton* (London, 1658; Wing R2097), pp. 13, 15.

21   Neil MacGregor, *Seeing Salvation: Images of Christ in Art* (New Haven: Yale University Press, 2000), p. 98.

22   For a detailed discussion of the origin and development of the Uncumber legend, see: David Williams, *Deformed Discourse: The Function of the Monster in Medieval Thought and Literature* (Montreal: McGill-Queen's University Press, 1996), pp. 309–22.

23   Harry S. Lipscomb and Hebbel E. Hoff, 'Saint Uncumber or *La Vierge Barbue*', *Bulletin of the History of Medicine*, 37 (1963): 523–27, (525). Important altars devoted to Saint Uncumber in England are found in Old St Paul's in London, and at Chew Stoke in Somerset. In John Heywood's earlier Tudor play, *The playe called the foure PP* (London, 1544; STC 13300), the character of the Palmer lists an altar devoted to the saint as one that he has visited on pilgrimage (sig. A1^V).

24   Thomas More, *A Dyaloge of Syr Thomas More* (London, 1529; STC 18084), fol. LX^V.

25   Jane T. Schulenburg, *Forgetful of Their Sex: Female Sanctity and Society, ca. 500–1100* (Chicago: University of Chicago Press, 1998), pp. 153–54.

26   The exact nature of the threat remains unclear. Some critics argue that the threat is sexual, in that the witch threatens to commit adultery with the sailor. Others suggest that the witch will harm the husband or the ship while in rat form.

27   John Bale, *A Comedy Concernynge Thre Lawes* (London, 1548; STC 1287), sig. B5^R.

28   John Banister, *The Historie of Man* (London, 1578; STC 1359), sig. B2^V.

29   Hippocrates, *Epidemics*, VI. 8. 32. The translation given is taken from the edition of *Epidemics II, IV–VII* by Wesley D. Smith (Cambridge: Harvard University Press, 1994), pp. 289–91.

30 Juan Huarte, *Examen de Ingenios, The Examination of Mens Wits*. trans. Richard Carew (London, 1594; STC 13890), p. 271.

31 Tomasa Garzoni, *The Hospital of Incvrable Fooles* (London, 1600; STC 11634), sig. B2ᵛ.

32 Antonio de Torquemada, *The Spanish Mandeuile of Miracles* (London, 1600; STC 24135), sig. K2ᴿ.

33 Torquemada, sig. K2ᵛ.

34 Michel de Montaigne, *The Essayes*, trans. John Florio (London, 1603; STC 18041), pp. 40–41. For an excellent examination of Montaigne's account, see Patricia Parker, 'Gender Ideology, Gender Change: The Case of Marie Germain', *Critical Inquiry*, 19.2 (1993): 337–64.

35 Francesco Maria Guazzo, *Compendium Maleficarum* (Milan, 1608), Book I, Chap. XVII. The translation is from the Montague Summers edition, translated by E. A. Ashwin (London: John Rodker, 1929), p. 57. Guazzo includes a number of accounts of women who have become men, as indicated by genital appearance or the growth of a beard. It should be noted that Guazzo and other continental demonologists differed in their opinion on the metamorphosis of human bodies into animals.

36 Joan Cadden, *Meanings of Sex Difference in the Middle Ages: Medicine, Science, and Culture* (Cambridge: Cambridge University Press, 1993), pp. 182–83.

37 Thomas Hill, *The Contemplation of Mankinde* (London, 1571; STC 13482), sig. 146ᵛ–147ᴿ.

38 Anglicus Bartholomaeus, *Batmann vppon Bartholome his book De proprietatibus rerum* (London, 1582; STC 1538), fol. 43ᴿ. The same argument occurs in Hill, sig. 147ᴿ⁻ᵛ. Hill goes on to argue that while children are also known to be hot and moist, they do not produce beards because 'the smokie superflouosnesse, which is the especiall matter of the heares … doth in them passe, and serue to their increase, and nourishment' (sig. 149ᴿ).

39 Bartholomaeus, fol. 43ᴿ. See also Bartolommeo della Rocca (Coccles), *A Briefe and Most Pleasaunt Epitomye of the Whole Art of Phisiognomie* (London, 1556; STC 5468), sig. Diiᴿ; and John Sadler, *The Sicke Womans Priuate Looking-Glasse* (London, 1636; STC 21544), pp. 16–17.

40 Scot, p. 54 (sig. F3ᵛ).

41 Pierre Le Loyer, *A Treatise of Specters or Straunge Sights, Visions and Apparitions*, trans. Zachary Jones (London, 1605; STC 15448), fol. 110ᴿ⁻ᵛ.

42 Claire Bartram, '"Melancholic Imaginations": Witchcraft and the Politics of Melancholia in Elizabethan Kent', *Journal of European Studies*, 33.3 (2003): 203–11, (203).

43 For a more detailed discussion, see Jenijoy La Belle, '"A Strange Infirmity": Lady Macbeth's Amenorrhea', *Shakespeare Quarterly*, 31.3 (1980): 381–86.

44 Thomas W. Laqueur, *Making Sex: Body and Gender from the Greeks to Freud* (Cambridge: Harvard University Press, 1990).

45 Mark A. Johnston, 'Playing with the Beard: Courtly and Commercial Economies in Richard Edwards's *Damon and Pithias* and John Lyly's *Midas*', *ELH*, 72 (2005): 79–103, (79).

46 Piero Valeriano, *Pro sacerdotum barbis* (London, 1553; STC 19902), sig. A7ᴿ⁻ᵛ.

47 Thomas Hall, *Comarum Akosmia, The Loathsomnesse of Longe Haire* (London, 1653; Wing H429), p. 48.

48 Heinrich Cornelius Agrippa, *The Glory of Women, or A Looking-Glasse for Ladies*, trans. Hugh Crompton (London, 1652; Wing A787), p. 14.

49 *Le Prince d'Amour; or The Prince of Love* (London, 1660; Wing R2189), p. 126.

50 John Bulwer, *Anthropometamorphosis: Man Transform'd, Or, The Artificial Changling* (London, 1653; Wing B5461), p. 198. Further citations are given parenthetically in the text.

51 For a brilliant discussion of the fear of effeminization that appears in anti-theatrical tracts, see: Laura Levine, *Men in Women's Clothing: Anti-Theatricality and Effeminization, 1579–1642* (Cambridge: Cambridge University Press, 1994); and Stephen Orgel, *Impersonations: The Performance of Gender in Shakespeare's England* (Cambridge: Cambridge University Press, 1996).

52 Philip Stubbes, *The Anatomie of Abuses* (London, 1583; STC 23376), sig. F5^V.

53 Elliott Horowitz, 'The New World and the Changing Face of Europe', *Sixteenth Century Journal*, 28.4 (1997): 1181–201, (1185). Further citations are given parenthetically in the text.

54 David Scott Kastan, *Shakespeare After Theory* (London: Routledge, 1999), p. 154.

55 Gerald of Wales, *The History and Topography of Ireland*, trans. John J. O'Meara (New York: Penguin, 1982), pp. 72–73. Gerald also mentions another woman with half a beard who was a hermaphrodite. Further citations are taken from this edition and are given parenthetically in the text.

56 Patricia Palmer, *Language and Conquest in Early Modern Ireland: English Renaissance Literature and Elizabethan Imperial Expansion* (Cambridge: Cambridge University Press, 2001), p. 92.

57 Barnabe Rich, *The Irish Hubbub, or The English Hue and Crie* (London, 1617; STC 20989), p. 4 (sig. B2^V).

58 Christopher Highley, 'The Place of Scots in the Scottish Play: *Macbeth* and the Politics of Language', in *Shakespeare and Scotland*, ed. Willy Maley and Andrew Murphy (Manchester: Manchester University Press, 2004), pp. 53-66, (62). Further citations are given parenthetically in the text.

59 Highley, p. 62.

60 John Block Friedman, *The Monstrous Races in Medieval Art and Thought* (Cambridge: Harvard University Press, 1981), p. 1.

61 Hartmann Schedel, *Liber Chronicarum* (Nuremberg, 1493), fol. XII^R. The Latin reads 'Item mulieres cum usque ad pectus sed capite plano sine crinibus'. Schedel's description is derived from the *Gesta Romanorum*, a medieval collection of anecdotes and commonplaces, which includes in its chapter 'De hominibus diversarum formarum', in turn based on Pliny and Augustine, the text that Schedel has copied almost verbatim: 'Item mulieres cum barbis usque ad pectus sed capite plano'.

62 Friedman, p. 1.

63 Christopher Wortham, 'Disorientation: The Case of *Othello*', in *The Touch of the Real: Essays in Early Modern Culture*, ed. Philippa Kelly (Nedlands: University of Western Australia Press, 2002), pp. 177–201, (192).

64 R. Malcolm Smuts, *Court Culture and the Origins of a Royalist Tradition in Early Stuart England* (Philadelphia: University of Pennsylvania Press, 1987), p. 29.

65 Smuts, p. 28. For a more detailed discussion of James, his English reception, and his treatment by historians, see: Jenny Wormald, 'James VI and I: Two Kings or One?' *History*, 68 (1983): 187–209; and Pauline Croft, 'The Reign of James VI and I: The Birth of Britain', *History Compass*, 1 (2003): BR 046, 1–13.

66 For a balanced discussion of contemporary representations of Scotland in early Stuart England, see William C. Carroll, 'The Cultural Construction of Scotland', in *Macbeth: Texts and Contexts* (New York: Bedford/St Martin's, 1999), pp. 271–99.

67 For a more detailed discussion of James's project of unification, and the literary and cultural responses to it, see: Joseph B. Rochon, *The King of Hearts: James VI and I, the 'Union of Love' and Images of Britain at the Anglo-Scottish Court, 1603–1608* (Ph.D. thesis, Queen's University, Ontario, 1999); and Sandra Bell, '"No Scot, No English Now": Literary and Cultural Responses to James VI and I's Policies on Union', *Renaissance Forum*, 7.1 (2004): 1–13.

68 On the wider question of James's influence on Shakespeare drama, including *Macbeth*, see: Jonathan Goldberg, *James I and the Politics of Literature: Jonson, Shakespeare, Donne and their Contemporaries* (Baltimore: Johns Hopkins University Press, 1983); Stephen Orgel, 'Making Greatness Familiar', in *Pageantry in the Shakespearean Theater*, ed. David M. Bergeron (Athens: University of Georgia Press, 1985), pp. 19–25; Leonard Tennenhouse, *Power on Display: The Politics of Shakespeare's Genres* (New York: Methuen, 1986); and Leeds Barroll, *Politics, Plague, and Shakespeare's Theater: The Stuart Years* (Ithaca: Cornell University Press, 1991).

69 Representative studies of this kind include: Henry N. Paul, *The Royal Play of Macbeth* (New York: Macmillan, 1950); Gary Wills, *Witches & Jesuits: Shakespeare's Macbeth* (Oxford: Oxford University Press, 1995); Alvin Kernan, *Shakespeare, the King's Playwright* (New Haven: Yale University Press, 1995); and Tristan Marshall, *Theatre and Empire: Great Britain on the London Stages under James VI and I* (Manchester: Manchester University Press, 2000), esp. pp. 61–65.

70 Representative readings of this kind include: Alan Sinfield, '*Macbeth:* History, Ideology, and Intellectuals', *Critical Quarterly*, 28 (1986): 63–77; Terry Eagleton, *William Shakespeare* (Oxford: Blackwell, 1986); David Norbrook, '*Macbeth* and the Politics of Historiography', in *Politics of Discourse: The Literature and History of Seventeenth-Century England*, ed. Kevin Sharpe and Steven N. Zwicker (Berkeley: University of California Press, 1987), pp. 78–116; and Kiernan Ryan, *Shakespeare*, 3rd edn (New York: Palgrave, 2002), esp. pp. 89–95.

71 Representative studies include: Curtis Perry, *The Making of Jacobean Culture: James I and the Renegotiation of Elizabethan Literary Practice* (Cambridge: Cambridge University Press, 1997), esp. pp. 111–52; David Scott Kastan, 'Is There a Class in This (Shakespearean) Text?', in *Shakespeare After Theory*; Robin Headlam Wells, '"Arms and the Man": *Macbeth*', in *Shakespeare on Masculinity* (Cambridge: Cambridge University Press, 2000); and Andrew Hadfield, 'Malcolm in the Middle: James VI and I, George Buchanan and the Divine Right of Kings', in *Shakespeare, Spenser and the Matter of Britain* (New York: Palgrave, 2004).

72 Jean E. Howard, 'Shakespeare, Geography, and the Work of Genre on the Early Modern Stage', *Modern Language Quarterly*, 64.3 (2003): 299–322, (319).

73 Richard Helgerson, *Forms of Nationhood: The Elizabethan Writing of England* (Chicago: University of Chicago Press, 1992). See also Laura Hunt Yungblut, *Strangers Settled Here Amongst Us: Policies, Perceptions and the Presence of Aliens in Elizabethan England* (New York: Routledge, 1996).

74 Of particular note is: A. J. Hoenselaars, *Images of Englishmen and Foreigners in the Drama of Shakespeare and His Contemporaries* (Madison: Fairleigh Dickinson University Press, 1992).

75 Highley, p. 62.

76 Jean E. Howard and Phyllis Rackin, *Engendering a Nation: A Feminist Account of Shakespeare's English Histories* (London: Routledge, 1997), p. 46.

77 1 Jac. I, c. 12 (1604), 'An acte against Coniuration Witchcrafte and dealinge with evill and wicked Spirits'. The text is reproduced in *Witch Hunting and Witch Trials*, ed. C. L'Estrange Ewen (London: K. Paul, Trench, Trubner, 1929), pp. 19–21.

Sam Johnson Corrected: *As You Like It* IV.2

Alan Brissenden

This 'noisy scene', said Samuel Johnson, who was tone deaf, 'was introduced only to fill up an interval, which is to represent two hours'.[1] Act four Scene two of *As You Like It* does carry out that function, but it has much more significance for the play than Johnson claimed. Other commentators have remarked, without always being specific, on its connection with folklore and ritual. In his note to the old New Cambridge edition Dover Wilson visualized 'a procession in which the deer-slayer shall be borne in triumph, like a Roman conqueror, to the Duke's presence: it will be fitting also that he wear the deer's horns and skin, as the insignia of victory. In all this, we do not doubt, Shakespeare had in mind folk-customs connected with the hunt and going back to the days of pre-Christian sacrifice which are now lost in oblivion'.[2] Annotating the scene in his edition of Shakespeare's complete works (1951), Hardin Craig considered it to be 'full of the customs of the chase, reflecting also the heathen background of the ceremony in the decking of the chief huntsman with the hide and horns of the slain deer as a fetish'. Michael Jamieson saw it as 'a tableau of a pagan rite in praise of hunting ... and the lusty choral singing is emblematic of the triumph of love and possibly of fertility also'.[3] For Chris Fitter, the scene is strongly political, offering 'its audiences the open celebration of illegally taken deer slain by outlaws ... [and becoming] an exultant ritual of demotic political transgression'.[4] In a detailed study, Edward Berry examines how Shakespeare keeps the 'processional and festive nature' of the return from the hunt, 'yet evokes complex overtones that almost certainly go beyond the original custom. For one thing', he continues, 'the event is directed by Jaques, who has not participated in the hunt and who has been described earlier ... weeping over the fate of a wounded deer. Jaques' comments, therefore, although not opposed to the celebration, place it in an ironical framework'.[5]

The nineteen-line scene is half dialogue, half song: Jaques enters with a group of lords dressed as foresters (i.e. forest-dwellers rather than officials in charge of a forest), and asks, 'Which is he that killed the deer?' On finding out, he suggests, 'Let's present him to the Duke like a Roman conqueror, and it would do well to set the deer's horns upon his head for a branch of victory'; he then calls for a song, and the song which follows is:

What shall he have that killed the deer?
His leather skin and horns to wear,
Then sing him home. The rest shall bear
This burden.
Take thou no scorn to wear the horn;
It was a crest ere thou wast born.
Thy father's father wore it,
            And thy father bore it.
            The horn, the horn, the lusty horn
            Is not a thing to laugh to scorn.

                                                                (IV. 2. 10–19)

Roman conquerors, however, were crowned with garlands of evergreen—laurel or bay—and Sir Thomas Elyot, in Book I, chapter viii of *The Governour* (1531), describes how 'To them which, in … hunting [deer] do show the most prowess and activity, a garland or some other like token to be given, in sign of victory, and with a joyful manner to be brought in the presence of him that is chief in the company; there to receive the condign praise for their good endeavour'.[6] When he meets the Duke, Shakespeare's huntsman is going to be wearing not a garland, but the skin and horns of the slain animal, and this kind of costume is generally accepted to be pictured in a rock painting found in the cave of Les Trois Frères in the Ariège, which is between 10,000 and 25,000 years old—a man with an animal skin on his back and antlers on his head, apparently dancing.

The Cambridge archaeologist Grahame Clarke describes it as 'a painting in black of a bearded figure wearing mask and antlers of a red deer, the skin of a horse or wolf and a long, bushy tail' and considers the 'suggestion that the dance was part of a magic ritual is inescapable'.[7] The survival of folk ritual over such a great length of time is of course unprovable, but in 578 (or 585) CE the Council of Auxerre forbade anyone 'to masquerade as a bull-calf or a stag on the first of January or to distribute devilish charms';[8] the *Malleus Maleficarum* (1584) refers to 'bad Christians [who] run about at time of Carnival with masks and jests and other superstitions' and in the note to his translation of this passage Montague Summers quotes the *Liber Poenitentialis* of St Theodore, seventh Archbishop of Canterbury: 'if anyone at the Kalends of January goeth about as a stag or a bull-calf, that is, making himself into a wild animal, and dressing in the skins of a herd animal, and putting on the heads of beasts; those who in such wise transform themselves into the appearance of a wild animal, let them do penance for three years, because this is devilish'.[9] And despite his strategy of mixing bits of clowning with his singing of hymns and gospel passages in public places, hoping thus to win men's ears and then their souls, St Aldhelm, Bishop of Sherborne (c. 640–709), condemned 'the donning of antlers or horns by human beings as part of the New Year festivities'.[10]

Such admonitions were however ineffective, and mummers were still wearing animal masks 600 years later, as seen in a border illustration by the Flemish illuminator Jehan de Grise for the *Romance of Alexander* (1338–44) (Figure 9). In sixteenth-century London ox horns carried on poles were a feature of the St Luke Day's Fair—the ox is a symbol of the saint—on 18 October, when dogs and women, and men dressed as women, were whipped during a procession from Cuckold's Point, on the Thames near Deptford, which according to Brewer's *Dictionary of Phrase and Fable*, has its name 'from a tradition that King John made there successful love to a labourer's wife', to Charlton, a distance of some five kilometres.[11] By the seventeenth century the celebration was known as the Horn Fair, and when the parade reached Charlton it marched three times around St Luke's church before getting down to the serious business of funmaking. In his book *Robin Hood: The Spirit of the Forest*, Steve Wilson says that Charlton village green was the site of a pagan festival which became known as the Horn Fair, during which 'The men would be dressed as women … all would wear horns, blow horns, carry horns'.[12] The Horn Fair continued until the authorities put a stop to it in 1872, but it has been revived in a modified form in recent times.

Figure 9: Mummers with beasts' heads. A marginal scene from the *Romance of Alexander*, by Flemish illuminator Jehan de Grise, 1388-1444. (MS Bodley 264 fol.181v. By courtesy of the Bodleian Library, Oxford.)

Well into the nineteenth century, dancers in the Horn Dance which was performed at Abbotts Bromley in Staffordshire carried antlers kept in the village hall. The antlers, large and heavy, were fixed on a frame with a short pole. Early in the twentieth century the folk dance and music collector Cecil Sharp wrote that 'within living memory, it was the custom in some Oxfordshire villages to kill an animal for the purposes of a feast at Whitsuntide and other festivals where Morris dancing took place—near the Forest of Wychwood, for example, the villagers joined in the Whit Hunt'; when the deer were caught, killed, and skinned, the heads and antlers went to the three men who were first in at the death, while pieces of skin were distributed as bringing luck.[13] Sharp suggests this was a relic of dressing in the skin and consequent metamorphoses. At not far distant Abingdon, Morris dancers were led by a man bearing ox horns on a pole.

By putting on the animal horns and skin, the huntsman in *As You Like It* symbolically transforms himself into the animal itself, but what the song is suggesting spreads beyond the confines of this scene, reaching throughout the play as a whole. It is, for example, a reflection on Jaques himself. At the beginning of II.7 Duke Senior, who has been looking for the melancholy courtier, says 'I think he be transform'd into a beast, / For I can nowhere find him like a man.' And later, when Jaques takes it on himself to 'cleanse the foul body of th'infected world' (II. 7. 60) the Duke rebukes him, saying he has been a libertine, 'As sensual as the brutish sting itself' (II. 7. 66), that is, his lust has had the power to turn him into a brute. This image of a person transformed is an image of that concept which is basic to theatre, metamorphosis, a concept that fascinated Shakespeare and many of his fellow-dramatists, and which especially informs the ethos of *As You Like It*.

It is obvious in the taking on of disguise by Rosalind and Celia soon after the beginning of the play, for instance, and at the end, in the sudden conversion of Duke Frederick at the edge of the forest. But it permeates the play's texture in various ways. Duke Senior's supposition about Jaques introduces a line of imagery which is continued later in II.7 when the starving Orlando bursts in upon the exiles with his sword drawn and Jaques queries, 'of what kind should this cock come of?' (90), and when Orlando, going to find Adam, sees himself a doe seeking her fawn (128). Transformation of people into beasts, plants and other things of nature was of course the stuff of Ovid's *Metamorphoses,* which Shakespeare knew well and drew on frequently. Touchstone refers to Ovid himself in III.3, making a pun on 'goats' and 'Goths'—and all puns depend on transformation of meaning. When Celia says that Orlando is 'furnished like a hunter', Rosalind puns, 'O ominous—he comes to kill my heart' (III. 2. 241), the pun accentuated for the eye in the Folio spelling of 'hart', and the exchange helps to develop the play's theme of the love hunt. Later in the same scene the transformation of humans into beasts through Pythagoras's theory of the transmigration of souls is matter for another witticism by Rosalind (III. 2.1

70–4). In the wider world of the play, the Forest of Arden is the place where Nature works its change on those who come there—some, like the exiled Duke and lords, Rosalind, Celia and Orlando, seeking refuge, others, like Oliver and Duke Frederick, intent on evil.

The idea of the chase is introduced in the first scene, when Charles the wrestler tells Oliver that Duke Senior is already in the Forest of Arden 'a many merry men with him, and there they live like the old Robin Hood of England' (I. 1. 110–11). Hunting scenes occur in several plays towards the end of the 1590s. There were two Robin Hood plays at the Rose in 1598, and some characters, like Falstaff in *The Merry Wives of Windsor* (1597) and Friar Tuck in Munday's Death of Robert Earl of Huntingdon (1598), either wear or carry deer horns on stage. The song of IV.2 suggests that in *As You Like It* Shakespeare is going one better than himself and other playwrights and putting his actor *into* a deer skin as well. If that were the case, then the idea of metamorphosis, which is talked of so much, and a constant in the play, becomes physically presented before us.

The other transformation imaged by the horns is the transformation of the married man into the cuckold, and R. S. White has pointed out that while the scene is a celebration of the hunt and that in this play it can be seen as a 'victory' after the hunt of love, 'the horns, although signifying victory, are also a symbol of marital uncertainty, a burden instead of a celebration'.[14] According to the song, according to popular belief, if one goes by the references in contemporary writing, and according to Touchstone and Rosalind cuckoldry was an inevitable event. While he is waiting with Audrey in III. 3 for Sir Oliver Martext to come and marry them, Touchstone meditates on the certainty of his future wife's infidelity: 'A man may, if he were of a fearful heart, stagger in this attempt: for here we have no temple but the wood, no assembly but horn-beasts. But what though? Courage. As horns are odious, they are necessary. It is said many a man knows no end of his goods. Right: many a man has good horns and knows no end of them. Well, that is the dowry of his wife, 'tis none of his own getting. Horns? Even so' (III. 3. 43–50). These days it can help if Touchstone makes the sign of the horns on 'many a man has good horns'; it can raise a laugh when the words themselves no longer do. In IV.1 Rosalind as Ganymede as Rosalind tells Orlando that a snail 'comes armed in his fortune, and prevents the slander of his wife' (IV. 1. 56–7): he already has his horns before he is married, and so after marriage no one can blame his wife for cuckolding him. Soon after this, she virtually coerces Celia into marrying her to Orlando, and thirty lines later she is making another joke about infidelity. And it is the next scene which contains the song in which men are urged to take 'no scorn to wear the horn' because all men have to wear it anyway.

As has already been remarked, Edward Berry links Act IV Scene 2 with Jaques's anti-hunting sentiments expressed in his empathy with the weeping deer described by the First Lord in II. 1. 25–63. Although Jaques has had no part in the hunt, he directs the celebration yet simultaneously mocks the nobility of it, even satirically echoing a classical reference such as that contained in Elyot's *The Governour* mentioned above by turning the crown of antlers into the cuckold's horns. As Berry notices, the spectacle is ambiguous, as the horn signals both phallic potency and marital impotence. In her Arden 3 edition of the play (2006), Juliet Dusinberre glosses 'bear' in the sentence 'the rest shall bear this burden' to encapsulate the word's conglomerate meanings: 'carry (horns); endure (cuckoldry); sing (the bass line or chorus)'. (Dusinberre, incidentally, emends the text to have the whole line not sung, but spoken alone by Jaques.)

However it may have been in popular lore, and pronounced from the stage, that one should not scorn to wear the horn—and Benedick in *Much Ado About Nothing* comforts himself with the thought that 'There is no staff more reverend than one tipped with horn' (V. 4. 122–3)—in real life cuckoldry was a matter for derision, and cuckolds were submitted to skimmington rides, or charivari; Francois Laroque illustrates a discussion of this custom with a woodcut of a riding of the cuckolds in Lyon (1587) (Figure 10) which shows a man being led through the streets 'seated facing the tail end of a donkey and wearing a cap with cock feathers … which

Figure 10: An anonymous woodcut of a riding of the cuckolds in Lyons (1587). (By courtesy of the Bibliothéque Nationale, Paris.)

Figure 11: A riding of a cuckold, with bells on, from the view of Seville by Georg Hoefnagel in Georg Braun, Civitatis Orbis Terrarum, vol. 5 (1593). Detail.

symbolize cuckoldry'.[15] The cock feathers were sometimes replaced with ass's ears, and both feathers and ears also symbolized fools. Bellows, in the picture being applied to the donkey's backside by a professional fool, were often associated with fools and figures representing folly, and fools, including Touchstone, were related to flatulence (see below [pun unavoidable]). Georg Hoefnagel's double-page illustration for the city of Seville in Volume 5 of Georg Braun's *Civitatis Orbis Terrarum* (1572–1618), shows a procession with a cuckold wearing a spectacular set of antlers, strung with bells, mounted on an ass and being mocked by bystanders making signs of horns (Figure 11). In England and Scotland, instead of being mounted on a real animal, the victim, or the victim's effigy or substitute, was placed on a pole, or 'stang', carried through the streets on willing shoulders, and might be pelted with filth and rubbish while the accompanying mob made raucous 'rough music' with instruments, pots and pans and even guns: a 'noisy scene' indeed.

In a discussion of 'Ridings, Rough Music and Mocking Rhymes in Early Modern Europe', Martin Ingram shows that the characteristic pretext for a riding was 'when a wife beat her husband or in some other noteworthy way proved that she wore the breeches … it was conventionally assumed—though not necessarily true in practice—that a husband who had been beaten by his wife was inevitably always a cuckold. Hence the prominence in ridings of horns and antlers'.[16] Rosalind's remark, already quoted, that a snail 'comes armed in his fortune, and prevents the slander of his wife' that is, deals with the slander before it is expressed, is a very gentle version of a real situation where a man marries a woman of doubtful reputation. Ingram cites an example of horns being nailed on to the gatepost of a newly married couple of whom the woman was held to be of loose morals.

A potent reason for the ridicule of cuckolds in this way was that horrific anomaly, the inversion of what was considered natural order, the authority of the husband overturned by the wife. It was appropriate that the punishment should take place at Shrovetide, Shrove Monday or Tuesday or Ash Wednesday, but more particularly on Shrove Tuesday, that time of carnival when social order was turned topsy-turvy and, in London, gangs of apprentices attacked brothels and theatres; that time of feasting before the Lenten fast began, when the pancake bell rang, and, in the vivid description of Firke in Dekker's *Shoemaker's Holiday*, 'There's cheer for the heavens—venison pasties walk up and down piping hot like sergeants; beef and brewis comes marching in dry [v]ats. Fritters and pancakes comes trolling in in wheelbarrows, hens and oranges hopping in porters' baskets, collops and eggs in scuttles, and tarts and custards come quavering in in malt shovels' (V. 2. 206–11).

Now all this eating can very easily lead to flatulence—another notable aspect of Shrove Tuesday—and Laroque quotes a description attributed to Nicholas Breton of Carnival as a character who is, among other things, 'chief Ganymede of the Guts … greatest Bashaw of the Batterbowls, Protector of the Pan-cakes … and in the least and last place, lower Warden of the Stink-ports'.[17] The link with *As You Like It* comes, not surprisingly, through that man fearful of but resigned to cuckoldry, Touchstone, the fool.

Touchstone's connection, and perhaps the whole play's connection, with Shrove Tuesday, and so with a reversal of order, is established on his first appearance, when he tells a joke to illustrate the corruption of correct order at the court which is ruled by Celia's father Frederick, who has usurped the dukedom of his brother, Rosalind's father—itself a violent reversal of order. The dialogue is as follows:

> *Touchstone* Mistress, you must come away to your father.
> *Celia* Were you made the messenger?
> *Touchstone* No, by mine honour, but I was bid to come for you.
> *Rosalind* Where learned you that oath, fool?
> *Touchstone* Of a certain knight that swore 'by his honour' they were good pancakes, and swore 'by his honour' the mustard was naught. Now I'll stand to it the pancakes were naught and the mustard was good, and yet was not the knight forsworn.
>
> (I. 2. 55–64)

When asked to prove it, Touchstone tells the girls to stroke their chins and swear by their beards he is a knave. Celia replies

> *Celia* By our beards—if we had them—thou art.
> *Touchstone* By my knavery—if I had it—then I were, but if you swear by that that

is not, you are not forsworn. No more was this knight, swearing by his honour, for he never had any; or if he had, he had sworn it away before ever he saw those pancakes or that mustard.

(I. 2. 70–76)

Twenty-live lines further on, Touchstone says in a different context, 'Nay, if I keep not my rank—', which Rosalind picks up with a pun, 'Thou loosest thy old smell' (I. 2. 100–1); he is talking about his standing in society, she is talking about a fart. (Editors usually emend the Folio 'loosest' to 'losest', which destroys the wordplay.) Fools were notorious for bad smells—it was part of their incapacity to contain themselves—and here Rosalind is paying Touchstone back for his joke at the expense of her uncle; although she may not have much reason to love Duke Frederick, the fool's comment on the court had earned a rebuke from Celia. But Rosalind is also making the connection between Touchstone and Shrove Tuesday, Pancake Day, that time of licence, and, among other things, of the punishment of cuckolds.

The relationship between cuckoldry and carnival is strongly made in George Chapman's brilliant version of the story of the woman of Ephesus, *The Widow's Tears* (c. 1605), written about five years after *As You Like It*. Here, the normal attitude of ridicule of the cuckold is reversed, and the play concludes with a riotous carnival where the mad ruler decrees that 'It shall be the only note of love to the husband to love the wife: and none shall be more kindly welcome to him than he that cuckolds him' (V. 1. 306–8); this is exactly the situation on which Thomas Middleton builds his greatest comedy, *A Chaste Maid in Cheapside* (1613), which is made all the more satirically powerful by being set not in a time of carnival, but in Lent.

A further connection with cuckoldry in *As You Like It* IV.2 can be made through the rituals of the chase. In the last act of the play, Touchstone refers to 'the fool's bolt, and such dulcet diseases' (V. 4. 63–4). This is a passage which has caused commentators much difficulty; a 'fool's bolt' is at one level of meaning a jibe, a shaft of wit; Robert Armin, who may well have played Touchstone, referred to his lengthy poem 'The Italian Tailor and his Boy', written probably in the 1590s though published in 1609, as 'this fool's bolt' (sig. H2ᵛ). The usual meaning ascribed to 'dulcet' is sweet, but why should a fool's joke be a sweet disease? The answer to that question is found in another pun. Touchstone is making an apt play on words. The word 'dulcet(s)' is a hunting term for the testicles of a deer (*OED* doucet 3). Since fools are noted for their lack of restraint, the saying 'a fool's bolt is soonest shot' can take on the phallic meaning of premature ejaculation. Touchstone, then, is saying that shooting his bolt, in that sense, is inconvenient, but as it is related to sexual activity it is a sweet inconvenience. To strengthen the case for such a sexual allusion we can turn to *Queen Anna's New World of Words* (1611), where John Florio gives 'a man's pillicocke' as a meaning for 'Dolcemelle', along with 'a musical instrument called a Dulcemell or Dulcemer. Also honey sweet.'

To go a little further: in *The Noble Arte of Venerie or Hunting* (1575), wrongly attributed to George Turberville, Chapter 42, headed 'How to Break up an hart in the French Manner', has the direction 'And before you go about to take off his [that is the hart's] skin, the first thing that must be taken from him are his stones which hunters call his doulcettes'.[18] When Jaques and the lords enter for IV. 2 it is after the kill and the breaking of the carcass, so not only are the horns the cuckold's horns, but the symbolic castration of the stag in the ritual cutting up of the carcass which has taken place can be taken as an allusion to the desexing of the husband by the unfaithful wife. It must be said that in a later chapter the translator of *The Noble Arte of Venerie* gives the English manner of breaking up the deer, which does not especially include the removing of the testicles as an initial move; however, the setting of *As You Like It* is French when it needs to be, and this could well be one of the occasions.

One further relationship between this scene and popular tradition can be suggested. As well as being borne along by rough music, skimmingtons were sometimes accompanied by the singing of scurrilous rhymes about the victim. The song in IV. 2 is not notably scurrilous, and it does not deal with an individual. Instead, it generalizes the plague of cuckoldry as the inevitable plight of the whole of male humankind. It makes a joke, and a song, out of a deepseated threat to male sexual dominance in marriage.

By the eighteenth century, when Johnson made his comment, it must be assumed that any connections such as I have been making between IV. 2, popular tradition, hunting ritual and other parts of the play had been lost, and the scene was omitted from all acting versions until Macready restored it in 1842. It was not always included in later nineteenth-century productions of the play, but when it was, it often became the excuse for rousing spectacle. At Stratford in 1879, for example, there was a procession with a slain deer, taken from among the descendants of the very herd at Charlecote from which Shakespeare, it was claimed, had poached a buck; the deer was subsequently stuffed and appeared regularly for forty years, becoming increasingly motheaten, apparently, until Nigel Playfair's production in 1919 got rid of it.

More recently, interest in folklore has led to the scene's being turned into a pagan rite, most notably in Peter Stein's 1977 production for the Schaubühne am Halleschen Ufer company in Berlin, which Michael Patterson called 'the most spectacular presentation of Shakespeare in Germany since Reinhardt and arguably the most significant Shakespeare production since Peter Brook's *A Midsummer Night's Dream*'.[19] A slain deer was brought in, skinned, and the hide draped over one of the lords; others holding horns on their heads danced in a circle. But Stein integrated the scene further into the play by having Orlando, who has been in the background painting his face like a woman, confront the skin-draped man and struggle violently with him while Rosalind and Celia, locked in a close embrace, rolled across the stage. Although Stein would not explain the episode, telling Patterson only that it 'formed a part of a dreamlike sequence which possessed musical and visual meaning rather than any narrow interpretable significance', Patterson plausibly saw it as part of the exploration of the play's blurring of sexual distinctions and its eroticism, discussed in Jan Kott's essay 'Bitter Arcadia': 'while Rosalind and Celia experienced the sexual embrace of two women, Orlando struggled with a wild, horned beast, emblematic of his violent masculine nature. Exhausted but victorious, he was now able to be truly worthy of Rosalind's love'.[20] John Dexter's 1979 National Theatre production in London turned the scene into a dark, bloodsoaked ritual in which Audrey's swain William (who is not even in the scene as written) has seemingly killed the deer, which is eviscerated on stage and William, in some initiatory rite, daubed with its blood and crowned with its antlers while the other men surround him wearing deer masks. William turned up again as Hymen in the play's final scene, wearing antlers and again surrounded by men in deer masks.[21] At Stratford's Royal Shakespeare Theatre in 1985 Adrian Noble made it the occasion of a dream of approaching adulthood by Celia, who remained asleep on stage throughout.

Lindy Davies, who directed *As You Like It* for the Sydney-based Bell Shakespeare company in 2003, considered the scene to be very important in showing the intrusion of male brutality into the forest. With a view of the play darker than usual, she saw Jaques as a compassionate and ironic figure, made fun of for his pitying the sobbing deer of II. 1, and in IV. 2 entering with an antlered deer's skull dripping with blood, disgusted and enraged at the brutality of the hunters who had committed such violence. His lines were spoken with heavy sarcasm, and the dance to the song which followed, during which he was thrust to the front of the stage, was strong, ritualistic, assertive: a pagan celebration of masculinity.

While there are directors who still omit IV. 2 altogether, the variety of interpretations by others is an indication of the richness that the scene offers. Some of the reasons for this richness are to be found in what has been proposed in this paper—that the idea of the horns of cuckoldry in the song draws on popular tradition; that by relating this idea so closely to hunting, Shakespeare also relates it to the theme of metamorphosis which is of such significance in the play; and that through the figure of the fool, Touchstone, the idea is related to carnival, particularly to Shrove Tuesday. It is quite clear that Act IV Scene 2 does far more than 'only ... fill up an interval, which is to represent two hours', as Dr Johnson thought.

Notes

1 Samuel Johnson, *Samuel Johnson on Shakespeare,* ed. H. R. Woudhuysen (Harmondsworth: Penguin, 1989), p. 179.
2 William Shakespeare, *As You Like It,* ed. John Dover Wilson (Cambridge: Cambridge University Press, 1926).
3 Michael Jamieson, *As You Like It* (London: Edward Arnold, 1965), pp. 57–58.
4 Chris Fitter, 'The Slain Deer and Political *Imperium*: *As You Like It* and Andrew Marvell's "Nymph Complaining for the Death of Her Fawn"', *JEGP*, 98 (1999), 207. For this reference I am indebted to Juliet Dusinberre, who generously sent me proof pages of her Arden 3 edition of *As You Like It* before its publication.
5 Edward Berry, *Shakespeare and the Hunt* (Cambridge: Cambridge University Press, 2001), p. 182.
6 Thomas Elyot, *The Governour,* ed. H. H. S. Croft, 2 vols (London: Kegan Paul, Trench and Company, 1880), vol. 1, p. 194.
7 Grahame Clark, 'The First Half-million Years', in *The Dawn of Civilization,* ed. Stuart Piggott (London: Thames and Hudson, 1961), p. 26.
8 Henricus Institoris and Jacob Sprenger, *Malleus Maleficarum,* trans. Montague Summers (London: Pushkin Press, 1948), p. 116.
9 Institoris, p. 116.
10 Cited in Ronald Hutton, *The Rise and Fall of Merry England: The Ritual Year 1400–1700* (Oxford: Oxford University Press, 1994), p. 47.
11 Brian Jewell, *Fairs and Revels* (Tonbridge Wells: Midas, 1976), p. 33.
12 Steve Wilson, *Robin Hood: The Spirit of the Forest* (London: Neptune Press, 1993), p. 13.
13 Cecil Sharp, *The Sword Dances of Northern England,* 3 vols (London: Novello, 1911–13), vol. I, pp. 13–14.
14 R. S. White, '"Now Mercy goes to Kill": Hunting in Shakespearean Comedy', *Durham University Journal,* 69 (1976), 28.
15 François Laroque, *Shakespeare's Festive World* (Cambridge: Cambridge University Press, 1991), pp. 296–97.
16 Martin Ingram, 'Ridings, Rough Music and Mocking Rhymes in Early Modern England', in *Popular Culture in Seventeenth-Century England,* ed. Barry Reay (London: Croom Helm, c. 1985), p. 169.
17 Laroque, p. 102.
18 George Turberville, [Anon. Not by Turberville; actually adapted by G. Gascoigne from J. de Fouilloux's *La Venerie,* 1573]. *The Noble Arte of Venerie or Hunting* (H. Bynnemann for C. Barker [1575]), p. 127.
19 Michael Patterson, *Peter Stein: Germany's Leading Theatre Director* (Cambridge: Cambridge University Press, 1981), p. 134.
20 Patterson, pp. 145–46.

21 Anthony B. Dawson, *Watching Shakespeare: A Playgoers' Guide* (Houndmills: Macmillan, 1988), pp. 44–45.

22 Cited in Seán Mac Mathúna, 'The Horn Fair in South London: London's First Carnival?' www.fantompowa.net.

Note: Earlier versions of this paper were given at the Twenty-fifth International Shakespeare Conference, Stratford-upon-Avon (1992), and the Third Conference of the Australian and New Zealand Shakespeare Association (Perth, 1994); I am grateful for the helpful discussions by conference delegates and to the University of Adelaide for financial support for research and travel which led to its completion.

Marlowe, Maps, and Might

Paige Newmark

The two most significant productions of *Tamburlaine* in the late twentieth century show us that cartography is as important to the play as it has ever been.[1] Peter Hall's 1976 production for the National Theatre starring Albert Finney, established how the cartographic theme is overpowering in the plays: it presented a bare stage in the pre-show, down-lit by a projected map of the known world that blurred into *terra incognita*. Terry Hands' 1992 RSC production starring Anthony Sher used a massive map as a backdrop for the whole of *Part 2*. The dominance of the map as a guiding force for Tamburlaine book-ended the production, since he died not saying his written line 'the Scourge of God must die', but pointing to the map and lamenting 'and shall I die and this unconquered? Unconquered?' The fact that the map was left onstage at the end was a wonderful *coup de théâtre*: it was at once a last great theatrical gesture for Tamburlaine and an image for the audience to take home with them after the play had finished. Sher's last words in combination with the image leave the audience musing on the ultimate nature of the map: is it a implement of power or a monument to Tamburlaine's failure? This essay will argue that the map's dualistic power was as essentially dramatic in the year 1587 as it was in 1992.

The desire to employ correct geography was part of an Early Modern discourse as exemplified by Jonson's famous concern for geographical verisimilitude in the theatre: 'Sheakspear in a play brought in a number of men saying they had suffered Shipwrack in Bohemia, wher y^r is no Sea neer by some 100 Miles.'[2] Only eight years after *The Winter's Tale* was first performed, not only was Shakespeare's credibility criticized, but also specifically his geographical reliability, since he gave Bohemia a seacoast, when it is in fact land-locked. The same problem had already been discussed onstage in such plays as *Henry V* and in *The Travailes of the Three English Brothers*, where the playwrights directly appealed to the audience to use their mind's eye. The self-conscious contrivance was used to ensure that the playgoers engage fully in the suspension of disbelief required of the theatre, lest the mapping of the stage has failed in any way to produce the desired *bona fide* effect:

> But would your apprehensions helpe poore art,
> Into three parts deuiding this our stage ...
> Thinke this Englande, this Spaine, this Persia.[3]

In *Tamburlaine* Marlowe went even further by giving detailed attention to geographical exactness: almost every scene very specifically establishes the geographic location of the action at the start. Marlowe's insistence on geographically framing the scene is a necessary dramatic pointer for the audience, in a play that moves so rapidly around the world. In *Part One* acts I and II start in Persia, act III moves to the Turkish empire, acts IV and V take place in Damascus; in *Part Two* acts III and IV occur in Aleppo, while act V takes place in Babylon. Throughout the play, the naming of cities, dominions and peoples is manifold: from the Western Isle, through Afric, Asia, Persia, Babylon, Egypt, the Armenian desert, to Graecia, and Mauritania. Even with today's modern, comprehensive atlases it can be hard to find all of Marlowe's place names on a map; the reception with which an Elizabethan audience must have greeted this long and exotic sounding list of names (which constantly and consistently appear throughout the play) must have been a heady cocktail of exoticism and foreign mystery.

Marlowe's use of maps in the play not only demonstrates that the playwright was a good student of geography, but that he uses it as a dramatic imperative. Ethel Seaton's significant article, 'Marlowe's Map', gives a meticulous and convincing argument in favour of Marlowe utilizing an Ortelius map as the source for both parts of *Tamburlaine*.[4] She points out that Ortelius' *Theatrum Orbis Terrarum* (1570) was so well known that it was used by all the great navigators and adventurers of the day, including Sir Humfrey Gilbert, Daniel Rogers, Camden, Hakluyt, and Dr Dee. She concludes that, 'the journeys of Tamburlaine's three generals (I. vi) were evidently planned by Marlowe with the *Theatrum* before him' (28). Thus, when Tamburlaine relives his life's conquests and laments what has yet to be achieved, he seems to be using a verbal description; in actuality he creates a mental map (as well as the physical one) in which to trace his wanderings in the mind's eye, making the accounts more graphic and substantially more believable.

If cartographical accuracy is important to dramatic credibility, the plays are arguably made less believable when geographic errors are encountered. Seaton provides persuasive explanations for each of Marlowe's geographical 'errors', and rationalizes why no answer can be provided for many others: 'Marlowe must have turned the atlas to and fro, and picked out a name here and there, attracted partly, but not entirely, by its sonority' (27–28). Her assumption that sometimes it is more important to be poetic than empirically correct is perhaps not as extemporary as one imagines since it is a reflection of a larger device in *Tamburlaine*. The playwright lists so many strange-sounding place names and describes them in such hyperbolic terms that, when Tamburlaine conquers them, he is fashioned into a marvellous character who is at once visionary and idealistic in his quixotic aims of world supremacy. Whether it is the 'paltry Scythian' fighting with five hundred men (1 I. ii. 102) whose army grows to twenty thousand (1 II. v. 91) and then eight hundred thousand (1 IV. i. 21–25), or Tamburlaine's taking over Eastern India 'laden with gold and precious stones', he becomes a romantic, strange, and yet powerful figure. The practical and thematic resonances to such a poetic construct are clear: Tamburlaine's powerful exoticism is first generated and then embellished to such a degree that his appeal becomes almost universal. It is fundamental to the play that there is a delicate balance of romantic poeticism and practical prudence in the main character in order for the audience to believe completely that he can conquer armies with or without raising his sword and still be a romantic hero capable of winning the heart of Zenocrate.

Despite identifying Marlowe's source map in the two plays, and the degree of certitude and scrutiny that Seaton applies to his text, recent cartographical and geographical studies of maps in relation to Early Modern drama provide alternative paradigms for understanding the employment of maps in the plays. Victor Morgan's 'The Literary Images of Globes and Maps in Early Modern England' explores the symbiotic relationship of maps and metaphor in the theatre, which would have been impossible without a familiarity with the new cartography by the Elizabethans and Jacobeans. J. B. Harley's 'Meaning and Ambiguity in Tudor Cartography' enumerates the ubiquity of the many types of map that emerged in the late sixteenth century and lays the foundation for interpreting maps as other than simple diagrammatic portrayals of landscape.[5] Harley foregrounds the subject of Early Modern cartography by analysing maps as practical, symbolic, and social agents. His approach is useful for ascertaining how the meaning of maps can vary when presented onstage, and most pertinent in re-assessing the various functions of mapping in *Tamburlaine*.

Richard Helgerson's 'The Land Speaks: Cartography, Chorography, and Subversion in Renaissance England' casts its net widely and situates the writings of Drayton, Spenser, and Sidney in a dialectic that is set at the power axis between mapping, patronage, and the land.[6] My essay considers how *Tamburlaine* resists Helgerson's belief that any anti-monarchical views expressed by the late-sixteenth-century writers and mapmakers still remain conventional in that they uphold an idea of nationhood in terms of the physical territory. Instead it explores how the play stages the tension between the ideological orthodoxy of British imperialism and the pervasive heterodoxy of Tamburlaine.[7] Tamburlaine's irreverent use of power to redraw the map for his own ends highlights his ego-centric view of the world and directly challenges the contemporary cartographic discourse by questioning whether ownership is contingent upon mapping or mapping upon possession. By examining how Tamburlaine assimilates the new cartographic orthodoxy to endorse his claims to territory we are made to question whether he undermines his entitlement by his anarchic means of acquisition. In addition the essay highlights how *Tamburlaine* appropriates the changing notion of maps from the symbolic medieval *mappae mundi* to representational modern physical geography, thereby epitomizing the uneasy shifting perceptions of the world in Marlowe's generation.

When the English stage witnessed a cartographic explosion only four years after the publication of Saxton's *Counties of Britain*, it was in *Tamburlaine* that a physical map first appeared onstage since the only known previous manifestation seventy years earlier in Rastells' *Four Elements* (c. 1517). Whereas maps were peripheral devices in the intellectual armoury of the medieval playgoer, they had become a cultural mainstay whose presence could be appreciated now that the cartographic explosion situated the maps within the *mentalité* of the Early Modern audience. Moreover they were powerful tools that Marlowe seamlessly incorporated into the fabric of the play by making them integral to the dramatic structure and fundamental signifiers of character.

Although no maps appear in either Henslowe's diary, nor any of the completed Records of Early English Drama (REED), nor any other extant lists of Elizabethan stage props, a map is first alluded to in *1 Tamburlaine*:

> I will confute those blind Geographers
> That make a triple region in the world,
> Excluding Regions which I meane to trace,
> And with this pen reduce them to a Map,
> Calling the Provinces, Citties and townes
> After my name and thine *Zenocrate*:
> Here at *Damascus* will I make the Point
> That shall be Perpendicular.

(1 IV.i v. 81–88)

In *2 Tamburlaine* an actual map (albeit a prop) is brought on after the title character cries out

> Give me a Map, then let me see how much
> Is left for me to conquer all the world,
> That these, my boies, may finish all my wantes,

(2 V. iii. 123–35)

The most noticeable characteristic, when comparing these two occurrences, is Marlowe's use of the map as a medieval device in the first instance and how he employs it from an Elizabethan point of view in the second. In *1 Tamburlaine* the 'triple region' refers to the old T–O maps, where the top half of the 'O' is Asia, the lower left-hand corner is Europe, and the lower-right hand corner is Africa. T–O maps, such as the Hereford *Mappa Mundi* (thirteenth century), or the Isidorean map (1472), were widely known at this time, as evidenced by the number of surviving manuscript T–Os.[8] What is significant about the use of T-O maps in this instance is that its function is purely symbolic and far from empirically accurate. In *2 Tamburlaine* the map is combined with a long list of place names that Tamburlaine has conquered and serves as a literal device whose primary role is to manifest his conquests practically. The shift in map usage reveals that Marlowe was not only making a point about the changing role of cartography, but also how maps mirror the altering conditions in the world of the play, and how characters similarly transform. Marlowe was able to illuminate the fundamental dramatic developments in the play in a particularly voguish way, by employing the transitional concept of mapping.

Tamburlaine invokes a map in the first instance (1 IV. iv. 81–88) to sanction his claim of absolute ownership over the entire world, including those territories that have not yet been mapped. In seeking to impress Zenocrate by his omnipotence, he claims that cartographers are 'blind'; he intends to prove their reductive view of the world as wrong by repositioning its centre as Damascus and naming his newly conquered/ mapped lands after himself and her. He invokes the map in a manner that parallels the real-world cartographic discourse of the late sixteenth century, where maps serve as objects of prestige and power in their own right.[9] His 'calling the Provinces, Citties and townes / After my name and thine *Zenocrate*' is an appropriation of both the Saxton's maps and the subsequent cartographic iconography which elides the depicted territories of England and the monarch who presides over them. The same orthodox relationship between the identity of the country and the monarch is propounded by Tamburlaine as a means of asserting his newfound entitlement over the conquered lands. At the same time, his claim is justified by appropriating the traditional T–O depiction of the world in redrawing and then renaming it. Cartographic convention places Jerusalem at the map's centre rather than Damascus. In repositioning the centre Tamburlaine is not only asserting that he controls the known world, but makes it known that he is happy to demonstrate as much on his new maps. His analogy (that he can as easily re-order the world with his sword as the cartographers can with their pens) takes the authority that maps contain, and uses it to legitimize his militaristic approach. In doing so, he rewrites the rules of power and ownership through the medium of the map. There is an irony in Tamburlaine's re-conception of the world: whether one looks at medieval T–O maps (or any contemporary atlas of Ortelius), Damascus is almost impossible to find; when it is identifiable, then its position is so close to Jerusalem as to be indistinguishable. Tamburlaine's bold reference to such a major shift in the centre of power is curious when one considers that it could never be actualized with any degree of certitude or observed by an audience. What this suggests is that Tamburlaine is less concerned with the practical or empirical notion of the map than its dramatic or poetical impact. Such a view is borne out when we consider how he manages to combine the purely symbolic idea of the God-given, immutable, biblical division of the T–O world map with the more contemporary concept of maps as unstable, changeable articulations of power.[10] Essentially the same God-like aspirations that we see Tamburlaine articulate numerous times in both plays, is asserted by re-ordering the world-view using the map. Where God was the centre of the world, now Tamburlaine takes on the characteristics of the deity, which he verbally propounds elsewhere in the play, by cartographically repositioning himself in Damascus as the new centre of the world. The newly cartographically aware audience would not interpret the idea of using maps as anachronistic for the historic Tamerlane (1336–1405), but rather be impressed by his use of a contrivance that possesses such latent power.

The juxtaposition of the two types of mapping reveals that Marlowe seems to be making a fundamental point about Tamburlaine's world through the play's structure. Cartographically *Tamburlaine* bridges the historical divide between the old symbolic T–O maps and the new cartography with its emphasis on geographical correctness and empirical verisimilitude. As mentioned Ortelius' *Theatrum* was the source for both parts of *Tamburlaine*; just as Ortelius combines the old maps in a supplement entitled *Parergon* with his new maps, so Marlowe also makes the two types of mapping in his play work in synchronization. In the atlas, Ortelius' historical maps come after the new mapping since he wants to keep his readership aware of the old world; in contrast, Marlowe self-consciously inverts this expectation, by placing the medieval map early on. Marlowe's use suggests that he was aware that the new geography sat uneasily with the audience, who were still steeped in a medieval tradition of mapping and only recently becoming aware of an alternative way of seeing the world. At the very beginning of *Tamburlaine* Cosroe institutes the idea that the perception of the world order is a medieval one. His lamentation of the passing of a 'former age' when Persia ruled over Africa and Europe (1 I. i. 6–10) combined with Tamburlaine's hope to 'reign in Asia' (1 I. i. 43) is specifically a T–O, tripartite conception of the world; the play immediately establishes itself as having a cartographically medieval scheme in place. In contrast when Cosroe shortly afterwards describes Tamburlaine and the swarming neighbours who threaten Persia from 'the farthest Equinoctiall line' (1 I. i. 119), he is invoking a modern cartographic allusion. What does this tell us about Tamburlaine? All the new maps emphasize verisimilitude and exactitude in order to show that legal precedence for landownership is founded on accurate mapping. Therefore when Tamburlaine is associated with the new mapping that calls upon such contrivances as an 'Equinoctiall line', he is immediately set up as representing part of the new world. Marlowe is juxtaposing the old world with its medieval cartographic conception and the new mapping to show who are the new power brokers.

Instead of imagining the world in bifurcated terms where there is either old or new mapping of the globe, Marlowe realized that one did not necessarily preclude the other and so managed to combine the two. He harnessed Ortelius' divided image and exploited the disparity to show that Tamburlaine embodies not only a changing world, but also a changing world order. The older, symbolic medieval T–O conception is used at first to emphasize an age when men respected traditional values, while the latter modern image is used to indicate the shift in world order to a new time when those values no longer exist. The result is a tension between a medieval Tamburlaine who wishes to 'conquere all the triple world' (2 IV. iii. 63) and 'to note me Emperour of the three fold world' (2 IV. iii. 118), and one who embodies an age when men rely on modern instruments, modern devices, and can substitute the idea of a God/Jerusalem-centred universe with a more humanist, self-centred world. Such a notion is introduced in the first mapping allusion, when Tamburlaine chooses to reject the old T–O symbolic representation of the world ('I will confute those blind Geographers / That make a triple region in the world') and substitute it with an empirically correct map with properly identifiable places:

> And with this pen reduce them to a Map,
> Calling the Provinces, Citties and townes
> After my name and thine *Zenocrate*.

The payoff occurs just before Tamburlaine dies: when assessing his landed achievements his modern cartographic imagery clearly echoes Cosroe's:

> Cutting the Tropicke line of *Capricorne*,
> I conquered all as far as *Zansibar* ...
> Looke here, my boies, see what a world of ground,
> Lies westward from the midst of *Cancers* line,
> Unto the rising of this earthly globe,
> Whereas the sun, declining from our sight,
> Begins the day with our Antypodes:
> And shall I die, and this unconquered?

(2 V. iii. 139–51)

As Tamburlaine grows more powerful, so his conception of the world correspondingly changes, and he leaves behind a medieval world vision that has nothing to offer him.

Tamburlaine's shifting expression of how he sees the world is consistent in one regard: it is predicated upon a language of universal possession. Questions of possession are very much to the fore in the play and constitute a recurring theme. From the beginning the 'natural right' of Mycetes as King of Persia is brought into question by the crowning of his brother Cosroe, while Callapine and Tamburlaine's sons also invoke their birthright to ownership of land (1 I. i; 2 I. i. 1–3; 2 I. ii. 1–3; 2 I. iii. 7–8; 2 III. i. 1–7). Tamburlaine's relentless war machine brings into question what ownership means, such as who and what determines the basis of tenure. For example natural ambition or 'Nature' (1 II. vii. 18–29) is cited as the reason for the attainment of 'the sweet fruition of an earthly crowne'. Luck is also cited as a rationale: 'Fortune that hath made him great' (2 I. i. 60). Tamburlaine (1 I. ii. 58–59; 1 III. iii. 98–99), Mycetes/Meander (1 II. ii. 30–32), and Callapine (2 I. ii. 66; 2 III. i. 69–78) all use kingdoms as rewards for good deeds throughout the play. However, most often the principles of ownership are based on might ('By murder raised to the Persean Crowne, / That Dares control us in our Territories' (1 I. ii. 64, 191–209, IV. i. 13–14); this recurrent image dominates the play's perception of who owns what land. The hiding of Mycetes' crown comically reduces the king's previously bombastic declaration of ownership of his kingdom to possession of a bauble (1 II. iv), further drawing attention to how 'might is right'. Similarly the value of land is reduced to a joke by Tamburlaine, who becomes so confident of his ability to win possession of the Persian kingdom that he challenges Cosroe for the crown as a jest (1 II. v. 98). Tamburlaine's power is so great that the contrary figures of God and Mahomet are used in conjunction in support of his supreme control of the land (1 V. i. 480–82). He is equally prepared to invoke the classical gods, as exemplified by his constant reference to Jove. Although it is Jove who sends Zenocrate as a sign that he 'shall be Monark of the East' (1 I. ii. 180–87), Tamburlaine explicitly takes on those same attributes of the 'God of war [who] resigns his roume to me, / Meaning to make me Generall of the world' (1 V. i. 451–52; 2 IV. iii. 33). An alternative viewpoint is presented by Theridamas, whose three rejections of kingdoms raises his status in the very same breath that it diminishes the importance of land over loyalty (1 II. v. 66; 1 IV. iv. 120–42; 2 I. iii. 13–17). The theme of land ownership as a manifestation of power is thus a constant that remains relevant to the end of the play when Tamburlaine is seen dividing his kingdom just before his death.

For Tamburlaine, possession of Zenocrate is predicated upon the same language as possession of the land. When they first meet he tells her that 'this faire face and heavenly hew / must grace his bed that conquers Asia' (1 I. ii. 36–37). He goes on to tell her that he has the power to 'invest you Empresse of the East' (l. 46), and that 'thy person is more worth to Tamburlaine / than possession of the Persean Crowne' (ll. 90–91). He takes complete possession of her and her country by rape and by military force. He continues in the same vein by refusing to marry her until her father has passed over possession to him. Although there is a turning point in his treatment of her ('the entertainment we have had of him … might … be counted princely' [1 III. ii. 37–39]), he still continues to integrate his perception of her with the land: when redrawing the world Tamburlaine does not simply choose to identify the land in his own image 'Calling the Provinces, Citties and townes / After my name' but also 'thine Zenocrate'. Even when he crowns Zenocrate and marries her, it is done over the bleeding bodies of Bajezeth, Zabina and Arabia, as if to complement his other triumphs of possession in a parallel—though ghoulish—manner (1 V. i. 507–35).

The confusing array of claims to ownership to land is solved by Marlowe with his recurrent references to modern maps: at the beginning of both plays the cartographical conceit is established; in *1 Tamburlaine* Cosroe complains how badly Persia has been pillaged by 'men from the farthest Equinoctiall line' (I. i. 119); again, in *2 Tamburlaine* (I. i. 25), Orcanes expresses in a cartographical manner the proposed advance of Tamburlaine 'from the shortest Northren Paralell'. Since the map represents such a powerful legal document for the Elizabethan audience, its repeated invocation reflects in a legal manner the extent of Tamburlaine's power.[11] Used in conjunction with his sword, Tamburlaine's citation of a map as proof of ownership therefore makes cartography a necessary and integral component of the dramatic structure. Tamburlaine's final use of the map to divide up his kingdom among his children legally parallels the redrawing of the world at the start of the plays. Such gestures are pointless unless the audience immediately accepts the convention, which, in turn is best exemplified in terms of a parallel contemporary discourse.

Tamburlaine's ambition for world dominance strongly echoes John Dee's imperialist philosophy in his manuscript *Brytanici Imperii Limites*. In the section 'Concerning a Reformed Location for the Islands of Estotilant & the region of Drogio', Dee proposes a 'geographical reformation' of Mercator and Ortelius, despite the fact that they are 'the two most celebrated geographers of this age'.[12] Dee seems careless of whatever geographic precedent has been established, preferring to found his imperial claims by simply redrawing the regional maps. We can see how Tamburlaine's solipsistic words are a glancing echo of Dee's later sentiment, that 'until this volume [*Discoveries*] can be elegantly and conveniently completed by the arts of the pen and the printing press, I thought that it would be not displeasing to your Serene Highness, if … I explained briefly what is worthy your attention among the rare and novel features shown in our diagram'.[13] Clearly Marlowe's use of the map in drama is a strong reflection of the utilization of cartography in the imperialistic discourse of the real world. Richard Wilson develops this argument further by showing the multiple connections between the main participants in the Muscovy Company, Walsingham, and Marlowe. Wilson contends that Marlowe's involvement in the realpolitik of the 'recent concern for trade and empire' was so elaborate that it ultimately led to his death.[14]

Dee was not the only person fashioning England into 'the incomparable Island of the Whole World' for Queen Elizabeth.[15] English imperialism manifested itself in other treatises, such as Thomas Digges' 'Arguments proving the Queenes Maties propertye in the sea landes, and salt shores thereof;'[16] explicitly imperialist chronicles appear in Hakluyt, while subtler manifestations occur in the iconography of the Ditchley and Armada portraits. Cartographically, the imperialist agenda emerged in examples such as Emery Molyneaux's 1592 terrestrial globe, which has the Queen's arms superimposed on Atlantis, representing England's claims to areas around Florida. Similarly, Tamburlaine uses geographic and cartographic language to express the extremity of his desire for world dominance: 'we meane to traveile to th' Antartique Pole, / Conquering the people underneath our feet' (1 IV. iv. 145–46). This sentence can be interpreted in two ways: either Tamburlaine means to travel to the south pole conquering everyone underfoot during his journey, or he is creating an imaginary picture of himself dominating the globe and everyone on earth. If one takes the second interpretation, then the similarity between Tamburlaine's speech and Elizabeth's imperialist manifesto is readily apparent. Although one is not necessarily inspired directly by the other, the correlation indicates a strong cultural surge that was taking place, whereby the numerous manifestations of cartographical symbolism clearly connected both the literature and the art.[17] The discourse occurring in both society and the drama, whereby Tamburlaine can refer to the reshaping of the world by cartographers, only makes sense to the audience if they comprehend what he means and understand maps as devices of imperial power and ownership.[18] Tamburlaine's final imploring his sons to conquer the new world 'westward from the midst of Cancer's line' with its 'golden Mines' (2 V. ii. 147–52) reflects this imperial discourse; just as it is as anachronistic for the historic Tamburlaine it is pertinent to the contemporary audience.

One of the unique aspects of *Tamburlaine* is how the play is the earliest example of drama appropriating the almost universal esteem that maps were held in society, and questioning their utility as orthodox instruments of administration by the government. Although *Tamburlaine* invokes maps as legal proof of ownership, on closer inspection we realize that the legal authority that the map is supposed to provide is actually being abused: its primary function as a constructive apparatus is turned into a negative one, and the map's hallowed status as a legally binding instrument of authority is inverted. Marlowe regularly challenged orthodoxy, and in this instance flexes his intellectual and moral muscle against the new mapping and the authority that they represented. In *Tamburlaine*, he is not so much disparaging the meaning of maps and what they represent, but availing himself of the new set of rich possibilities which maps provide. This challenging of authority says as much about the power of the theatre to contend accepted forms of behaviour as it does about Marlowe's writing, which regularly questions the exercise of power.[19]

Such a misappropriation of authoritarian means is characteristic of Tamburlaine and has been well documented: he takes the conventional and expected norms of society and inverts them.[20] For example, his treatment of Bajazeth is antithetical to the expected conventions of warfare (1 IV. ii. 56–65). His degradation of Bajazeth in using him as a footstool is made particularly humiliating since Tamburlaine is dressed in white—ironically symbolizing his traditional chivalric code of behaviour. His sacrilegious burning of the Koran (which was interpreted at the time as symbolizing the Bible) is followed by even greater glory.[21] In his challenge to Mahomet ('Whom I have thought a god') to rescue the Koran, Tamburlaine rejects the deity; likewise he invokes both Gods in his bid for world supremacy and yet rejects both their existences after he has achieved his aim (2 V. i. 179–202).[22] Equally perplexing is how his cold-blooded murder of the virgins is followed by his most poetic speech in the play ruminating on the beauty of Zenocrate; again he emphasizes his contradictory nature by dressing himself in black in contrast to the virgins' white. There is an irony about the way in which Marlowe uses this inversion: one would expect that Tamburlaine's appalling treatment of prisoners and blasphemies would make him into a figure of contempt and dislike, a villain.[23] Yet paradoxically it is his very ability to invert expectations that makes him successful: just as 'the slave usurps the glorious name of war' (1 IV. i. 67) he becomes the most powerful military leader. Similarly he commandeers the law by redrawing the map and thereby 'usurps' the glories of mapping to become sole landowner. Tamburlaine's debasing the map for his own ends would be interpreted by the audience as anti-social, unlawful and disruptive; yet it has the opposite effect, since his actions only prove that his claims to earthly power are left unchallenged, or when challenged remain uncastigated.

In a similar fashion, the choice of Tamburlaine, rather than anyone else, to bring maps into play is intrinsic to Marlowe's paradoxical conception of the character. Like most of the audience, Tamburlaine understands the value of ocular proof, and his lack of education does not prohibit him from understanding the impact that the visual representation embodied in a map can have. On the contrary, the lack of learning seems to work in Tamburlaine's favour in the same way as the poetic resonance in Enobarbus's 'barge' speech, where the words (or in this case image) invoked are uncharacteristically sophisticated. The self-conscious use of an educated man's motif in the mouth of an untutored man draws attention to the charged nature of the image. The irony is most apparent in the final moments of the play, when Tamburlaine self-consciously characterizes himself as 'the Scourge of God' as he lies dying next to (or beneath) the map of his conquests.

Marlowe could simply conclude his *Tamburlaine* verbally but instead brings on an authoritative theatrical emblem to visually establish exactly what has occurred during the two dramas. The map, as a physical manifestation of his life's work, serves the practical function of delineating all the places that he has subjugated:

Here I began to martch towards *Persea*,
Along *Armenia* and the Caspian sea …
And from th'Antartique Pole, Eastward behold
As much more land, which never was descried,
Wherein are rockes of pearle, that shine as bright
As all the Lamps, that beautifie the Sky,
And shal I die, and this unconquered?

(2 V. iii. 127–59)

Tamburlaine then dies leaving the map as the only visual evidence of his sweeping achievements. The audience would experience his use of the map as wholly in character, since he is someone whose language and actions are at once hyperbolic and grandiloquent. Correspondingly the map provides a similarly powerful and articulate statement, as it is not simply a minor prop but a major theatrical device that is both authoritative and resonant.

Equally important to the utilitarian function, Elizabethan audiences simultaneously understood Tamburlaine's map emblematically: it represents what he can pass on to the next generation (as King Lear does) and remains a clear visual symbol of his prestige and power. Two examples that are most analogous are the wall-maps of Queen Elizabeth and Lord Burleigh that so prominently announce their office and indisputably proclaim their power, and Sir Henry Unton's map-like memorial picture.[24] Just as Unton's picture is a static manifestation of his life's journey represented in one place, so the travels which Tamburlaine proudly traces, embody his powerful exploits; Tamburlaine's map thus represents a memorial of his power and a tribute to his success. However, Stephen Greenblatt posits the opposite point, suggesting that the map could be interpreted as a symbol of failure rather than attainment, since it simultaneously represents all that Tamburlaine has left 'unconquered.'[25] Greenblatt's interpretation is consistent with Tamburlaine's response in his rare moments of loss: Tamburlaine's keeping the dead body of his other possession, Zenocrate, after her soul has departed is a similarly futile gesture in the face of defeat. The common aspect in both scenes is how Tamburlaine's world disintegrates in the face of death; where he can control making someone die, he has no power in stopping death. His unwavering desire to attain complete control over the entire world is frustrated by death. If the play were simply a moral tale then perhaps we could interpret Tamburlaine's use of the map as an emblem of his life's deficiency, since he is not rewarded for his deeds. Unlike traditional morality plays that portray man's passage through life as a moral journey, Tamburlaine is not accompanied by his good deeds, but leaves them behind in the form of a map. The map thus represents a truncated symbol of aspiration whereby his desire for omnipotence is illustrated by an incomplete representation of world domination.

However, *Tamburlaine* presents an unusual ethical scenario, since protagonists traditionally 'fall' after the kinds of acts of barbarity, cruelty, and acquisitiveness that Tamburlaine perpetrates. This time the protagonist does not have a moral epiphany, but augments his crimes by further sins resulting in even greater glory. Instead, Tamburlaine as anti-hero succeeds in spite of his heinous actions. His map serves as a memorial, and is akin to those contemporary maps-in-Bibles which trace the wanderings of Moses in Exodus; they provide the cartographic template for illustrating the idea of narrative progress in a relative spatial stasis.[26] More importantly, they delineate not only the geographical travels, but also the moral travails of Moses. As Catherine Delano Smith has shown the salient part of the Exodus maps lay in their status as seminal moral maps representing Luther's new reformist church entering a new holy land and holy era.[27] The escape from Egypt was a symbol of Luther's call to a renewed and redefined faith unavailable before, while the Exodus was also seen as a metaphor of the journey from ignorance to knowledge and freedom from the bondage of Rome. Since Tamburlaine loves to make highly symbolic and theatrical gestures (such as the changing colours of his tents in 1 IV. i. 49–93), his emblematic use of the map is entirely in character. Bringing out a map that is so alike to those seen in Bibles strongly suggests that the association raises his status to that of a prophet.

Further light is shed on the question of whether the map is an object of triumph or disappointment if we look at the timing of when the map is brought onstage in *Part 2*. Our point of view is influenced by the fact that Tamburlaine has just arrived on his chariot, pulled by the kings of the same conquests he boasts about. Our perspective is therefore not solely Tamburlaine's but tainted by the kings' as we see his successes on the map through their eyes: looking at them we are reminded that his triumphs are gained at the loss of their kingdoms. Although we cannot know if he is jubilant, cruel, or petty in his use of the map, any playing (or reading) which suggests that Tamburlaine is revelling in their loss might diminish his stature at such a decisive point in the play. Placed in the final moment, the map is a manifestation of all that the character and the play have striven for. Its presence is the apotheosis of Tamburlaine's career that completes the dramatic arc of both character and play. As such a crucial signifier in Tamburlaine's journey, we can see the map's presence is not only desirable but also necessary for audience and readership alike. Whether we choose to accept Tamburlaine's map as a symbol of failure or success, there remains an irony in his obsessive invocation of the map at the end of his life, when he displayed such 'contempt of earthly fortune' (1 V. i. 366) earlier in *Part 1*. What also seems ironic is that his legal appeal to the map is an embracement of the very tool of law that he so comprehensively rejected at start of play. The irony is furthermore compounded by the fact that he cannot take the map with him after death; his reference to so many conquests eventually starts to sound hollow and the map mocking.

The duality of Tamburlaine's character reflects the duality of the plays, which in turn is reflected in the duality of the map usage. The repetition of cartographic references perfectly embodies our perception of Tamburlaine and is crucial for understanding the multiple layers of the play as both realistic and poetic. *Prima facie*, the practical aspect of introducing maps for functional purposes makes the plays seem that much more immediate to the audience. On a more ideological level, by alleging that the geography within the plays is empirically correct, the tales are lent an aura of truth. The plays therefore are made more believable, and consequently emotionally and ideologically more powerful. In a legal context the maps are also invoked in a dualistic manner: on the one hand Tamburlaine's fighting drives his quest for domination of the mapped world, yet he needs to invoke a more philosophical notion of a map as a binding legal tool in order to assert that same claim. Likewise, Tamburlaine's antithetical desire for omnipotence and fear of failure are simultaneously demonstrated in his final map. The play manages to exemplify the real world discourse between the status of T–O maps and modern empirical maps, in Tamburlaine's rejection of one in favour of the other. This bridge is made poignant in light of the fact that the previous manifestation of maps on the English stage (*Elements*) failed to reconcile the two types of mapping. Where *Elements* looked forward in its attempt to harness the map as a practical device, *Tamburlaine* looks back to the medieval drama and its use of symbolism. The resolution for the duality of how maps were perceived was only possible after they became part of a cultural normalcy. Only after establishing themselves as part of the intellectual landscape could they then become essential components of the literary and theatrical vocabulary.

Notes

1   All quotations taken from *The Complete Works of Christopher Marlowe*, ed. Roma Gill, 5 vols (Oxford: Clarendon Press, 1987–98), vol. V: *Tamburlaine Parts 1 and 2*, ed. David Fuller (1998).
2   *Ben Jonson*, ed. C. H. Herford, Percy and Evelyn Simpson, 9 vols (Oxford: Oxford University Press, 1925–52), vol. I, p. 138, ll. 208–10.
3   J. Day, W. Rowley and G. Wilkins, *The Travailes of the Three English Brothers* (London: Wright, 1607), sig. H4[r-v], Epilogue, ll. 8–11. The issue continued to be debated as late as 1641, when Georges de Scudéry pertinently wrote in his preface to *Ibrahim*, 'how shall I be touched by the misfortunes of the Queen of Guindaye and the King of Astrobacia, if I know that their very realms are not on the map of the world?' Georges de Scudéry, *Ibrahim* (Paris, 1641).
4   Ethel Seaton, 'Marlowe's Map', *The English Association: Essays and Studies*, 10 (1924): 13–35.
5   *English Map-Making 1500–1650*, ed. Sarah Tyacke (London: British Library, 1983), pp. 22–56.
6   Richard Helgerson, *Forms of Nationhood: the Elizabethan Writing of England* (Chicago and London: Chicago University Press, 1992), pp. 105–48. Helgerson's application of the theoretical approaches to cartography are used to assert that maps and chorographies are not ideologically neutral but contribute to Britain's views of itself, which progressively place greater emphasis on the land than the monarch.
7   John Gillies refers to this in '*Tamburlaine* and Renaissance Geography', *Early Modern English Drama*, ed. Garret A Sullivan, Patrick Cheney and Andrew Hadfield (New York and Oxford: Oxford University Press, 2006), p. 36. Gillies' 'Marlowe, the Timur Myth, and the Motives of Geography', in John Gillies and Virginia Mason Vaughan eds,

Playing the Globe: Genre and Geography in English Renaissance Drama (Madison, NJ and London: Fairleigh Dickinson University Press and Associated University Presses, 1998), pp. 203–29, also appears relevant to this chapter. However, it focuses on how the 'motif of cartographic expansionism is … juxtaposed with … a set of more ritually-based paradigms of spatial practice deriving from ancient geographic lore'; its deliberation on ritualistic structures and spatiality has little to offer this particular study.

8   Marcel Destombes, *Mappemondes A.D. 1200–1500* (Amsterdam: Israel, 1964), lists 1,106 extant T–O maps, 21, 23, and illustrations i–xxxvii at end of volume; David Woodward, 'Medieval *Mappaemundi*', in *The History of Cartography*, I, ed. J. B. Harley and David Woodward (Chicago: University of Chicago Press, 1987), pp. 286–370.

9   Helgerson; David Buisseret ed., *Monarchs, Ministers and Maps: the Emergence of Cartography as a Tool of Government in Early Modern Europe* (Chicago and London: University of Chicago Press, 1992); John Gillies, *Shakespeare and the Geography of Difference* (Cambridge: Cambridge University Press, 1994).

10 Naomi Reed Kline, *Maps of Medieval Thought* (Woodbridge: Boydell, 2001), pp. 13, 228–29.

11 For more on the legal efficacy of maps in Elizabethan England, see Peter Barber, 'England I: Pageantry, Defense, and Government: Maps at Court to 1550' and 'England II: Monarchs, Ministers, and Maps, 1550–1625', in Buisseret, pp. 26–98; P. D. A. Harvey, *Maps in Tudor England* (London: British Library and PRO, 1993), pp. 31, 45, 84–85, 98, 110–11.

12 John Dee, *Brytanici Imperii Limites* (ms., 1576), in William Sherman, *John Dee: the Politics of Reading and Writing in the English Renaissance* (Amherst, Mass.: University of Massachusetts Press, 1995), p. 184.

13 In the second section of *Limites*, entitled 'Unto youer Ma:tis tytle Royall to these forene Regions, & Ilands do appertayne .4. poyntes'. The preface is headed 'A briefe Remembraunce of Sondrye foreyne Regions, discovered, inhabited, and partlie Conquered by the Subjects of this *Brytish Monarchie*: And so your lawfull Tytle … for the dewe Clayme, and just recovery of the same disclosed …', in Sherman, pp. 184–85.

14 Richard Wilson, 'Visible Bullets: *Tamburlaine the Great* and Ivan the Terrible', in *Christopher Marlowe*, ed. Richard Wilson (London and New York: Longman, 1999), pp. 120–39.

15 Dee, *Discoveries*, fol. 206v; see also John Dee, *Thalattokratia Brettanika* (ms., 1597); both in Sherman, pp. 181, 191 and 194.

16 MS, undated in Lansdowne Collection.

17 See my article 'Mapping the Theatre, Mapping the Body' in *Shakespeare in Southern Africa*, the journal of Shakespeare Society of Southern Africa, vol. 16, 2004, 15–28.

18 For discussions of Early Modern notions of empire and Britain see A. F. Pollard, 'The Elizabethans and the Empire', *Proceedings of the British Academy*, X (1921): 1–20; Frances Yates, *Astraea: The Imperial Theme in the Sixteenth Century* (London and Boston: Routledge & Kegan Paul, 1975), especially pp. 38–54, and 74–76; Tristan Marshall's *Theatre and Empire. Great Britain on the London Stages under James VI and I* (Manchester and New York: Manchester University Press, 2000).

19 Stevie Simkin, *Marlowe* (Harlow: Longman, 2000), p. 52; Antony Easthope, *Literary into Cultural Studies* (London: Routledge, 1991), p. 5; Alan Sinfield, *Cultural Politics—*

Queer Reading (London: Routledge, 1994), p. viii. Leonard Tennenhouse, *Power on Display* (New York and London: Methuen, 1986); Stephen Greenblatt, *Renaissance Self-Fashioning from More to Shakespeare* (Chicago: Chicago University Press, 1980); Greenblatt, 'Invisible Bullets: Renaissance Authority and its Subversion, *Henry IV* and *Henry V*', in Richard Wilson and Richard Dutton, eds, *New Historicism and Renaissance Drama* (London and New York: Longman, 1992), pp. 97–98, 107–8.

20 Gill, pp. xxvii–xliv; Eugene M. Waith, *The Herculean Hero* (London: Chatto & Windus, 1962).

21 Robert Green condemned Marlowe as blasphemous in 1588 for 'daring God out of heauen with that Atheist Tamurlan', Millar Maclure ed., *Marlowe: The Critical Heritage 1588–1896* (London: Routledge, 1979), p. 29.

22 For further discussion of Tamburlaine's confusing interaction with the gods see Simkin, pp. 92–95.

23 'The ambiguity of moral impact in Tamburlaine has led to widely varying interpretations', David M. Bevington, *Mankind to Marlowe* (Cambridge, Mass.: Harvard University Press, 1962), pp. 212–15, 257–62.

24 Barber, pp. 26, 76–79.

25 Stephen Greenblatt, 'Marlowe and the Will to Absolute Play', in Richard Wilson and Richard Dutton, eds, *New Historicism and Renaissance Drama* (London and New York: Longman, 1992), p. 62.

26 Two other rare theatrical examples of maps portraying narrative progress in spatial stasis are Ben Jonson's *Pans Anniversarie; or, The Shepherds Holy-Day* (1620?) in Herford, vol. VII, pp. 533–34, ll. 143–45, and *The Honorable Entertainment Gieven to the Quene's Majestie, in Progresse, at Elvetham in Hampshire, by the Right Hon'ble the Earle of Hertford, 1591*. The Elvetham drawing is the only extant printed map that accompanies an entertainment of any sort; see John Nichols, *The Progresses and Public Processions of Queen Elizabeth*, 3 vols (London: Nichols, 1823), vol. III, p. 101.

27 Catherine Delano-Smith, 'Maps in Bibles in the Sixteenth Century', *The Map Collector*, 39 (1987): 2–14.

Ben Jonson and 'the proper passion of Mettalls'

Anthony Miller

No early modern writer shows more curiosity than Jonson about the everyday materials of life, especially urban life, from food and clothing to the fairground and the news sheet. None shows greater pleasure in every kind of *virtù* and inventiveness, from the heroic to the nefarious. One aspect of his catholic curiosity and knowledge that has been little explored is Jonson's poetic and dramatic use of metals and of the related technologies and myths. *The Alchemist* has of course directed attention to Jonson's treatment of alchemical science, but the present essay seeks to direct attention toward the play's knowledge of other branches of early modern metallurgy. The essay also begins with Jonson's unusual blacksmithing metaphor for the work of the poet, in his poem to Shakespeare, and ends with his most extended version of the myth of the Golden Age and the Iron Age. In these cases, too, it seeks to establish that Jonson has a sound knowledge of the technologies involved and a clear-headed understanding of the role of metals in civilized life, an understanding that unexpectedly puts him at odds with classical prescript or precedent in these areas.

When praising Shakespeare for the art which he also applies to his surpassingly natural plays, Jonson chooses the blacksmith's forge as his metaphor for the poet's rigorous and laborious shaping of his materials:

> And, that he,
> Who casts to write a living line, must sweat,
> (Such as thine are) and strike the second heat
> Upon the *Muses* anvile: turne the same,
> (And himself with it), that he thinkes to frame.[1]

Hammering away sweatily in his poetic smithy, the poet must be thorough and meticulous. 'A heat' was a term both for a single operation of heating in a furnace and also for the metal thus treated; if metal could not be worked satisfactorily after a first heat, it would be returned to the furnace, emerging as the 'second heat'. Jonson therefore envisages the poet beating his lines into shape on a second attempt. In this prescription, his verses implicitly contradict Heminge's and Condell's praise, on the preceding page of the First Folio, of Shakespeare's easiness of composition, witnessed by the fact that 'wee have scarse received from him a blot in his papers'.[2]

Jonson elsewhere shows himself irritated by this praise: 'My answer hath beene, Would he had blotted a thousand'.[3] Himself notorious for his slow working methods, Jonson defended poetic revision:

> For all that wee invent doth please us in the conception, or birth; else we would never set it downe. But the safest is to returne to our Judgement, and handle over againe those things, the easinesse of which might make them justly suspected.[4]

In the poem, he therefore partly praises Shakespeare, but also partly instructs him retrospectively, or reshapes him in the mould of the true poet.

Jonson varies his metaphor a little, keeping it in the realm of the workshop, if not necessarily of the forge, when he declares that the poet must also 'turne' his lines, as one turns material on a lathe, giving them a smoothed-out regularity. At the same time, the poet must turn himself, by which Jonson probably means that he must discipline and perfect his own ethical nature.[5] The activity of smoothing returns to the smithy when Jonson calls Shakespeare's lines not only 'well torned' but also 'true-filed' (l. 68), smoothed with the metalworker's file so that they are 'true', correctly shaped and fitting neatly into the working mechanism of his poetry. When all this is done, the poet is in a position to achieve the 'framing', the overall fabrication of his poetic artefact. That Jonson envisages this process in terms of early modern light industry is clear from the parallel language of Joseph Moxon:

> you must take a piece of Iron thick enough, and with the *Pen* of your *Hammer* ... batter it out; ... and so by several *Heats*, if your Work require them, frame it into Form and Size ... if it be not throughly *welded* at the first *Heat*, you must reiterate your *Heats* so oft, till they be throughly *welded*.[6]

The Muses are not usually associated with a blacksmith's workshop: Jonson's conceit creates an almost oxymoronic contrast between the poet's labour and the conventional belief that he may write almost effortlessly, from the direct dictation of the Muses. A more apt divine model for Jonson's laborious poet is the blacksmith god Vulcan. Even this model is surprising: elsewhere in Jonson's writings Vulcan's lameness associates him with the limping incompetence of the false poet, and the idea of an eloquent Vulcan is matter for witty paradoxes.[7] Likewise, Jonson's usual link between wit and the products of the smithy is a negative one, as when his Captain Bobbadill dismisses the wit of another as 'old iron, and rusty proverbes! a good commoditie for some smith, to make hob-nailes of'.[8]

The anomaly of the '*Muses* anvile' may be summed up as Jonson's treating the liberal art of poetry in terms of the mechanical art of blacksmithing. These two branches of the arts are generally opposed to one another, notably by Seneca, who opposes the mechanical art of metalworking to the liberal art of philosophy. For Seneca, an inventor of practical arts, like Daedalus, is the adversary of a philosopher, like Diogenes, since he distracts men from the quest for simplicity or sufficiency. Seneca argues that mines and iron tools were the invention of men 'of active and keen but not of great or elevated mind', that the mechanical arts, which have generated a false sense of need in men, 'were devised by reason, it is true, but not by right reason'. Remembering the most familiar and durable of the blacksmith's products, Seneca asks, 'was it philosophy that taught the use of locks and keys?'[9]

Generally Jonson, too, valorizes the liberal arts over the mechanical. His frequent attacks on his associate in the creation of Jacobean masques, Inigo Jones, are based on the charge that Jones's contributions were those of a mere mechanic, like the 'Cooke' of *Neptunes Triumph* (originally written in the year of Jonson's Shakespeare poem), or the dauber and carpenter of the 'Expostulacion with Inigo Jones', of the early 1630s, which ironically condemns poetry to the role of a pedlar in comparison with those newly elevated arts:

> Painting and Carpentry are the Soule of Masque.
> Pack with your pedling Poetry to the Stage,
> This is the money-gett, Mechanick Age![10]

When it is related to the other attitudes and tensions already noted in the poem, the fact that Jonson's poem on Shakespeare places the activity of the poet in the smithy suggests therefore a complex of attitudes, both to the role of poet in general and to the status of Shakespeare in particular. Jonson vindicates the poet's labours, partly by way of an implicit rebuke to Shakespeare for his natural easiness or lack of industrious labour. But in amplifying this line of thought, Jonson places the poet in the category of artisan, a position that he is determined to deny in his disputes with Jones. This determination itself perhaps betrays an anxiety about the status of the poet, to which Jonson is known to have been sensitive, for example when the Earl of Rutland rebuked his wife for keeping table to poets.[11] In instructing Shakespeare, Jonson may unconsciously be seeking to consign his crowd-pleasing rival to the place of a mechanic artist, a counterweight to the surprisingly hyperbolical praises that Jonson bestows elsewhere in his poem.

A metallurgical term that has more general circulation in Jonson is that of 'temper'. The concept of temper evolved simultaneously in ethical teaching and in metallurgical practice; there are continual crossovers between the two areas of usage, seen as early as Plutarch, whose treatise *De cohibenda ira* instructs the reader how to improve the conduct of a friend by skilfully tempering praise with reproof:

> at the first to be willing and most readie to praise; but afterwards we must doe as the Smithes who temper yron: For when they have given it a fire, and made it by

that meanes soft, loose and pliable, they drench and dip it in cold water, whereby it becommeth compact and hard, taking thereby the due temperature of stiffe steele; even so, when we perceive that our friends be well heat and relaxed (as it were) by hearing themselves praised by us, then we may come upon them by little and little with a tincture (as I may so say) of reproofe, and telling them of their faults.[12]

As Plutarch shows, tempering is both what is taught by the moralist (and therefore by the Jonsonian poet) and also a principle of the art by which he teaches. Jonson invokes the ethical ideal in the figure of Crites in *Cynthia's Revels*, 'A creature of a most perfect and divine temper. One, in whom the humours and elements are peaceably met, without emulation of precedencie'. He invokes the artistic principle for his *Epigrammes*, where the 'wiser temper' of his poems will disappoint those who expect from epigrams nothing but abusive 'Wormewood, and sulphure'. He invokes the two together in *Hymenæi*, where Reason discerns an ideal temper both in the art of the masquers' dancing and (too hopefully) in the union of temperaments between the Earl of Essex and Lady Frances Howard:

> Such was the Golden Chaine let downe from Heaven;
> And not those linkes more even
> Than these: so sweetly temper'd, so combin'd
> By UNION, and refin'd.[13]

Good tempering also sustains a well ordered polity, as in Jonson's *Panegyre* for King James, where the joy of the different social ranks, the people's love and the nobles' zeal, keep alive each other's flame, 'as doth the wike and waxe, / That friendly temper'd, one pure taper makes'.[14]

Virtue and vice in Jonson are, however, always near to one another, and apt to transform into one another. The virtues of true tempering, and the useful arts of the forge and furnace, are answered by the vicious danger of false tempering, and by the use of furnace and forge for counterfeit purposes. In the political realm, the metaphor of the forge is applied to the two antagonists of *Sejanus*, as the place of deceitful fashioning. Sejanus' scheming brain is 'This sparkling forge' in which he creates 'an armor' against Caesar; the Senate is another 'forge' in which he frames his political deceptions; for his part, Caesar's legal devices are 'A net of VULCANES filing' in which to take his enemies.[15] At the downfall of Sejanus, the metallurgical locale shifts from the forge to the foundry, in which his statues will be melted down:

> The fornace, and the bellowes shall to worke,
> The great SEJANUS crack, and piece, by piece
> Drop i' the founders pit.[16]

In likening Sejanus' tragic fall to the destruction of a statue, Jonson exemplifies the mutability that characterizes even the seeming stability of metals, and also suggests that Sejanus never was the master of Rome, as he thought himself, but rather a simulacrum. The final proof of this fact is provided by the furnace's fire, which connotes both the Christian Hell and the trying or testing function of the poet.

The other capital abuse of the technological and ethical ideals of tempering is the activity of alchemists, in whose hands those ideals turn into the materials of fraud. According to the deluded Sir Epicure Mammon, the alchemist

> can extract
> The soules of all things, by his art; call all
> The vertues, and the miracles of the Sunne,
> Into a temperate fornace: teach dull nature
> What her owne forces are.[17]

All that is true, but in an ironical sense: Subtle, Face, and Doll do extract from their gulls their peculiar vanities, and do teach those dull self-deceivers what they truly are; they do call down cosmic forces into their furnace, though their victims fail to ask, with Shakespeare's Hotspur, 'will they come when you do call for them?'. In *The Alchemist*, Jonson exposes the fraudulence of his false metallurgists, and their inversion of the ethical ideals of tempering and of labour. At the same time, the comic poet shows himself half in love with the skills of his charlatans, partly, one supposes, because they resemble the skills of the poet, who himself has a discomfiting affinity with the illusionist as well as with the instructor. As it follows through these complex dramatic strands, many aspects of Jonson's comedy can be linked to early modern writings on mining and metallurgy, and not only in the area of alchemy.

The alchemist is one of Jonson's favourite versions of the *alazon* figure, the trickster or mountebank or projector.[18] The rogues of *The Alchemist* dazzle and fleece their interlocutors with impressive catalogues of fraudulent equipment, materials, and techniques, though it is their opponent Surly who, in satirical mode, reels off the best of these catalogues:

> your *elixir*, your *lac virginis*,
> Your *stone*, your *med'cine*, and your *chrysosperme*,
> Your *sal*, your *sulphur*, and your *mercurie*,
> Your *oyle of height*, your *tree of life*, your *bloud*,
> Your *marchesite*, your *tutie*, your *magnesia* ...
>
> (II. 3. 184–88)

The art of alchemy, which has at any rate a theoretical respectability, is further adulterated by Jonson's rogues with more and more suspect pseudo-sciences—magic, necromancy, astrology, phrenology, chiromancy, 'metascopy' (I. 2. 104–1. 3. 67; IV. 2. 44–49). The abuses of the rogue alchemists depend for their efficaciousness, of course, on the desires of their victims, a mix of corruption and pathos, which render them so gullible. These desires are summed up in their relation to the delusive philosopher's stone of the alchemists. The simple tobacconist Drugger has hopes of himself aspiring to the quest for the stone (I. 3. 77–82). Subtle promises the Puritan brethren that the stone will deliver them a wide range of political allies, raise them armies in the field, and save them from the subterfuges of false piety that Jonson mercilessly catalogues (III. 2). Sir Epicure Mammon has an orgy of desires that will be fulfilled by the stone, but the most pressing and tangible is sexual possession of Doll Common, which Mammon imagines in terms that altogether confound giving and receiving, action and talk, mineral gold and human flesh:

> Now, EPICURE,
> Heighten thy selfe, talke to her, all in gold;
> Raine her as many showers, as JOVE did drops
> Unto his DANAE: Shew the *God* a miser,
> Compar'd with MAMMON. What? the *stone* will do't.
> Shee shall feele gold, tast gold, heare gold, sleepe gold:
> Nay, we will *concumbere* gold.
>
> (IV. 1. 24–30)

The nugatory promises of the rogues and the vain hopes of their gulls are summed up in the explosion of the 'laboratory' and the ragged remnants that it leaves: 'A few crack'd pots, and glasses, and a fornace' (V. 5. 40).

In all these ways, *The Alchemist* displays the lineaments of a comedy written according to classical critical precept. But there are elements in the play that render it more problematic, and these elements too relate to Jonson's treatment of the metallurgical arts. The rogue alchemists thrive, and their gulls are deluded, by what is a merely mechanic art—or (another complicating factor) the pretence of one. Jonson's satirical comedy depends partly on the absurdity of anyone's believing that the mechanic arts could deliver the happiness that Jonson's characters invest in the art of alchemy. Face represents himself as the miner, bringing home the victims of fraud, with Subtle as the refiner, working on his gullible material with his alchemical equipment (I. 3. 99–109). What, then, of the honest labours of the blacksmith? On the evidence of the poem to Shakespeare, the labours of the poet and of the true metallurgist might be expected to contrast to hopes of easy wealth. It might be that the audience of *The Alchemist* is expected to recognize the contrast between the honourable labours of the workman and the fake labours of the rogue alchemists, and indeed to see that the ethical strenuousness traditionally claimed by alchemists, is claimed by Jonson for the poet.

But this possibility is contradicted by a further complicating factor—the ways in which the shape of the action of *The Alchemist* evinces admiration for its trickster figures, and an association between them and the poet. This tendency is most apparent when the seeming *raisonneur* figure Surly fails in his attempt to engineer an ethical dénouement in Act IV, and when the trickster Face survives the actual dénouement of Act V, and thrives by forming an alliance with the expected justicer figure of Lovewit. In these ways, the play refuses to conform to the exemplary ethical design of comedy. Not only that, but in the epilogue, Face makes an association between the 'pelf' won by the fake alchemists and the entertainment that is offered to the audience:

> this pelfe,
> Which I have got, if you doe quit me, rests
> To feast you often, and invite new ghests.

(V. 5. 163–65)

As often in Jonson's greatest work, the boundaries between seemingly opposed forces and values prove disconcertingly unstable.

To place Jonson's text in the context of early modern writings on a range of metallurgical technologies will help clarify some of the issues here, if not necessarily resolve them. Contrary to what is assumed or claimed by some modern scholars of literature and alchemy, a boundary did exist between the practice of alchemy and the practice of more empirically based forms of metallurgy. It is true that the chemical theory that underlay all forms of metallurgy was in general terms alchemy, but many early modern metallurgists advanced their technologies on an empirical basis, without relating them to chemical theory, and some pointed out emphatically that the theoretical promises of alchemy were empirically unsustainable. Early modern writers on the subject resemble Jonson in their ridicule of the claims of alchemy and their suspicion of alchemists. For Vanocchio Biringuccio the art is 'una volonta vana, et un pensiero immaginata' [a vain wish and fanciful dream], in which 'le speranze dele lor fabulose scritture sieno ombre di maschare composte da certi Romiti herbolari per darsi credito, over da altra gente otiosa' [the hopes of their fantastic writings are but masked shadows, composed by certain itinerant herbalists in order to accredit themselves or else by other lazy people].[19] Likewise, whatever might be said for their theory and for their predecessors, Georgius Agricola has no doubt that contemporary alchemists are charlatans and thieves.[20]

Early modern metallurgists might well have assented to the chemical theory expounded by Subtle to Surly, but they might equally have agreed with Surly's sceptical riposte about its practical methods and outcomes (II. 3. 142–98). Jonson's hostility to alchemy is not necessarily the prejudice of a conservative humanist towards an adventurous branch of science or towards mechanic arts as such; it is at least as likely to show a broad and up-to-date knowledge of the early modern literature on mining and metallurgy. This likelihood is confirmed by further correspondences between *The Alchemist* and the technical literature. For it was not only alchemists who made large claims and promises. Writers on the Americas detail their prodigious wealth, and the 'projectors' of early modern England make lavish predictions about undeveloped mines or new metallurgical processes, usually with the aim of winning monopolies or patents, and frequently offering no credible evidence for their claims. In their optimism or fraudulence, these writers resemble Jonson's alchemists, and the resemblance brings *The Alchemist* into closer rapport with everyday and conspicuous technologies, that were sharing in the 'proto-industrial revolution' of the sixteenth and seventeenth centuries.[21]

Sir Epicure's extravagant dreams of the wealth and power that he will win from the philosopher's stone echo not only the promises of alchemy but also the reports and promises of the mineral wealth of the Americas. The Midas-like state in which he will talk to Doll all in gold, in which 'Shee shall feele gold, tast gold, heare gold, sleepe gold', his imagined ability to bestow largesse at will ('I will pronounce the happy word, *be rich. /* This day, you shall be *spectatissimi*'; II. 1. 7–8): all this conforms to the accounts of the fabled wealth of the Americas. According to Alvaro Barba, La Paz is a domain of Midas similar to Sir Epicure's imaginings:

> the Country is so largely reported to be rich in Gold, that it were incredible, unless so many eye-witnesses had affirmed it: ... in the time of the rains the Boys often pick up Gold in the streets in small bits, like the kernels of apples'.[22]

Pietro Martire d'Anghiera reports the discovery in Hispaniola of a piece of gold of 3310 pounds weight, which was sent to the King of Spain, 'the ship with all the men beeing drowned by the way, by reason it was over laden with the weight of gold'.[23] Cristóbal de Acuña populates the Peruvian mining city of Potosi with grandees of Epicurean proportions: 'there are some reckon'd to be worth, Two, some Three, and some Four Millions of Crowns'; at festivals, such men 'had the prodigality to throw away Two or Three Thousand Crowns a Man among the Mob.'[24] As Sir Epicure promises Doll Common that she will 'tast the aire of palaces', dress in 'the iewells / Of twentie states', and dine on 'cockles, boild in silver shells' (IV. 1. 135, 141–42, 158), so in Potosi wealth overturns state in the same ways:

> The common People do live much at their ease, but are all proud and haughty, and always go very fine, either in cloth of Gold and Silver, or in Scarlet, or Silk trimmed with a great deal of Gold and Silver-Lace. The Furniture of their Houses is very Rich, for they are generally serv'd in Plate.'[25]

Sir Epicure believes that Subtle the alchemist has transported such sites of fabled wealth to London's Blackfriars:

> Now, you set your foot on shore
> In *novo orbe;* Here's the rich *Peru:*
> And there within, sir, are the golden mines,
> Great SALOMON'S *Ophir!*

(II. 1. 1–4)

This is a common kind of claim among early modern writers on mining and metals. Pietro Martire reports that Spanish explorers identified Hispaniola with the Biblical Ophir, and that gold mines in Hispaniola were found to contain 'deepe pits, which had been digged in old time, out of these pittes, the Admirall ... supposeth that Solomon the king of *Hierusalem* had his great riches of gold, whereof we read in the olde Testament'.[26] Sir Epicure's hopes of seeing these American wonders transported to Blackfriars correspond also to the writings of English projectors. Thomas Bushell prophesies that the mines of Wales will prove 'a second *Indies*';[27] Dud Dudley avers that the British Isles are really the 'North Indies', and promises, with a largesse worthy of Sir Epicure, to make work for 'twenty thousand Smiths or Naylors at the least dwelling near these parts, and taking of Prentices'.[28] Simon Sturtevant gives calculations to prove that his inventions 'will bee worth *per annum* 330. thousand pounds, immediatly after the two first yeares'.[29]

Though they are bold in their general claims, metallurgical projectors rarely give specific details—in order, they say, not to divulge their secrets to competitors. The result is that they speak like Jonson's alchemists, claiming the knowledge of arcane secrets that are always just beyond tangible reach. Dudley's new smelting technology works

> by wayes not yet in use, which the Authour will make known, hereafter, if God permit him health, time and space ... to declare unto this latter Age of the World, in which God is pleased to manifest many of his Secrets; *Qui vult secreta scire, secreta secrete sciat custodire.'*[30]

Sturtevant bewilders the reader with an extraordinary catalogue of inventions—Heterocresious and Homeocresious, primative and derivative, organicall and emporeuticall, tryable and untryable, conformable and incomformable.[31] His claims climax in a mix of jargon and hyperbole worthy of Subtle: 'The plegnick Rhombus is an Engin of extraordinary and admirable power and faculty, and in regard of quick and speedy motion there was never any Machin yet devised, which commeth neere unto it.'[32]

The most influential treatment of the historical and ethical status of metals for the early modern period was Ovid's account of the four ages in the first book of his *Metamorphoses*. Ovid traces a descent from gold through silver and bronze to iron, though his emphasis falls on the contrast between the first and the last, golden age and iron age:

> Aurea prima sata est aetas, quae vindice nullo,
> sponte sua, sine lege fidem rectumque colebat. ...
>   de duro est ultima ferro ...
> iamque nocens ferrum ferroque nocentius aurum
> prodierat, prodit bellum, quod pugnat utroque.
> [Golden was that first age, which, with no one to compel, without a law, of its own
> will, kept faith, and did the right. ... The age of hard iron came last. ... And now
> baneful iron had come, and gold more baneful than iron; war came, which fights with
> both.][33]

A feature of Ovid's history is its disjunction between metals as metaphoric markers of historical decline and metals in actual use. The iron age is defined partly by the advent of mining and the first use of metals. The golden age was *metaphorically* golden because it did not know *actual* gold; it is only in the iron age that gold is mined and used as a medium of exchange. Iron appears at the same time, and the two metals together introduce avarice, treachery, and war. Ovid's use of metallic terms introduces a paradoxical element into his mythical history. The terms are used to chart decline, but at the same time they evince the unavoidable importance, the defining character, of metals in human civilization. In order to conceptualize his ages of perfect and comparative innocence—the ages of gold, silver, and bronze—Ovid must use a metaphor drawn from the experience of his age of catastrophic decline. He conspicuously links iron and gold in his denunciation of mining and war. It is as if in Ovid the conceptual separation of the ages will not quite work when the history is looked at close up.

The Golden Age Restor'd turns on Jonson's understanding and reinterpretation of Ovid's myth.[34] The central brief action of the masque shows the Iron Age personified, leading a rebellion by his issue Avarice, Fraud, Slander, and other vices. This outrage brings a new degeneration, in which 'The iron-age is turn'd to steele'.[35] The rebellion is overthrown by the simple act of Pallas showing her shield, which turns the rebels to stone. After this action, Astraea and the personification of the Golden Age descend, to take possession of their restored kingdom. In this new dispensation, by a witty Ovidian metamorphosis, Astraea finds herself rooted in the earth, unable again to flee, as she once fled at the advent of the Iron Age.[36] The new Golden Age is planted in the first instance by the rule of Jove—who, in the context of a masque, of course signifies King James. It is a special accomplishment for this Jove to rule over the Golden Age, since Jove originally ruled over the Silver Age. The historical revision has a defensive intention, to show Envy that the Golden Age is not confined to the reign of Jove's father. Mythically, Jove is matching Saturn, but historically James is matching Elizabeth, ruler over an English Golden Age that was remembered with increasing nostalgia in the Jacobean period.

In accordance with masque convention, it is proclaimed at the beginning that Jove has restored the Golden Age by his own choice and grace to an undeserving world.[37] But in the rest of the text this magical effortlessness is complemented by effortful action, in which the metals and the labours associated with the Iron Age are required to build a Golden Age. In contending with the age of steel, Pallas is armed with a shield, which signifies her wisdom, but which itself is presumably of steel. It is only the virtuous use of steel that can fight off the vices of the giants' age of steel. At any rate, Pallas requires the arms that Ovid locates solely in the Iron Age. Once Pallas has won her victory, the Golden Age requires the instruction of poets, who are given notable prominence at the centre of the masque. Poets, we know, must apply the blacksmith's art of laboriously turning lines and turning selves to perform their teaching function. The Golden Age now requires even Astraea to labour: 'Who vowes, against or heat or cold, / To spin you garments of her gold', a precaution unnecessary in Ovid's Golden Age, when spring was perpetual, 'ver erat aeternum'.[38] The last words of the masque declare that it would be Astraea's prayer to live in the Golden Age of James's England, where she might 'Unbought with grace or feare unsold, / The law to mortals give'.[39] This is an age whose metaphorical gold readily turns into the actual gold of venality, and which must therefore submit to a 'law' that was unnecessary in Ovid's Golden Age.

Jonson revises Ovid's historical myth of metals to accommodate the actual use of metals. Even in the complimentary context of a court masque, he acknowledges a traffic between the King's ideal Golden Age and the degenerated Iron Age that it supposedly replaces; the Golden Age is revived within history. And within history, it behoves every man to refine his teaching and his virtue on the model of the labourer in metals.

Notes

1   'To the memory of my beloved, The Author Mr. William Shakespeare', ll. 58–62, in *Ben Jonson*, ed. C. H. Herford and Percy and Evelyn Simpson, 11 vols (Oxford: Clarendon Press, 1925–52), vol. 8, p. 392. Since at the time of writing, *The Cambridge Edition of the Works of Ben Jonson* is still a year from publication, Jonson is quoted throughout from the Herford-Simpson edition. In all quotations, contractions are expanded and u/v, i/j, and long s are regularized.

2   *Mr. William Shakespeares Comedies, Histories, and Tragedies* (1623), sig. *A*3. In references to books before 1800, place of publication is London unless otherwise stated.

3   *Timber: or, Discoveries*, ll. 649–50.

4   *Discoveries*, ll. 1719–23; cf. *Volpone*, Prologue, ll. 11–12.

5   Cf., e.g., Jonson's assumption of 'the impossibility of any mans being the good Poet, without first being a good man', *Volpone*, Dedication, 'To … the Two Famous Universities', ll. 22–23. The origin of the English word 'turn' in all its senses is the Latin *tornus*, lathe; as Jonson may have known, the Latin in turn derived from the Greek τορνος, compasses, the tool that Jonson adopted as his personal *impresa*.

6   Joseph Moxon, *Mechanick Exercises: … Applied to the Art of Smithing in General* (1693), pp. 8, 9.

7   *Every Man out of his Humour*, Induction, ll. 71–72; *Poetaster*, IV. 5. 127–44.

8   *Every Man in his Humour*, Folio Version, I. 5. 96–98. In the same play, however, Cob exercises his wit, albeit comically, in 'hammering, hammering revenge'.

9   Arthur O. Lovejoy and George Boas, *Primitivism and Related Ideas in Antiquity* (Baltimore: Johns Hopkins University Press, 1935), p. 270.

10 'An Expostulacion with Inigo Jones', ll. 50–52.

11 'Ben Jonson's *Conversations with William Drummond* of Hawthornden', ll. 361–64, in *Ben Jonson: The Complete Poems*, ed. George Parfitt (Harmondsworth: Penguin, 1975), p. 470.

12 Plutarch, *The Philosophie, commonlie called, The Morals*, trans. Philemon Holland (1603), p. 115.

13 *Cynthias Revels*, II. 3. 123–25; *Epigrammes*, II. 4, 8; *Hymenæi*, ll. 320–23.

14 *A Panegyre, on the Happie Entrance of James, Our Soveraigne*, ll. 71–72. Since the 'Panegyre' was written to greet James on his way to his first Parliament, it is likely that the interrelation of nobles and people stands for an ideal harmony between Lords and Commons.

15 *Sejanus*, III. 494, II. 495, III. 245.

16 *Sejanus*, V. 774–76.

17 *The Alchemist*, IV. 1. 85–89. Further line references to this play are incorporated in the text.

18 When Volpone plays the role of mountebank, he uses the jargon of alchemy and claims its discipline (always a parody discipline for Jonson): *Volpone*, II. 2. 147–70. In the masque *Mercurie Vindicated from the Alchemists at Court*, alchemists are unrespectable, deluded, or fraudulent, this time persecuting poor Mercury.

19 *De la Pirotechnia* (Venice, 1540), fols 5ᵛ, 7ᵛ; translation from *The Pirotechnia of Vannoccio Biringuccio*, trans. Cyril Stanley Smith and Martha Teach Gnudi (New York: American Institute of Mining and Metallurgical Engineers, 1942), pp. 35, 41. As in Jonson's *Mercurie Vindicated*, Biringuccio also shows a Mercury who also takes flight from the ministrations of alchemists, and 'quasi ridendo li suoi adversarii tutti sbeffati et scherniti lassa con le boccie et lor borse vacue' (fol. 23ᵛ) [Almost laughing, it leaves all its adversaries mocked and scorned with their phials and filters empty (p. 80)].

20 *De re metallica* (Basel, 1556), sigs. α2ᵛ–α3; translation from *De re metallica libri XII: Basle, 1556*, trans. Herbert Clark Hoover and Lou Henry Hoover (London: The Mining Magazine, 1912, repr. New York: Dover, 1950), pp. xxvii–xxix.

21 The idea of proto-industrialism was introduced by John U. Nef in a famous series of publications, culminating in *The Conquest of the Material World* (Chicago: University

of Chicago Press, 1964). For a recent reconsideration, see Michael Zell, *Industry in the Countryside: Wealden Society in the Sixteenth Century*, Cambridge Studies in Population, Economy and Society in Past Time, 22 (Cambridge: Cambridge University Press, 2004), especially Ch. 8.

22   *The Art of Metals ... in Two Books* (1674), p. 110. For further marvels, see pp. 95–96, 121–22. Barba's book was published in Spanish in 1640. Though this and some of the other writings on mining and metallurgy quoted in the present discussion postdate Jonson's writings, the printed texts that have survived undoubtedly typify the discourse concerning exploration, patents, and monopolies, that prevailed earlier in the century and that would not have escaped Jonson's alert ear for hyperbole.

23   *De nouo orbe* (1612), fol. 56ᵛ. There were earlier Latin and English editions, dating from 1530.

24   *Voyages and Discoveries in South-America* (1698), pp. 45, 61.

25   *Voyages and Discoveries*, p. 46.

26   *De nouo orbe*, fols. 18ʳ, 27ʳ.

27   *A Just and True Remonstrance of His Majesties Mines-Royall in the Principality of Wales* (1641), sig. A3, cf. sig. A4, p. 16.

28   *Metallum martis* (1665), sigs. A4ᵛ, E4.

29   *Metallica* (1612), sig. *3.

30   *Metallum martis*, sig. D7ᵛ. The Latin means 'Who would know secrets, let him know how to keep secrets secretly'.

31   *Metallica*, pp. 72–78.

32   *Metallica*, p. 103.

33   Ovid, *Metamorphoses*, trans. Frank Justus Miller, Loeb Classical Library, 2nd edn., 2 vols. (London: William Heinemann, and Cambridge, Mass.: Harvard University Press, 1921), vol. 1, pp. 89–90, 127, 141–42. In Ovid, our age is not, strictly speaking, the iron age, because the denizens of the iron age were destroyed by flood, and the present human race was created out of stones cast by Pyrrha and Deucalion. Nevertheless, Ovid does seem to intend that readers will recognize themselves and their world in his iron age.

34   This masque has been the subject of excellent though divergent political readings: Leah Marcus, 'City Mettle and Country Mettle: The Occasion of Ben Jonson's *Golden Age Restored*', in *Pageantry in the Shakespearean Theater*, ed. David M. Bergeron (Athens: University of Georgia Press, 1985), pp. 26–47; David Riggs, *Ben Jonson: A Life* (Cambridge, Mass.: Harvard University Press, 1989), pp. 215–18; Martin Butler and David Lindley, 'Restoring Astraea: Jonson's Masque for the Fall of Somerset', *ELH*, 61 (1994), 807–27. The present discussion seeks to complement this work by approaching the masque from a different angle.

35   *Golden Age Restor'd*, l. 61.

36   *Golden Age Restor'd*, ll. 221–27.

37   *Golden Age Restor'd*, ll. 1–14.

38   *Golden Age Restor'd*, ll. 212–13; *Metamorphoses*, l. 107.

39   *Golden Age Restor'd*, ll. 238–39.

Note: This essay was first printed in *Parergon* 23.2 (2006).

Madness in *A Yorkshire Tragedy* and *The Pilgrim*

Joost Daalder

I. Introduction

In my work on madness in Renaissance drama so far,[1] I have been particularly concerned to demonstrate that a number of the playwrights are interested in madness as a psychological phenomenon rather than anything else. For example, they usually, unlike many of their contemporaries, do not see it as caused by demonic possession. Similarly, I argued concerning *Twelfth Night* that Shakespeare's view of madness seems to be singularly at odds with platitudinous Renaissance concepts of it as a matter of the four humours. So-called humoral psychology, we all learned as undergraduates, derives from classical antiquity, namely Hippocrates and Galen. According to this way of looking at things, madness, like any disease, is the result of a disordered state of the four fluids in our bodies which were called humours. Much modern discussion of madness in the Renaissance has been based on the assumption that there were no people who could look beyond this psychology, in which both cause and treatment tend to be described in physical terms.

It is true, of course, that Shakespeare at times uses the language of humoral medicine, but on the whole not, I think, in such a way as to inspire us with the feeling that he himself strongly believed in it. What is conspicuous about a play like *Twelfth Night* is that terms like 'madness' are so frequent in it, while those to do with the humours are not. The obvious explanation must be, therefore, that Shakespeare was interested in madness as a mental phenomenon, as regards both cause and effect.

In my discussion of *Twelfth Night* I also took issue with a book written by Duncan Salkeld, which had struck me as thoroughly misled by Foucault.[2] Salkeld had contended that madness in the Renaissance is to be seen as a physical matter, in tune with Foucault's view that there was no clear distinction made between mind and body until Descartes did so in the mid-seventeenth century. Hence, thus Salkeld argued, what strikes us as madness in drama before 1650 must have a physical cause, and hence, too, we can ultimately see it as political, because the microcosm is linked with the macrocosm. I suggested that a play like *Twelfth Night* does not subscribe to any such view of things at all. On the contrary, it makes fun of orthodox beliefs about physical connections.

Of late there have been several other studies based on Foucault's highly influential work on madness.[3] Thus Derek Peat has written an admirably lucid essay in which he correctly points out that 'Shakespeare is interested in the working of the individual mind affected by madness', but he focuses his discussion largely, as does Foucault, on questions of institutionalization of patients and the way they were treated.[4] The essay is excellent for what it does, but it leaves me dissatisfied for what it omits, viz. a discussion of the psychology of those considered mad. I think a similar problem arises in the case of two other recent studies influenced by—even if at times strongly disagreeing with—Foucault, by Carol Thomas Neely and Ken Jackson.[5] Both are interesting and valuable (even if quite controversial) works, which have much to contribute about attitudes to madness, its treatment, its presentation on stage, and similar 'external' matters, but they do not seem to me to reveal much about what happens within the minds of mad characters whom Renaissance dramatists present to us. Neither does the superb study by Michael Macdonald, which concentrates on a minute examination of what we might call 'psychiatric case notes' of the period.[6] These enable us to see what a Renaissance doctor recorded, but they do not explain much of what happens in Renaissance plays.

In principle, one might think that of all the approaches adopted in modern studies the psychoanalytical one would best analyse the psychology of characters in Renaissance plays. In its fullest form, though, psychoanalysis runs the risk of importing an enormously complicated and much-attacked modern system into the plays, and of 'finding' much that many readers see as far-fetched, whether as conceived by the author's mind or by ours. In my opinion, the best discussion of these issues, demonstrating the failings of excessive, full-blown psychoanalytical probings, remains that of Brian Vickers.[7] Yet, though it is difficult to accept the thinking of Freud and his followers wholeheartedly either by itself or as a satisfactory means of analysing madness in Renaissance drama, there is one important way in which several of the more penetrating Renaissance dramatists are so to speak 'proto-Freudian', namely in their understanding of the relationship, in an individual's psyche, between madness and what Freud called (to use the English term) 'the unconscious'.

I have argued at length in my edition of Middleton and Rowley's *The Changeling*[8] that such a play presents madness thoroughly as a matter of the psyche, as regards both cause and effect, and I believe that the same is true of, for example, Webster's *The Duchess of Malfi*. Both of these plays show a quite stunning grasp of the way madness may come about, particularly as a result of characters not understanding what lives in their unconscious, so that their consciousness comes to be warped as a result, and their minds move into the territory of what we call fantasy. Beatrice in *The Changeling*, and Ferdinand in *The Duchess*, strike me as perhaps the most potent examples in Renaissance drama of such diseased minds. Plays like *The Changeling* and *The Duchess of Malfi* are ahead of their time, not circumscribed by it.

I am not *guided* by Freud's thinking about these matters. On the contrary, I believe that such plays establish their own sophisticated structure of thought, and that it so happens that their authors are to some extent precursors to Freud. It is in this area of overlap, I believe, that Renaissance dramatists introduced something quite new, and showed a powerful understanding which does not occur in any Renaissance treatises on madness, such as the major 'handbook' of the time, Robert Burton's *The Anatomy of Melancholy* (1621). Or, for that matter, in Foucault's *Madness and Civilization.*

To my mind, the role of the unconscious plays an important part in several Renaissance plays concerned with madness, but not in all. I should now like to examine two Renaissance plays explicitly concerned with madness—*A Yorkshire Tragedy* (1605) and, more briefly, *The Pilgrim* (1621)—to see whether or not, to what extent, and in what ways, either or both of them attach importance to the unconscious.

II. Thomas Middleton: *A Yorkshire Tragedy*

The story in this play[9] is based on a real incident, described in a pamphlet which is the prose source for *A Yorkshire Tragedy*, namely *Two most unnatural and bloodie Murthers*, published in London in 1605, soon after Walter Calverley, a member of a distinguished Yorkshire family, killed two of his very young three sons. Usually such pamphlets were published in much the same way as a newspaper article might be today: to take advantage of the interest the story would arouse—or perhaps, through word of mouth, had already created—among potential readers. There is no way of knowing how many people watching the play in performance actually knew the pamphlet, or even the story. The dramatist may have felt that many would not know the story or that, if they did, a dramatic presentation would stimulate new interest. There is enough similarity between the pamphlet and the play to make it likely that Middleton assumed that many had *not* read the pamphlet. But even for those who had, he presented much that cannot be found in that source. It is improbable that Middleton would have assumed that *all* members of the audience were acquainted with the story as such, leave alone with the pamphlet. So the proper procedure is to consider the play *per se* first. Afterwards I shall briefly consider the relationship between the play and the pamphlet, though only for the purposes of my discussion.

Analysis of the play *per se*

The story presented is that of a man who degenerates into a dissolute shadow of his former self. He comes to murder two of his three sons, and attacks his wife in the process. Yet he exhibits something like an enigmatic repentance before he is taken to prison.

The author shows himself aware of the view that the protagonist may be insane because the devil has taken possession of him. It is well known even today that there was a widespread belief in the Renaissance that madness resulted from such an action by the devil, and it is only too tempting to believe that the playwright is convinced that we need think no further than this explanation.[10] Yet it seems to me that on closer inspection this attitude is that of some of the characters in the play rather than Middleton himself. In any case, whatever the precise origin of the protagonist's insanity, the author allows us important insight into the *nature* of his condition.

In this respect the first scene offers a material contribution. It shows us two serving-men commenting on the fact that their 'young mistress is in such a pitiful, passionate humour for the long absence of her love [i.e. beloved]' (i. 1–2). It later becomes obvious that her 'love'—the protagonist of the play to whom she was betrothed—has left her, and, as one of the serving-men comments, 'mad wenches, because they are not gathered in time, are fain to drop of themselves' (i. 5–6). The young woman is like an apple which should be gathered in time, but, because this has not happened and nature's course has been withheld, she is frustrated, and the coarse idea that she may 'drop' of her own accord does not do away with the fact that her 'mad' infatuation ('mad' often meant 'madly in love') cannot find its proper outlet and is thus likely to make her mad indeed. Thus within a few lines Middleton gives us an example of a nearly mad person without leaving us at all uncertain as to how her madness originates. This young woman is to be compared with the protagonist: we are at once alerted to the possibility that other characters in the play may be mad too, and the origin of madness in the young woman's instance is not presented as having anything to do with the devil. If we find that the protagonist is mad, there is no need to assume that the devil has caused his condition, for the madness of the young woman offers an alternative interpretation.

The protagonist is not sexually deprived like the young woman, and if there *is* a cause for his madness, a comparison between the two characters is obviously intended to make us look for something different. Interestingly, in the man's case, there does not appear to be anything as tangible to discover. I think that Middleton wishes us to see his madness as the stronger and the more dangerous as a result. Seemingly, his insanity, unlike the 'madness' of the young woman in scene i, is not caused by a specific event, but self-generated. We hear that he has married another woman, but no reason is given why he should commit, in essence, bigamy, exactly because there *is* no apparent reason: his insanity, we feel, consists of doing totally illogical, whimsical things which go against our sense of what is normal and natural. This point is conveyed, almost jocularly, in the statement of Sam, a serving-man who reports on the marriage:

Why, did you not know that till now? Why, he's married, beats his wife, and has two or three children by her. For you must note that any woman bears the more when she is beaten.

(i. 39–42)

From Sam's point of view, the last sentence is of course meant to be jocular, but Middleton also appears to satirize the protagonist's conduct by drawing attention to the absurdity of the proverbial notion that a woman's fertility is increased by beating her; the author's tone is almost funny, but his wit does not disguise his sense of outrage implied by the sequence 'he's married'—'beats his wife'—'and [therefore] has two or three children by her'. This husband has an insane concept, not only of his role as husband (in both marriages), but also of the connection between cause and effect.

Scene ii gives us the new wife's observation of her husband. The man, contrary to 'the virtues that his youth did promise' (ii. 6), and for no apparent reason at all, wastes money on gambling, is engaged in voluptuous meetings, midnight revels, and so forth. Nor, as she sees matters, is his reaction to his own conduct sane. He shows himself dejected, 'Not as a man repentant but half mad / His fortunes cannot answer his expense' (ii. 13–14). The husband's attitude is not that of a stupid man, but someone half-insane (not just 'angry') at the thought that he has too little money for his wasteful expenses; the normal and natural idea that he might be seriously at fault does not occur to him. We are not informed, and cannot guess, what makes him like this: all we are given is the enigmatic, inexplicable fact of his half-insane behaviour. And at this stage the text has not even hinted at the possibility that the devil has anything to do with him.

That he is not just half-mad, however, is revealed shortly afterwards; once he appears on stage it becomes obvious that the wife has described him to us in too mild a way. When she first asks him to tell her the cause of his discontent he replies:

A vengeance strip thee naked, thou art cause,
Effect, quality, property; thou, thou, thou!

(ii. 34–5)

This accusation does not rest on any fact offered by him or which we can see; it is totally fanciful and at odds with our developing notion of what his wife is truly like: the picture of patient forbearance and altruism. Soon after, he raises a yet more serious and specific charge:

If marriage be honourable, then cuckolds are honourable, for they cannot be made without marriage.

(ii. 42–3)

The insane notion that his wife is adulterous is one that he brings up at several points throughout the play. And if there is one thing about which he appears to be at all consistent in his madness it is the sense that somehow his wife is the source of his malaise. Although it should be apparent to him that money makes him unhappy, and that there is no reason whatever, in any case, why his wife should supply it, he answers to her second query as to what causes his discontent: 'Money, money, money; and thou must supply me' (ii. 57).

Here we must pause to wonder whether the play does not perhaps produce a hint as to *why* this man should hate his wife so much. It is just possible that we are given some insight into what started the whole process: in ii. 74–5 the husband says that he 'never could abide' her, and married her only 'for fashion sake'. Middleton may here imply that the husband married this woman because she was with child by him. Perhaps, then, we are to imagine that he did not love her, and that he has come to hate her the more since: he blames her for the fact that his own disloyalty to his betrothed has led him into what he now sees as a prison. This would also account for his hatred of his children. But such an attitude is of course unreasonable and insane to begin with, and we would still be without an ultimate cause other than the husband's inherent psychological make-up. Nevertheless, the marriage 'for fashion sake' (if that is what it was) may have provided a strong stimulus for the development of his insanity, which appears to have been markedly evident from the moment he married. At all events, his character is unstable and his perception of reality is impaired. Later in scene ii, the husband is admonished by a well-meaning gentleman, who says:

>   ... of all the worst,
> Thy virtuous wife, right honourably allied,
> Thou hast proclaimed a strumpet.

To which the husband replies:

> Nay, then I know thee.
> Thou art her champion, thou, her private friend,
> The party you wot on.
>
> (ii. 147–52)

Here 'private friend' means 'secret lover', and the husband's warped imagination tells him that the gentleman's defence of his wife must imply dishonourable conduct. Psychologically this is of course convincing as there is a mad logic to it: the husband assumes that his wife is adulterous (which may be based on his by now unconscious knowledge that *he* has been adulterous from the moment he left his betrothed); and any praise of her by a male 'proves' that she is disloyal (for, presumably, anyone who is not her lover would hate her, like the husband himself). Thus, as the play unfolds, the husband's madness, though still puzzling as to its origin, becomes more comprehensible in its nature than it was at first. In fact, Middleton shows a very penetrating and persuasive insight into the way a mad mind operates.

So far, the evidence suggests that the husband is an intrinsically unstable man, whose insanity has come to be focused obsessively on his wife. We may suspect that his wife or anyone to do with her will come in for continued attack; and it remains an open question whether the husband is still able to function at all effectively in a context which he sees as unrelated to her. In this respect the next two scenes are extremely interesting.

In scene iii we see the wife upon her return from a trip to London, where she has been to see her uncle. Her husband had insisted that her dowry should be sold (ii. 88ff.), but her uncle, already familiar with his prodigal life before her arrival, has instead promised to get the husband a place at court. This would seem to be the kind of prospect that should please a rational man, but the husband, when hearing about it, flies into a rage, complaining, for example: 'Shall I that dedicated myself to pleasure be now confined in service?' (iii. 51–2). In his view of things, his own selfish pleasure is all that counts, and his wife's (and her uncle's) good attempts to help him to earn money are merely an unreasonable imposition. This behaviour, after what we have seen from him before, does not really surprise us.

But scene iv does offer a surprise. Here, the master of the university college where his brother has been an exceptionally promising student explains that this brother is in exceedingly serious trouble on the husband's account. It comes as something of a real shock to hear the husband exclaim 'O God, O!' (iv. 22), and 'I never had sense till now; your syllables have cleft me' (iv. 33–4). 'I never had sense till now' augurs well as a possible sign of repentance and insight. But why this sudden conversion? I think the answer must be that the husband has an obsession about his wife which prevents him from seeing *her* in a sane light, while his relationship with *his brother* is something different altogether. Thus, although the change may justifiably strike us as very odd and irrational, it can be understood if we attempt to see things through the husband's mad eyes.

In a way the conversion seems authentic enough. When left on his own, the husband soliloquizes: 'O, thou confused man, thy pleasant sins have undone thee, thy damnation has beggared thee!' (iv. 55–6). The use of the word 'confused,' particularly, gives us hope; it probably means both 'ruined' and 'confused' in the usual modern sense, and appears to indicate that the husband is beginning to obtain a good understanding of his situation. As he notes: 'My riot is now my brother's jailor, my wife's sighing, my three boys' penury, and my own confusion!' (iv. 78–9). It seems as though his brother's problems have suddenly and illuminatingly made him aware of what he has done to his wife, his three sons, and himself. We expect a return to sanity.

However, that is not what we get. When he catches sight of his oldest son, we do not see what ordinary mortals consider kindness. The father draws a dagger, tells his son that he will not live to be a beggar, that therefore ''Tis charity to brain you' (iv. 102-3), and stabs him. This notion that it is better for the child to be killed than to beg is likely to strike the audience as showing madness because it inverts values that we see as normal; and no one in the play accepts the husband's reasoning.

Where does he get this new bout of madness from? I think we may surmise that something like the following takes place in his mind. At first his brother's suffering triggers off a seemingly 'normal' reaction, in that he realizes that he has been gravely at fault. When he sees the child, however, he is reminded of his wife's existence, though from here on his 'thoughts' are partly unconscious. His self-loathing should, if anything, make him destroy himself. But as soon as he is reminded of his wife his persistent inclination—in the form of rationalization—to blame her for his own misdoing eclipses his momentary sanity, and, facing a choice between utter condemnation of himself or of his wife, his aggression turns towards her and becomes all-consuming. The reason why his destructiveness now knows no bounds is that he feels he has lost everything he valued, and must punish his wife and everyone associated with her.

If my analysis is correct, it would seem that, at this stage at any rate, Middleton provides us not only with an insight into the nature of the husband's madness, but also into its origin inasmuch as that appears to lie in his desertion of his betrothed and his later marriage to another woman. We are coming to understand the husband's growing resentment of his wife since the unwelcome wedding took place, and his unconscious wish to blame her, which gets expressed as mental and physical violence towards her. Middleton clearly shows a brilliant awareness of the relationship between the husband's consciously shown aggression (the vehement manifestation of his repressed libido) and its unconscious source. This particular obsession is the more firmly delineated by the contrasting attitude which Middleton makes the husband adopt towards his brother.

But it would be a mistake to see the whole play in these terms. The ultimate cause for the husband's insanity is not to be found just in any particular event but in his general psychological make-up. Middleton started his play with a presentation of an enigmatic action on the husband's part, and that is also how he finishes it. At the beginning, that action is the husband's decision to leave his betrothed pining at home, and to embark on another relationship, which leads to bigamy. We never discover why he abandons his betrothed, even though we do appear to get an indication of the 'reason' for his violent hatred of his wife. At the end, however, Middleton startles us by supplying yet another unexpected twist to his drama. This husband commits various atrocities before he is caught and taken to jail. In scene x, the last, he asks to see his wife before his imprisonment and execution. When she shows nothing other than kindness to him, he reacts in a completely surprising fashion. Previously (ix. 20–1) he had expressed repentance 'that one's left unkilled, / My brat at nurse'; he did not express any regret about the fact that he had killed his other children and wounded his wife. Now, he turns to his wife with the words:

> How now, kind to me?
> Did I not wound thee, left thee for dead?
>
> (x. 9–10)

And subsequently he claims 'now glides the devil from me' (x. 18), in a speech which reveals a man apparently so transformed that his wife exclaims:

> O my repentant husband!
>
> (x. 28)

Are we to take it, then, that the husband really *is* a different man? Perhaps the answer should be 'yes' on the one hand but 'no' on the other. A play written in 1605 may well have been intended as, at least in part, a tragi-comedy. Nothing can erase the tragedy of death in the play—particularly that of the husband's children, but also his own impending demise. If the husband is to be seen as sincerely repentant, and cured of his madness, then there is tragic pathos in the fact that his repentance comes too late to save him from capital punishment, and his wife from losing him for ever. But the final upsurge of good in the husband would provide a comic—i.e. happy—final note which leaves us with a sense of hope despite the tragic events which have occurred. I believe that the play can be read in this way to an extent, but that our response is not complete unless we consider also another possibility, namely that the husband is in no sense saved.

For him to be saved, the husband, like Faustus, would have to show that he believes in God's forgiveness. Although within his limits he seems repentant, he appears to have no faith in God's mercy. This lack of faith is, in Middleton's vision, presumably characteristic of his lack of insight in general: the play apparently signals to us, in the final analysis, that the husband is neither saved from eternal punishment nor cured psychologically. The repentance he now shows should probably ultimately not be seen as evidence of increased insight any more than the repentance which he exhibited when he was informed about his brother's malaise.

Middleton may well still to some extent share the old belief that insanity is caused by demonic possession, but on the whole I see him as working on something new in this masterpiece. Prior to this play, few Renaissance dramatists had realized the importance of the contrast between what a person appears to be like on the surface and what in fact—unbeknownst to that person—happens in the unconscious. Ophelia's singing about a woman losing her virginity (an unconscious allusion to her own preoccupations) is an exception rather than the rule. In this play we see a man blaming his wife for faults which unconsciously—but *only* unconsciously—he must know are his own. And it is mainly from this disjunction in his psyche that his insanity springs. In other words, an essential strand of this play is Freudian.

The play in relation to the pamphlet

More than one character in the play, including the husband himself, relates his madness to demonic possession. This element is absent from the pamphlet, and has led the editors of the Revels edition, A. C. Cawley and Barry Gaines, to argue that demonic madness is the cause of the husband's insanity. We have, however, found a very different explanation in our analysis of *A Yorkshire Tragedy*, and a very different reason for Middleton's inclusion of demonic possession as something mentioned by characters in the play. My contention is that the concept of demonic possession does little to explain the husband's psychology, and that Middleton has introduced this concept mainly as a red herring. He has something more searching and innovative to offer, and in order to stress the importance of the unconscious in the husband's mental make-up, he offers us demonic possession as an old-fashioned and inadequate concept that some of *his characters* resort to, but which *he* does not believe in, or at most only partly.

The main problem to be found in the Cawley–Gaines discussion is that it does not enable them to make sense of the first scene. They in effect dispose of this problem by claiming that 'it seems safe to infer that Scene i was added by a later playwright. The irrelevant allusion in the opening scene to a young woman forsaken by the 'young master (l. 9) who is 'her love' … is unlikely to have been made by the playwright (or playwrights) responsible for the rest of the play' (p. 15). There are difficulties here. The claim that the allusion to the young woman is 'irrelevant' is one that according to my argument does not stand up. I see the young woman's role as pivotal because, like the husband, the young woman ends up mad, and, as in his case, the madness has to do with the sexual side of our nature: the young woman is sexually frustrated, while the husband's hatred of his wife as allegedly adulterous finds its ultimate origin in his unconscious discomfort about his desertion of—and disloyalty to—his betrothed.

But the main problem with the idea that scene i is 'irrelevant' is that it is part of the story as found in the pamphlet, which Cawley and Gaines enable us to read by reprinting it (Appendix A, pp. 96–110). Why would we have to imagine that one author wrote scenes ii–x of the play in the belief that the story about the young woman as found in the pamphlet is 'irrelevant' to his concerns while a later author would subsequently have wished to add a scene based on material in the pamphlet that *he*, obviously, did find relevant? Once the material, both in the pamphlet and in the play, is found to be part of a sequential and logical, organized whole, the basis for claiming that the scene must have been written by someone else simply disappears.

Indeed, one of the most interesting aspects of the pamphlet is that it provides all the central material which Middleton needed in order to construct a play of great psychological depth to which the notion of demonic possession contributes little. The pamphlet, even by itself, makes fascinating reading, but it is Middleton's merit that he saw in its material the potential for a coherently structured play which would gradually reveal to us the nature of the husband's madness. For example, once the husband has deserted his betrothed, he is described, in the pamphlet, as profoundly 'altered in disposition from that which he was' (l. 82), so that 'he grew into a discontent' (l. 92). I feel that to Middleton, as it may to us, the change must have seemed due to the fact that there is a connection between the young man's desertion of his first love and his lack of satisfaction resulting from that act of betrayal. One thing the pamphlet constantly stresses is that the husband considers his wife a 'strumpet' and his children 'bastards'; even the notion that he married her but 'never loved' her is mentioned by him (l. 128), though it is Middleton who later adds, in the play, the idea that the marriage was 'for fashion sake' (ii. 74).

Thus the pamphlet was obviously studied by Middleton with great care, and he consistently emphasizes those oddities in the husband's behaviour and statements which stand out in the pamphlet, but in such a way as to enable the reader to see more clearly how they all form part of a complex yet intelligible psychological pattern. One's overall impression is that he viewed the pamphlet as offering a very detailed tale, which was no doubt an accurate rendering of what had in fact happened, and which presented him with an opportunity to use it for the creation of a unified artistic whole, permeated by his own extraordinary insight.

One further remarkable thing needs to be added. Cawley and Gaines also reprint a document called 'Calverley's Examination before the Justices' (Appendix B, pp. 111–12). Calverley was examined on 24 April 1605, and the account given shows that he firmly believed that his wife had herself indicated to him by means of signs and tokens that his children were not begotten by him. This instance of delusion would no doubt have interested Middleton greatly, but there is no evidence that he was aware of the document when writing his play.

III. John Fletcher: *The Pilgrim*

The Pilgrim was written late in 1621, just before Middleton and Rowley's *The Changeling*, which it influences in some minor matters of detail, but not at all substantially. The main general resemblance is that both plays contain scenes set in an asylum, but while in *The Changeling* these scenes make a crucial contribution to the meaning of the play, such is hardly the case in *The Pilgrim*. And even if considered by themselves the madhouse scenes in *The Pilgrim* are less satisfying and illuminating. Nevertheless, they are interesting and important enough to examine in some detail, even if they contain the strange mixture of cleverness and superficiality which appears to me characteristic of this author's handling of a serious subject. The play as a whole also needs to be taken into account.

We are first introduced to the asylum in III. vi, by a 'Gentleman'; I quote lines 9–16 from his speech:

> Tis a house here
> Where people of all sorts, that have been visited
> With lunacies and follies waite their cures:
> There's fancies of a thousand stamps and fashions,
> Like flies in severall shapes buze round about ye,
> And twice as many gestures; some of pitty,
> That it would make ye melt to see their passions:
> And some as light againe, that would content ye.[11]

> (III.vi. 9–16)

There is obviously no clear distinction in the Gentleman's mind between 'lunacies' and 'follies'. In both cases, people exhibit them because they have been 'visited' by them, and apparently both lunatics and fools can be cured. Both kinds of people, it seems, are in the grip of 'fancies'. In the play as a whole, Fletcher himself does not seem to be confident that many of the patients can be cured, but he does appear to uphold the Gentleman's attitude otherwise.

The Gentleman's ambivalence in his attitude to the patients also appears to be shared by the author. Prior to this speech, the Gentleman has already warned that a visit to the asylum may affect one with 'sadnesse' (III. vi. 7). He proposes the visit to Pedro, a morally admirable character who perhaps more than anyone can lay claim to being the kind of person to which the title refers. Pedro is keen to visit the patients: 'I never had such a mind yet to see misery' (III. vi. 23). As the Gentleman explains in his speech, the patients' delusions ('fancies') and the accompanying 'gestures' inspire 'pitty' in some cases. However, in other instances madness/folly is apparently to be seen as a cause for 'light' amusement. The reason why Fletcher was fond of tragi-comedy (a form to which *The Pilgrim* fairly closely approximates) is that it enables him to raise serious matters which ultimately—so he appears to feel—his happy endings do not require him to think through.

Still, to say that Fletcher is only partly serious is not to say that he offers us nothing worthwhile along the way. His fondness for dramatic effect is not always incompatible with an ability to probe things. Thus, for example, we are given, in III. vii, an interesting and persuasive picture of a mad (and 'mad' is what he is appropriately called) scholar, a young man whose presence in the asylum seems at first inexplicable. When first mentioned, he is described as apparently 'in his right wits' (III. vii. 12) by the second keeper. The impression that he may be in the wrong place is reinforced when a Gentleman says:

Ile assure ye sir, the Cardinal's angry with ye
For keeping this young man.

The Master (of the madhouse) replies:

I am heartily sorry.
If ye allow him sound, pray ye take him with ye.

(III. vii. 52–4)

Obviously the Master has little medical judgement, and can easily be swayed by those in authority. He does however have some conviction as to the true state of his patient, for when a second Gentleman asserts there is nothing wrong with him, he says: 'Be not deceived sir, / Marke but his looke' (III. vii. 59–60). Clearly he feels—however vaguely—that there is some real evidence to go on. And indeed there is. For when the scholar is about to be released, some accidental conversation about the weather changes the seemingly normal young man, and the second Gentleman comments that his eyes are 'altered' (III. vii. 92). It turns out that the scholar believes he is Neptune (III. vii. 103).

The Master's judgement and professionalism may not be beyond reproach, but he is certainly not always wrong, and he and the Gentlemen agree fully that the scholar's delusion constitutes proof of his insanity. The Master is not aware of how it comes to the fore after periods of seeming normalcy:

Many have sworn him right, and I have thought so:
Yet on a sudden, from some word, or other,
When no man could expect a fit, he has flown out.

(III. vii. 127–9)

In fact, however, Fletcher himself clearly implies what brings on a 'fit'. It is not an arbitrary event. The young man had heard about bad weather, and especially about what he calls 'Strange work at sea' (III. vii. 88); his imagination—always ready to absorb anything that confirms him in his self-conceived role—becomes active, and he talks about the sea and his power as its god in a way which seems to him just as 'normal' as any other conversation. It is not, therefore, as though *he* has actually changed. Fletcher quite brilliantly hints that a lunatic can seem sane so long as a conversation between him and others seems 'normal' to both. For example, the first Gentleman asks him: 'Doe you sleep a nights?' (III. vii. 68). Someone who thinks of himself as Neptune may just as truthfully answer in the affirmative to this as any 'normal' person. Therefore the answer will mislead the person who thinks that he is conducting a thorough examination of the patient's health.

The questions asked are nevertheless interesting, because they no doubt indicate what, in Fletcher's view, is the conventional procedure adopted for the probing involved. I select one of these questions as potentially interesting from a psychological point of view, as it is concerned with possible causes of madness:

> Is there no unkindnesse
> You have conceiv'd from any friend or parent?
> Or scorne from what ye lov'd?

(III. vii. 71–3)

Apparently the idea is that someone who has been deprived of affection *must* be mad. But the interest is more in ascertaining whether the patient *is* mad than in deeply examining the origin of the disease. Fletcher demonstrates how these various questions in the end reveal nothing about the patient's condition. Indeed, when the symptoms become all too obvious, we still do not learn *how* the scholar has come to think of himself as Neptune.

It is the dramatic effect which interests Fletcher rather than an exploration of causes, but the episode effectively shows how plausible a lunatic may seem until—by accident—something is brought into play which proves that his imagination is not, after all, in tune with our view of reality. There are also times, however, when even Fletcher's picture of a mad person *per se* is less convincing—and we do not learn anything about the underlying cause. We do not doubt that the scholar is mad. But the 'English Madman' seems much less mad. The first keeper claims 'These English are so Malt-mad, there's no medling with 'em' (III. vii. 22), and the notion appears to be that cause and symptom are in fact one and the same: this madman is obsessed with beer, and that is what his madness consists of. But, although it is true that the madman's obsession leads him to take account of very little else in reality, he is not confused in any such way as the scholar is, and Fletcher does not stress the difference enough. Rather, this character appears to be introduced for the purpose of clowning.

There is no firm connection between the psychology of the main characters in the play and those in the madhouse. The scenes in the madhouse are not altogether justified, and to a large extent they are an excuse for the purpose of entertainment. Fletcher does have some—not very profound—notion as to how madness may be caused. But, in contrast to Middleton, he certainly has no awareness of the role of the unconscious. In his view, madness may be, at times, a matter of character, but in the main it is caused by a process of cumulative stress. Madness is most typically a state in which the lunatic's vision of reality is seriously distorted by his fantasy.[12] But on the whole Fletcher is more interested with what is on the surface than with any such probing as Middleton engages in.

IV. Conclusion

My discussion reveals that *A Yorkshire Tragedy* is to a substantial extent, in its handling of the unconscious, a 'proto-Freudian' play, but that *The Pilgrim* is not. To determine to what extent and in which ways Renaissance plays presenting madness introduce the concept of the unconscious we must—in a currently unfashionable way—try to read the play faithfully with attention to what the author's view appears to be. We shall then find that in some plays authors do reveal an intense interest, and of a 'modern' kind, in the unconscious, but that in others they do not. Those plays which do are exciting because they embody something new. However, this does not mean, of course, that *all* authors should view *all* forms of madness in terms of the unconscious. 'Abnormal psychology' is far too complex and controversial an area for that. However, if we are interested in the way Renaissance drama presents the psychology of madness, then in many cases we shall find that the unconscious, whether we choose to see that as 'proto-Freudian' or not, plays an important part. In this respect, we shall find ourselves closer to Freud than Foucault, with his emphasis on institutionalization and his refusal to separate the physical and the mental.

Notes

1   'Folly and Madness in *The Changeling'*, *Essays in Criticism*, 38.1 (1988), 1–21, later adapted for the Introduction of my edition of *The Changeling* (London: A & C Black (Publishers) Ltd., and New York: W. W. Norton & Co., 1990); 'William Shakespeare: *Othello'*, in *Making Connections II*, ed. Annie Greet (Adelaide: English Discipline of the Flinders University of South Australia, 1991), pp. 69–77; 'Madness in Jasper Heywood's 1560 Version of Seneca's *Thyestes'*, *Classical and Modern Literature*, 16.2 (1996), 119–29; 'Madness in Parts *1* and *2* of *The Honest Whore'*, *AUMLA*, 86 (1996), 63–79; 'Perspectives of Madness in *Twelfth Night'*, *English Studies*, 78.2 (1997), 105–10.

2   Duncan Salkeld, *Madness and Drama in the Age of Shakespeare* (Manchester: Manchester University Press, 1993).

3   Michel Foucault, *Madness and Civilization: a History of Insanity in the Age of Reason*, trans. Richard Howard (New York: Random House, 1965).

4   Derek Peat, 'Mad for Shakespeare: a Reconsideration of the Importance of Bedlam', *Parergon*, 21.1 (2004), 113–32.

5   Carol Thomas Neely, *Distracted Subjects: Madness and Gender in Shakespeare and Early Modern Culture* (Ithaca and London: Cornell University Press, 2004); Ken Jackson, *Separate Theaters: Bethlem ('Bedlam') Hospital and the Shakespearean Stage* (Newark: University of Delaware Press, 2005).

6   Michael Macdonald, *Mystical Bedlam: Madness, Anxiety and Healing in Seventeenth-Century England* (Cambridge: Cambridge University Press, 1981). The case notes are those of the clergyman and astrological physician Richard Napier (1559–1634): what

Macdonald examines is not so much 'Bedlam', in any form, as Napier's psychiatric practice.

7 Brian Vickers, *Appropriating Shakespeare: Contemporary Critical Quarrels* (New Haven and London: Yale University Press, 1993), ch. 5, 'Psychocriticism: Finding the Fault', pp. 272–324.

8 See note 1 above.

9 It is now generally accepted that this play (1605) was written by Thomas Middleton. See the pioneering work in the relevant sections of David J. Lake, *The Canon of Thomas Middleton's Plays* (Cambridge: Cambridge University Press, 1975), and Macdonald P. Jackson, *Studies in Attribution: Middleton and Shakespeare* (Salzburg: Universität Salzburg, 1979). Later scholars have generally concurred with Lake and Jackson. I see no reason for doubting that the whole of *A Yorkshire Tragedy* is by Middleton.

10 See the edition by A. C. Cawley and Barry Gaines for the 'Revels' series (Manchester: Manchester University Press, 1986), from which I quote throughout. The explanatory comments are particularly helpful, and I have drawn on them in the course of my discussion. However, the critical approach adopted in the Introduction seems to me less perceptive, notably when it discusses madness in terms of demonic possession (pp. 15–21). The best recent discussion of the play, though not focused on madness, is Lisa Hopkins' '*A Yorkshire Tragedy* and Middleton's Tragic Aesthetic,' *Early Modern Literary Studies: A Journal [on-line] of Sixteenth- and Seventeenth-Century English Literature*, 8.3 (January 2003), 15 paragraphs. She also offers a fine, full bibliography.

11 The edition I quote from is that by Cyrus Hoy, in Fredson Bowers, gen. ed., *The Dramatic Works in The Beaumont and Fletcher Canon*, Vol. VI (Cambridge: Cambridge University Press, 1985). This is an 'old-spelling' text, but reasonably easy to find, and probably very reliable. I know of no reliable modernized edition, nor of one that offers much explanatory material. There is as far as I know no substantive discussion of madness (or for that matter anything else) in this play.

12 The idea of demonic possession as a cause for madness does occur in the play, but only as a silly mistaken notion which needs to be exposed. Hence it is attributed, ironically, to the Master of the asylum (cf. IV. iii. 183).

Les 'contraires seiours': Scève's Use of the Diana Myth in the *Délie* of 1544

Jane Southwood

Maurice Scève's *Délie* of 1544 is the first *canzoniere* of the French sixteenth century.[1] It is also the first emblem book in French. As such it is a significant work, but it is significant in other ways. Published some five years before the poet Du Bellay's apology for vernacular poetry, *Défence et illustration de la langue française* (*Defence and Illustration of the French Language*), in which Du Bellay advocates the use of French rather than Latin as a vehicle for poetic utterance, the *Délie* anticipates many of the ideas of the *Défence*.

Scève wrote other works as well as the *Délie*: neo-Latin verse, several eclogues in French, including *La Saulsaye, églogue de la vie solitaire,* published in Lyon in 1547, and one on the death of the dauphin, the eldest son of François Premier, who was believed to have been poisoned: *Arion, églogue sur le trépas du dauphin, fils de François Ier,* published in Lyon in 1536. As his contribution to a poetry competition—which he won—he also composed *blasons,* poems in praise of various parts of a woman's body, his *blasons* being rather more elevated than most. His subjects are the forehead, the eyebrow, the tear, the sigh and the throat. Evidences of his *blasons* are to be found in the love-sequence under consideration here. He also wrote a long philosophical poem called the *Microcosme,* published in Lyon in 1562.

But it is the *Délie* which has earned him the greatest respect. These four hundred and forty-nine poems, or *dizains* as they are called, each comprising ten lines of ten syllables, are remarkable for their intellectual, scholarly and emotional density. This very density accounts for the reputation he had among his contemporaries (and subsequently) as a difficult poet. His verse uses Latinate syntax and vocabulary and requires a knowledge of the Bible, of mythology, of classical writers, of Neo-platonic doctrine and of iconological lore. Once these obstacles are overcome, however, the freshness and vigour of his vision become apparent.

Central to the *Délie* is the identification of the Beloved with the goddess Diana, or 'Delia', a name which comes from her birth place, the island of Delos, hence the title of the love sequence. The first critic to spell out the significance of the title was V.-L. Saulnier in his masterly two-volume work on the poet, published in 1948.[2] Saulnier points out that in the sequence Scève is exploring all the resonances of the

Diana myth and playing on the multiple aspects of the goddess. Since Saulnier's work other critics have considered the question.³ This essay reviews the use of the myth in the portrayal of the fundamental contradictions of that experience, the 'contraires seiours' (D 216) or contrary states in which the lover is held captive in the sequence.

* * *

The pre-eminent characteristic of Diana, a characteristic underlying the whole love-sequence, is her chastity. Délie, like her namesake, is chaste and, for the main, unattainable: the poet's love remains essentially unrequited. It is this which fits her to be a new Laura. The more chaste and pure she is, the more worthy of the lover's adulation. Moreover Diana's chastity befits the Platonic character of a woman who, on the title page of the *Délie,* is called 'obiect de plus haulte vertu' ('object of a higher virtue'). Linked to her chastity are her hardness and coldness towards men. Unburdened by the yoke of men, Diana is insensitive to male suffering, in this way paralleling the cruel, hard Lady of the Petrarchan tradition. These Delian traits of hardness and coldness are found in D 185, in which the poet draws together abstract and concrete in a poem which anticipates the sonnets of Shakespeare:

> Le Cœur surpris du froict de ta durté
> S'est retiré au fons de sa fortune:
> Dont a l'espoir de tes glassons hurté
> Tu verrois cheoir les fueilles vne a vne.
> Et ne trouuant moyen, ny voye aulcune
> Pour obuier a ton Nouembre froit,
> La voulenté se voit en tel destroict,
> Que delaissée & du iour, & de l'heure,
> Qu'on luy deburoit ayder a son endroict,
> Comme l'Année, a sa fin ià labeure.

> My heart, surprised by your coldness and harshness,
> Has taken refuge in the depths of its misfortune:
> Thus would you see the leaves of my hope, struck by your hail,
> Fall one by one.
>   And finding neither means nor way
> Of fortifying itself against your November cold,
> My will finds itself in such a distressing situation,
> That, deprived of both the day [light] and the moment,
> When considerable help should be forthcoming,
> Like the year, it toils to its imminent end.⁴

Here the hardness of the Beloved towards her lover is expressed in an image of extreme cold, that of approaching winter. Her intransigence corresponds to the ravages of the elements on fragile Nature as autumn passes into winter. Surprised by this unexpected coldness, just as, towards the end of autumn, one is surprised by the cold, the lover's heart seeks refuge in the depths of his suffering, as an animal hibernates in a cave. The vigorous imagery of leaves which fall, as the lover's hope is struck by Délie's hail (lines 2-4), speaks forcefully of her hardness and coldness and the corresponding fragility of the lover. One is reminded of Shakespeare's sonnet 73:

> That time of year thou mayest in me behold
> When yellow leaves, or none, or few, do hang
> Upon these boughs which shake against the cold [5]

in which the bard suggests his approaching old age by means of the Roman commonplace of expressing the human cycle in terms of the seasons.

In the poem of Scève's the green leaves of hope and survival—an image frequently employed in the *Délie*—have become the dead leaves of despair, symbol of the lover's decline. The richly imagic language of the quatrain combines with a vigorous and difficult syntax (lines 3-4), whose carefully controlled tempo evokes not only the Lady's assault on the lover's hope, but also the progressive diminution of his strength, conveyed by the lingering 'vne a vne', evoking the leaves which fall, one by one.[6] The elegiac tone of the quatrain is prolonged in the *sizain*. The Lady's coldness is that of the end of the year; deprived of the light and life he seeks in her, the lover's will gradually succumbs.

The theme of Délie's chastity is pursued in a group of four poems which introduce the nymph Daphne. Ovid tells us (*Metamorphoses*, 1) that Daphne was pursued by Apollo and changed into a laurel tree by her father just as the god was on the point of ravishing her. Daphne is linked with Diana in two ways. Like the goddess, a chaste virgin, at certain moments the nymph lends her name to Diana, who, in Laconia, is worshipped as Artemis *Daphnaia,* to whom Daphne's tree, the laurel, is sacred.[7] This association of Diana and Daphne allows Scève to explore one of the fundamental tensions of the sequence in D 102:

> Bien qu'on me voye oultre mode esiouir,
> Ce mien trauail toutesfois peine endure,
> I'ay certes ioye a ta parolle ouir
> A mon ouye asses tendrement dure:
> Et ie m'y pene affin que tousiours dure
> L'intention de nostre long discours.
> Mais quand au but de mon vouloir ie cours,

Tes voulentez sont ailleurs declinées,
Parquoy tousiours en mon trauaillé cours
Tu fuys, Daphnes, ardeurs Apollinées.

Although I may be seen to be enjoying myself immoderately,
This is not without continual suffering on my part,
Certainly I take pleasure in hearing your words
So tenderly harsh to my ears:
And I strive to prolong these long talks of ours.
But when I rush towards the consummation of my desires,
Your wishes are elsewhere inclined,
And so it is that in my tormented course,
You flee, Daphne, my [Apollonian] ardours.

The subject of the *dizain* is a conversation with Délie which the lover tries in vain to prolong, a conversation in which, following the Petrarchan antithesis, there is both pleasure and suffering. Their desires seem to be the same, but when the poet seeks to realize his, he notices that the Lady's wishes are elsewhere inclined. This pursuit of a Lady who resists him at the last moment gives rise to the image of Daphne and Apollo, the chaste and unattainable nymph and the enflamed lover who pursues her. The metaphor illustrates beautifully the Lady's evasive character and the carnal nature of the lover's pursuit,[8] the force of which is resumed in the key words 'fuys' and 'ardeur', 'flight' and 'burning passion'.

Elsewhere Scève draws on the motif of the nymph transformed into a laurel tree. In two poems he reminds us of Apollo's frustration at not being able to satisfy his lust. Instead of the fruit he desires, there is nothing but a bitter-tasting tree.[9] In D 310, a *carpe diem,* the poet evokes the body of Délie ravaged by time—a vision which elsewhere he contrasts with the survival of her virtue—then shifts his attention to the lover, who, from the green youth of his Beloved, will only have retained the boughs and bitter leaves, symbol of unrequited love. The boughs and leaves of the laurel also symbolize the poem that our poet, a new Apollo, will have created on the subject of his love and the renown he will earn through his poem. From the Lady's refusal is born the work of poetry which, like the evergreen laurel, will assure his glory and survival. However, this is a bitter recompense.

This *dizain* links Scève with Petrarch who, similarly, is unable to satisfy his love for the chaste nymph Laura and uses the legend of Daphne and Apollo to express the theme. In D 388 Scève refers to Petrarch in connection with the bitter taste of the laurel in a play on words on the name Laura/laurier which echoes the Italian poet's use of the same image, his pun on Laura/lauro and his comparison of himself to Apollo.[10] Lines 6-8 of another *dizain,* D 417, refer to Petrarch and to:

... celle terre heureuse,
Ou ce Thuscan Apollo sa ieunesse
Si bien forma, qu'a iamais sa vieillesse
Verdoyera a toute eternité.

... this happy earth
Where that Tuscan Apollo
Formed his youth so well, that his old age
Will be forever green [for] all eternity.

The vision of Petrarch here is of a Tuscan Apollo immortalized by the lines he created on Laura/laurel; the lines recall the crown of laurel which he received in 1341 in acknowledgement of his poetic achievement.[11]

In D 407—a sort of inverted *carpe diem*—the reference to Daphne again recalls Petrarch's use of the myth to suggest the virtue of Laura:

En moy saisons, & aages finissantz
De iour en iour descouurent leurs fallaces.
Tournant les Iours, & Moys, & ans glissantz,
Rides arantz defformeront ta face.
    Mais ta vertu, qui par temps ne s'esface,
Comme la Bise en allant acquiert force,
Incessamment de plus en plus s'esforce
A illustrer tes yeulx par mort terniz.
    Parquoy, viuant soubz verdoyante escorce,
S'esgallera aux Siecles infiniz.

Seasons and ages going by in me
From day to day reveal their perfidy.
As the Days and Months and gliding years turn,
Furrowing wrinkles will deform your face.
    But your virtue, which is not effaced by time,
Acquires strength as it goes, like the North wind,
And ceaselessly strives with greater and greater effort
To give light to your eyes dimmed by death.
    Thus living under ... green bark,
It will be the equal of all the centuries to come.

Here, metamorphosed by the poem, in the same way as Daphne is changed into an evergreen tree, Délie will live forever. Her chaste virtue—which incites the poet's love and brings about the genesis of lines about this love—this immortal virtue, is symbolized by the image of the life which continues under the green bark, as Coleman points out (*Maurice Scève*, p. 132), an idea expressed in Ovid, who stresses how the soul of Daphne continues to live 'novo sub cortice'. As Daphne, transformed into a tree, never dies, so the chaste Délie, transformed by the poem, will remain forever alive. This *dizain* belongs with other poems of the sequence which use evergreen plants to suggest the lasting quality of Délie's virtue, often contrasted with the decay of her physical form.

By means of the myth of Daphne and Apollo Scève is able to evoke the fundamental conflict of Délie's chastity and his burning desire; unrequited love, symbolized by the bitter laurel tree; and the virtue of his Beloved, which, like the evergreen tree into which Daphne is transformed, will remain forever alive. The myth allows him to assimilate himself to Apollo as Petrarch did in his verse and in this way to pay homage to the great Italian poet. Symbol of chastity and poetic fame, the laurel is also an emblem of the Lady's immortal virtue. Praise of the Beloved and of her chastity, themes of her survival beyond death and of poetic fame are fused in the image of the laurel, an integral part of the myth of Daphne, chaste nymph linked to the goddess Diana.

So far we have seen Scève concerned with Délie's chastity, purity and virtue. However, at times in the sequence Délie is also sensual. This accords well with the nature of Diana, who, though usually of an intransigent chastity, nevertheless, on occasion, reveals a discrete sensuality, witness her relations with Pan and Endymion. Scève's treatment of the Endymion legend allows him in D 126 to introduce the theme of the dream of love, so important in the literature of later poets in the sixteenth century, particularly for those who belonged to the so-called 'Pléiade' (Ronsard, du Bellay, Rémy Belleau, Jodelle, Baïf, Pontus de Tyard and Jacques Peletier du Mans):[12]

A l'embrunir des heures tenebreuses,
Que Somnus lent pacifie la Terre [,]
Enseuely soubz Cortines vmbreuses,
Songe a moy vient, qui mon esprit desserre,
Et tout aupres de celle là le serre,
Qu'il reueroit pour son royal maintien.
        Mais par son doulx, & priué entretien
L'attraict tant sien, que puis sans craincte aulcune
Il m'est aduis, certes, que ie la tien,
Mais ainsi, comme Endimion la Lune.

As the hours of darkness gather,
When Somnus slowly stills the earth,
Buried under dark Curtains,
Dream comes to me and frees my spirit,

> And presses it to her,
> The one my spirit revered so for her royal bearing.
> But by her sweet and gentle manner
> She so attracts my spirit as to make it hers,
> with the result that without any fear,
> It seems to me that [, in fact,] I hold her,
> But only as Endymion the moon.

This impressive beginning reveals Scève's masterly treatment of moments of transition in the day, between twilight and night, or night and dawn.[13] These moments of transition grow out of Délie's function as source of light. They also link the poet to Ovid, whose love poetry evokes above all dawn or twilight.[14] The sonorous beginning introduces the theme of night which brings felicity after the tribulations and anguish of the day. It is a Petrarchan theme based on Virgil which Scève explores elsewhere in poems, in which night, which should bring comfort to the lover, only increases his anguish. In these lines of D 127 the poet hints at the sweetness that this night will bring him as it fills his void, for the night is accompanied by dreams of voluptuousness in which the lover possesses his Beloved. The softness of the repeated sonorities in 'heures', 'tenebreuses', 'vmbreuses', and the beauty of the infinitive become noun, 'embrunir', create an ambiance of peace and tranquillity propitious to dream. The evocation of this peaceful night and the traditional reference to the god of sleep, in bed behind black curtains, suggest the harmony of the dream which comes in line 4. The syntax of this line evokes a real approach, 'Songe a moy vient ...', whose firmness anticipates that of line 9. Consoling Dream, perhaps that which comes out of the ivory gates in Book VI of *The Aeneid,* approaching the bed of the sleeping lover, frees his oppressed spirit. The expressive quality of this verse—the lightness created by the repeated 's' sounds and by the verb in final position ('Songe a moy vient, qui mon esprit desserre')—enhances the impression of the soaring of the liberated spirit. Having freed the lover's spirit, dream reunites it with the Lady. Inexorable, distant and majestic by day, in the dream world of night Délie proves welcoming, tenderly receiving the lover's spirit and revealing a gentleness which gives her lover the illusory impression of embracing her, 'Il m'est aduis, certes, que ie la tien'. The certainty of having her in his arms collapses with the painful return to reality as the poet realizes that it is only in dream that he holds her, 'Mais ainsi, comme Endimion la Lune'. The myth of Endymion, recounted by Lucian in *The Dialogue of the Gods,* is of a beautiful young man condemned by Jupiter to eternal sleep in exchange for perpetual youth, and who, as he sleeps, incites the love of the moon goddess Selene, later identified with Diana, who visits him nightly.[15]

This fragilely seductive vision on which the poem ends, of a lunar Délie, who embraces for all eternity the beautiful sleeping youth, or who is embraced by him,[16] resumes the themes of sleep, introduced at the beginning, of the love between goddess and mortal and of the impossibility of their union other than in the illusory world of dream. The encounter with Délie in the dream world of night is linked to other *dizains* in which she momentarily shows a more gentle side towards the lover, according him slight physical favours. However these poems in which a more sensual Délie emerges are tinged with a delicateness, fragility and purity, seen already in the Endymion poem. They suggest how rare are these moments of union between the lovers, how fleeting the pleasures the Lady offers and how pre-eminent Délie's chastity in their relationship. Throughout the sequence it is a question of infinitesimal variations in the proportions of the chaste and the sensual.

Perhaps the most perfect example of a rare moment of union with the Beloved is that offered by D 367 in which the alliance of chastity and sensuality which characterizes Délie maintains in perfect equilibrium the fragility and joy of a love so fraught with contradictions:

> Asses plus long, qu'vn Siecle platonique,
> Me fut le moys, que sans toy suis esté:
> Mais quand ton front ie reuy pacifique,
> Seiour treshault de toute honnesteté,
> Ou l'empire est du conseil arresté
> Mes songes lors ie creus estre deuins.
>   Car en *mon corps*: mon ame, tu reuins,
> Sentant ses mains, mains celestement blanches,
> Auec leurs bras mortellement diuins
> L'vn coronner mon col, l'aultre mes hanches.

> Longer to me than a Platonic century.
> Was the month that I was without you.
> But when I saw again your peaceful forehead,
> Lofty abode of all probity,
> Whose authority is beyond the powers of human apprehension and judgement,
> My dreams then I believed prophetic.
>   For into my body, my soul, you returned;
> Feeling her hands, hands celestially white,
> With their arms mortally divine
> One crowning my neck, the other my [hips].

The themes introduced by the first six lines are of absence and presence, of the necessity of the Lady to her lover and of her perfection which passes beyond the power of human judgement, a frequent theme in the sequence. By the allusion to the 'Siecle Platonique' the poet introduces the notion of time which, because of the Lady's absence, is painfully prolonged, the Platonic year being the amount of time necessary for all the heavenly bodies to return to their original position. The allusion also introduces the theme of the difficulty of following the Platonic ideal of love, which advocates the apprehension of beauty by the intellect and underlines the necessity for the lover to do without the physical presence of the Beloved. The rest of the *dizain* constitutes, in some measure, a refusal to follow this ideal. The theme of the absence of the Lady, drily treated in the first two lines, is followed by the theme of her presence: the veneration of her forehead, seen at a distance, a theme which recalls Scève, the *blasonneur*, creator of a *blason* on the forehead. The physical intimacy of the latter part of the poem, with its opening-out of the language, suggests the ecstasy of the lover. It is from line 6 and the conjunction 'car', which links the two parts of the poem, that the physical presence of the Lady makes itself gloriously felt, as the lover's soul, separated from his body, is reintegrated into the latter. It is then, as McFarlane points out (*The 'Délie*, p. 39) 'that the poem catches fire and is transformed.'

This reuniting of body and soul, a process accompanied by the reunion of the two lovers, gives rise to a delicious sensuality which increases progressively across the quatrain. First of all there is the suggestion of a caress implicit in the reference to hands, where the repetition of the word, 'mains', creates a lingering impression[17] as Délie touches the lover delicately. In this description of her hands, which are 'celestially white', is intermingled the divine or spiritual and the sensual, these hands which invite the lover to revere them as befits a goddess, and to touch their whiteness. There follows the arms that are 'mortally divine' of this woman who is both unapproachable goddess and palpable mortal, who, in accordance with Petrarchan precepts, brings both life and death, who incites in the lover a love which leads to a higher good—and so to eternity—and a sensual love, subject to time. Then comes the moment in line 10 to which the whole poem moves slowly and perfectly: the embrace, voluptuously sculpted by the arch of the two arms which pass around the lover's neck and hips, the verb 'coronner' ('crown') suggesting the dignity of the gesture and how this precarious and precious moment is the culmination of the lover's dreams. Contrasting with the evocation of time spent without the Beloved, the embrace marks a moment of utter felicity in which time is dissolved in her presence.

Goddess of chastity, Diana is also goddess of *la chasse* or hunting, expending in this way the energy she might otherwise expend in amorous liaisons. Around the theme of Diana the huntress, Scève develops the Petrarchan themes of the cruelty, wounding, suffering and death associated with cynegetic activity. Armed with bow and arrow which she uses against wild animals and against foolhardy mortals such as Acteon, the virgin huntress is an apt figure to represent the chaste Petrarchan Lady, whose beauty wounds and kills, from whose eyes are unleashed wounding arrows and who captures prey in her nets. Lighter poems of Alexandrian inspiration are to be found around this theme in the *Délie*, as is a *dizain* which treats the Acteon myth. The *innamoramento,* or birth of love, from which the whole series of poems derives, dwells too, in the first instance, on a vocabulary of wounding and death reminiscent of the hunt. The first *dizain* of the sequence, which employs the image of the legendary basilisk whose look is fatal, recalls indirectly the goddess of the hunt in various ways, firstly, by using the motif of the eye,[18] which, like that of Acteon, looks at the forbidden goddess, and secondly, by invoking the wounding characteristics of the goddess of the hunt, her sway over death and the cult that is dedicated to her:

> L'Œil trop ardent en mes ieunes erreurs[19]
> Girouettoit, mal cault, a l'impourueue:
> Voicy (ô paour d'agreables terreurs)
> Mon Basilisque auec sa poingnant'veue
> Perçant Corps, Cœur, & Raison despourueue,
> Vint penetrer en l'Ame de mon Ame.
>   Grand fut le coup, qui sans tranchante lame
> Fait, que viuant le Corps, l'Esprit desuie,
> Piteuse hostie au conspect de toy, Dame,
> Constituée Idole de ma vie.

> My eye, too ardent, in its youthful wanderings
> Turned around like a weather vane, imprudently, idly;
> Then (O fear of agreeable terrors)
> My basilisk with its cutting sight
> Piercing Body, Heart and unprepared Reason,
> Came and penetrated to the innermost part of my soul.
>   Great was the blow, such that without cutting blade
> The body living still, the Spirit dies,
> Pitiful victim [gazing] with admiration on you, Lady,
> … henceforth Idol of my life.

The identification of the Beloved with Diana allows the poet to use in a particularly powerful and original way the Petrarchan commonplace, of Virgilian origin, of the hunt of love in which the lover is a wounded hart or stag, the favourite prey of the goddess. One of the *dizains* which best uses this conceit is one which also draws upon the *materia medica* of Diana, reminding us that she is a goddess who not only wounds, but also heals, attested to by the numerous Greek epithets which reveal her healing function: *alexíkakos,* warder off of evil; *hygiastikos,* capable of restoring health; *paeonikos,* healing.[20] The alliance of wounding and healing in D 422 exposes an important Petrarchan tension central to the *Délie:*

> Touché au vif & de ma conscience,
> Et du remords de mon petit merite,

Ie ne scay art, & moins propre science,
Pour me garder, qu'en moy ie ne m'irrite,
Tant ceste aigreur estrangement despite
En vains souhaitz me rend si variable.
    Fust elle, aumoins, par vertu pitoyable
Mon dictamnum, comme aux Cerfz Artemide,
Tirant le traict de ma playe incurable,
Qui fait mon mal ardemment humide.

Wounded to the quick both by my conscience
And by remorse caused by my own lack of worth,
I know of no art nor proper science
To guard against internal hurt,
So much does this sharp, strangely angry pain
Make me irresolute and given to vain desires.
    Would that she were, at least through virtue steeped [in] pity,
My dittany, as Diana to the Stags,
Drawing the shaft from my incurable wound,
Which makes my hurt burningly [damp].

In the first two lines the poet states that he is profoundly wounded by his conscience—perhaps the fact that his love towards Délie is carnal in nature—and by his realisation that he is unworthy of her. This causes him remorse. In line 3 we find the Ovidian commonplace, reiterated in line 9, that there is no remedy for love's wounds.[21] In the first three lines the poet evokes the passage of the wounding arrow, which sinks deep into the flesh and causes the resulting wound. He also evokes in a more abstract way the condition of the lover moved by his love experience. Lines 4-5, which expose the irritation and intense pain the lover suffers, anticipate the enflamed wound of line 9.

    In the quatrain the afflicted lover is compared to a wounded stag, thus recalling Diana the huntress. The lover/stag expresses the wish that Délie cure him by her virtue, that is, as Beverley Ormerod points out, by her moral excellence and her power to heal, similar to that of a medicinal herb.[22] He wishes that Délie were the dittany which would extract the iron from his body, as Diana/Artemis cures the stags, an illusion which has links with several traditions. Dittany is the herb sacred to Diana in her manifestation as Lucina, goddess of childbirth.[23] According to the mythographers of the sixteenth century, statues of Lucina are crowned by garlands of a herb believed to be a powerful vulnerary and capable of drawing out arrows from the bodies of stags or wild goats, this function recalling that of the midwife.[24] The writers of antiquity who mention the healing capacities of dittany, and from whom the sixteenth-century mythographers derived their lore, include Aristotle,[25] Cicero,[26] Pliny the Elder[27] and Virgil, who in Book XII of *The Aeneid* (vv. 411-24) speaks of the infusion of dittany prepared by Venus to draw out the arrow lodged in the body of her son Aeneas, a herb Virgil points out is eaten by wild goats for this purpose. Emblem writers include dittany to exemplify the dictum that love is incurable. Treatises from the fifteenth and sixteenth centuries which draw on the tradition from antiquity and proclaim the curative qualities of dittany and its capacity to extract arrows are also discussed by McFarlane.[28]

The lover's wish in the Scève *dizain* encapsulates several tensions. Firstly, he wishes that Délie feel pity for him, but Délie, like her namesake, is only rarely inclined to pity her suffering lover. Secondly, he wishes she were his dittany as Artemis is to the stags. However, Diana/Artemis who heals is also she who unrelentingly pursues the stag in order to destroy it. This tension is increased by the lover begging Délie to cure him of a malady which she herself has caused, underlined by the fact that the lover has taken on two attributes of the goddess, her mutability (line 6) and her humidity (line 10).[29] In this way Scève portrays the Petrarchan tension that she who causes the suffering is the only one who can heal it, just as Diana/Artemis, who wounds the stag, is the only one who can cure the animal with her healing herb.

D 422 is an important poem in several ways. By its image of dittany and the lover/ stag, linked via the central figure of Délie/Diana, the poet evokes the Beloved as both source of joy and pain. D 422 forms part of a larger body of poems built around the theme of the 'mal d'amour', of love as sickness—a fever or ulcer. Sometimes this sickness is unfulfilled sexual desire and Délie's role is to remove that desire by sublimating it. The dittany, too, is part of a network of herbs and plants associated with Diana/Artemis. There is the cedar of D 372, which recalls the title, *Cedreatis* Diana:[30]

Tu *m'es* le Cedre encontre le venin
De ce Serpent en moy continuel,

You are my cedar againt the venom
Of this Serpent which is always inside me

Like Délie/Diana herself, cedar has both positive and negative qualities. Here Scève is drawing on a tradition in which cedar was believed to act as an antidote to snake venom and to drive out snakes, a tradition mentioned by Virgil in the *Georgics* (Book 3, line 414) and subsequently by French writers such as Vincent de Beauvais[31] and Glanville.[32] In D 372 the serpent's venom symbolizes the poison of sexual desire[33] which the lover hopes a transcendent Délie can counteract, as she sometimes does in the sequence. However, cedar is also harmful to men[34] and in this poem, rather than inhibiting sexual desire, Délie nourishes it. The poem closes with the lover succumbing to the fragrance which emanates from Délie's mouth, a fragrance which surpasses all the perfumes of Arabia:[35]

... spire (ô Dieux) trop plus suaue alaine,
Que n'est Zephire en l'Arabie heureuse.

... breathe in (O gods) a far sweeter breath,
Than Zephir in Arabia felix.[36]

In D 50 and D 70 wormwood or absinthe appears, like the laurel tree, a familiar Petrarchan symbol of the bitterness of unrequited love.[37] By virtue of its botanical name, *Artemisia*, it is also associated with Diana/Artemis.[38] The evergreen juniper, too, part of the *materia medica* of the goddess[39] and considered in the Renaissance to be a remedy against snake venom,[40] appears in D 449, the last *dizain* of the sequence, where it suggests the eternal nature of the poet's love for Délie, the life she gives him and poetic renown, similar to that of Petrarch, whose *Trionfo del Tempo* is recalled in the final image:[41]

Nostre Geneure ainsi doncues viura
Non offensé d'aulcun mortel Letharge.

In this way our Juniper will live on
Not threatened by any mortal Lethargy.

The symbolic function of juniper resembles that of myrrh, the precious aromatic plant which embalms, and thus, like Délie, promises eternal life.[42] The plant also recalls Myrrha, the chaste nymph in Diana's train, who is transformed into a tree. In D 378, a poem discussed at length by Coleman (*Maurice Scève,* pp. 157-60), the poet addresses his Beloved thus:

Tu me seras la Myrrhe incorruptible
Contre les vers de ma mortalité (lines 9-10)

You will be [for me] the incorruptible myrrh
Against the worms [and 'verses'?] of my mortality

Finally there is the image of 'Dorion' in D 30, possibly the 'daucus' or 'docion' mentioned by Pliny, like dittany, reputed to remove arrows sunk in the flesh and to help snakes slough their skin.[43] In this poem, the heart, a serpent wounded by Délie's arrow, dares not seek the remedy offered by the herb, for it is only the re-assertion of chaste thoughts in the lover which can save him.

Diana, goddess of healing and wounding, is also a goddess of life, in her role as Lucina, and death, in her role as Oulia. This latter attribute allows Scève to explore the Orphic theme of love as death. In D 2 a figure linked to Hecate appears to suggest the deadly nature of the Beloved:

Le Naturant par ses haultes Idées
Rendit de soy la Nature admirable.
Par les vertus de sa vertu guidées
S'esuertua en œuure esmerueillable.
        Car de tout bien, voyre es Dieux desirable,
Parfeit vn corps en sa parfection,
Mouuant aux Cieulx telle admiration,
Qu'au premier œil mon ame l'adora,
Comme de tous la delectation,
Et de moy seul fatale Pandora.

The Creator, through his high Ideas,
Made Nature admirable in her own right.
She through virtues guided by His virtue
Strove to create a miraculous work.
        For from every good the gods might desire,
[Was] created a body perfect in its perfection,
Exciting such admiration in the Heavens,
That [at first sight] my soul adored it,
As the [delectation] of [all],
And for me alone … fatal Pandora.

The first six lines of this *dizain*, which employs scholastic terminology and rhetorical devices of an earlier tradition, trace the descending movement of creation according to Neo-platonic theory.[44] From God the Creator ('le Naturant', *Natura Naturans*) emanates the beauty which the Ideas then transmit to Nature (*Natura Naturata*),[45] who, in turn creates a perfect being, Délie, in effect, 'obiect de plus haulte vertu', whose physical charms mirror her spiritual perfection and whose perfection, descending in a chain from God, reflects the divinity. The *adnominato*, 'Par les *vertus* de sa *vertu* ... s'esuertua*[46] reinforces the descending chain. This creation of a beneficent Creator has an extraordinary effect on the whole universe. In a charming reversal the poet states (line 7) that Délie influences the celestial world, whose proper function is to illumine and control the earth. The effect on the poet/lover of this woman is that of Pandora on Epimetheus, who also adored her at first sight, for Pandora was endowed with multiple gifts by the gods (mentioned by Scève in line 5) and her seductive charms enchanted all mortals ('Comme de tous la delectation', line 9).[47]

However, Pandora has negative connotations and these it is that Scève evokes in the last line of his poem. It was she who, in opening the *pithos* or urn, brought evil into the world, a legend which made of her a pagan Eve in the eyes of the early Church Fathers.[48] In Orphic legend Pandora is also associated with Hecate, infernal goddess of death, linked to Diana. Thus it is that Scève presents the ambivalence of the Lady he loves. Four hammered-out syllables, 'Et de moy seul ...' introduce Délie as Pandora, she who is not only gentle, but hard; not only beautiful, but deadly. It is this image which, as McFarlane says (*The 'Délie'*, p.85), ensures the success of the poem.

It is above all ambivalence which characterizes the Beloved. This ambivalence is beautifully illustrated by D 22 in which Scève plays on the notion of Diana as *dea triformis* : Diana, Luna, Hecate:

> Comme Hecaté tu me feras errer
> Et vif, & mort cent ans parmy les Vmbres:
> Comme Diane au Ciel me resserrer,
> D'ou descendis en ces mortelz encombres:
> Comme regnante aux infernalles vmbres
> Amoindriras, ou accroistras mes peines.
>> Mais comme Lune infuse dans mes veines
> Celle tu fus, es & seras DELIE.
> Qu'Amour a ioinct a mes pensées vaines
> Si fort, que Mort iamais ne l'en deslie.

> As Hecate you will make me wander
> Both alive and dead, a hundred years among the [S]hades ...
> As Diana you will enclose me in the Heavens,
> Whence you descended to these mortal miseries.
> As one reigning over the infernal darkness
> You will lessen or increase my torment.
>> But as the moon flowing in my veins
> ... You were, are and will be DELIE
> Whom Love has joined to my mortal thoughts
> So strongly, that Death can never part us.

Lines 1-2 depict the torments, that, as Hecate, the Beloved metes out to the lover. Like the Shades who have received no burial rites, those beings both dead and alive, who are not permitted to enter Charon's boat in order to reach the other side, but who are forced to wander for a hundred years before resting in the tranquil dwelling-place of the dead (Virgil, *The Aeneid*, VI, v. 329 and v. 371), the lover will be forced by Délie/Hecate, goddess of the number one hundred,[49] to wander on the shores of hell in a state which is that of the living death of the Petrarchan tradition. This torment is perhaps that of sexual desire, which throughout the *Délie* is linked to Hecate.[50] Opposed to this vision of suffering and death is that of Délie/Diana, celestial divinity, whose role is to lift the lover up towards the light (lines 3-4).[51]

In lines 5-6 the lover is consigned to darkness and infernal punishment by Délie/ Proserpina, judge of the underworld. Then the image of Délie as Moon infused in his veins appears, with overtones of sensuality, of the influence of the moon on human health and destiny and of the madness that is this love. The Beloved's power is reinforced by the echo of the *Gloria Patri*: just as Délie/Diana reigns over the three worlds, infernal, terrestrial and celestial, so she exercizes her power over past, present and future. Her domination is such that the poet/lover will never untie the knot which ties him to her, the play on words 'deslie (untie)/Délie' and the repetition of sounds, 'Si <u>fort</u>, que <u>Mort</u>', accentuating the power of this love which will unite them beyond death.

Délie, source of both joy and torment, is herself an image of the contradictory nature of the feelings she incites: spiritual love and carnal desire. It is via the Platonic equation of light as spiritual love, and darkness as carnal desire that Scève often explores this conflict. The identification of his Beloved with the moon goddess allows him to do this, as he himself says in D 59:

> … ie te cele en ce surnom louable,
> Pource qu'en moy tu luys la nuict obscure.

> I conceal you in this praiseworthy name
> Since you light up in me the dark night.

The light/darkness motif is one of the most important and frequent of the whole *recueil*. It allows Scève to exploit the Petrarchan model of light as presence and darkness as absence, the waxing and waning of the moon and her daily return suggesting the theme. It also allows him to treat the Platonic cave and love as illumination. For it is not only as moon that Délie appears. Radiating from this metaphor are others which make use of the natural rhythms of other luminaries: the sun and the stars. Many poems reveal Délie as the sun which illuminates the lover in the fullest sense of the word, for she brings him light and life and awakens him from the torpor in which he languishes before her arrival.

But if, in keeping with her Platonic function, Délie is a source of light to the lover, she is also a source of darkness, inciting physical desire in him. This ambivalence is perhaps best illustrated in D 7:

> Celle beaulté, qui embellit le Monde
> Quand nasquit celle en qui mourant ie vis,
> A imprimé en ma lumiere ronde
> Non seulement ses lineamentz vifz:
> Mais tellement tient mes espritz rauiz,
> En admirant sa mirable merveille,
> Que presque mort, sa Deité m'esueille
> En la clarté de mes desirs funebres,
> Ou plus m'allume, & plus, dont m'esmerueille,
> Elle m'abysme en profondes tenebres.

This beauty which embellished the World
When she was born, in whom dying I live,
Has imprinted in my eyes
Not only her living features:
But so keeps my faculties in a state of captivation
In admiration of the marvellous miracle that she is
That even on the point of her death, her divinity awakens me
Into the light of my dark desires
And the more illumined I am, the more whereat I marvel,
She casts me into deepest darkness.

The vision of Délie's luminous beauty with which the poem opens suggests once more that she is a quasi-divine being. Her luminous presence has come to establish itself in the terrestrial darkness of the lover (line 2): like Christ (*Romans* 6, vv. 3-5), she will redeem the lover, by allowing him to live in her. Equally this line is the expression of a Neo-platonic commonplace: the death of the lovers and their rebirth, one in the other.[52] (The sixteenth-century significance of death in a sexual sense is not present in this poem).

The mystical beauty of Délie holds the lover enslaved in amazement at her qualities (lines 5-6). Like the resplendent beauty of Sophie in Leone Hebreo's *Dialogues of Love,* which Eugène Parturier, an earlier editor of *Délie,* sees as a model for this *dizain,*[53] Délie's beauty penetrates the eyes, pierces the heart and finally seizes the mind or 'espritz' of the lover. It is in the last four lines that the Beloved's capacity to incite contradictory tendencies in her lover is revealed, by the opposition of darkness and light. His ecstasy in beholding Délie is such that he is on the point of death. It is at this point that, like Christ who descends into hell to lead the souls back to light, his Beloved awakens him.[54] But her luminous beauty also awakens in him a desire which links him to the world of matter and darkness. The antitheses of life and death, of light and darkness suggest a co-existence of physical desire and of a higher aspiration. The poet marvels at this co-existence, which creates a moment of respite in the poem (line 9), before he is plunged into the dark abyss, into the elemental chaos of the human condition. Physical desire does not allow him to cross the distance that separates him from this radiant divinity and ascend towards the domain of pure spirit. Thus it is that this perfect woman casts him into darkness.

* * *

In this essay I have taken as a basis for discussion the identification of the Beloved with the goddess Diana. I have examined some of the ways in which Scève has exploited the myth in order to portray the tensions of his relationship with his *Dame*, tensions which, as the poet confirms in D 216, are inseparable from his love:

> At different times, several days, many hours,
> From hour to moment, from moment to [forever],
> In my soul, O Lady, you dwell,
> Entirely taken up in contrary states.

> En diuers temps, plusieurs iours, maintes heures,
> D'heure en moment, de moment a tousiours
> Dedans mon Ame, ô Dame, tu demeures
> Toute occupée en contraires seiours.

Notes

1   The critical edition of the *Délie* used throughout is that of I.D.McFarlane, *The 'Délie' of Maurice Scève* (Cambridge: Cambridge University Press, 1966). Following on the convention established by McFarlane, each *dizain* is cited with its numbering in the sequence preceded by the letter 'D'.

2   V.-L. Saulnier, *Maurice Scève*, 2 vols (Paris: Klincksieck, 1948), I, pp. 148-50, p. 281.

3   McFarlane, *The 'Délie'*, pp. 15-16; Dorothy Coleman, 'Scève's Choice of the Name "Délie"', *French Studies*, 18 (1964), 1-16; Dorothy Coleman, *Maurice Scève: Poet of Love* (Cambridge: Cambridge University Press, 1975), pp.118-40; Beverley Ormerod, 'Scève's *"Délie"* and the mythographers' Diana', *Studi Francesi*, n.67 (1979), 86-93.

4   Unless otherwise stated, the translations into English of each *dizain* are taken from Ronald A. Hallett, *A Translation with Introduction and Notes of the 'Délie' of Maurice Scève* (unpublished doctoral thesis, University of Pennsylvania State University, 1973). My modifications of Hallett's translations are enclosed in square brackets.

5   William Shakespeare, *Complete Works*, Sonnet LXIII (London: Oxford University Press, 1964). p. 1116.

6   McFarlane, *The 'Délie'*, p. 66.

7   Coleman, 'Scève's Choice of the Name "Délie"', p. 5.

8   Coleman, *Maurice Scève*, p. 132.

9   Coleman, *Maurice Scève*, reminds us (p. 132) of the frustration of the god at the moment of the transformation of the nymph into a tree.

10 Petrarch, Sonnets VI, CVII, CLXXXVIII, CCLV.

11 Marius Piéri, *Pétrarque et Ronsard ou De l'influence de Pétrarque sur la Pléiade française* (1896; repr. New York: Burt Franklin, 1968).

12 For a discussion of the dream of love in the work of the poets of the 'Pléiade', see Henri Weber, *La Création poétique au seizième siècle en France: De Maurice Scève à Agrippa d'Aubigné* (Paris: Nizet, 1955), pp. 356-369 and Gisèle Mathieu-Castellani, *Les thèmes*

amoureux dans la poésie française 1570-1600 (Paris: Presses Universitaires de France, 1981), who treats (pp. 147-62 and pp. 435-55) the origins of the theme and its use by Ronsard and by the later Baroque poets.

13 These moments of the metaphoric or real transition from night to day (D 79, D 266, D 304, D 355, D 378) and from day to night (D 98, D 106, D 111, D 133, D 355, D 356), which grow out of the assimilation of the Beloved to Diana, are amongst the finest in the love-sequence.

14 W.S.M. Nicol, 'Ovid, *Amores*, 1 5', *Mnemosyne* 30 (1977): 40-48, speaks (p. 46) of a poetry of meetings which take place 'quiddam nubis opacae', between *lux* and *tenebrae*. Mathieu-Castellani, *Les Thèmes amoureux*, points out (p. 148) the importance of Ovid's invocation 'Ad Aurorem' for the poetic tradition of the dream of love.

15 James Hall, *Dictionary of Subjects & Symbols in Art* (London: John Murray, 1974), p. 103, note 6.

16 Coleman, *Maurice Scève* suggests (p. 127) that this verse is ambiguous and could mean 'as the Moon holds Endymion' or 'as Endymion holds the Moon', thus suggesting the possibility of a reciprocal love.

17 McFarlane, *The 'Délie'*, p. 39.

18 Certain critics consider it is the eye which launches the whole love-sequence. Hans Staub, *Le Curieux désir: Scève et Peletier du Mans, poètes de la connaissance* (Geneva: Droz, 1967) points out (p. 37) that Scève is a poet of looking in a work which begins with 'L' 'il'. Dorothy Coleman, *Maurice Scève,* states (p. 194): 'This is the basis of the view adopted by McFarlane and Staub that the whole cycle is, as it were, triggered off by the Eye'.

19 This is, as McFarlane points out (*The 'Délie'*, p. 35 and p. 367, note to D 1, 1), an echo of Petrarch's *Rime* 1, 3: '*in su 'l mio primo giovenile errore …*' He adds 'It is not without significance that a Petrarchan echo should be found in the first and the last lines of the sequence (cf. D 449, 10).'

20 For a list of the epithets of the goddess see W.H. Roscher, *Ausführliches Lexikon der Griechischen und Römischen Mythologie* (Leipzig: Teubner, 1884-1924), sv 'Artemis', 1, 560-592.

21 The plaintive exclamation uttered by Apollo in Ovid's *Metamorphoses* (1, books 1-V) recalls this dictum: the god declares that, while the medicine is one of his inventions and that he governs the world of plants, there is no plant capable of curing love.

22 'Scève's *Délie* and the mythographers' Diana', p. 88. This article has proved invaluable for my discussion on the herbs associated with Délie/Diana.

23 Ormerod, 'Scève's "*Délie*" and the mythographers' Diana', p. 87.

24 Ibid, p. 87.

25 Aristotle, *Historia Animalium*, vol III, book IX, paragraph VI.

26 Cicero, *De Natura Deorum*, volume II, book 2, paragraph 126.

27 Pliny the Elder, *Natural History,* book XXVI, paragraph 142; book VIII, paragraph 97.

28 McFarlane, *The 'Délie'*, cites (p. 477, note to D 422, 8) a passage from St. François de Sales taken from E. Huguet, *Dictionnaire de la langue française du seizième siècle* (Paris: Champion, 1925-)

29 Ormerod, 'Scève's "*Délie*" and the mythographers' Diana', p. 88.

30 Ormerod, 'Scève's "*Délie*" and the mythographers' Diana', p. 88.

31 McFarlane, *The 'Délie'*, mentions (p. 464, note to D 372,1) the quotation on cedar as an antidote to snake bite from Vincent de Beauvais' *Speculum naturale* XII, appearing in an earlier edition of the *'Délie'* edited by Eugène Parturier (1939; repr. Paris: Didier, 1961).

32 Ormerod, 'Scève's "*Délie*" and the mythographers' Diana', p. 88.

33 Coleman, *Maurice Scève*, p. 150.

34 McFarlane, *The 'Délie'*, mentions (p. 464, note to D 372, 1) that Saulnier states (Scève, I, p. 282) that cedar was also believed to be harmful to man.

35 For a discussion of *Arabia felix* see Jean Hubux and Maxime Leroy, *Le Mythe du phénix dans les littératures grecques et latines,* Bibliothèque de la Faculté de Philosophie et Lettres de l'Université de Liège, fascicule LXXXII (Paris: Droz, 1939), pp. 85-95 and Coleman, *Maurice Scève*, p. 150, note 1.

36 The translation is my own.

37 McFarlane, *The 'Délie'*, mentions (p. 385, note to D. 50, 10) that the metaphor of absinthe appears in the *Canzionere*. Under the section 'Style', Piéri, *Pétrarque et Ronsard,* speaks (p. 481) of the lover in Petrarch who 'se repaît à la fois de miel et d'absinthe' (feeds on honey and absinthe); Ormerod, 'Scève's "*Délie*" and the mythographers' Diana', mentions (p. 86) that Cesare Ripa, the well-known Renaissance mythographer, cites Petrarch's lament for the lover feeding on wormwood ('il cibo assentio')—a familiar metaphor for the unhappy lover—to justify his depiction of *Affano* (Affliction) with sprays of wormwood in her hands.

38 Ormerod, 'Scève's "*Délie*" and the mythographers' Diana', p. 86.

39 '… were included in her *materia medica* … among plants, the juniper, and the white and black hellebore, the healing properties in these being Artemis herself, counteracting the power of Artemis the cause of the disease', quoted in Simone de Couvreur Ferguson, *La Religion de Diane dans la poésie française du XVIe siècle* (unpublished doctoral thesis, University of Connecticut: 1975), p. 78.

40 Ormerod, 'Scève's "*Délie*" and the mythographers' Diana', p.89.

41 McFarlane, *The 'Délie'*, states (p. 481, note to D 449, 10) that this image is a reminiscence of Petrarch and cites two lines from his *Trionfo del Tempo*, lines 74-5: 'Ma io v'annunzio che voi siete offesi / Da uno grave e mortifero lethargo' and adds (p. 481) 'Thus does the *Délie* open and end with a discreet homage to Petrarch'.

42 'On dit que le buis, le cedre, l'ebene, l'if, le geneure … n'en vieillissent jamais', quoted in Ferguson, *La Religion de Diane dans la poésie française du XVIe siècle*, p. 77.

43 See Jane M. Drake-Brockman (Southwood), 'Scève, the Snake and the Herb', *French Studies* 33 (1979): 129-136.

44 Leo Spitzer , 'The Poetic Treatment of a Platonic Christian Theme', *Comparative Literature* 6 (1954): 193-217; Weber, *La Création poétique,* p. 181, note 3; Coleman, 'Scève's Choice of the Name 'Délie''', p. 8 and *Maurice Scève,* p. 136; McFarlane, *The 'Délie'*, introduction, p. 84 and pp. 367-368, note to D 2; Staub, *Le Curieux désir*, p. 50.

45 Spitzer , 'The Poetic Treatment of a Platonic Christian Theme', p. 202, note 11 and McFarlane, *The 'Délie'*, p. 368, note to D 2, 1, who observes that the verb 'naturer' means 'create', 'form' in old French.

46 McFarlane, *The 'Délie'*, p. 368, note to D 2, 4.

47 For an analysis of the different versions of the myth of Pandora from Hesiod on, and its use in art and literature, see Dora and Erwin Panofsky, *Pandora's Box: The Changing*

Aspects of a Mythical Symbol, 2nd edn (New York: Pantheon, 1969). Other poets who use the image of Pandora include Du Bellay, *Les Antiquités de Rome*, XIX and Ronsard, *Sonets pour Hélène*, II and XVIII. For a discussion of the use of the image in sixteenth-century poets, see Guy Demerson, *La Mythologie classique dans l'œuvre lyrique de la 'Pléiade'* (Geneva: Droz, 1972), sv. 'Pandore'.

48 Panofsky and Panofsky, *Pandora's Box*, mention (p. 61) the painting of Jean Cousin, *Eva Prima Pandora*.

49 Gisèle Mathieu-Castellani, 'La figure mythique de Diane dans *L'Hécatombe* d'Aubigné', *Revue d'Histoire Littéraire de la France* 78 (1978): 3-18, p. 9.

50 Beverley Ormerod, 'Délie and the Hare', *French Studies* 30 (1976): 385-92, p. 390.

51 According to Coleman (*Maurice Scève*, p.139) this verse could also constitute a discreet allusion to the myth of Endymion and would then evoke the ecstasy of the union, contrasted with the torment inflicted by Délie/Hecate.

52 Henri Weber, 'Platonisme et sensualité dans la poésie amoureuse de la Pléiade', *Lumières de la Pléiade* (Paris: Vrin, 1966), p. 172.

53 Parturier, *Délie*, pp. 9-10.

54 Weber, *La Création poétique*, pp. 182-83.

Playing with Worldly Things:
The Dialogues of the Little Academy
at Little Gidding

Kate Riley

Amongst the papers of the Ferrar family is a collection of dialogues: transcripts of the proceedings of an educational circle at Little Gidding made up of many of the daughters of Susanna Ferrar and John Collet and called the Little Academy.[1] The sisters met to participate in a form of loosely Socratic or Platonic-style dialogues through which it was supposed they should gain pleasure and moral edification, each participant having composed and memorized the content of her part of the dialogue before they assembled.[2] Rational enquiry was encouraged in their 'survey of those opinions and practizes which the world recommends or disallows', within the limits of a notion of 'true and right Reason' that discerned 'according to the weights and by the standard of Scripture' rather than using 'the scales of common Judgement'.[3] A likeness with the Erasmian and broader humanist thought and pedagogical strategies that had informed the curricula of English (boys') schools for more than a century is discernable here in the adoption of the classical medium of dialogue and in the emphasis placed on the concord of faith and reason.[4] Appropriately monitored writing and study were deemed worthwhile pursuits for the young women of Little Gidding, being both morally instructive and useful for developing practical literacy, which had a range of everyday applications from correspondence to household account-keeping.[5] In the context of Ursula Potter's claim that many early modern English boys left school with excellent reading skills but only a rudimentary grasp of writing, 'a 'mechanical art' not considered appropriate to the superior grammar school program or to the education of a gentleman', it is particularly notable that the Ferrar girls were encouraged to write this way.

Despite historians' long-held assumption that the dialogues are Nicholas Ferrar's work, it makes sense that the Collet sisters wrote the dialogues themselves. Simple research and composition based upon a controlled body of literature available in the household would likely have been condoned, if not integral to the 'storying' practice (as the Ferrars dubbed it) as a whole. Historians following Turner in the late 1670s have tended to attribute authorship of the dialogues to Nicholas, arguing that the women who recited them did so from memory and had no part in their composition.[6] Perhaps they are swayed by John Ferrar's determination to give witness to his brother's hand having guided all matters of consequence, including his assertion that 'Nicholas Ferrar contrived a book of fitting stories and lessons for the training up of young people' in reference to his provisions for the boys' schoolroom.[7] However there is no evidence in the Ferrar papers or the dialogue texts to suggest that Nicholas did anything other than supervise the storying from time to time. And as Muir and White attest, though John Ferrar zealously adds credit to his brother in his biography and describes Nicholas's provisions for the education of the children, in particular the boys, in some detail, nowhere does he mention Nicholas in conjunction with the dialogues. Nicholas took notes when he was present at storying and later transcribed the proceedings, and thus perhaps exercised editorial discretion, but during the Academy's most active period from 1631–32 he was often absent from Little Gidding.[8] Five manuscript volumes of the dialogues are extant, made and bound by the sisters from the transcripts.[9] The first volume was completed by the February 1632 anniversary of the Academy's establishment, when it was presented to Mrs Ferrar, and then was forwarded at her bidding to her granddaughter Susanna Mapletoft at Margaretting.[10]

In keeping with the early modern maxim that examples had greater purchase on the imagination than did precepts, the sisters drew vignettes from the store of books in the household (of which no record survives), both relatively recent and from the distant past, which, recounted in turn, illustrated the moral strengths and shortcomings of their protagonists:

> good Histories, whereof wee ought not in truth to bee unfurnished, considering the opportunity that GOD hath given us to grow rich in these kind of jewells; for Jewells they are indeed, especially when they are well sett by a gracefull delivery and a seasonable application.[11]

A variety of personages from a range of contexts, secular and religious, populates the dialogue transcripts. Amongst them are: classical heroes such as Trajan and Alexander; an assortment of desert fathers—clear favourites, a source respected by members of Lancelot Andrewes' circle[12] amongst English Protestants and whose example affirmed the wisdom of the Ferrars' project of retirement in particular— and their heathen contemporaries of the Alexandrian patriciate; Bede's early English Christians like Oswin, King of Northumberland and the bishop Aidan; and fifteenth-, sixteenth- and seventeenth-century figures including Cosimo de' Medici, Popes Marcellus II and Adrian VI, Katherine of Aragon and Maurice of Orange. The presence of tales such as 'The Lady of the Lights' suggests that the sisters occasionally dipped into the annals of romance, territory conventionally spurned for its ungodliness (Vives, for example, maintains in this regard 'What shulde a mayde do with armour? ... Hit can nat lyghtly be a chaste mynde, that is occupied with thynkyng on armour, and turnay, and mannes valiaunce') and specifically condemned in the storying of 31 December 1631.[13] Themes resounding throughout the dialogues relate to the central premise that worldly things pale in significance when compared with spiritual concerns; seeking virtue is a matter of immediate consequence, not something easily deferred till later in life, and should include practising temperance, patience, moderation, devotion and resistance to the urges of the 'weaker affections'.

Reportedly established at the behest of the participants' grandmother, Mary Ferrar, on the Feast of the Purification (Candlemas, 2 February) in 1631, the Little Academy operated until 1634. Its core members were the four eldest Collet sisters resident at Little Gidding, Mary, Anna, Hester and Margaret, who performed the majority of the stories and shared responsibility for the functioning of the group. Their ages in 1631 were: Mary, thirty; Anna, twenty-eight; Hester, approximately twenty-four; and Margaret, approximately twenty-three. Two younger sisters, Elizabeth and Joyce, offered shorter stories in keeping with their junior status, despite the fact that at approximately nineteen and sixteen years of age respectively they would have been completely capable of full participation. Each member of the Academy bore a fixed title and took part in the dialogues under that alias, as if in character. Mary, the eldest and very much the dominant presence among the sisters, was called the 'Cheife' and her younger sister Anna was called the 'Patient'. Hester and Margaret were the 'Cheerefull' and the 'Affectionate', and Elizabeth and Joyce were the 'Obedient' and the 'Submisse'; it is not clear which sister took which name in either pair. Their sister Susanna Mapletoft was given the honorary title of the 'Goodwife', but living at a distance she did not participate in the storying. The sisters' grandmother (who made no verbal contribution), their parents Susanna and John Collet, and their uncles John and Nicholas Ferrar all had titles in the Academy—respectively the 'Founder' or 'Mother', the 'Moderatour', the 'Resolved', the 'Visitour' and the 'Guardian'. At least one of them was present at each meeting session, largely in the capacity of commentators and supervisors rather than storytellers with the exception of Mrs Collet, who presented stories alongside her daughters from time to time. The rationale behind the Academy's character names is discussed below.

At first envisaged as a daily practice, the Academy soon fell to meeting only during holiday periods (apart from a very busy first summer monopolized by the protracted case of Charles V's retirement),[14] in particular Christmastide when storying functioned as a godly alternative to the customary gaming and feasting of the season. Sometimes there was a significant degree of congruence between the festival and the lesson behind the stories recited on a given day—the importance of an appropriate disposition towards death was communicated throughout the discussion on Holy Innocents' Day (28 December) 1631, for example.[15] But more often than not the connection between the lot or example of the saint nominally being commemorated and the moral of the story was abstruse, and it seems likely that the sisters agreed upon a specific but not directly correlated theme or themes for reflection prior to each dialogue.

During Christmastide 1631 the storying was held upstairs in the 'Sisters' Chamber',[16] presumably one of the 'chambers and closets' that Nicholas had provided for his nieces, rather than downstairs in the great chamber where most communal activities such as meals and regular prayer gatherings took place.[17] The performance had an audience of 'most of the Family', though it is not clear whether an audience was a constant or a prerequisite for storying.[18] The sessions stalled after the 1632 Christmas season, but, following a long hiatus and moved by old Mrs Ferrar's wish to see the Academy active again, the group reconvened in 1634 subsequent to her May death. The transcript of the 'Winding Sheet' dialogue then performed—on mortality, in which reference is made also to George Herbert, who had died on 1 March 1633[19]—is the last indication of the Academy's activity.[20] The precise date of this gathering is difficult to determine; Williams suggests some two years after Christmastide 1632, late in 1634.[21] By this reckoning, the active lifespan of the Little Academy was only about two years, from the end of the Christmas season early in 1631 to the end of the Christmas season early in 1633, with one outlying performance towards the end of 1634.

The Little Academy is an unusual phenomenon; it is not typical to find oratorical activities in the schooling or leisure pursuits of young women outside of aristocratic or court circles in the early Stuart period, for the obvious reasons that women's public speech and their possession and demonstration of knowledge were not ideologically condoned. It begs investigation on a number of fronts. The present study concentrates on the dialogues performed during 1631 and 1632 when the Little Academy was functioning at its peak and the meetings were relatively frequent. Transcripts appear in Sharland's *Story Books*. The discussion shows how dramatic performance was incorporated into the Ferrars' devotional and didactic routine through the dialogues. Storying provided suitably moral entertainment and, by representing events from the history of the outside world, was a regulated means of bringing secular knowledge to women in the secluded religious household. The rejection of worldly things in favour of simplicity and the inner life of the spirit were precepts fundamental to the design for Christian living at Little Gidding, and a high proportion of the exempla are instances that turn on the choice between bodily or material indulgence and renunciation. In so far as the Collet sisters' knowledge of history and the world beyond their household was augmented through their storying, the process was weighted such that they were compelled to reject these glimpses at other ways of life as inferior to their path of self-denial and devotion.

Most emphasis is placed on the significance of the Academy's role as a key site within the household where a process of mediating and dispersing values occurred: in this instance, young women identified and defined moral precepts for themselves by viewing events of the recent and distant past through a Christian filter. Importantly, this included settling on appropriate standards with regard to the gender-specific constructs and states of matriarchy, maternity and virginity. All of this was done in accordance with the notions promulgated as orthodox within the family (and thus compatible with the Ferrars' social status and confessional identity), matters substantially determined via Nicholas's influence. The Collet sisters rationally constructed and furthermore acted out the contours of the confinement that their family and culture prescribed, defrayed through the dialogue tropes, which offset seriousness with spectacle or a note of humour.

The dialogues are an example of a mechanism through which values were internalized in an early modern domestic context, one to which female literacy was critical; the reader observes how the sisters learned and moreover became advocates for the discourses that effected their subjugation. Both the medium and the context of their 'playing' were controlled. Generic convention was deployed with acute effect to shape their sense of proper conduct and achieve conformity, at least of mind, with 'family' values. And the routine of composing and then reciting their stories before an audience, comprising supervisors of the parental generation and younger children in whom virtue had to be instilled by example, bound the young women with the threat of charges of failure or hypocrisy if they did not apply in their daily or future actions the principles they championed. As the Cheerefull said, 'To know these things and not to follow them will procure double stripes.'[22]

I. Why establish the Little Academy?
Motivations for and functions of the storying

That Nicholas anticipated the effectiveness of the dialogues as a method of inculcating values, in keeping with pedagogical theories of the time, is one possible explanation for why the Little Academy was set up in the first place. Other factors impinged on its creation too. In establishing the Little Academy the Ferrars were dealing with the problem, in contemporary terms, of having a large number of daughters in the household, most of them awaiting marriage but too old for the schoolroom.[23] It was important that they were not idle and that their time was filled with fitting pursuits. In storying, moral and intellectual content were combined with the opportunity to perfect skills of vocal and bodily deportment and decorum, forming an entirely wholesome, improving activity.[24] The research and composition process and the careful work of copying and binding the transcripts likewise constituted disciplined, devout uses of time, culminating in a tangible product. It was gender-specific training. The Academy was part of a broader project to prepare the Collet sisters for life as married gentlewomen, but moreover as godly wives.

For it is highly probable that, likely by Nicholas's design, the sisters were raised with a view to their marrying priests, an end which would secure them sound futures in the feminine roles of wife and mother but in circumstances where the religious orientation was perhaps greater than in a lay household of appropriate station. By becoming entrenched in clerical families the young women would stand a better chance of continuing with their lives of pious observance at a pitch approximating that to which they had become accustomed at Little Gidding, thereby individually conveying the Ferrar mission of living to Godwards into the wider world. A seventeenth-century parson's wife had special pastoral and in some cases evangelical responsibilities in the parish, visiting and ministering to the frail and ill, for example, much as the Ferrar women did through the infirmary, soup kitchen and widows' lodgings at Little Gidding. Most significantly, the clerical family was a model to the rest of the community; thus the minister's wife had to embody feminine virtue as an obedient and devout wife and mother, taking care of her children's religious and moral training and maintaining effective government of household and family. A century after the necessity of clerical celibacy was first questioned in the process of the English Reformation, clerical marriage had become an accepted institution, but one only just beginning to establish its respectability. In part this was because many clergymen could not claim any particular wealth or distinction of lineage. For the Ferrar-Collets, the task of finding suitable husbands and providing dowries for so many daughters was a social and financial burden. Clergymen might have lacked gentle birth and money, but with any luck they could boast personal holiness and a university education as standard, and could offer their prospective wives the promise of a godly home and a share in the respect that their position earned them in the neighbourhood. Perhaps these benefits would offset their shortcomings, in the long term paving the way for clergymen to become eligible partners for gentlewomen. But the centuries-old stigma attached to 'priest's whores' was slow to dissipate in the (relatively) newly Protestant nation, and as a consequence there was considerable pressure upon clergy wives to demonstrate scrupulous feminine conduct and to establish the social cachet of their families.

The degree to which women who married clerics in the Elizabethan and early Stuart era were moulding a new social role and the possibility that they experienced empowerment in the process of doing so merits further research, but is beyond the scope of the present discussion. However, it is worth considering whether, having priest-husbands identified as their future goal, a sort of anticipatory marital relationship was established through the Collet sisters' relationships with their unmarried uncle, Nicholas Ferrar. The devout deacon so revered in the household was also its head and was central to their spiritual formation, maintaining close individual bonds with his nieces. Perhaps Nicholas was as it were a sort of proto-husband, not quite a husband, not quite a father, and not quite a priest, who was only properly displaced when the sisters married other men. In this case, conditioned to be receptive to and respectful of their godly profession and consequent authority, the girls could have developed an emotional inclination towards clerics. The proximity of their ages should be borne in mind also when considering the nature of the extremely close relationships, however chastely sublimated, that Nicholas pursued with his nieces, in particular with his favourites, Mary and Anna. Nicholas was thirty-eight in 1631 when the Academy was founded, and Mary and Anna were respectively thirty and twenty-eight years old. By July of that year Anna had sought the approval of Nicholas and their parents to spend the rest of her life unmarried, as Mary had done somewhat earlier. While Nicholas's support of Anna in her resistance to repeated attempts to marry her to Arthur Woodnoth (the kinsman and London goldsmith who acted as the Ferrars' city agent, then aged about forty) does not prove a countervailing attachment between them, it does suggest sympathy, and the letters between Anna and Nicholas, like those between Mary and Nicholas, testify to their psychological intimacy and his encouragement of both in their decision to live as celibates.

Regardless of whether its members married laymen or ministers, the Little Academy was designed to address the particular needs of women according to notions of what was proper for their present and future conduct and bearing in mind the weaknesses generally associated with being female. It was characterized as a feminine institution from the outset:

> It was the same Day wherein the Church celebrates that great Festivall of the Purification, that the Mayden Sisters, longing to bee Imitatours of those glorious Saints by whose Names they were called (for all bare Saints Names, and shee that was elected CHEIFE, that of Blessed Virgin Mary) having entered into a joint Covenant betweene themselves and some others of neerest Blood ... for the performance of divers religious exercizes ... they therefore resolved, together with the Practize of Devotion, to intermingle the study of wisedome, searching and enquiring diligently into the knowledge of those things which appertaine to their Condition and Sex.[25]

Founded according to the will of the matriarch, Mary Ferrar, to whom the dialogue transcripts are dedicated, it was hardly coincidental the inaugural session of the Little Academy was held on the Feast of the Purification, 2 February 1631. By that date, the Ferrars would have been quite settled at Little Gidding, having first arrived there in May 1625, and all of the Collet sisters then involved with the Academy over the age of fourteen—roughly the point at which girls would conventionally have been considered mature or at least too old for school. The Marian connotations were explicit, and consequence was attributed to the other female saints' names with which the Collet sisters were christened, including Anna and Elizabeth. Furthermore, as has been noted, the participants assumed names representing desirable feminine character traits. The object of these sobriquets was to identify a quality in which each was lacking but to which she was particularly enjoined to aspire, according to her personality and her role in the household. 'Alas, then,' said John Collet of one of his daughters, probably Joyce, '... I perceive this Lovely Name is not imposed on our Submisse for desert; but Instruction to teach her, what shee ought to bee, rather then to tell others what shee is.'[26] The titles were exhortatory rather than complimentary, although given her prominent role in the family and the respect with which she was generally held, the Cheife seems to have been an epithet Mary Collet properly deserved. 'Finding in themselves, and observing in others that doe sincerely pursue virtue, that the greatest barre of Perfection was Ignorance of the truth',[27] it behoved them to settle on a path of study, but of course only where the matter was reckoned fitting for women's consumption and restricted to examples that might cultivate virtues which they were typically deemed to lack. The circumscription of women's reading material was customary, particularly in the context of their education. Authors of prescriptive texts recommended suitable reading, such as the heading on books for young women to read during their formative years that Juan Luis Vives included in *The Instruction of a Christen Woman*. Vives condemned romance and the profane poetry of the Greeks and Romans, in particular unchaste amorous verse, and endorsed biblical and patristic reading as well as select classical authors such as Plato, Seneca, and Cicero.[28] The dialogues of the Academy bear out similar priorities in the Collet sisters' reading. In general, fiction is eschewed and factual works such as histories are favoured.

In their dedicatory epistle to the transcripts of the dialogues, Mary and Anna Collet describe their purpose as follows: 'that whereunto this particular exercise is chiefly intended: the Discoverie of those false Opinions wherewith the world misleads all Mankind, especially our weaker sex'.[29] They set up a clear opposition between the snares and evils of worldly concerns and the goodness of spiritual things, citing their grandmother's conduct as their model in the pursuit of virtue, stating: 'You have forsaken all those Affections, Imploiments, and Delights, wherein the world perswades the cheif content of womens minds should ly, and you have censured them as vanities at the best, as sins and great ones, as they are commonly pursued.' They credit Mary Ferrar with suggesting and sanctioning this means of studying virtue within the context of the household regimen, but also attribute to her their very capacity to undertake this rational endeavour. They refer to intellect almost as if it were a simple matter of biological inheritance, helping them to strive after that which is good as much as the moral conditioning which took place in the godly environment that their grandmother fostered. Matriarchy was significant in the Ferrars' family culture. The opening line of John Ferrar's biography of his brother Nicholas reads: 'Nicholas Ferrar's mother was of the ancient Cheshire family of the Woodnoths of Shavinton ...' and continues with a substantial excursus on her exceptional qualities both of body and character before moving to a description of her husband, Nicholas Ferrar the elder. The distinction of her gentry status was a valuable source of establishment identity for the family; Nicholas Ferrar the elder was, after all, only a Hertford draper's son who had found fortune trading in London. While Mary Ferrar was alive the rituals of daily life at Little Gidding revolved around her actual and symbolic seniority, as both embodiment and emblem of family heritage and order. Each day she sat enthroned as overseer of her grandchildren's education and play in the great hall, a beneficent but revered presence, a constant symbol of lineage and feminine virtue imprinting on the minds of the next generation, and the figurehead of a household at least numerically dominated by females.[30] Her grand-daughters were not alone in remarking on her outstanding mental acumen and virtue. Augustine Lindsell, Bishop of Hereford and earlier Nicholas' tutor at Clare, 'would say of her, that he knew no woman that passed her in eloquency (which was natural to her), in judgment and in wisdom, as he did ever admire her, and for her devotion towards God'.[31] Were acclaim from such an elevated personage promoted in the household, it would surely have added to the sisters' respect for the matriarch. It is significant, too, that her intellect is mentioned before her piety, and represented as 'naturally' compatible with it.

Given the main purpose of the dialogues was to edify the young female participants, there is a preponderance of male exemplars in the stories. Notwithstanding the Marian connotations evoked in the Academy's opening session, there are few female role models, and moreover those women who do feature are generally in situations quite divorced from the Collet sisters, not only in time and place but also in condition of life and virtue. Pagan harlots who came to God through encounters with hermits (often not entirely dispassionate themselves) the daughters of Little Gidding were not, though it is tempting to speculate as to the existence of any projected likeness between such instances from the early church and the situation of the unmarried Nicholas Ferrar and his spinster nieces. Why should this be the case? Comparable early-modern prescriptive literature abounds in references to 'the fortitude and wifely faithfulness of Penelope and the patience of Griselda … the helping Lydia, the chaste Susannah, the judicious Deborah, the housewifely Martha, the pious Mary, sister of Martha, the steadfast Mary Magdalene and, above all, the Blessed Virgin Mary'.[32] The predominance of male role models both historical and legendary in the literature from which the Collet sisters worked is a likely explanation; the notion that exceptional behaviour was less to be expected from women with their intrinsic inclination towards weakness and error was powerful. The surrender of public engagement in favour of a life of pious retirement, a theme most relevant to the Ferrar–Collet family, was also a more remarkable and arguably a more difficult choice for men, and thus the individuals recorded as exemplars of renunciation were especially likely to be male. (Perhaps too this suggests that the presence of an audience of mixed gender was an important part of the dialogues' edifying function.)

More simply, the sisters might have found the exploits and praiseworthy acts of distinguished men of greater interest than the available cases of feminine virtue.

Mary Ferrar resigned her position as convenor of the Little Academy on St Luke's Day (18 October) 1632, owing to advanced age—she was about seventy-eight years old—and illness. The members of the group debated who should be installed in her stead (they chose Mary Collet and installed her with great ceremony as the new Mother on 1 November 1632)[33] and amongst their assertions the position of the Affectionate is most noteworthy.

> 'So it may serve to our own purpose, it little matters what others censure (sayd the Affectionate). Wee are too farre already engaged to have the worlds good word, and therefore I think it great Folly for feare or satisfaction of men to turn back to that which may lead us on the better to GOD. Wherefore I beseech you, without giving way to further traverse of this business, to goe immediately to the choise, not of a Lord, but of a Lady; for so you have resolved, and so the constitution of our Family requires, it being the woman sex that exceeds both in Number and faultines amongst us.'[34]

As contrived as the record of the deliberations concerning the appointment of the leader may be, the passage is revealing insofar as it betrays anxiety surrounding their female-led practices, in spite of the celebratory matriarchal rhetoric demonstrated at other points, such as in the dedicatory letters to the volume of dialogues. The Affectionate's statement shows that the assumption of women's particular inclination to sin was current in the family and was a reason for instituting measures for their education (or at the very least a means of justifying their more intellectual endeavours). Her assertion is an indication, unparalleled in its frankness, both of the state of the family and the purpose of the Little Academy.

Storying was meant to be enjoyable as well as morally instructive, nonetheless, and as such it offered an alternative to the fleshly indulgence that was a part of many conventional forms of leisure and celebration. The Little Academy's role at Christmastime is a case in point. In 1631 old Mrs Ferrar imposed a ban on customary festivities such as card-playing and feasting in favour of more solemn observance and, according to the Cheife, charged the Academy with the 'hard task' of 'mak[ing] it a merry and true Christmas, both together, to your household by delightfull and vertuous exercises, that they should have no Cause to envy others greater Liberty or better Cheere'.[35] The Cheerefull called for a similarly ascetic Christmas in Advent 1632, and summoned a meeting of the Academy at during which temperance and corporal denial were discussed.[36]

II. Performance, entertainment and education:
the Little Academy in context

Enthusiasm for theatre and display in the early Stuart period was matched by reservation and outright hostility, and the matter of women appearing onstage incited particular controversy. The participation of high-ranking women in festive masques held at court and in the private households of the affluent met with the censure of theatre-detractors such as William Prynne and William Ames.[37] In his colossal jeremiad *Histrio-Mastix*, published in 1633, shortly after the inception of the Little Academy, Prynne famously branded all 'women actors, notorious whores'. By allegedly levelling the indictment at Henrietta Maria, who was rehearsing a production at the time, he forfeited to the king his legal career, his liberty, the tops of his ears and more besides.[38] Ames's reproachful gaze meanwhile comprehended acting and play-going, Christmas festivities, gaming, drinking, oaths and myriad other transgressions. Yet the existence of the Little Academy would seem to demonstrate the fact that the godly Ferrars approved of acting and performance in an edificatory context, unlike some other pious parties. It is worth considering, then, historical and contemporary examples of the use of drama and performance for didactic purposes, before assessing whether indeed the Ferrars regarded the dialogues to be dramatic or theatrical, and how the function of entertainment related to that of instruction.

Plenty of precedent was available for reference should the Ferrars have needed to justify the existence of the Little Academy. Comparable applications of performance to those of the Little Academy are identifiable in boys' education in early modern England and in contemporary European institutions. The use of drama as a didactic tool in western culture is ancient. More particularly, the familiar Socratic mode of the dialogue, turning on the model of the witty sage engaging in conversation with a naive interlocutor (or interlocutors) from whom rational insights are coaxed progressively, has continued effectively unbroken since Plato's adoption of the form as the basis of philosophical practice.[39] The use of drama and dialogue in schools was strengthened in the early modern era through the advocacy of humanist educators such as Erasmus and Vives. Erasmus believed in the value of drama as an educational tool and embedded this principle in his programme for St Paul's School, which influenced the curricula of grammar schools throughout the realm.[40] Drama helped to develop the skills of oratory that were prioritized as training for men's public and professional roles, not least amongst these clerical office, in the classical model.[41] It may be presumed that their tutor incorporated oratory into the boys' 'schooling and learning the Latin tongue' at Little Gidding. [42] It is not surprising that it does not appear to have figured in the programme of their sisters, given a culture that prescribed and to some extent enforced feminine silence in public, and in which women were barred from oratorical employment in pulpit, parliament and courtroom as well as on stage. For girls and for the majority of English boys who did not have the privilege of attending grammar school, dialogue would have been most recognizable from the question-and-answer format of the prayer book's catechesis.[43] Yet it is still possible that Nicholas Ferrar had participated in dramatic activities during his own schooling (or at university) and promoted the concept amongst his nieces.

In European schools, humanist drama designed to teach as well as to delight 'was sufficiently established by the start of the sixteenth century for there to be at hand a valuable instrument for the spread of the ideas of the Reformation'.[44] Similarly, by the seventeenth century playing was entrenched as a pastime for enclosed nuns and a feature of boys' schooling in Catholic Europe, and growing in its missions and colonies. Despite the mixed responses and monitoring activities of ecclesiastical authorities who imposed regulations governing the conduct of devotional plays and intermittently objected to various aspects of the practice—for example, they were keen to see that sisters did not grow their hair for playing female parts and did not wear secular costumes for performing, in particular men's clothes—drama subsisted even in the strict environs of the post-Tridentine cloister.[45] The Jesuits utilized drama in boys' schooling and in the training of recruits to the Society. Role-playing, projecting into biblical episodes or into hypothetical situations with which a contemporary religious might meet worked as an engaging preparation for ministry and, bolstered by the immediacy of drama, rendered it an effective means of fostering mission in men's orders.[46] Many scholars have attested to the spectacular quality of various rituals of Catholic observance, and worship of this kind as well as plays reinforced the impassioned, demonstrative and affective quality of Counter-Reformation devotion.

A few notable exceptions to the general pattern of excluding girls from dramatic activities in early modern England exist which may be compared with the Little Academy. As far as school dramatics are concerned, the case of some pupils from Ladies Hall in Deptford who appeared in Robert White's masque *Cupid's Banishment* is outstanding. Probably cast as the eight singing wood-nymphs attendant on Diana, their performance in front of Anne of Denmark at court at Greenwich in 1617 was sponsored by Lucy (Russell, née Harington), countess of Bedford, a renowned patron of the arts and even with her godly convictions a keen participant in masques.[47] In contrast, it is most likely that the Ferrars would have looked askance at these exuberant spectacles; their storying involved nothing like the costumes, dancing and stage machinery of the masques.

The Collet sisters in the Little Academy were already very much of age and their storying had little in common with the masque's voluptuous 'celebration of the development of the girls of Ladies Hall into graceful and worthy young women'.[48] Neither were they at school. In terms of the underlying seriousness of the storying, its edificatory ends and factual content, it is possible to draw parallels with Lettice,

Lady Falkland's idea for a 'women's retreat', influenced by the learned circle at Great Tew.[49] The Academy was in its ideals perhaps a little closer to prefiguring Mary Astell's *Serious Proposal* of a 'Monastery' for women's devotion and study.[50] But at Little Gidding, religious endeavour ultimately outweighed rational enquiry. The sisters were engaged in a structured, corporate routine by which, above all, each learned how to behave as a godly woman should and how to effect her own and her family's spiritual improvement.

Although the participatory and cerebral nature of dialogues might disincline a reader of the transcripts to classify them as dramatic performances, there was clearly a performative aspect (beyond that of collective role-playing) to the storying. The Collet sisters clearly understood themselves to be acting: 'Weele now come downe to the represention of some of those things in Actions which you have heard of in the Abstract' said the Cheerefull, having completed a lengthy scriptural prologue to the storying.[51] They usually performed before a small, variable audience of non-participant family members. The attendance of an audience meant the dialogues could be conceived of as having a didactic function that extended beyond the experience of Academy members alone. It was also a measure of transparency, invoking the sanction and endorsement implicit in supervision by uninvolved observers.

Further, the transcripts reflect the sense of occasion that surrounded dialogue sessions, consistent with their taking place on holidays. The report of the enthusiastic, unusually large gathering on St John the Evangelist's Day (27 December) in 1631 following the previous day's storying suggests that the performances excited the attendees to anticipation, despite the fact of the obvious vindicatory construction of the account: using the family member's eager enjoyment of the dialogues to reassert the legitimacy of the practice and the claim to its efficacy as a means of moral instruction.

> The Remembrance of the former Daies Pleasure having after a quicker dispatch then ordinary, though of extraordinary cheere, carried up most of the Family to the SISTERS Chamber, the GUARDIAN, seeing unusuall Lonelines in the Dining Roome, himselfe onely and one or two more being left, smilingly sayd to his MOTHER that it might well now bee seene that there is as great delight to bee found in good things and profitable as in pernicious Vanities. For I doe not think any Gamesters within twenty Miles more egerly bent upon their Play then our Family on their Stories.[52]

The description also communicates a sense of the immediacy of spectacle. The 'Company' were busily recounting the stories of the day before, 'sharpening their Appetites for that they were to hear', when the sisters 'instantly appeared' and the Cheerefull began to sing.[53]

Musical interludes are noted occasionally too, and these, together with the inclusion of the sort of dramatic entrances and pauses that can best be likened to stage tropes rather than rhetorical or oratorical strategies, must have added to the sense of performance.[54] The Cheife concluded her Ash Wednesday 1631 tale of Pirrhus and Cineas with a pause, as follows, adding gravity to the ultimate statement of the moral of the story and enabling her to exploit the modesty topos, conventional etiquette for cognoscenti and a frequent recourse of women writers but especially important in this context where women perform, and moreover perform in such a way that demonstrates their knowledge. She sustains what must inevitably be a delicate balancing act:

> 'If it will be honourable and good in our gray haires, how much more now in youth, to bee wise and virtuous?'
> Here the CHEIFE stayd, and having for a good space sett her eies on the ground, at last with a cheerefull eie viewing the Company round about—Your thoughtfull Countenances (sayd shee) give Testimony that I have sayd too much, and perhaps in other manner then I ought, and therefore I will no further increase your wearinessse or my owne fault.[55]

Learning to play and sing were amongst the activities allotted time in the daily schedule at Little Gidding, and a letter records the purchase of an organ, but it is only in the Little Academy transcripts that the presence of a music master in the household is revealed. '[T]he Master of their Musique played on the Vyoll' whilst the Cheife sang a hymn as a prelude to the St Stephen's Day storying in 1631. The song, it seems, was intended to evoke a sense of solemnity and settle the holiday audience, 'refreshing to the Memories the ground of this Daies solemnity'.[56] Similarly, the Cheerefull, 'to whom the Guidance of that Day fell, made an enterance by singing' a hymn to the accompaniment of the viol to open proceedings the following day, again as a way of inclining the audience to a holy attitude.[57] Most sessions include at least one song or hymn (the absence of the music master and therefore the music is sufficiently unusual to be noted on 31 December 1631[58]), generally early on as a means of introducing the day's theme. Sometimes the exposition is framed with music: the dialogue of 29 December 1631 on the question of the afterlife opens with a song by the Submisse and ends with one by the Obedient, 'excusing [them] for the stories which they otherwise were bound to have told'.[59] Songs therefore could be substituted for the standard moral tales.

The dialogues pursued by the young women of the Little Academy bear a strong relation in style and functions to the practices of storytelling and scriptural reading at Little Gidding. Storying complemented and in some regards echoed the conventional public, locutionary aspects of their communal religious observance. Every morning 'each person (the sons and daughters of the family) according to their ages and discretions repeated to [Nicholas] what chapters and psalms they had learned without book'[60] that week. Ritualized reading of scripture aloud featured at various points in the working day and during meals on Sundays.[61] 'While they were thus in feeding their bodies' the children took turns 'to read a chapter in the Bible ... that so also their ears and hearts might not want the best spiritual food'.[62] On weekdays 'the two younger daughters and four boys' read 'either some chronicles of nations, journeys by land, sea voyages and the like ... because the minds then being in most men altogether intent upon the refreshment of their bodies doth not willingly admit any serious speculation, it is thought fitting that the reading shall be always of some easy and delightful matters'.[63] The meal over, a further story set by Nicholas would be told 'without book' by one of the boys.

> They were short, pleasant, and profitable, good language and no less good in matter, teaching them something of worth, exciting to virtue and the hatred of vice, and by this the young ones learned to speak gracefully and courageously.[64]

Just as transcripts were made of the Academy's dialogues, a 'summary collection' of the most salient details of the children's stories was prepared. A schoolmaster kept notes from which a fair copy was written by one of the children then reviewed after the midday meal, much as the dialogue transcripts Nicholas took were copied and gathered into volumes by the participating sisters. John Ferrar described the process as constituting 'exercises' made under the supervision of 'directors' (himself and Mary Collet), indicating unmistakably that it was understood to be an educational activity.[65] The ends of scripture readings, mealtime stories and the Academy's dialogues alike were moral edification and entertainment, and further, building conversancy with the events of the world's history.

Apart from providing diversion for those at table, an opportunity to practise public speaking, and a deterrent to idle conversation, storytelling was a means of informing the secluded family about the concerns of the wider world.

> And by this means it so came to pass that, though they seemed to live privately and had not much commerce with people, yet they were well acquainted with the forme and latter passages of the world and what was done in it at home and abroad, and had gained knowledge of many actions of note and passages of consequence, and the manners of other countries and nations, and affairs of their own country.[66]

Yet, as has been stated, the rejection of worldly things is a core motif of the dialogues. The purpose of the storying of Holy Innocents' Day 1631, for example, on mortality, was

> by representing Death on the stage in his owne dreadfulness, to perswade you to make timely provision for his entertainment; and by representing the world on the other side in its owne Nakednes to withdraw you from further lose of Time and paines in the

pursuit thereof: since, however largely the world promiseth, you shall clearly see it is not able to performe anything touching that content which you seek after.[67]

A preoccupation with death and renunciation makes sense given the reasonably heavy mortality that corresponded with the Collets' and Ferrars' high fertility; most family members would have been bereaved of relatives, especially children or siblings, and acquaintances. The impression of recent deaths is discernable in some of the stories too; for example, as mentioned previously, Mary Ferrar and George Herbert are remembered in the 'Winding Sheet' dialogue. In addition, substantial weight was placed upon preparing for a good death in early modern Protestant culture. Talking about mortality, self-denial, and the superiority of spiritual things reflected their conscientious piety, and in itself constituted a pious practice (which is not to say their concerns were insincere). The Little Academy was a venue in which the Collet sisters examined and confirmed the theory of devout living, but simply doing so was also a pious act.

Why did the Ferrars seek to acquaint themselves and their children with terrestrial matters then, given their retirement and their declared contempt for material existence? Notwithstanding their godly ideals, a practical perspective governed their preparation for present and future social interaction. The sons and daughters of Little Gidding were raised in the expectation of entering the world, taking up professions and/or getting married according to gender. Maintaining connections with kin, friends and acquaintances such as former business associates was necessary to safeguard the immediate material interests of the household and facilitated the negotiation of good marriages for their children and the placement of sons in apprenticeship or employment, for example. Knowledge *per se* was not shunned, consistent with their humanist-influenced Protestant, gentry beliefs in the value of education and civic responsibility, no doubt inflected with the pragmatic spirit of enterprise. A corresponding regard for moderation is plausible too. Sons in particular would be better equipped to succeed in business, scholarship or the service of the English people as churchmen or in public life if they were familiar with historical and contemporary events; better officers of patriarchy. And regardless of sex, learning about the righteousness and the folly of humanity through such examples helped to hone the moral sense and ideally could lead individuals towards a state of humble wisdom, and responsibility. They would be fitter parents, set to impart values to the next generation (mothers, after all, were responsible for their children's religious education and the formation of their characters), all the while putting their trust in redemption. Commerce with the world could be avoided only temporarily; a thorough drilling in avoiding its snares and a conscientious frame of mind would equip them for the encounter.

Bearing the vindicatory force of precedent and principle in mind then, to understand why storying was deemed appropriate for the young women of Little

Gidding it is also necessary to recognize that the context in which the dialogues were performed was controlled in a number of important ways. They took place in the confines of the household, and there is no evidence to suggest that the performance ever transgressed this space. No record exists of playing in front of an audience of anyone other than family members, and even amongst the sisters participation in the dialogue circle was restricted to those deemed sufficiently mature.[68] The dialogues were always superintended by adults, parental figures, and intermittently subject to auditing by Nicholas Ferrar, the self-styled 'Visitour' of the Little Academy. Further, the dialogues took place in a festive space. Construed as a special occasion within the household and with pleasure an intended outcome, it may be argued that anything untoward that emerged in the goings on would have been safely encapsulated in these exceptional circumstances. So in spite *and* because of being constructed as a space for leisure, rather than offering intermittent respite from the unrelenting mutual checking and regulation of self that the household regimen encouraged, the Little Academy was another site of moral regulation and control, its idiosyncratic format and the participants' opportunities for enjoyment notwithstanding.

The dialogues were a process of learning to know the enemy. In a paradoxical turn, the company of sisters staged the world, letting it into the confines of the godly household by relating and re-enacting episodes from history. Through interpreting the stories and assimilating the lessons drawn from them, they persuaded themselves and their audience to renounce the world, to shut it out again: at least its corrupting aspects, and at least in principle. For the rest, they learned from the examples of the righteous how to endure its perils and temptations. Storying was a process through which the young women had leave to experiment with knowledge and performance that was nevertheless controlled and contained. They researched, composed and presented the dialogues when scholarly reading and writing (moreover in a classical mode) and performance were still regarded as being properly the business of men. But they did so only with the approbation of their same-gender patron, the matriarch of the family, organized hierarchically, labelled according to the qualities they lacked, and whilst supervised by members of their parents' generation, including adult men. The storying was a very effective means of reinforcing in the young women the precepts of their Protestant culture, in accordance with their gender and social rank, which were doubtless familiar from childhood and now nuanced consistent with the prioritisation of piety at Little Gidding. It was fundamentally conservative. As the Affectionate put it,

> Wee are necessitated to be better then ordinarily Christians are, or els our case wilbe farre worse, in that wee know the way and the reward of weldoing; of both which points, as far as I can perceive, the world is utterly ignorant. If our stories be right, the practize of the world is very wrong.[69]

Finally, it is reasonable to surmise that a desirable consequence of the Academy's operation was developing the habit of mutual moral policing amongst participants in the dialogues, in keeping with the family rhetoric of working in common towards salvation, thereby encouraging the perpetuation of the values the process sought to instil.

Appendix: Little Academy Characters

Participants' ages in 1631, the year the Little Academy was founded, are listed.

The Founder/Mother	Mrs Mary Ferrar, 77
The Guardian	John Ferrar, 43
The Visitour	Nicholas Ferrar, 38
The Moderatour	Susanna Collet (née Ferrar), 50
The Resolved	John Collet, 53

'The Foure Mayden Sisters'

The Cheife [later Mother]	Mary Collet, 30
The Patient	Anna Collet, 28
The Cheerefull	Hester Collet, 24
The Affectionate	Margaret Collet, 23

The Obedient	Elizabeth Collet, 19
The Submisse	Joyce Collet, 16

The Humble	Ann Mapletoft, 3

The Goodwife [later Well-married]	Susanna Mapletoft, 29

There is no record of Mrs Ferrar's character actually participating in the dialogues, though she was probably an observer. She stood down as Mother on St Luke's Day (18 October) 1632. Mary Collet was installed in her place on All Saints' Day (1 November) 1632, taking on the title of Mother. She continued to play a dominant part in the dialogues under her new name.

John Collet, the Resolved, 'who in the want of Roome at first gave way to others for the better Exercize of their Vertues' during the storying sessions, is listed as committing himself to the group at the beginning of 'The Winding Sheet' and figures in the discussion 'On the Retirement of Charles V'.[70]

It is unclear from the records which sisters were the Cheerefull and the Affectionate. Sharland (p. xliv) and Blackstone suggest Margaret and Elizabeth, but are not sure who took which role. Williams makes Hester the Cheerefull and Margaret the Affectionate; his conclusion is followed here.[71]

Ann (Nan) was the daughter of Susanna and Joshua Mapletoft. As a small child she came to live at Little Gidding where her aunt Mary Collet took charge of her care. Nan entered the Little Academy on 1 November 1632 as the Humble, the seventh virtual 'daughter' Mary Collet attained that day when she was installed as the new Mother of the Academy.[72] Sharland calls Nan the 'seventh child of Mrs. Joshua Mapletoft (née Susanna Collet)' (p. xliv); this is incorrect, as Susanna and Joshua Mapletoft had only married in 1628 and by 1632 had at most four children. The Humble cannot have been more than four years old at this time, and her membership of the Academy was symbolic.

The Good Wife is a non-participant character mentioned rarely in the dialogues. The role was probably created for Susanna Mapletoft, the second-eldest Collet sister who was married in 1628 and lived with her husband, the Reverend Joshua Mapletoft, and their children in Margaretting, Essex. Susanna received frequent letters from the family at Little Gidding and, in line with old Mrs Ferrar's bidding, was sent the first volume of the Academy's proceedings on the anniversary of its foundation.[73]

Notes

1   Girls' boarding schools, established to cater for the daughters of the gentry from the late sixteenth century onwards, were known as academies. Kenneth Charlton, *Women, Religion and Education in Early Modern England* (London & New York: Routledge, 1999), pp. 131–41. The children of Little Gidding did not leave the household for their education: the boys had a schoolhouse and schoolmasters on site, and the Little Academy was for their older sisters.

2   Reading a story rather than telling it from memory was regarded as exceptional. For example, the Moderatour is noted as having 'obtained the privilege for that once to read her story, which shortnes of time and other occasions had not given leave fully to finish, much lesse to committ to memory,' 29 Dec 1631, E. Cruwys Sharland, ed. & introd., *The Story Books of Little Gidding* (London: Seeley & Co., 1899), p. 82.

3   Feast of the Purification 1631, Sharland, *Story Books*, p. 2.

4   For a parallel argument concerning the continuity of Erasmus's ideals, including the notion of exemplary lives, transmitted via a rhetorical tradition into English Protestant biography, see Patrick Collinson, '"A Magazine of Religious Patterns": An Erasmian topic transposed in English Protestantism', in *Renaissance and Renewal in Christian History*, ed. Derek Baker (Oxford: Basil Blackwell for the Ecclesiastical History Society, 1997), pp. 223–49.

5   Ursula Potter, 'Performing Arts in the Tudor Classroom', in Lloyd Kermode, Jason Scott-Warren and Martine Van Elk (eds), *Tudor Drama Before Shakespeare, 1495–1590: New Directions for Research, Criticism, and Pedagogy* (Houndmills: Palgrave Macmillan, 2004), p. 148.

6   Lynette R. Muir and John A. White, eds, *Materials for the Life of Nicholas Ferrar*, (Leeds: Leeds Philosophical and Literary Society, 1996), p. 6.
7   Ferrar, *Life*, in Muir and White, *Materials*, p. 82.
8   Muir and White, *Materials*, pp. 17–18.
9   Nicholas Ferrar was not always present to transcribe the dialogues; presumably the sisters worked from their own drafts where his copies were not available.
10 See the letters of 2 Feb 1632 in Sharland, *Story Books*, pp. liii–liv.
11 St Stephen's 1631, Sharland, *Story Books*, p. 20.
12 Blackstone, *Ferrar Papers*, p. 6.
13 'The Lady of the Lights': Ash Wednesday 1631, Sharland, *Story Books*, pp. 8–9; 31 December 1631, pp. 119–22. Juan Luis Vives, *De Institutione Foeminae Christianae*, 1524, trans. Richard Hyrde as *The Instruction of A Christen Woman*, (London, 1529). A digital rendering of Hyrde's 1529 edition together with introductory essays is available from the University of Illinois Press at http://www.press.uillinois.edu/epub/books/vives/toc.html. Quote: 'What bokes be to be redde, and / what nat. The .v. Chapter.' The Ferrars' definition of 'chivalrous tales' was capacious; 'Virgill and Homere ... Ariosto and Spencer' are reviled in a breath on p. 119 of Muir and White, *Materials*. Shortly before his death in 1637, Nicholas Ferrar ordered the immolation of his cache of books, doubtless including romances, on the site where soon he would be interred; he also made written record of the act from his deathbed. See Ferrar, *Life* in Muir and White, *Materials*, pp. 109–10. Nicholas's statement disavowing the books is on p. 111. Evidently he had expressed his intention to burn the collection, which comprised 'many hundreds [of books, in several languages ... comedies, tragedies, love hymns, heroical poems, and such like things' (p. 110), much earlier. The Cheife refers to '... that Bone-fire which is resolved, as soone as Conveniency permitts, to be made of all these kinds of Bookes [like Ariosto's 'Orlando'] by our Visitour' in the dialogue of 31 December 1631, Sharland, *Story Books*, p. 119.
14 See the first paragraph of St Stephen's 1631, Sharland, *Story Books*, p. 19, where the story's omission from the first volume is explained. The dialogue 'On the Retirement of Charles V' is printed in Williams, *Conversations*, pp. 1–156.
15 Holy Innocents' 1631, Sharland, *Story Books*, pp. 59–71.
16 St John the Evangelist 1631, Sharland, *Story Books*, p. 39.
17 Ferrar, *Life* in Muir and White, *Materials*, p. 82. Blackstone (*Ferrar Papers*, p. 100) and Sharland (*Story Books*, title page) claim that the dialogues were held in the great chamber, though no evidence supports their assumption.
18 St John the Evangelist 1631, Sharland, *Story Books*, p. 39.
19 'The Winding Sheet' in Blackstone, *Ferrar Papers*, pp. 197–98 & note.
20 Williams discusses the chronology of the dialogues in his introduction to *Conversations*, pp. xx–xxxiii. For Mrs Ferrar's exhortation and the resolution to re-establish the dialogues, see 'The Winding Sheet' in Blackstone, *Ferrar Papers*, pp. 108–9.
21 Williams, *Conversations*, p. xxix.
22 St Andrew's 1632, Sharland, *Story Books*, p. 242. As a measure of the consequence of their commitment, consider the case of the Resolved (John Collet) in the preamble to the 'Winding Sheet'. He suggested that the participants should be bound to enacting in reality what they recommended in the stories, going so far as to state that doing so was as important a public testimony of faith as their baptismal vows (Blackstone, *Ferrar Papers*,

p. 110).

23 It appears that the younger girls at Little Gidding stopped attending lessons with their brothers, for whom schoolmasters were engaged, around the age of puberty.

24 The dialogue transcripts contain comparatively little reference to the physical aspects of performance, such as gesture, bodily deportment, dance or grace of movement, however, given the emphasis conventionally accorded them in prescriptions for boys' schooling, for example. Actions of this sort were associated with oratory and commercial theatre; neither were approved activities or occupations for women. 'It would be difficult to overstate the extraordinary value Tudor grammar schools placed on action;' on *chironomia* or 'rhetorical dancing' see Potter, 'Performing Arts in the Tudor Classroom', pp. 152–54 (quote: p. 153). See also McCabe, *Introduction to Jesuit Theater*, p. 20.

25 Sharland, *Story Books*, p. 2.

26 'On The Retirement of Charles V', in Williams, *Conversations*, p. 137 and quoted by him on p. xxxiii. In the footnote to the dialogue text (n. 1, p. 137) Williams identifies the Submisse as Judith Collet, whereas the Submisse is Joyce Collet in his introduction (p. xxxiii). Joyce or her sister Elizabeth must have been the Submisse, as Judith was born in 1624 and therefore would have been too young to participate in the dialogues.

27 Sharland, *Story Books*, p. 2.

28 Vives, *Instruction of A Christen Woman*, trans. Hyrde, 1529. http://www.press.uillinois.edu/epub/books/vives/ch1.html#1.7.

29 Sharland, *Story Books*, p. lii.

30 'The old gentlewoman set herself down in her chair and this was her constant place; some or other of her daughters or her grandchildren were always there. Some too young to go to school sat there in great silence either at their books or otherwise, and the elder, some to their needleworks, others to learn what they were to say next day…', Ferrar, *Life* in Muir and White, *Materials*, pp. 82–83.

31 Ferrar, *Life* in Muir and White, *Materials*, p. 41.

32 Charlton, *Women, Religion and Education*, p. 96.

33 For the description of the installation ritual: All Saints' 1632, Sharland, *Story Books*, pp. 173–84.

34 St Luke 1632, Sharland, *Story Books*, p. 163.

35 St Stephen 1631, Sharland, *Story Books*, p. 19.

36 'On the Austere Life' in Williams, *Conversations*, pp. 159–315; see also Williams' Introduction, pp. xxviii–xxix.

37 Edmund S. Morgan, 'Puritan Hostility to the Theatre', *Proceedings of the American Philosophical Society*, 110.5 (Oct. 1966), 340–347, is the seminal work on anti-theatrical sentiment in Elizabethan and early Stuart England.

38 William Prynne, *Histrio-Mastix: The Player's Scourge; or, Actor's Tragedy* (London, 1633).

39 See, for example, Andrea Wilson Nightingale, *Genres in Dialogue: Plato and the Construct of Philosophy* (Cambridge: Cambridge University Press, 1995); Francisco J. Gonzalez, *Dialectic and Dialogue: Plato's Practice of Philosophical Inquiry* (Evanston: Northwestern University Press, 1998).

40 Potter, 'Performing Arts in the Tudor Classroom', p. 144.

41 On school drama, see Ursula Potter, 'Pedagogy and Parenting in English Drama,

1560–1610: Flogging Schoolmasters and Cockering Mothers', unpublished PhD thesis, University of Sydney, 2001, available at http://hdl.handle.net/2123/356.

42   Ferrar, *Life* in Muir and White, *Materials*, p. 82.

43   A catechism was attached to the order for confirmation from the first edition of the *Book of Common Prayer* (1549) and an extended version remained a feature of the 1662 prayer book. Ian Green's three-part study is the definitive work on catechesis and education in the Protestant faith in England following the reformation: *'The Christian's ABC': Catechisms and Catechizing in England c. 1530–1730* (Oxford: Oxford University Press, 1996); *Print and Protestantism in Early Modern England* (Oxford: Oxford University Press, 2000); *Word, Image and Ritual: Protestant Instruction in Early Modern England* (provisional title) (Oxford: Oxford University Press, forthcoming). On catechesis as a method of religious education, see Charlton, *Women, Religion and Education*, pp. 89–92.

44   John Warrack, *German Opera: from the Beginnings to Wagner* (Cambridge: Cambridge University Press, 2001), p. 4.

45   Elissa B. Weaver, *Convent Theatre in Early Modern Italy: Spiritual Fun and Learning for Women* (Cambridge: Cambridge University Press, 2002), pp. 54–55.

46   On Jesuit drama: William H. McCabe, *An Introduction to the Jesuit Theater*, ed. Louis J. Oldani (St Louis: The Institute of Jesuit Sources, 1983). For a fascinating study of 'autodidactic drama' in Jesuit education, the power of performance in stirring up devotion in young people, and the role of children or youths as exemplary figures, see Alison Shell, *"'Furor juvenilis"*: post-Reformation English Catholicism and exemplary youthful behaviour', in *Catholics and the 'Protestant Nation'*, ed. Ethan Shagan (Manchester and New York: Manchester University Press, 2005), pp. 185–206.

47   Robert White, *Cupid's Banishment: A Masque Presented to Her Majesty by the Young Gentlewomen of the Ladies Hall, Deptford, May 4, 1617*, ed. and intro. C.E. McGee, *Renaissance Drama*, n.s., 19 (1988), pp. 227–64. The play text is also reproduced in S. P. Cerasano and Marion Wynne-Davies eds, *Renaissance Drama by Women: Texts and Documents* (London and New York: Routledge, 1996), pp. 76–89. Cf. I. A. Shapiro, who suggests that 'Ladies Hall' refers to the accommodations of the younger gentlewomen who attended the great ladies of the queen's entourage, not an independent school, and thus the players in *Cupid's Banishment* were young ladies-in-waiting. Letter to the editor, *Review of English Studies*, n.s., 21.84 (Nov. 1970), 472–73.

48   McGee, Introduction to *'Cupid's Banishment'*, pp. 228–29. The masque's conventional veneration of chaste love celebrated the girls' readiness for marriage, implying sexual maturity and invoking the managed conjugal sexuality supposedly epitomized by the royal couple.

49   Bridget Hill, 'A Refuge from Men: The Idea of a Protestant Nunnery', *Past and Present*, 117 (Nov 1987), 111–12. For Hill's comments on Little Gidding, see pp. 110–11. For the Great Tew Circle, see Hugh Trevor-Roper, *Catholics, Anglicans and Puritans: Seventeenth-Century Essays* (London: Secker and Warburg, 1987), pp. 166–230.

50   Mary Astell, *A Serious Proposal to the Ladies, for the advancement of their true and greatest interest by a lover of her sex* (London, 1694).

51   St John the Evangelist 1631, Sharland, *Story Books*, p. 44.

52 St John the Evangelist 1631, Sharland, *Story Books*, p. 39. The church at Little Gidding is dedicated to St John the Evangelist, so it is possible that the feast was one of particular consequence for the family.

53 St John the Evangelist 1631, Sharland, *Story Books*, p. 39.

54 The distinction may be quibbling: Andrew Gurr argues that 'in the sixteenth century the term "acting" was originally used to describe the "action" itself of the orator, his art of gesture. What the common stages offered was "playing".' *The Shakespearean Stage 1574–1642*, third edn (Cambridge: Cambridge University Press, 1992), p. 99.

55 Ash Wednesday 1631, Sharland, *Story Books*, p. 6.

56 St Stephen's 1631, Sharland, *Story Books*, pp. 20–21.

57 St John the Evangelist 1631, Sharland, *Story Books*, p. 39.

58 31 Dec 1631, Sharland, *Story Books*, p. 103.

59 29 Dec 1631, Sharland, *Story Books*, pp. 72–73, 88–89.

60 Ferrar, *Life*, in Muir and White, *Materials*, pp. 70, 75. Contemporary educationalists stressed the importance of memorizing texts, particularly in learning religion; for example John Brinsley, *Ludus Literarius: or, The grammar schoole* ... (London, 1612), described by Rosemary O'Day in her *Education and Society 1500–1800: The Social Foundations of Education in Early Modern Britain* (London & New York: Longman, 1982), p. 51.

61 For example, reading from the Gospel concordance. Ferrar, *Life* in Muir and White, *Materials*, pp. 76, 81.

62 Ferrar, *Life* in Muir and White, *Materials*, p. 73.

63 Ferrar, *Life* in Muir and White, *Materials*, pp. 83–84.

64 Ferrar, *Life* in Muir and White, *Materials*, p. 84.

65 Ferrar, *Life* in Muir and White, *Materials*, p. 84.

66 Ferrar, *Life* in Muir and White, *Materials*, p. 84.

67 Sharland, *Story Books*, p. 61.

68 The exception to the rule was the Humble, Nan Mapletoft, who was initiated into the Academy as the seventh 'daughter' of Mary Collet on 1 November 1632. See: All Saints' 1632, Sharland, *Story Books*, pp. 181–82. Nan cannot have been more than four at this time; her parents, Susanna Collet and Joshua Mapletoft, having married in 1628 (see the Appendix to this essay).

69 St Andrew's 1632, Sharland, *Story Books*, p. 243.

70 'The Winding Sheet' (preamble), in Blackstone, *Ferrar Papers*, p. 110. 'On the Retirement of Charles V' in Williams, *Conversations*, pp. 1–156.

71 Williams, *Conversations*, p. xxxii.

72 All Saints' 1632, Sharland, *Story Books*, pp. 181–82.

73 See the letters of 2 Feb. 1632 in Sharland, *Story Books*, pp. liii–liv.

Seeking a Voice:
Lady Grace Mildmay and the Constraints
of Conduct Literature

Philippa Kelly

'My father could not abide to see a woman unstable or light in her carriage, to hold her head one way and her hands another and her feet a third way, her eyes tossing about in every place and the features of her face disfigured by evil countenances', writes Lady Grace Mildmay in the later life autobiography that she wills to her grandchildren (1617). 'But he liked a woman well graced with a constant and settled countenance and good behaviour throughout her whole parts, which presenteth to all men a good hope of an established mind and virtuous disposition to be in her.'[1] Thus emerges an impeccable image of Grace Mildmay herself, a seventeenth-century English gentlewoman with exemplary physical and social containment—perfectly ordered, nothing out of place, all of her features and gestures suggesting a composite harmony.[2] In a patriarchal society—one in which many woman read but did not write, and in which a woman's writings were sometimes managed by a male editorial hand[3]—Lady Grace's voice is strong, bolstered by the confidence that she is writing for the glory of God. Repeatedly seeking for her words to be 'approved', she turns first to God—'This book of mine is the consolation of my soul, the joy of my heart and the stability of my mind, as they are approved by the word of God' (p. 25)—and then to her descendants: '[T]here is nothing [which] hath happened unto me in the course of my life ... but the like may fall out to some other, wherein my comforts and remedies may be approved unto them as they have been unto me' (p. 25).

Anticipating at every turn her temporal and divine audiences, Lady Grace's autobiography bears the constant weight of biblical allusions and instructional purposes, so that any search for psychological inwardness—for a sense of *who* she was as an individual—yields little more than a patchwork of formalized commonplaces. To simply call such discourse 'autobiography' or 'life-writing' raises intriguing and complicated questions. What motivates this gentlewoman, at an advanced age, to record the events of her life? What does she intend her readers to see? Strained by the freight of worldly and eternal concerns, how do her words reveal, or conceal, elements that we might deem 'autobiographical'? And a larger question hovers over these particulars: how might this private, upper-class gentlewoman speak, if at all, to the category, 'early modern Englishwoman'?

People's lives are, and always have been, subject to interpretation through conjecture. This is even more the case with the lives of early modern women because of their culturally encoded silence.[4] In the effort to tease out the quieted voices of women who lived four hundred years ago, approaches have been made from many different places, including the liberties and permissions granted by gendered identity and, more specifically, by gendered writing, which, in devotional contexts, associates supplication with a conventionally feminine narrative stance;[5] analyses of the socially-constructed meanings of women's deaths;[6] discussions of childbirth,[7] work,[8] and literacy,[9] as well as attempts to discern a voice amongst the many women who could neither read nor write. Amidst the huge wealth of material by early modern women that could possibly direct our attention, and an even more dizzying variety of possible critical perspectives, this contribution to the volume takes Mildmay as its subject, relating her life-writings to the blueprint offered by her understanding of her generational continuum, by her biblical education, and by the conduct literature—unyielding, instructional, and narrowly focused—from which she took guidance (and to which, indeed, she contributed through her own autobiographical writings). An understanding of these highly formulaic influences can enable us to contemplate 'self-representation' in terms of the strict moral, educational, generational and social functions through which Mildmay knows and expresses herself.

Invoking a blueprint

'There is nothing that hath so much power to poison the world as the press', says Joseph Hall, Bishop of Norwich,

> which is able, in one day's warning, to scatter an heresy over the whole face of the earth. In the times of our forefathers, when every page and line was to pass the leisure and pains of a single pen, books were geason [scarce] and, if offensive, could not so easily light into many hands to work a speedy mischief. Error, that could but creep then, doth now fly, and in a moment cuts the air of several regions ... we have reasons to rue the inconveniences that have followed upon the abuses of this so beneficial a practice. For, as all men are apt to write their own fancies, so they have, by this means [of print], had the opportunity to divulge their conceits to all eyes and ears: whence it hath come to pass, that those monstrous opinions, which had been fit only to be condemned to perpetual darkness, have at once both visited and infected the public light ... Never age or nation hath had more cause to cry out of this mischief than this age of ours.[10]

Written in 1640, Hall's words give shape to the fears that grew along with the expansion of print culture. Acknowledging in all men the impulse for some kind of life-writing or self-expression ('all men are apt to write their own fancies'), he sees the press as turning such fancies from private self-gratification to devilish proliferation. Important for this discussion is firstly the acknowledgement of private life-writing as an impulse and a practice; and secondly the counsel not to cancel out such fancies, but to curb their distribution. These fancies are, Hall ruefully acknowledges, an unfortunate part of human nature, and should be designated to darkness as to a latrine—it is only when aired that they spread infection. Against the judicious singularity of his forefathers' careful pens, therefore, Hall counterbalances the 'mischief[s]' wrought by those who facilitate easy distribution; to the former he ascribes the word of God, while to the latter he attributes the spread of 'monstrous opinions'.

Lady Grace's autobiography contributes to the war about words that accelerates, in the early seventeenth century, toward Hall's gloomy conclusions. The autobiography follows in the tradition of the 'godlie' conduct book convention that was developed amongst Puritan gatekeepers as a counterweight to the corrupting influence of secular publications. As increasing numbers of women—many of whom could read even if they did not write—had access to printed matter, such 'godlie' books were designed to confirm right conduct as well as right relations between husbands and wives, parents and children, masters and servants, matrons and maids.[11] The main focus of instruction was what Patrick Hannay called the 'weake sexe' of womankind, requiring firm direction.[12] 'I would haue her if she reade', says Thomas Salter, 'to reade no other bookes but suche as bee written by godlie fathers, to our instruction and soules healthe, and not suche lasciuious Songes, filthie Ballades, and undecent bookes as be moste commonly now a daies sette to sale, to the greate infection of youth' (p. 39). The words of such fathers were divine instruments, able to 'delight' women *and* to 'pricke and incite their hartes, to follow vertue, and haue vice in horror and disdaine, yea their mindes ... wilbe come noble and magnanimous thereby' (p. 23). Lady Grace's intention is in concert with such opinions: she desires that 'whosoever readeth them [her words] may make good use of them, especially seeing they shall find every point of doctrine confirmed and approved by the scriptures' (p. 24).

Against the proliferation of idle words, then, Lady Grace adds her own trenchant avowal of the indisputable word of God. 'Books of idle plays' she sees as 'fruitless and unprofitable matter which will pervert and carry the mind from all goodness and is an introduction to all evil' (p. 24). At the outset of her autobiography she declares that she will never 'receive any doctrine from men which proceedeth not from God according to the truth of his word in all sanctity and true holiness' (p. 23). Words provide a direct connection between God's will and earthly acts; and the task of humankind is to defend them against abuse and misapprehension. It is to this purpose that her own words are dedicated; and she describes her clear intention to map 'the best course to set ourselves in from the beginning to the end of our lives', alluding to the need to understand, and to be obedient to, the laws of God and 'the chronicles of the land' (p. 23).

The larger framework of the generational continuum to which Lady Grace constantly alludes provides a justification for her own life-writing. '[T]he Lady Despencer ... hath endowed you with her ancient and noble blood', she writes to her grand-daughter, Mildmay Fane. 'Preserve that blood unspotted evermore as she hath done, chaste and upright in all her virtuous conversation from her youth unto her old age' (p. 43). Such is Lady Grace's own purpose: justifying her memoir through her duty to memorialize the venerable conduct of her ancestors and to pass down their counsel to her descendants, she records her own life as a commendable part of this God-fearing lineage. And in the very ordinariness of her reflections, strung together as they are through biblical allusions and the sage commonplaces that she draws from the conduct literature of her time, she reflects the entire lineage of worthy individuals within its proper larger picture, which is 'a testimony of the love and presence of God', a God who will 'be with them forever and increase and multiply the gifts of his holy spirit in them'. Her memoir provides a means of ordering both the retrospective and proleptic dimensions of her life, documenting 'the perfection of a good life in this world and everlasting blessedness in the kingdom of heaven' (p. 24).

Like a curator at the door of a museum, then, Lady Grace guides us through her life, proffering her age and experience as the correct vantage point for examining its value. Constantly underscored by passages from the Bible, her narrative insists that the record of her life—and of all lives past and future—remains ultimately with God, and that to record her life at all is not just a temporal event but an eternal one. It is this understanding of the eternal within the temporal that grants plausibility to an account that appears, at times, wilfully misrepresentational. As we will see in the section following, the author practices a wilful concealment or 'alternative construction' of events because it is the *template* of the past that is essential to her own literary self-expression, requiring all who visit its pages to accept the conditions of the time-honoured model on which she draws. And this is a strong feature of early modern Protestant women's life-stories—those written by them and on their behalf—in which the self-assertion permitted by the narrative form necessitates self-effacement, a constantly remarked-upon subjection to God's design that becomes, in effect, the 'statement' of selfhood.[13]

I. The gendering of spiritual identity

Elspeth Graham has identified two important themes pertaining to recent studies on early modern women: one that represents women as negatively defined and lacking positive identity; and the other that focuses on the degree of empowerment permitted to them through flexible gender constructions. Because of the fluidity permitted by a perceived lack of gender definition, women had room to manipulate their identities.

So, for instance, as many accounts of cross-dressing indicate, women—understood to be frailer and more impressionable—could appropriate masculine signs of power, and thus masculine power *itself*, by dressing as men. And this fluidity in turn highlighted the very 'constructedness' of identity: masculine superiority was understood to be imposed rather than intrinsic, a social interpretation rather than a biological necessity. Uncertainty prevailed about the very marks of gender that were relied upon for the functioning of domestic/public duties, and for understandings of propagation and laws of inheritance.[14] This gendered frailty provides a useful way into a perception of the gendering of religious beliefs. Firstly, the privacy of devotion is seen as commensurate with a woman's 'natural' private space, the home, and the attitude of supplication with her 'naturally' gendered piety.[15] 'My beloved is as a bundle of myrrh unto me, he shall lie between my breasts', says Lady Grace, echoing the Song of Solomon.[16] 'His mouth is as sweet things and he is wholly delectable'.[17] 'Oh, let my wellbeloved lay his left hand under my head and with his right hand let him embrace me' (75).[18] The sexualization of devotional language grants to women a certain power: their 'naturally' passive role demeanour serves as a model for mortals who seek unity with God.[19] Thus we see men, as well as women, expressing themselves as wedded to God with the lavish adoration of a corporeal lover.[20]

But if on the one hand femininity provides an ideal posture for devotion—one that men readily adopt in their conversations with God—running counter to this is the strain of rigidity identified as inherently 'masculine'. And this very identification depends upon the clear subordination of woman as the 'weaker' gender. William Gouge represents such negative reliance in his determination of man's 'superioritie and authoritie' as deriving directly from God. God is the true husband upon whom a woman's first 'hopes and desires' are fixed, and 'the sweet Bridegroom' of a woman's soul.[21] 'An honeste woman ought not behynde her husbandes back to haunt any evell company', counsels Thomas Becon, while Thomas Salter warns against contact with 'kitchine seruauntes' and 'idle housewiues', who should be 'shonned, as infectious diseases' (p. 25). For William Whately, likewise, a woman's 'impudency and unwomanhood, doth track the way to the harlots house'.[22] And in looking to Lady Grace's writings, we see the careful self-subordination of a strong, resourceful woman as manifesting this very contradiction between gendered form and frailty. A woman who (as we shall see in subsequent paragraphs) has coped self-reliantly with domestic and financial handicaps, yet insists on modelling the ideal for silent and dutiful self-comportment: learning from man 'with silence, and all subjection' is a woman's earthly place. 'Let not a woman teach', she advises, paraphrasing St Paul to Timothy, 'neither usurp authority over the man, but be in silence' (p. 45).

The gendered relationships in Lady Grace's life are fascinating for the ingenious way in which she was able to manipulate gender conventions to create a devotional frame for her 'self' and her life. Having been promised much by his father, Sir Walter Mildmay, her future husband, Sir Anthony, reluctantly entered into marriage, only to find that he and his bride were kept as virtual paupers in his father's house. While it was common among aristocratic families for a newly married couple to live as guests of the groom's parents for a few months or even a few years, Lady Grace—living, with her husband, on a combined allowance of 130 pounds per year to cover their clothing as well as the cost of personal servants and other household needs—was kept in this situation for the next twenty years. Sir Anthony stayed at large for a half of each year, leaving Lady Grace to make her own life in her father-in-law's home. It is clear that her record of her life is not motivated by familiar modern-day sensibilities, the interest of which is likely to be, for example, in the revelation of her own, or her husband's, or her father-in-law's, psychology. Rather, her struggle is to match the events and relationships in her life to the proportions of godly living. And it is this feature—the way in which she subordinates a highly neglectful situation (an absent husband, a shallow and mean-minded father-in-law) to the requirements of her spiritual journey—that permits some access to *who* Lady Grace is.

First and foremost, Lady Grace sees herself as an exemplary Christian figure, and wishes to contribute this fact to an ongoing communication with future generations. To this end, the all-too evident shortcomings of the Mildmay men are remarked upon, but not puzzled over, because their function is representational rather than revelatory. While Lady Grace declares the primacy of both men in her life, they have only a figurative connection to the consummate narrative of her relationship with God. 'The goodness of the Lord … hath ever followed me so from time to time … [and] is worthy to be remembered of me and all that discerned of me, from one generation to another', she says, adding to the generational mix an ancient strain of Psalm 100. 5: 'For the Lord is good; his mercy is everlasting; and his truth endureth to all generations' (p. 85). Neatly triangulating her relationship to God, husband and father-in-law, of her husband she notes that 'I have observed an extraordinary favour of God toward him divers ways wherein appeared the love, mercy and protection of God over him' (p. 41), and of her father-in-law she says, 'I thought myself in the house of God all the time of my abode with my father-in-law, for that no evil company was permitted to resort to his house nor to appear in his presence, whereby I was preserved from the sight or hearing of evil' (p. 34).

II. Spiritual identity and double time

In narrating the events of her life in this way, Lady Grace links her identity to the awareness of what can be called 'double time'. The various events of her temporal life are mentioned as points of absorption into the reality that *matters*: the union with God that goes beyond time. This is the reality that she derives through her own lineage, and that she, in turn, bequeaths to her descendants. Indeed, *not* to bequeath it would be a mark of gross spiritual failure. Lady Grace's material life, it should be noted, is very much taken up with financial matters: the shortfall in the funds promised by Sir Walter and the paltry inheritance that Sir Anthony receives from him; the expectation of inheritance from her own father, broken at the very last moment by his rewriting of his will under the persuasions of her sister; the recovery of the original will, the battle with her sister to have this former will validated, and the getting together of a dowry for her daughter, which is complicated by the parsimony of her deceased father and father-in-law. In all of this, however, the devoutness of her path remains central. She is the servant, and the supplicant, of God, patiently expecting the bounty that runs through, and beyond, the events of this world, and discerning in the apparent arbitrariness of temporal life an enduring divine wisdom. Having been taught from her childhood days 'to look for troubles, which appertaineth to all the children of God' (p. 28), she sees adversity as an opportunity, given by God, to be resourceful: 'There was never any thing more blessed unto me in this life than mine afflictions and trials which were never greater than God enabled me to bear' (p. 39). Keeping this in mind, her gift of a dowry to her daughter without any care for her own straitened means provides evidence of faith in 'the abundance of God's blessing' (p. 36). And she sees her blessings as many: 'as I gave myself wholly into God ... so he received me graciously and preserved me in safety and diverted and prospered me' (p. 34).

God's blessing is thus given not only 'ever', but everywhere, in the life depicted by Lady Grace (p. 72). 'For whensoever we receive this holy sacrament of our Lord Jesus Christ his blessed body and blood, worthily, faithfully and according to his holy institution; the fountains of the gardens are broken unto us, the well of living waters floweth out unto us and the springs of Lebanon runneth swiftly unto us throughout all our parts; from our head unto our feet, so that no part is left unwashed or unrefreshed' (p. 77). Here she paraphrases the Song of Solomon (4. 15–16) to express the organic, and highly sexualized, union between God's eternal life and her own mortal body. The point about this—and about practically every other of her quotations cited here—is that she expresses her spirituality in terms of constant textual pastiche, pasting it together from the archives of the spiritual education she gleans from her readings in the Bible and conduct literature, and echoing the Hebrew erotic poem as an allegory of Christ's relationship to the Christian soul. Distinctively derivative, imitative and allusive, her prose strains after quasi-biblical authenticity through the layering of linguistic analogy.

But if this (borrowed) language can merge body and soul, it can also effect a radical splitting between them; and this rupture is, for Lady Grace, a hazard of corporeal existence, in which the beating of 'my heart' is 'the original of all the desires and evil carriage of my mortal body' (p. 74). Her autobiography, derivative as it is, continually reminds us of the strain of this division: 'Oh, my stubborn and crooked heart, weaker and much worse than my corrupt and sinful flesh' (p. 74). In the record of her life the division is, in a sense, 'healed' by the author's constant reminder to herself of the eternal meaning that underscores temporal affairs. Describing her solicitousness towards relatives and servants and their ungrateful plotting against her, for example, she understands that they 'rendered me evil for good' (p. 86). Their injustice, and the suffering woman's righteousness, are already anticipated by, and resolved within, her integrative narrative: its devotional blueprint gives her a 'natural' claim to the role of suffering, righteous being as chosen by God. And God, quite unsurprisingly, 'turned his loving countenance towards me' (p. 37).

Lady Grace's autobiography can in this sense be seen as a means of knitting up the inexplicable, the erratic, or the inexcusable, within the seamless horizon of eternal justice. Again and again, in addressing the double dimensions of her existence, she draws on the generational continuum that connects her life in the world to her life beyond it. Her 'unspotted garment' is a state of innocence, preserved against the evils of the world: 'I spent the best part of my youth in solitariness, shunning all opportunities to run into company least I might be enticed and drawn away by some evil suggestions to stain mine unspotted garment and so be robbed of mine innocency' (p. 34). This image recalls the 'chaste and upright' bearing of her 'unspotted' forbear, Lady Despencer, as well as the 'unspotted carriage' of Sir Walter Mildmay: 'the Lord so led and carried me in all my ways and preserved mine innocency so unspotted' (p. 38). And in her typically Protestant caution about the insinuating presence of evil, she joins a wider epistolary movement by women whose purpose in writing letters to their descendants was to endorse the path of spirituality and to bolster them against the workings of the devil.[23]

In appreciating Lady Grace's relationship to the temporal and the eternal—and, more specifically, her insistence upon integrating the temporal *within* the larger frame of the eternal—there emerges a striking parallel between the 'materials' of metaphor and corporeality. The unspotted metaphysical apparel of herself and her ancestors— her insistence upon a clean and unadorned spirituality—are consonant with her physical bearing. Of women's dress she echoes 1 Peter 3. 3–4 in a conspicuous conjunction of corporeal and spiritual quiet composure: 'For even after this manner in time past did ... the holy women which trusted in God attire themselves and were subject to their husbands' (p. 44). She also cites the advice of her mother, Lady Sherrington, who 'said that she could give me jewels and pearl and costly apparel. But she would not until I were furnished with virtue in my mind and decked inwardly and willed me first to seek the kingdom of God' (p. 28). In recruiting her generational continuum to assist in preserving the chastity of body and soul, Lady Grace follows those conduct writers who deplored the stereotype of worldly women, prone 'idlely and wanto[n]ly to gad abrod' (Becon, p. 281), 'scorn[ing] to be closed vp in any obscure place' (Rich, p. 249), and whose garish clothing and makeup flouts their husbands' gravity (Gouge, p.115). 'It is the guise of … harlots to prancke and pricke up themselves to inueigle men's affections', says Snawsel's well-spoken character Eulalie, whereas 'honest and religious matrons, we are neat inough, if we be cleanly, and can please our husbands' (p. 117). In response to these stereotypes, Lady Grace suggests that a woman's apparel, like her mind, must be modest and subordinate to her husband, and, echoing her mother, she quotes approvingly from 1 Timothy 2. 9–10, 'let women array themselves in comely apparel with shamefastness and modesty, not with braided hair or gold or pearl or costly apparel, but (as becometh women that profess the fear of God) with good works' (p. 45).

It is perhaps entirely predictable that women like Lady Grace are inclined to define themselves counter to the stereotype of the woman who dresses with attention to detail and gads about town. Her interest is not in examining what is *in* the world, but in its contributive effect on her eternal life. Claiming little interest in getting herself up for the temporal world, it is somewhat ironic that she does indeed 'get herself up' just as meticulously for the masculine spiritual judge who takes great notice of her studious asceticism. Indeed, advice books of the period are embellished again and again with the image of bodily asceticism as God's mirror. Dorothy Leigh says for example:

> for who so is truly chaste, is free from idlenesse and from all vaine delights, full of humility, and all good Christian vertues: who so is chaste, is not giuen to pride in apparel, nor any vanity, but is alwaies either reading, meditating, or practising some good thing which she hath learned in the Scripture.[24]

'The vnchaste woman', she adds, 'is proud, and always decking her selfe with vanity … but also so much wickednesse' (p. 27). She likens such women to 'strumpets and whores, who for couetousnesse sake sell their soules and bodies, and make themselues such filthie vessels in this earth, that it is most loathsome to thinke of'. They 'bragge as well of their jewels and costly apparel that the world bestoweth upon them' (p. 50). In an advice book to her unborn child, Elizabeth Jocelin laments the fact that such women are praised before those of true merit: '[I]f the time mends not before you come to understanding', she says, 'you will heare a well drest woman … more commended than a wise or honest, or religious woman'.[25] Asceticism for Mildmay, as for Leigh and Jocelin, exists as a visible, and necessary, sign of rectitude. For such women themselves, dressing and acting with modesty signals the (modest) expectation of their own understandings. 'Let wives submit themselves unto their husbands as unto the lord', Lady Grace recites from the epistles, 'as the church is in subjection unto Christ, even so let the wives be to the husbands in every thing' (p. 44). She praises 'time past' when 'the holy women which trusted in God attire[d] themselves and were subject to their husbands' (p. 44). Through this understanding of God's will as mediated on earth, they express themselves and, indeed, justify their thoughts as 'worth' expressing.

III. 'God had placed me in this house': the meaning of domestic life

Historians and literary critics have devoted a good deal of attention to the nature and scope of women's occupation in Lady Grace's times.[26] This subject was also heavily debated by her contemporaries, with several writers dramatizing debates about upper-class women's entitlement to expansive social roles.[27] Sir Thomas Elyot's Platonic dialogue, *The Defence of Good Women* (1545), reflects the wish of humanists to promote women's capacity for virtuous action, and to suggest that the compass of such action should not be confined to the home.[28] Nicholas Breton's *The Praise of Virtuous Ladies* (1580) offers a more light-hearted, and highly rhetorical, defence of women's sense and virtue; while Robert Snawsel's *A Looking-glasse for married folks* (1610) dramatizes a debate between various women about the ideal extent of their social and domestic roles.[29] In arguing for the benefits of women's learning, Richard Hyrde examines the various reasons against it, countering each negative with a positive: 'I never heard tell nor read of any woman well learned that ever was (as plenteous as evil tongues be) spotted or infamed as vicious. But on the other side, many by their learning taken such increase of goodness that many may bear them witness of their virtue.'[30] Jane Anger's 'Protection for Women' (1589)[31] argues strongly for women's right to action and self-government. And the debate about women's capacities and capabilities is staged not only in pamphlets and conduct manuals, but also in journals and commonplace books left to descendants. William Dethick, for example, leaves us this diary note:

> God hath created a woman, to be an helper to man, and made hir of his fleshe and bone, therefore above all mortale things is she to be honored, no less than Man, having in hir, all [pure extollments] as may be founde in Man viz fortitude ... [the capacity] to distinguishe good from evill. God hath also given to woman, and man, indifferently, knowledge of his miraculous workes, [and they] both, doe glorifye his name. Yea by Women, men are honored, and may not be [divorced] from them ... Adam was composed of earthe, or claye: But Eve was made of a man's ribb ... And honoring the vertue of ffortitude (no more commended in Man) by great and good examples, it may be proved, that woman['s virtue should be] extolled, no lesse than Man. The magnanimity of Minerva, Mother to Apollo, appeared in manye bloodye battalls.[32]

No matter how trenchant the arguments for women's independence, however, it remained that men, in the main, mistrusted women's capacity for prudent judgement. 'He who lets his wife go to every feast and his horse drinke at every water, shall have neither good wife nor goode horse', facetiously wrote Sir Francis Fane, husband to Lady Grace's daughter Mary, in a commonplace manuscript now lodged at the

Folger Library.[33] Thomas Burton notoriously linked the thinking gentlewoman to an increased susceptibility to mental defect and depression: 'For seldom should you see an hired servant, a poor handmaid, though ancient, that is kept hard to her work and bodily labour, a coarse country wench troubled in this kind.'[34] Excellence in housewifery—not simply 'the art of keeping house as a wife' but also the art of house-management—was a means by which to usefully evaluate women of varying ranks and occupations.[35] And the writers of advice books—even if they avoided accusations of madness, or the extremes of Joseph Swetnam's misogynistic *The arraignment of lewde, idle, froward and unconstant women*[36] (first published in 1615 as a response to Anger's 'Protection for Women')—did much to entrench this view about women's domestic suitability and accountability. According to Heinrich Bullinger, for example, the honest woman should never 'go eny where without her husbandes knowledge and leaue' or 'take upon her anye farre iourney. And yf hir husband be gone forth or be not at home, let hir holde hirselfe as a wedow and lyue quiet'.[37] In his *Catechisme*, Thomas Becon exhorts women 'continually to remain at home in their house, diligentlye and vertuously occupied, except urgent, waighty and necessary causes compell her to go forth, as to go unto the church, to pray or to hear the worde of God, to help with sick neighbors or to … go to the market to bie things necessary for her houshold'.[38] Thomas Salter counsels 'a Maiden, beyng become wife, by the instruction and teachying of her prudent Mistres', to 'be sufficient to gouerne a houshold and familie discretely' (p. 39). For Patrick Hannay, 'It befits not Man for to imbrace/Domesticke charge, so its not Womans place/For to be busied with affairs abroad:/For that weake sexe, it is too great a load' (p. 376). And Richard Braithwaite urges women, where possible, not to venture out at all: 'for divers maine respects, a custome very irregular and undecent, that *Women* should frequent places of *Publike* resort, as Stage-playes, Wakes, solemne Feasts, and the like'.[39]

Lady Grace's self-identity complies firmly with the outlines of such manuals: 'God had placed me in this house, and if I found no comfort here, I would never seek it out of this house and this was my certain resolution' (p. 34). All of her activities in the home—her morning studies in divinity, her singing ('I … practiced my voice in singing of psalms and in making my prayers to God and confessing my sins' [p. 35]), her drawing and needlework ('I found in myself that God wrought with me in all' [p. 35])—are illustrated as acts of piety. Prominent amongst her worthy household acts is her medical practice. Despite the disdain expressed by (predictably male) physicians for those 'inauthentical' women whose claims to medical knowledge amounted to 'dangerous whisperings about the sick',[40] administering 'physick' within the limits of womanly skill was seen as an important aspect of a housewife's training. In his tract, *The English Housewife,* Gervase Markham, who, in early 1615, published one of the most comprehensive guides for women's household instruction, recommends for housewives 'a physical kind of knowledge; how to administer many wholesome receipts or medicines' to household members and (for the gentry) to servants and field workers. 'The depths and secrets of this most excellent art of physic', he adds, 'is far beyond the capacity of the most skillful woman, as lodging only in the breast of the learned professors; yet that our housewife may from them receive some ordinary rules and medicines which may avail for the benefit of her family is ... no derogation to that worthy art.'[41] It was acceptable for a woman to learn some physic from her father, as in the case of Mary Trye, for example.[42] And during her lifetime Lady Grace acquired a good deal of medical knowledge. Having read, in her youth, 'Dr Turner's herbal and in Bartholomew Vigoe' [a work of surgery]' (p. 26), she records her own medical contributions as a form of praise for God, who has given humankind 'precious gums for medicine' as well as the 'wisdom and knowledge to use them' (p. 84). But unlike some of her contemporaries who developed similar skills and interests—Anne Harcourt and Margaret Hoby, for instance—Lady Grace did not go out to treat the sick. Rather, all her work was done within the home, under the strict guidance of the medical experts with whom she corresponded. Her memoirs evidence no disapprobation from them, nor from any other men (including God), in response to her use of medical knowledge: 'every day I spent some time in the herbal and books of physic and in ministering to one or other by the directions of the best physicians of mine acquaintance, and ever God gave a blessing thereunto' (p. 35).

What words mean

In comparing the diary mode with that of autobiography, Dean Ebner makes the important point that an autobiography is a 'life-review' in which an individual undertakes to examine a personal life-history. A diary, in contrast, generally purports to record a life in progress.[43] Elaine McKay concludes on this basis that as readers we do not expect the same level of retrospective analysis in a diary that we do in an autobiography.[44] Taking the vantage of hindsight to organize and cohere her life, Lady Grace is able to retrospectively map her experience, presenting it as an entirety fit for the divine. Rounding up days and years within the thrust of an ongoing narrative, she firmly establishes the temporal (adversities, triumphs, celebrations and practices) as an ongoing exercise in the service of God. She emerges as a clearly delineated figure, providing a stout narrative encasement in which to preserve the piety of herself and her family. She might be seen to reveal her Protestant devotion, as well as her sense, as her life draws to a close, of the subordination of temporal concerns to the providential pattern of eternity.

In the process, however, there emerge intriguing questions about Lady Grace's identity. Given that her marriage occurred fifty years before her diary was written, do her late-life reminiscences efface the emotions she might have entertained at the time of, for example, her marriage to a man whose main goal was to be absent from home, as well as her subjection to the caprices of a parsimonious father, a treacherous sister and a deceptive father-in-law? If Lady Grace's autobiography is to be taken at face value, these adverse events afford opportunities for her to grow closer to God. But how did she respond to the injustices at the time, and how did she express her responses in words and actions? These are questions that leak out of a memoir's compressed chronology, questions to which answers might never be found, or to which answers might sometimes be pieced together from the written records of others who knew the writer. The few letters written to Lady Grace by servants and doctors reflect little more than the class boundaries that mark communications of the time, so that the civilities of 'your humble servant', and so on, forbid any genuine opinion of her person. And the epitaph written for Lady Grace by her daughter, Lady Mary Fane, simply repeats for the mother the kind of descriptions that she has herself afforded others: 'Here also lieth Grace Lady Mildmay ... she was most devout, unspottedly chaste maid, wife and widow' (p. 21).

In assessing how her life-writings take shape and what they mean—what they say about her life, how they might relate to the term, 'individuality'—we might notice an inclusiveness that is common to many diaries of this period. Lady Grace writes of the will to be included rather than to be extraordinary; the will to establish oneself as a functional and worthy part of an ancestrally predestined community. 'Self', for her, is always composite, never separate: and the realization of selfhood is the understanding of how fully to inhabit—whether through prayer, through rightful inheritance of property, or through rightful expression of virtue—the place that one is born to.

Notes

1   *With Faith and Physic: the Life of a Tudor Gentlewoman, Lady Grace Mildmay, 1552–1620*, ed. Linda Pollock (London: Collins and Brown, 1993), p. 27. See also Retha M. Warnicke, 'Lady Mildmay's Journal: A Study in Autobiography and Meditation in Reformation England', *The Sixteenth Century Journal: Journal of Early Modern Studies*, 20.1 (Spring 1989), 55–68.

2   The composition of the ideal gentlewoman—whose every part connoted the grace of the entire person—was adopted by English sonneteers, and was reflected in the comportment and carriage of the ideal English gentlewoman embodied here by Lady Mildmay. Nancy J. Vickers, in 'Diana Described: Scattered Women and Scattered Rhymes', *Critical Inquiry*, 8.2 (Winter 1981), 265–79, describes the Petrarchan depiction of women as 'a composite of details' (p. 267) which formed the model for European gentlewomen, as described, for example, by Nicholas Caussin in France: 'A Lady well accomplished is like a starre with fiue rays, which are the fiue virtues, of Deuotion, Modesty, Chastity, Discretion, and Charity. Devotion formeth the interiour; modesty makes it appeare in the exteriour with a requisite comlinesse; Chastity perfecteth both the one, and the other; Discretion applyeth

it to the direction of others; and Charity crowneth all her actions'. (Nicholas Caussin, extract from 'The holy court, second tome' (1631.) Caussin's text, along with many others to be used in this discussion, is quoted from the facsimile collection *Conduct Literature for Women, 1500–1640,* ed. William St Clair and Irmgard Maasen, 6 vols (London: Pickering and Chatto, 2000), vol. 6 (pp. 51–97), p. 79. (Please note: this six-volume text has been reproduced in facsimile. For the sake of a legible script, the Elizabethan '*f*' has been modernized in quotations cited from the facsimiles compiled in these volumes.)

3   We might look to Anne Askew's 'Examinations', edited and 'elucidated' by John Bale: *The Examinations of Anne Askew,* ed. Elaine V. Beilin (New York: Oxford University Press, 1996), or to Richard Hyrde's 'Approbation' attached to Elizabeth Jocelin's *The Mother's Legacy, To her Vnborne Childe, Conduct Literature,* vol. 5, pp. 275–432.

4   Christina Luckyj explores the relationship between silence and gender in the second chapter of *A Moving Rhetoricke: Gender and Silence in Early Modern England* (Manchester: Manchester University Press, 2002).

5   This point will be elaborated on later when I address the feminized union between body and soul that was the contemporary convention for devotional writing, both male and female. For now, it is useful to mention the work of Helen Wilcox, who has written extensively on the kind of female proactivity that might be gleaned from women's devotional writing. Wilcox pays attention, for example, to the effect of inverted syntax, which may accentuate a woman's narrative voice although the overt narrative intention is to highlight a scriptural text. As an instance of this kind of female self-assertion, see Wilcox's analysis of the voice of the Quaker missionary Katherine Evans, in 'Selves in Strange Lands: Autobiography and Exile in the Mid-Seventeenth Century', Bedford, Davis and Kelly eds, *Early Modern Autobiography* (Ann Arbor: University of Michigan Press, 2006), p. 143.

6   Such analyses at times reveal more about the retrospective analyst than about the event of a particular death itself. Consider, for example, Lucinda Becker's discussion of Ralph Josselin's distaste for a widower's over-hasty wish to remarry. Becker cites Josselin's consecutive diary notes: his counseling of the man to postpone remarriage; the timely death of the woman he wished to remarry; his planting of an apricot tree. Becker concludes that the planting of the tree represents Josselin's gesture of smug satisfaction that God's will has been done. This is wildly speculative, given that Josselin, whose diary entries are filled with *non sequiturs,* may have planted an apricot tree for reasons completely unrelated to the matter in hand (Lucinda M. Becker, *Death and the Early Modern Englishwoman* [London: Ashgate, 2003], pp. 71–72). For a moving discussion of two women's deaths (Katherine Brettargh and Mary Gunter), see Robert Watson, *The Rest is Silence: Death as Annihilation in the English Renaissance* (Berkeley: University of California Press, 1994), pp. 305–22.

7   For a useful article on the perils of childbirth, see Sharon Howard's discussion of the discourse of martyrdom in Alice Thornton's perilous and painful childbirth: 'Imagining the Pain and Peril of Seventeenth-century Childbirth: Travail and Deliverance in the Making of an Early Modern World', *Social History of Medicine,* 16.3 (2003), 367–82. If figures like Lady Ann Fanshawe indicate something of a norm, the approach of childbirth was a perilous event. Of Fanshawe's fourteen pregnancies, only three survived all the way through to maturity. She gave birth to three daughters whom she named Elizabeth, four

named Richard, and two named Henry. An interesting light is thrown on the difficulties encountered in pregnancy at the time when we consider that Fanshawe's three children who did survive—Katherine, Margaret and Anne—were all born within the period when she did not have to undergo the exertion of travelling abroad with her husband.

8   For accounts of this, see Christine Peters, *Women in Early Modern Britain, 1450–1640* (Basingstoke: Palgrave, 2003), pp. 45–67; Alison Sim, *The Tudor Housewife* (Montreal and Kingston: McGill–Queen's University Press, 1996), pp. 94–107, and Amy Louise Erickson, *Women and Property in Early Modern England* (London: Routledge, 1993), where she analyses property law, upbringing and expectations of boys and girls, marriage settlements and inheritance. See also Judith M. Bennett, who takes the involvement of women in brewing as paradigmatic of women's access to, and involvement in, work during the rise of capitalism, and the low social status they were accorded, *Ale, Beer, and Brewsters in England: Women's Work in a Changing World, 1300–1600* (Oxford: Oxford University Press, 1996). One of the most concise and informative accounts of women's employment remains that given by Carol Camden in 1952: *The Elizabethan Woman* (New York and London: Elsevier Press, 1952), pp. 145–48.

9   See Eve Rachele Sanders, *Gender and Literacy in Early Modern England* (Cambridge: Cambridge University Press, 1998), who argues that literacy 'helped to engender new and profoundly different forms of subjectivity' (p. 2). Helen Hackett also offers some useful speculations on women's literacy in *Women and Romance Fiction in the English Renaissance* (Cambridge: Cambridge University Press, 2000). Thomas Salter voices a typical view of women's ideal self-employment when he says, 'how far more conuenient the Distaffe, and Spindle, Nedle and Thimble were for them with a good and honest reputation, then the skill of well ---[word unclear] a penne or wrightyng a loftie vearce with disshame and dishonour, if in the same there be more erudition than vertue …', 'A mirrhor mete for all mothers, matrons, and maidens, intituled the mirrhor of modestie' (1579), *Conduct Literature*, vol. 5 (pp. 1–72), p. 37.

10   Bishop Joseph Hall, *The Works of the Right Reverend Joseph Hall*, a new ed. rev. and corr. with some additions, by Philip Wynter. 10 vols (Oxford: Oxford University Press, 1863), p. 644.

11   For a discussion of the expectations of women articulated by conduct publications, see Effie Botonaki, *Seventeenth-Century English Women's Autobiographical Writings: Disclosing Enclosures, Studies in British Literature*, vol. 88 (Lewiston: Edwin Mellon Press, 2004). See Introduction, pp. 1–42.

12   Patrick Hannay, 'A happy husband' (1618), *Conduct Literature*, vol. 4 (pp. 351–80), p. 376.

13   Sylvia Brown in *Women's Writing in Stuart England* (Phoenix Mill: Sutton Publishing, 1999) has referred to a similar feature in the Mother's Legacy genre. She suggests that the authors of these legacies 'are themselves caught between the contradictory self-assertion which the genre allows, and the self-negation it demands' (p. vii).

14   Elspeth Graham, 'Women's Writing and the Self', *Women and Literature in Britain, 1500–1700*, ed. Helen Wilcox (Cambridge: Cambridge University Press, 1996), pp. 209–33.

15   Helen Wilcox calls this 'a feminized soul dependent on the power of grace', 'My Soule in Silence', *Representing Women*, p. 14.

16   Song of Solomon, 1. 13: 'A bundle of myrrh is my wellbeloved unto me; he shall lie all
     night betwixt my breasts.'
17   Song of Solomon, 1. 2: 'Let him kiss me with the kisses of his mouth: for thy love is
     better than wine.'
18   In describing God's nurturing love her voice chimes with those of other, later women,
     often of very different social standings and religious persuasions, for whom God is able
     to 'annointe' a woman's 'teate', as Elizabeth Grymston puts it. 'For where he purposeth
     to heale, he spareth not to launce: and if he see thou be fostered by the world thy naturall
     nurse, he can annoint hir teate with the bitternesse of discontent, to weane thee from hir:
     for he that bindes the franticke, and awakes the lethargee, is troublesome, but friendly
     to both', Elizabeth Grymeston, 'Miscellanea, Meditations, Memoratives' (1604), *Brown
     University Women Writers Project first electronic edition*, 2001. Source copy owned by
     the Bodleian Library, shelfmark: Quarto.E.31.Th.Bs. STC 12407. Later in the century
     the Quaker Margaret Fell, wife of George Fox, employs God's 'tenderness and the
     bowels of love' towards women as a powerful argument for female speech and female
     agency as primary carriers of the Gospel, transforming Mildmay's Tudor conservatism
     into the radical and revolutionary, Margaret Fell, *Women's Speaking Justified*, 1667.
     Brown University Women Writers Project first electronic edition, 2002. http://www.wwp.
     brown.edu/encoding/research/NASSR/WWP.html. Source copy owned by Henry E.
     Huntington Library, shelfmark: 94232, Wing F643. See also Margaret Askew Fell (Fox),
     'Women's Speaking Justified: Epistle from the women's yearly meeting at York, 1688'
     (Los Angeles: Clark Memorial Library, 1979), and Catie Gill, *Women in the Seventeenth-
     Century Quaker Community* (Aldershot: Ashgate, 2005).
19   See Sylvia Brown, 'General Introduction: The Mother's Legacy', *Women's Writing in
     Stuart England*, p. vii. C. W. Bynum aptly describes the female model for the religious
     man: 'The male writer who saw his soul as a bride of God or his religious role as womanly
     submission and humility was conscious of using an image of reversal. He sought reversal
     because reversal and renunciation were at the heart of a religion whose dominant symbol
     is the cross—life achieved through death', *Fragmentation and Redemption: Essays on
     Gender and the Human Body in Medieval Religion* (New York: Zone Books, 1991), p.
     171.
20   Henry Constable asks, 'Give me then purity instead of power, / And let my soul,
     made chaste, pass for a maid', *Female and Male Voices in Early Modern England:
     An Anthology of Renaissance Writing*, ed. Betty S. Travitsky and Anne Lake Prescott
     (New York: Columbia University Press, 2000). Male devotional poetry of this period—
     in Donne, George Herbert, Herrick, Crashaw—is deeply and famously informed by a
     willing displacement of gender. Confirming the feminization of Donne's 'Batter my
     heart' sonnet, Bishop Joseph Hall, quoting Matthew 5. 6 ('Blessed are they which hunger
     and thirst after righteousness: for they shall be filled', praises the God who 'ravishest my
     soul' [p. 547]), while in a more domestic context Richard Rogers writes of the pre-marital
     years in which 'sighes and plaints' to God 'were more sweet to me than hony', lamenting,
     since his marriage, the loss of time and space for communing with God, Richard Rogers,
     Two Puritan Diaries, By Richard Rogers and Samuel Ward, ed. with an introduction by
     M. M. Knappen (1933) (Gloucester Mass.: P. Smith, 1966), p. 101.

21 Gouge says that a husband's 'superioritie and authoritie hath power to command his wife'. He later stipulates, however, that 'If her husband command her to doe that which God hath expresly forbidden, then ought she by no means to yeeld vnto it: if she doe, it may rather be termed a joint conspiracie of husband and wife together against Gods will', Gouge, Of Domesticall Duties', *Conduct Literature*, vol. 5 (pp. 73–182), p. 171; p. 173.

22 Becon wrote the preface to Miles Coverdale's first English translation of 'The christen state of matrimonye', by Heinrich Bullinger (1541), which went through eight English translations over the next thirty-five years, *Conduct Literature*, vol. 2. (pp. 1–199), p. 162; 'A Bride-Bush: or, A Direction for Married Persons' (1619), *Conduct Literature*, vol. 5 (pp. 183–274), p. 252.

23 Dorothy Leigh writes to her children of the devil who inhabits the waking world: ' doe not sleepe at night', she says, 'till thou hast humbled they selfe before God on thy knees in prayer; for night is a time when the world leaues a man (as it were) for a while, and when the world leaues him, the diuell hath not so much power ouer him; for the world is a great Instrument for the diuell to worke by. Therefore when the world is asleepe (as it were) the diuells power is weakened, and then bee sure thou prayest to God to deliuer thee from the diuell, and from the world'. 'The Mother's Blessing', in *Women's Writing in Stuart England*, p. 36. Elizabeth Richardson writes of the devil who pervades 'the vaine world', 'my corrupt flesh', and 'sinfull thoughts', tempting her to 'offend with my tongue, or in my actions', *A Ladies Legacie to Her Daughters* (1645), in *Women's Writing*, pp. 199–200. And Elizabeth Jocelin forewarns her unborn child that the devil is lurking the minute one opens one's eyes: 'At thy first wakinge in the morninge, be carefull of thy selfe that thou harbor in thy brayn no vayn or unprofitable but of all no ungodly fancy … but straight frame thy selfe to meditate on the mercies of god … The devils malice is easily perceived for even now he lyes lurkynge … The infinit malice of the divell and your own exceedinge weaknes how do you thinke you wear preserved from his snares while you slept or do you thinke he only besets you when you are awake? No be not deceived he is not so fayr an enemy', *Mother's Legacy*, in *Women's Writing*, p. 112.

24 *Women's Writing in Stuart England*, p.27.

25 *Conduct Literature for Women*, pp. 355–56.

26 In her famous discourse on the virtues of breastfeeding, the Countess of Lincoln condemns those who rely on wetnurses in order to preserve their own strength and beauty: a woman who refuses to nurse her own children betrays her God-given duty (while also potentially compromising the character of the child, which was believed to be shaped by the milk it suckled—see Christine Peters, *Women in Early Modern Britain*, p. 66.) Women, it was insisted, could learn all they needed from their home-coming husbands.

27 While conduct books exhorted women to confine themselves to the home, working guilds were open to young women and to women who continued at least nominally to run them when their husbands deceased. Marriage to a member of a guild conferred rights upon a wife, which she was permitted to retain beyond her husband's death. A few women operated sizeable businesses, although most female shop owners were widows who ran those left to them by their late husbands. Steve Rappaport also makes the point that, given the nature of pre-industrial forms of production, 'most women were actively engaged in the production and distribution of goods and services, often working in shops alongside

male members of the household', learning economic skills not through apprenticeship but through informal 'on the job' experience, 'Reconsidering Apprenticeship in Sixteenth-Century London', *Renaissance Society and Culture*, ed. John Monfasani and Ronald G. Musto (New York: Italica Press, 1991), p. 240, f. 2. But it is also true that women's work—the major part of which was of low status, like searching the bodies of suspected plague victims, or as an 'unchaste' taverner's servant—'conferred different degrees of status and economic independence', Peters, *Women in Early Modern Britain*, p. 65.

28   Sir Thomas Elyot, *The defence of good women, deuised and made by Sir Thomas Elyot knight*, *Conduct Literature*, vol. 2, pp. 201–66. Elyot's misogynistic character, Caninius, for example, says that 'in woman kinde faithe neuer rested, yet be you still as blinde as your litell god Cupide, for the childish affections which ye beare to your ladies, causeth you to think the thinges which ye se, to be nothing but vanities' (pp. 209–10). Candidus defends the reputation of women against this assault, arguing, 'I haue found women much blamed for their inconstancy: but for mine own knowlage I neuer perceiued any suche lacke to be in them, but rather the contrary' (p. 210).

29   Xantip, the scold, asks what she should do about her stingy, disrespectful husband, who does not allow her to behave well because he 'will not let me haue that which is necessary, but spend that we haue in tipling and swilling ... and amongst whores and harlots'. This attitude attacks the heart of current opinion about the superior wisdom of husbands, whose wishes should not be contradicted by women's whims, *A Looking-Glasse for Maried Folkes* (1610), *Conduct Literature*, vol. 4 (pp. 87–204), p. 118.

30   See Travitsky and Prescott, *Female and Male Voices*, p. 82.

31   *Jane Anger Her Protection for Women*. PDF document rendering of STC 644 prepared in March 2000 by Wes Folkerth, Dept of English, McGill University. On-line access: http://www.shakespeare.mcgill.ca/anger.pdf.

32   William Dethick, *The Excellencie of man, his nobilitie, praise, glory, honour and dignitie*, section titled 'Of the Praise and Glorye of Women', Folger Library MS V.b.125, ascribed to Sir William Dethick, c. 1610, pp. 40v–41r.

33   Sir Francis Fane, in Folger MS V.a.180. Commonplace book, compiled c. 1655–56, p. 41.

34   See Carol Thomas Neely, 'Shakespeare's Tragedies and Early Modern Culture', in *Shakespearean Tragedy and Gender*, ed. Shirley Nelson Garner and Madelon Sprengnether (Bloomington: Indiana University Press, 1996), p. 79.

35   See Amy Louise Erickson, *Women and Property*, pp. 53–54. Erickson provides a very good discussion of the range of expectations put upon housewives, as well as the cultivation of housewifery as an art that was not confined to marital situations (pp. 53–55).

36   Joseph Swetnam *The Arraignment of lewde, idle, froward and unconstant women or, the vanity of them, chuse you whether with a commendation of the wise, virtuous, and honest women. Pleasant for married-men, profitable for young-men, and hurtfull to none* (London: Printed by E.C. for F. Grove, on Snow-Hill, near the Sarazenshead, 1660).

37   Heinrich Bullinger, *The christen state of matrimonye* (1541), *Conduct Literature*, vol. 2 (pp. 1–200), p. 162.

38   Thomas Becon, *Catechisme*, *Conduct Literature*, vol. 2 (pp. 269–327), p. 281.

39   Richard Braithwaite, 'The English Gentlewoman' (1641), *Conduct Literature*, vol. 6 (pp. 97–364), p. 153.

40 John Cotta, quoted by Linda Pollock, *With Faith and Physic*, p. 93.

41 Gervase Markham, *The English Housewife: Containing the inward and Outward virtues which ought to be in a complete woman; as her skill in physic, cookery, banqueting-stuff, distillation, perfumes, wool, hemp, flax, dairies, brewing, baking, and all other things belonging to a household*. Ed. Michael Best (Kingston and Montreal: McGill–Queen's University Press, 1986), p. 8.

42 Mary Trye notes how she inherited her medical skills: 'abiding the late great and never-to-be-forgotten pestilential calamity of this city, and undergoing that mortal stroke, in which I lost two of my dearest friends, my father and mother, but surviving them myself, I received a medicinal talent from my father, which by the instruction of so excellent a tutor as he was to me, and my constant preparation and observation of medicines, together with my daily experience by reason of this very great practice; as also being mistress of a reasonable share of that knowledge and discretion other women attain; I made myself capable of disposing such noble and successful medicines, and managing so weighty and great a concern', 'Medicatrix, OR The woman physician', in *English Women's Voices, 1540–1700*, ed. Charlotte F. Otten, (Miami: Florida International University Press, 1992), p. 193.

43 Dean Ebner, *Autobiography in Seventeenth Century England* (The Hague: Mouton, 1971), p. 20.

44 'The Diary Network in Sixteenth and Seventeenth Century England', Monash University School of Historical Studies, 2001. on-line access: http://www.arts.monash.edu.au/eras/edition_2/mckay.htm.

Paradises Lost:
Invaded Houses in Donne's Poetry

Heather Dubrow

I

The seventeenth century witnessed the development of the antimasque, a supplement in the several senses of that fraught but still useful term.[1] Antimasquers invade a space that both is and is not the court, and they invade as well a text that is apparently devoted to very different values; in some instances those incursions are literalized spatially by associating these transgressive figures with another geographical locale, such as Ireland. The same era witnessed as well the birth of the country house poem, a genre that displaces and replaces potential invasions—by discontented neighbours of a lower social status, by cold weather, by the snake whose presence in the original Eden is arguably troped by threats like those—with its celebration of hospitality. Invaders push their way in, on their own terms. In contrast, in this genre guests are invited in, according to a shared social code, or, in the instance of the poor in 'Upon Appleton House', safely and statically positioned at the threshold.[2] Of course, much as masques include antimasques, country house poems on occasion incorporate instances of the alternative to hospitality that they are devoted to controlling; returning to 'Upon Appleton House', for example, Marvell's Thestylis performs a fascinating linguistic analogue to other types of invasion when she breaks into the narrative, an interruption that not coincidentally is Othered by being gendered female. Such developments in these two literary forms, then, crystallize the preoccupation with intruders that characterizes so many other texts of the early modern period.

Nowhere is that preoccupation more recurrent or more revealing than in the canon of John Donne. Donne writes—and, as I will suggest, is written by—scenarios of invasion, especially though not exclusively plots involving invaded houses. A telling number of the love poems, such as 'The Sunne Rising' (to which I will return in more detail), 'The Apparition', 'The Funerall', and 'The Relique' open on such intrusions. So too does 'Satyre I', where that 'fondling motley humorist' (1) trespasses into the speaker's 'standing wooden chest' (2) of a study.[3] Versions of invasion occur within the bodies, as it were, of many other texts; notice, for example, the words that 'would teare / The tender labyrinth of a soft maids eare' ('Satyre II', 57–58). In the eclogue to the Somerset epithalamion, Idios denies that his poem was intended 'Either the Court or mens hearts to invade' (100).[4] And in the *Devotions*

Donne writes of 'break[ing] into houses where the plague is' (I. 'Expostulation') in a characteristic reversal assuming the role of the disease that is often presented as an invader itself.[5] Although one has to avoid the temptation to make of one little trope an everywhere, linguistic and stylistic analogies to invasion also recur throughout the canon; for example, Donne's predilection for disjunctive conjunctions like 'but' or 'yet' creates a syntax in which a discordant element invades the rest of the sentence ('Yet this enjoyes before it wooe ... Yet thou triumph'st' ['The Flea', 7, 23], 'Loves mysteries in soules doe grow, / But yet the body is his booke' ['The Exstasie', 71–72], 'And this is the cause, why I do sin; but why I should sin, there is none at all' [Sermon No. 4]).[6]

Why and how, then, does Donne so often refer to invasions in general and invaded houses in particular? Studying that preoccupation can variously provide new perspectives on familiar passages in his canon and clarify his reactions to such issues as the engendering of sexual guilt and the relationship of public and private. And scrutinizing this issue can also illuminate more general problems ranging from the structures of narrative to the workings of our own critical practices to the anxieties that shape, and I believe misshape certain public policies in the twenty-first century.

II

To begin with, then, Donne's preoccupation with invaded houses participates in the matrix of cultural and literary history and needs to be read against other representations of invasion. As I have argued elsewhere, some of the deepest anxieties in his culture pivoted on three related forms of domestic intrusion—burglary, the entrance of step-parents, and fire—with burglary especially relevant to this essay.[7] Thus the fears of invasive foreign powers and especially of putatively foreign priests were powerfully staged in the domestic arena as well, as studies by Richard Helgerson and Linda Woodbridge cogently demonstrate.[8]

Thievery in general and burglary in particular were arguably the most feared and most prototypical of all crimes in early modern England. Egeus tellingly accuses his would-be son-in-law Lysander of it:

> And stol'n the impression of her fantasy
> With bracelets of thy hair,
>
> ...   ...
>
> With cunning hast thou filch't my daughter's heart.
>
> (*A Midsummer Night's Dream*, I. i. 32–33, 36)[9]

Inflamed by Stella's refusal to quench his flames, Sir Philip Sidney's Astrophil declares, 'Yet worse then worst, I say thou art a theefe, a theefe? / Now God forbid. A theefe, and of worst theeves the cheefe' ('Fift Song', 43–44).[10]

One of many reasons thievery was indeed the 'worse then worst' was its prevalence. In Essex, one historian reports, ninety per cent of all reported crimes were against property, and stealing in its many forms was certainly the predominant offence throughout the Tudor and Stuart periods, at least in the counties for which records are available.[11] Another reason for tensions about such felonies is that one type of thief, the burglar, challenges a distinction crucial in Donne's writings as well as elsewhere in his culture, the divide between *inside* and *outside* and between *mine* and *yours*; if all crime figures transgression, the burglar literally transgresses in the sense of stepping over a boundary. Moreover, the perpetrator of such crimes intrudes into a 'forfended place' (*King Lear*, V. i. 11), an expression that Regan deploys in relation to that invader Edmund's adulteries; victims of burglary in our own culture often report that they feel contaminated, violated, and the connections between violating a house and a woman's body become explicit in many early modern texts, including some poems by Donne to which I will turn shortly.

Because of the frequency of the early death of parents and the prevalence of rapid remarriage in many social groups, the early modern version of what is today sometimes termed 'blended families' was common. Although always complicated by regional variations and sometimes impeded by the paucity or inaccuracy of records, the invaluable work of the Cambridge Group for the History of Population and Social Structure has demonstrated how many children were liable to be raised by a step-parent; the extent to which that situation was perceived in terms of invasion is suggested by the warnings about second marriages in marriage manuals. Texts of the period witness these events as well. If *1 Henry VI* opens with the coffin of the country's father on stage, the death of a parent impels many comedies and tragedies by its author. The ghost of Old Hamlet is the most famous of such spectral visitors, but many other revenants play a more subterranean but nonetheless significant role. Witness, for example, Sir Rowland, who figures the several paradises lost of *As You Like It*. The result of such untimely demises, the entrance of the step-parent, is famously figured by Claudius; though often described as Hamlet's uncle, both that mourning prince and his diegetic and non-diegetic audiences would have viewed the nefarious monarch primarily as a stepfather. Similarly, the parallels between Sir Rowland's replacement, Orlando's brother Oliver, and the evil stepfather or stepmother would have been apparent to Shakespeare's original audience. Yet plays like *Hamlet* and *As You Like It* may tempt us into readings of its culture that are more convenient for the purposes of this essay than correct for the texts in question: whereas step-parents were indubitably perceived and represented as a clear and present danger under many circumstances, it is likely that under others they were welcomed.

Finally, it is not coincidental that a Renaissance translation of Petrarch's *Phisike against Fortune* describes introducing a stepmother into the house as setting it on fire: all these types of invasion were connected in the cultural unconscious of early modern England.[12] Architectural practices, such as the open hearths, thatched roofs, and the use of wood as the predominant building material intensified the likelihood of a conflagration.

Intrigued with the early modern anxiety about invasion, about a decade ago I began to investigate that fear largely in terms of the triad above, that is, burglary, the death of parents, and the loss of the literal, material home, especially through fire. Two other forms of invasion, I have recently come to believe, are no less significant in the culture or rather cultures of early modern England. First, in a book tellingly and wittingly entitled *Foreign Bodies and the Body Politic*, Jonathan Gil Harris deploys medical discourses to show how often illness was seen as a type of invasion.[13] As Harris points out, newer concepts of disease, unlike the humoral models inherited from Galen, saw it as an outside agent infiltrating the body. Substantiating and supplementing Harris's analysis is an intriguing passage about the plague. The seventeenth-century Scottish doctor John Makluire, wishing to stress the extraordinary agency of air, observes:

> it passeth so quickly through the body, that it printeth presently the qualities wherewith it is indued in the parts of the same, and therefore there is nothing able to change more shortly the body than it ... A good air ... revives the spirits, purifieth the blood, procureth appetite ... A contaminate aire with filthy exhalations, arysing from standing waters, dead carcases, middings, gutters, closets, and the filth of the streets, (all which if any where are to bee found heere, which argueth a great oversight of the magistrats, bringeth a great hurt to the inhabitants, and a great good to the Physicians, Apothecaries, and bel-man) corrupteth the spirits, and humors, and engendereth often a deadly contagion or pest.[14]

If that text the body was liable to invasion by what Harris cleverly terms 'foreign bodies', so too were texts in the more literal sense. Indeed, all the forms of incursion I have catalogued thus far troped and were troped by the workings of texts. A collection devoted to celebrating the work of an Australian academic is an appropriate venue for discussing this issue, for the scholarship of another Australian, Harold Love, is among the most important—and most judicious—of the many commentaries on manuscript and print culture.[15] If lyric itself is inherently dialogic, as some Bakhtinian scholars and arguably Bakhtin himself assert, its conditions of production were dialogic as well.[16] Commonplace books and other collections often juxtaposed texts in ways that established a conversation between them. Answer poems thus represent an extreme and overt version of common practices. Ashmole 1486, as Marcy North demonstrates in her important work, in effect presents Marlowe's 'Passionate Shepherd to his Love' and Raleigh's reply as a single poem: Simon Forman places the word 'finis' only at the end of the second poem, not at the conclusion of the first as it does with other lyrics.[17] Such conversations could be present in print as well, as Herrick's arrangement of his *Hesperides* reminds us. And to return to manuscripts, we recall that copyists and readers often added yet more texts or commentaries on pre-existing ones. Under what circumstances were such additions seen as an invasion, and under what circumstances an enrichment? Our poststructuralist hermeneutics of suspicion impels the former reading, and no doubt it is often just. Yet, as in the case of step-parents, we need to allow for variety and lability, remembering that one man's invasion could be another man's, or the same man's, invitation as well.

III

Indeed, the movement from invasion to invitation structures 'The Sunne Rising', the lyric that best introduces and encapsulates Donne's engagement with the dynamics of invasion. The speaker famously opens this poem by lamenting the sun's intrusion into the chamber he shares with his beloved—'Busie old foole, unruly Sunne, / Why dost thou thus, / Through windowes, and through curtaines call on us?' (1–3). By the end, he invites that unruly visitor in: 'Shine here to us, and thou art every where' (29). Intrusion becomes invitation; surveillance becomes submission.

If the issue of invasion in Donne's poetry has been largely overlooked, this lyric has hardly suffered from comparable neglect. Incisive earlier readings of 'The Sunne Rising' by such Donne scholars as J. B. Leishman and Clay Hunt have recently been supplemented by a range of interpretations, some of which crystallize shifts in the profession since the work of those scholars.[18] Thus, for example, Meg Lota Brown traces its desperation about and celebration of the power of language; Arthur F. Marotti offers a biographical reading rooted in Donne's fear of social disapproval and failure; Ben Saunders connects it with the Lacanian Imaginary.[19] Especially complementary to my own generic commentary is A. D. Cousins's acute demonstration of how Donne fashions a utopian anti-aubade.[20]

But despite all the intelligent attention the poem has enjoyed, the assumption that its principal classical source is Ovid's address to Aurora in *Amores* I. xiii, notably propounded by J. B. Leishman, has seldom been questioned.[21] I do not want to underestimate the influence of that text or indulge in a old critical game whose sources and tonalities are best clarified by the label, 'My source is bigger than your source'; but the conventional wisdom about I. xiii may have distracted us from acknowledging another Ovidian source, which pivots on invaded dwellings.

For Ovid's *Amores* I. vi exemplifies the *paraklausithyron* (or 'by the closed door'), a classical motif generally neglected by students of early modern poetry, though enthusiastically imitated by certain authors of it.[22] In it, an unfortunate and importunate lover waits on the threshold, trying to gain entrance to a closed or locked house that clearly figures the female body. Often he argues with an unrelenting gatekeeper; in other texts, the door itself participates in the dialogue. The motif, which appears in both drama and lyric, assumes a wide range of forms, including an inverted variant particularly germane to my purposes—that is, in several poems by Propertius, a lover within the lady's chamber contrasts his happy situation with that of rivals outside the door.[23] Other classical instances include Theocritus' *Idyll* 3, Catullus 67, and Tibullis 1.5. (Such poems, incidentally, find their counterpart in the medieval tradition exemplified by the *Romance of the Rose*, where the enclosed blossom is guarded by such figures as Daunger and Shame.) In any event, Donne's intense interest in Ovid and in the Latin elegy in general, a literary type in which the motif flourished, makes it likely he was very aware of its potentialities.

One of the principal versions of the *paraklausithyron* in the English Renaissance is the fourth song in *Astrophil and Stella*. And like their classical antecedents, many other texts from the period allude to the tradition obliquely or playfully; one might, for example, cite Romeo's balcony scene and the intriguing inversions of the motif in Herbert's 'Love (III)'. Arguably this literary type, which focuses on a lover seeking admittance, was attractive to certain Renaissance writers and their audiences in part because it both expressed and deflected the situation of other petitioners in the culture, whether they be young men seeking patronage or merchants seeking entrance into the gentry. The tradition did not, however, die after the early modern period. The folk song 'Silver Dagger' incorporates it, as does the song aptly named 'Locked Out', performed by Crowded House.

'The Sunne Rising' does not participate in the *paraklausithyron* tradition in the straightforward way we find in some of those versions—but that is precisely what makes the connection so intriguing. Donne is characteristically evoking the tradition largely to reverse it—to signify on it—here, and he does so in ways that exemplify the Mannerist delight in display on which L. E. Semler has written so cogently.[24] That is, the male lover, rather than pleading in vain to get in, has gained admission both to the house and the female body it tropes in the convention; and having done so he has in effect assumed the role of gatekeeper or other authority who attempts to deny entrance to the sun. Or, to extend A. D. Cousins's analysis of utopian and dystopian elements in Donne, the lover becomes the guard at the door of a utopia, policing the threshold between that world and its dystopian opposite outside.[25]

Acknowledging elements from the *paraklausithyron* in 'The Sunne Rising' crystallizes the ways the poem comments on invaded houses, at once supporting some familiar interpretations of the lyric and questioning others. First, the tradition in question foregrounds certain characteristics of the sun's behaviour. Reinforced by the reference to windows and curtains, the paraklausithyron convention underscores the sun's role as a would-be invader, an undertow to the apparent civility of 'call on us' (3). The intrusive sun, normally associated with regulating, is, as Donne puts it, unruly, as unruly as literal burglars. More specifically, in the many versions of the *paraklausithyron* closely related to the classical *komos* tradition, which describes processions and revels, the lover is, as it were, drunk and disorderly; arguably Donne's deployment of his adjective 'unruly' associates the sun with such figures, thus further demeaning him.

More speculatively, arguably his hints of the *paraklausithyron* convention also encourage us to read the sun as a rival lover. In any event, it is clear that the *paraklausithyron* also illuminates the speaker's role. To begin with, the lover's position as insider in more senses than one is emphasized by the implicit but effective contrast with the situation in which he, like the sun, would be the outsider clamouring to get in. Instead, he is the insider who excludes three threats: the sun, the versions of the *paraklausithyron* in which he himself would be excluded, and the Petrarchan traditions that would also position him outside the house, clamouring for admission. Similarly, normally the excluded lover delivers the lament that constitutes the poem; Donne's speakers often delight in drowning out the voices of others, whether female lovers or male rivals, and in a sense this poem demonstrates that same predilection. The poem controls the 'Busie old foole' (1) verbally as well as spatially, thus creating the equivalent of an exclusive and excluding version of pastoral within his chamber.[26]

In any event, in 'The Sunne Rising' if the sun takes the place of the unsuccessful lover its desired entrance also represents the invasion of narrativity. Donne's celestial alarm clock brings time into the poem in the obvious senses long recognized by many readers and immortalized in the ideology of the aubade. On another level, however, it introduces time in the sense that its entrance creates narrativity in a situation previously exemplary of lyric stasis. That is, not only does the poem in effect tell a story about the sun, but the sun's entrance carries with it the preconditions for narrative, the assumption of a before and an after, in this case the unchanging world of consummated love and the subsequent time when it has been threatened. Hence it is telling that both the challenges to the sun's power and the closural assertion that such challenges have triumphed banish the grammar of action verbs and substitute the stasis of predication: 'She'is all States, and all Princes, I', Donne famously writes in line 21, and the poem concludes on another instance of predication: 'This bed thy center is, these walls, thy spheare' (30).

If the poem parries potential invasion by substituting the timelessness of predication, it also accomplishes that end by enclosing, encircling would-be threats. Witness again line 21, 'She'is all States, and all Princes, I', an assertion that has rightly engendered so much feminist criticism. However we resolve those important debates, it's clear that the states and princes are literally enclosed between the pronouns, much as the text itself attempts to enclose and contain the power of the sun by transforming its narrative before and after into a forever and an everywhere. Notice too that this containment is effected not only through the linguistic changes in question but also through redefinitions in role and position. The invader in effect becomes an observer.

Invasion is also contested through the workings of apostrophe and other forms of address: that figure does its work not merely by calling up, the function commonly emphasized by its celebrants, but also, as is in fact often the case with apostrophes, by renaming. Thus the sun is labelled a busy old fool, a process echoed when the lovers are renamed as all states and princes. No less telling and more germane to us, however, is the parallel strategy of shifting power by shifting the sun among various types of auditory and the consequent authorial position. My point is not merely or mainly that the sun is associated with speech, apostrophe thus becoming prosopopoeia, but rather that its speech derives from and is tellingly represented in terms of fluid auditory positions in particular. Obviously, at the beginning of the poem the poet counters the situation of in effect being object to the sun's gaze by turning the sun itself into the object of and audience to a complaint. But he then intensifies the denigration of his busy old fool by making it the ventriloquizer of the words he assigns ('Goe tell Court-huntsmen' [7]), thus interpellating the sun into a subsidiary position similar to that of the huntsmen and the ants. Again, later in the poem the sun is commanded to answer questions, but ones where the answer is already known, to which he has already been an audience. Thus the manipulation of the sun's spatial and social position, acutely charted by many critics, is troped and enabled by shifts in its discursive position. Apparently subalterns, celestial and otherwise, can indeed speak as long as they voice the words assigned to or expected from them.

IV

In 'The Sunne Rising', then, Donne associates invasion with rivalry, certainly that of competing plots and traditions and conceivably that of a rival lover. Invasion is also associated with space and place, in this case a house. And it is connected with eroticism and narrativity, the latter of course itself seen as a form of eroticism by Peter Brooks and others.[27] Echoes of and analogues to these patterns recur elsewhere when Donne evokes invaded houses. He sometimes tropes competition, the driving force behind so many of his lyrics (and, one suspects, so much of his behavior) in terms of an invaded dwelling; witness in particular the invasive ghost in 'The Apparition'. Often such invasions are connected to sexual intercourse, presented in terms of invading a vulnerable space; witness the 'Epithalamion made at Lincolnes Inne', where the bridegroom-cum-priest is described in terms of not the disembowelment more customarily associated with his profession but its reverse ('The priest comes on his knees t'embowell her' [90]). Similarly, in the line from 'Satyre II' that I quoted earlier, 'words, words, which would teare / The tender labyrinth of a soft maids eare' (57–58), the words surely figure and, the lover hopes, prefigure entrance into the labyrinth of the woman's body.

'The Sunne Rising' is the clearest example of the *paraklausithyron* in the canon, but it is not unique: another but very different study of verbal and spatial control, the *Holy Sonnet* beginning 'Batter my heart' also plays on and with the *paraklausithyron*.[28] God is indeed a lover locked out of that well defended structure the speaker's heart, and Donne's poem, like Ovid's *Amores* I. vi, adduces the parallel with beleaguered towns. But Donne's text draws attention to its most central tensions precisely through divagations from the typical *paraklausithyron*. For Donne is at once the gatekeeper who cannot let in the importunate lover and the beloved who desperately wants to; and he at once has the potential agency of that gatekeeper ('Labour to'admit you' [6]) and the inability to act effectively ('but Oh, to no end' [6]). Thus the pull between Catholicism and Protestantism that I, like many other critics, find in the poem is enacted through its allusions to the literary tradition of the invaded, or potentially invaded, edifice.

Moreover, elsewhere in the canon, as in 'The Sunne Rising', the protagonist characteristically triumphs by turning an actual or potential invader into a spectator. James's voyeuristic delight in the sexual exploits of newly married couples are translated in the 'Epithalamion ... on the Lady Elizabeth and Count Palatine' into those who wait to see which member of the couple opens the curtains. If 'The Canonization' opens on a critical onlooker, it famously concludes on a whole world respectfully observing the exemplary lovers. This reinterpretation of invasion is, I suggest, the dynamic behind the emphasis on observation that Donne scholars have noted in many of his poems: he typically transforms would-be invaders into observers. And these obedient and respectful onlookers impel us to qualify the Foucauldian suggestion that observation no less than knowledge is power with the recognition that observers may be entranced, enthralled or in any event coopted, as potential invaders typically are when Donne transforms them to spectators (a recognition that supports second-generation challenges to earlier theories of the cinematic gaze). Or compare the twentieth item in Kafka's *Collected Aphorisms*: 'Leopards break into the temple and drink the sacrificial vessels dry; this is repeated over and over again; finally it can be calculated in advance and it becomes part of the ceremony'.[29]

Most recurrent and most intriguing, however, is the connection throughout Donne's canon between invaded houses and invaded or interrupted narratives. On the one hand, an interruption may set a narrative in motion, as does the entrance of the satiric antagonist in 'Satyre I'. But on the other hand, enacted and staged interruptions may mirror the ways a narrative itself struggles to contain unruly traces of conflicting genres or tonalities. If divergent and distracting generic echoes interrupt *Metempsychosis*, a point pursued by Cora Fox in her paper 'Enclosing Sin',[30] their workings are mirrored diegetically by the invasive entrances of the peregrinating soul. Sir Philip Sidney gives those who criticize his love some if not equal air time, so to speak; Donne typically attempts to counter such potential interruptions by interrupting and answering them before they can get a word in. They are allowed only to shine silently on the lovers.

V

Why, then, does Donne so often write about invaded houses, and why does he do so in the ways I have been sketching? To begin with, the three threats I outlined earlier—burglars, step-parents, and fires—were a clear and present danger to him, as to so many members of his culture. As noted above, Donne himself had a stepfather, and given the prevalence of fire and of thievery in urban areas he is likely to have had some knowledge of those particular invaders. The frequent references to fire in his sermons and other prose works, though traceable to multiple etiologies, are suggestive.

Donne's preoccupation with invasion is surely also related to, as it were, his memories of a Catholic boyhood—but related in ways as difficult to assess as they are important to acknowledge. We have seen that the type of domestic invasions traced in this paper echo and are echoed by the fear of invading foreign powers, and it is intriguing to speculate though impossible to ascertain how Donne the Catholic and Donne the ex-Catholic would have viewed the threatened incursions by Catholic countries. In any event those potentialities are likely to have heightened his preoccupation with invasion.

Even more intriguing and even more speculative is how he viewed a cognate phenomenon, the surreptitious invasions of priests into England and perhaps into his own literal house. Dennis Flynn argues that Jasper Heywood, Donne's uncle, called often at Donne's boyhood home, thus heightening his nephew's engagement with the mission of introducing priests.[31] Invaluable though Flynn's extensive research is, here as at a few other junctures he slides from an appropriately cautious hypothesis to a series of assertions that treat that hypothesis as fact. Thus he moves from saying that it is likely Heywood often visited his sister's home to the firmer claim that 'Donne would have had fairly frequent contact with his uncle since London became the natural center of Heywood's missionary activities over the next two years'.[32] But what if Heywood didn't have the time or patience for children? what if he and his nephew didn't take to each other? and so on.

In any event, it is certainly safe to say that the presence of priests in England and the price Donne's brother paid for that presence further intensified the emotional valences of invaded houses for Donne. To what extent did he see England as a house invaded by Heywood and other priests? To what extent did he see the harbouring of priests as yielding to or participating in an invasion—to what extent as a holy mission? Above all, it is likely that his position on such issues was inconsistent and shifting—Annabel Patterson's points about his divided and unresolved responses to censorship are relevant to these cognate questions.[33]

In general, indeed, Donne is attracted to invasion, that narrative where spatial and subject positions shift so rapidly, in part because of imputed shifting positions in his own life, especially between invader and invaded. The bodily permeability that John Carey traces persuasively suggests that Donne would have perceived his own flesh as liable to invasion.[34] If the fears of that intrusion intensified by step-parents were a clear and present danger for him, so too were the concerns about the incursions of disease traced by Harris.[35] Yet in the *Devotions* he repeatedly emphasizes that illness is in a sense an invader that is always already within—'Is this the honour which man hath by being a little world, that he hath these earthquakes in himself, sudden shakings' (I. 'Meditation').[36] The body, like the burglar, confounds the distinction between inside and outside, even self and other.

As these physiological versions of invasion imply, Donne saw himself as invader, would-be or otherwise, as well as invaded. He was clearly attempting to break into the patronage system and into court circles, a process so often frustrated and frustrating. Moreover, I have already suggested that he sometimes represents the male role in sexual intercourse as that of invader into a vulnerable space, a pattern no doubt intensified by the paraklausithyron trope and the many Latin elegies that describe courtship in terms of entering a house. Are not his fears of the rivals who invade a relationship and his attacks on unfaithful women in part at least a deflection of the anxiety that the male lover is always in some sense an intruder?

Much of what this essay has anatomized thus far concerns invasion in general, but there are many additional reasons Donne is interested in invaded houses in particular. It is obvious that the division between *us* and *them* recurs repeatedly throughout his texts, whether in the epistles to patronesses that contrast less worthy recipients and poets or in the many love poems that disparage 'Dull sublunary lovers' ('A Valediction: forbidding Mourning', 13). The motif of the invaded house, I suggested, functions by casting the divide between us and them into the spatial terms of inside and outside. This is significant because it reminds us that Donne, product of a culture that still often defined wealth largely in terms of land, tends to see power as the control of literal or metaphoric space, a viewpoint anatomized by theorists of space, especially Henri Lefebvre.[37] 'We'll build in sonnets pretty roomes' ('The Canonization', 32), he insists, and the epistles to male friends often trope the control or lack of control of one's subjectivity in spatial terms.

Such connections between space and subjectivity are evident in Donne's preoccupation with boundaries and borders. He is, as I have written elsewhere, the poet of marginal states, of cusps, of present participles—the poet of 'the yeares midnight ... and the dayes' ('A Nocturnall upon S. Lucies Day', 1), of a migrating soul breaking from one body to another, of a 'playes last scene' (*Holy Sonnets* ['This is my playes']), of a Christian who is on the threshold of 'that Holy roome, /

Where … I shall be made thy Musique' ('Hymne to God my God, in my sicknesse', 1–3).[38] The image of the invaded house provides a literal, material analogue to his preoccupation with other borders.

That image participates as well in a concern even pervasive in Donne and recent Donne criticism, the relationship of public and private.[39] Much as some recent studies of patriarchalism have demonstrated that the line between public and private was not clearcut in early modern England, so my commentaries on invaded houses direct our attention to the ways Donne blurs that line. To be sure, he does repeatedly construct the autonomous world of love so many critics have written about; but he typically compromises its autonomy. The world of love is always under threat, always liable to invasion and intrusion, whether by the critic in the opening stanza of 'The Canonization' or the initially uncomprehending observer of that 'bracelet of bright haire about the bone' ('The Relique', 6), probably the most famous piece of jewellery in literature. Or, to put it another way, for Donne the relationship of public and private, like so much else, is a process rather than a state—a process that sometimes transforms would-be intruders into respectful observers.

V

The invaded houses in Donne's texts and his culture carry with them many implications for broader literary issues, as well as for tensions in our own cultures. A number of critics are attempting to rethink the workings of narrative in light of critical developments of the last three decades, and the invaded house casts light on that mode. I have already suggested connections between intrusion into a dwelling place and into a text, and those connections can help us to reconfigure the speech act of storytelling. While students of narrative have traced its origins to situations ranging from the pressures of desire to the imperative to found a city, the agenda of forestalling the interruptions of an alternative genre, an alternative story, an alternative mode of closure is an equally powerful drive behind narrative. For telling a tale authorizes prolonged speech, holding at bay potential invaders. Or, to put it another way, much as Donne's 'Sunne Rising' transforms invasion into invitation, so storyteller repositions someone who is potentially a rival storyteller and an interrupter of the current narrative in the less threatening role of listener or even supporter of the tale at hand.[40]

More broadly, further analyses of invasion would be appropriate in this opening decade of the twenty-first century because so many cultural anxieties are represented in terms of that putative act. Fears about immigrants and terrorists are often cast, and even more often concealed, in scenarios of invasion. Witness all the science fiction movies about aliens who pass as natives. Although he presumably would not share the prejudices impelling such films, Steven Spielberg does share their preoccupation with invading and its opposite number, being shut out: those concerns are as pervasive in his films as the lost home, to which they are closely related. Finally, and more to my purposes here, an essay on invasion is an appropriate tribute to Chris Wortham, whose many contributions to the profession include an edition of *Dr Faustus,* that play that stages so many versions of intrusion, and a co-edited edition of the pastoral poems of Andrew Marvell, texts that repeatedly return to the invaded garden to which there is no return.

Notes

1   I am grateful to my research assistant, Kimberly Huth, as well as to audiences at the University of Sydney and Macalester College for their contributions to this essay.

2   On hospitality in the country house poem, see my essay 'Guess Who's Coming to Dinner?: Reinterpreting Formalism and the Country House Poem', *MLQ,* 61 (2000): esp. 68–70; in the reprinted and expanded version, 'The Politics of Aesthetics: Recuperating Formalism and the Country House Poem', in *Renaissance Literature and Its Formal Engagements,* ed. Mark David Rasmussen (New York: Palgrave, 2002), see esp. pp. 74–81.

3   John Donne, *The Satires, Epigrams and Verse Letters,* ed. W[esley] Milgate (Oxford: Clarendon Press, 1967). I cite this edition throughout.

4   All citations are to John Donne, *The Epithalamions, Anniversaries and Epicedes,* ed. W[esley] Milgate (Oxford: Clarendon, 1978).

5   John Donne, *Devotions upon Emergent Occasions* (Ann Arbor: University of Michigan Press, 1959), p. 9. All citations are to this edition.

6   John Donne, *The Elegies and The Songs and Sonnets,* ed. Helen Gardner (Oxford: Clarendon, 1965); I cite this edition throughout. John Donne, *The Sermons of John Donne,* ed. George R. Potter and Evelyn M. Simpson (Berkeley: University of California Press, 1962), vol. I, p. 227.

7   For an expanded version of this argument about burglars, step-parents and the early death of parents, and the loss of dwellings, especially from fire, see my book *Shakespeare and Domestic Loss: Forms of Deprivation, Mourning, and Recuperation* (Cambridge: Cambridge University Press, 1999), on which the ensuing discussion of these issues is in part based.

8   The fear of those domestic invaders is traced in Richard Helgerson, *Adulterous Alliances: Home, State, and History in Early Modern European Drama and Painting* (Chicago: University of Chicago Press, 2000); in *Vagrancy, Homelessness, and English Renaissance Literature* (Urbana: University of Illinois Press, 2001), Linda Woodbridge analyzes the significance of vagrants' mobility.

9   Throughout this essay I cite *The Riverside Shakespeare,* ed. G. Blakemore Evans, 2nd ed. (Boston: Houghton Mifflin, 1997).

10 *The Poems of Sir Philip Sidney,* ed. W. A. Ringler, Jr. (Oxford: Clarendon, 1962).

11 On the prevalence of crimes against property in Essex, see Joel Samaha, *Law and Order in Historical Perspective: The Case of Elizabethan Essex* (New York: Academic Press, 1974), p. 22.

12 Francesco Petrarch, *Phisicke against Fortune,* trans. Thomas Twyne (London, 1579),

Nviii^v^.

13 Jonathan Gil Harris, *Foreign Bodies and the Body Politic: Discourses of Social Pathology in Early Modern England* (Cambridge: Cambridge University Press, 1998).

14 John Makluire, *The Buckler of Bodilie Health* (Edinburgh, 1630), pp. 64–66.

15 See esp. Harold Love, *Scribal Publication in Seventeenth-Century England* (Oxford: Clarendon Press, 1993).

16 Among the many studies of dialogism in lyric are Don H. Bialostosky, *Wordsworth, Dialogics, and the Practice of Criticism* (Cambridge: Cambridge University Press, 1992). On the issue of whether Bakhtin himself or one of his followers modified his earlier contrast between the putative dialogism of the novel and its absence in lyric, see my book, provisionally entitled, *The Challenges of Orpheus: Lyric in Early Modern England*.

17 See the paper Marcy North delivered at the 2000 Modern Language Association meeting in Washington DC, 'Finis: Manuscript Lyrics and the Problem of Endings'. I am grateful to the author for making her work available to me before publication.

18 For these earlier approaches to the poem, see J. B. Leishman, *The Monarch of Wit: An Analytical and Comparative Study of the Poetry of John Donne,* 7th ed. (New York: Harper and Row, 1965), esp. pp. 188–191; Clay Hunt, *Donne's Poetry: Essays in Literary Analysis* (New Haven, CT: Yale University Press, 1954), pp. 91–93.

19 Meg Lota Brown, 'Absorbing Difference in Donne's Malediction Forbidding Mourning', *John Donne Journal,* 20 (2001): 289–92; Arthur F. Marotti, *John Donne, Coterie Poet* (Madison: University of Wisconsin Press, 1986), pp. 156–57; Ben Saunders, *Desiring Donne: Poetry, Sexuality, Interpretation* (Cambridge, MA: Harvard University Press, forthcoming).

20 A. D. Cousins, 'Donne and the Resources of Kind', in *Donne and the Resources of Kind,* ed. A. D. Cousins and Damian Grace (Madison, New Jersey: Associated University Presses, 2002), pp. 13–15.

21 Leishman, *Monarch,* esp. pp. 188–190.

22 I am indebted to Sarah Monette for useful information about the paraklausithyron tradition.

23 With her customary erudition, Stella P. Revard traces links between Donne and Propertius in 'Donne and Propertius: Love and Death in London and Rome', in *The Eagle and the Dove: Reassessing John Donne,* ed. Claude J. Summers and Ted-Larry Pebworth (Columbia, MO: University of Missouri Press, 1986), pp. 69–79. She does not comment explicitly on the *paraklausithyron* tradition (though she does cite from a different perspective, the rendition of a female viewpoint, one poem in which a version of it appears, Propertius I.3); her demonstration of Donne's other debts to Propertius implicitly supports my argument that the early modern poet would have been aware of his predecessor's reinterpretations of the *paraklausithyron* as well.

24 L. E. Semler, 'Mannerist Donne: Showing Art in the Descriptive Verse Epistles and the Elegies', in *Donne and the Resources of Kind,* ed. Cousins and Grace.

25 Cousins, 'Donne and the Resources of Kind', pp. 13–15.

26 I am very grateful to my undergraduate student Abram Foley for suggesting this connection with pastoral to me.

27 See esp. Peter Brooks, *Reading for the Plot: Design and Intention in Narrative* (New York: Alfred A. Knopf, 1985), esp. Ch. 2.

28 Because of the controversies associated with numbering and ordering these poems, I identify them by their opening words.

29 Franz Kafka, *Shorter Works*, vol. 1, trans. and ed. Malcolm Pasley (London: Secker and Warburg, 1973), p. 87.

30 Cora Fox, 'Enclosing Sin: Formal Transgression and Misogyny in Donne's *Metempsychosis*' (paper presentation, Modern Language Association Convention, Washington, D. C., December 1996).

31 Dennis Flynn, *John Donne and the Ancient Catholic Nobility* (Bloomington: Indiana University Press, 1995), esp. pp. 101–4.

32 Flynn, *John Donne*, p. 102.

33 Annabel Patterson, *Censorship and Interpretation: The Conditions of Writing and Reading in Early Modern England* (Madison: University of Wisconsin Press, 1984), esp. pp. 102–5.

34 On bodily permeability, see John Carey, *John Donne: Life, Mind and Art*, 2nd ed. (London: Faber and Faber, 1990), esp. Ch. 5.

35 Harris, *Foreign Bodies*.

36 Donne, *Devotions*, p. 8.

37 See esp. Henri Lefebvre, *The Production of Space*, trans. Donald Nicholson-Smith (Oxford: Blackwell, 1991).

38 On Donne's predilection for marginal states, see my study *Echoes of Desire: English Petrarchism and Its Counterdiscourses* (Ithaca, NY: Cornell University Press, 1995), pp. 207–8.

39 See, e.g., the reading of 'The Canonization' in Ronald Corthell, *Ideology and Desire in Renaissance Poetry: The Subject of Donne* (Detroit: Wayne State University Press, 1997), pp. 88–100.

40 See my lengthier discussion of storytelling as an invitation to complicity and a defence against rival stories in '"Lending soft audience to my sweet design": Shifting Roles and Shifting Readings of Shakespeare's "A Lover's Complaint"', in *Shakespeare Survey, 58* (2005): esp. 24–30, 32.

Marvell's 'Horatian Ode on Cromwell's Return from Ireland' and the Context of the Engagement Controversy

Conal Condren

'Charles I was the Basil Fawlty of the Seventeenth Century.'
C. J. Wortham

The weighty presence of Charles I in Marvell's Horatian Ode has allowed the praise of Cromwell to be construed as doubtful or disingenuous, even, as C. J. Wortham has argued, for it to be mistaken as an expression of royalism.[1] The poem has come to epitomize that pervasive subtlety that can make any straightforward reading of Marvell's work seem like critical incompetence. [2] Hence Wortham's demand for clarifying contextualization. To this end he has placed the poem in the partial context of the Engagement controversy of 1649–52 and drawn suggestive connections between it and Hobbes's political theory.[3] Yet patterns of ambivalence might well be expected from a time of such intense dislocation, with the untoward status of the Commonwealth a principal source of ethical agonizing.[4] So while some parliamentarians were dismayed at the execution of Charles, the pugnaciously royalist Hobbes was prepared to accept the new Republic. But what if the fault-lines of argument have been misconstrued? How does a reconsideration affect the interpretation of Marvell's Ode?

The argument here is austerely limited. It is only about one poem and I do not wish to claim that a knowledge of the Engagement controversy is sufficient for its understanding. Indeed, despite the attractions of contextualization, the results are rarely as conclusive as we might hope. What are posited as contexts are themselves functions of our predispositions to read texts in certain ways, so privileging some sorts of extra-textual relationships above others, processes that can come perilously close to circularity. Certainly, to ask for a new context is to invite a new reading not to contemplate something that leaves established meanings untouched. Moreover, the closer a text is studied, the more contexts might be generated. The more they are conjured from undifferentiated background, the more difficult it becomes to keep them impervious to patterns of implication and marginal possibility that may ultimately destabilize what was thought secure. Even where we have no good reason to worry about such contextual porosity, a relatively stable context may operate as a counterpoint to a text; contexts do not determine how their materials are used. Marvell's use of complex rhetorical *topoi* has been much discussed; the Ode plays with forms characteristic of royalist writing;[5] it reverberates with echoes classical and contemporary, poetic and propagandistic; but whether they are grace notes and residua, or heavily freighted with the author's principal meaning is another matter. Little wonder that we have ways of making the poem inconclusive if we choose and cannot be stopped from fashioning the poet in our own image.[6]

Consider an incontrovertible fact. The poem is a formal praise and may be seen as working within a highly conventionalized epideictic genre of poetics, with propensities towards hyperbole, that readily reveal distance between image and evidence. In measuring any such credibility gap there is ample room to infer dissonance or even a litotic contradiction between, in John Austin's terms, locution and illocutionary force. Indeed, the less worthy a subject, the more skill is displayed in the panegyric. The disgruntled courtier Sir William Cornwallis had demonstrated his ingenuity precisely by celebrating the impossible, syphilis. But when he lauded that notorious image of tyranny Richard III, it is less certain whether the praise was an oblique criticism of the rulers who followed him or was pretty free of critical gravitas.[7] Is one essay a destabilizing context for the other, or are they simply separate exercises? In short, the very dexterity epideictic demands also allows the dogged ambiguator to reintroduce inconclusiveness despite the words on the page. When all else fails we can always make hermeneutic hay with irony.[8]

The necessities of contexualization, then, can raise as many problems as they settle; yet with this qualification in mind, the argument here is that if the Engagement controversy is one salient context, its understanding does diminish that 'exactly pitched ambivalence' Blair Worden thought he had found in the Ode; rather, the poem offers a forceful moral endorsement of a brave new world.[9] Marvell's hopes may have been dashed by the time his 'accidental triptych' on Cromwell was finished, but as Wortham shows, we need stronger arguments than have been provided to erase a Commonwealth commitment from its first panel.[10]

In 1649 Charles I was executed for tyranny and, in order to prevent any repetition, Cromwell's army and its parliamentary supporters abolished the office of the monarch and the House of Lords. The 'kingdoms old', were indeed 'cast into another mould' (35–36).[11] After much debate, the leaders of the new Commonwealth imposed an Engagement, first on ministers of state and then upon all adult males who might hold some form of subordinate office. The point of this calculatedly evasive pseudo-oath was to assert symbolically the continuity of rule, law and justice and to flush out malignants. Refusal to engage carried the danger of losing property and being put beyond the protection of the state. It was, perhaps, naively believed that those deeply antipathetic to Parliament would expose themselves by a refusal to engage. What the Engagement did, however, was to excite conscientious disquiet over the propriety of abandoning sacred oaths of allegiance to Charles for a new oath or something suspiciously like it. What was it, what did it mean and what right did the men in Parliament have to impose such a demand?[12]

The ensuing debate has pretty uniformly been understood as being between the supporters of the new de facto power urging the acceptance of the Engagement for the sake of peace and those justifying refusal in the name of the 'helpless right' (62) of de jure rule.[13] On this simple breakdown of the arguments, it was a matter of the basic self-interest of recognizing power versus adherence to a principle: might versus right. Once this taxonomy is accepted, writers like Marvell and Hobbes can be seen as bowing to the realities of a violent world even if they found it all morally distasteful—hence one contextual grounding for the imputed aura of ambivalence in the Ode.[14] Wortham, for example, suggests that Marvell saw Cromwell's 'career as an instance of a rise to power, rather than as an ethical issue'.[15] After all, the peremptoriness of Cromwell's rising star, burning through the heavens, his irresistible force in overturning tradition before crushing the Irish, are all conveyed with no conspicuous sense of outrage. Instead, he is portrayed as something beyond ethical censure; blame and resistance are alike, 'madness' (25). The mechanism for sustaining the balance within the poem is to be sought in the wistful appreciation that right and justice were nevertheless on the side of the morally impeccable Charles. Hence, to put it crudely, if the debate was over right versus might, comely Charles is the poetic image of right, restless Oliver of might.

Such an overview, however, requires that modern conceptions of power are mistaken for seventeenth-century usage; and in fact, predominantly the word power referred to a moral right, a responsibility of exercising an office. The words power and office could be synonyms.[16] For moral condemnation, terms like force, oppression, violence, tyranny were preferred. This should forewarn us that argument did not turn on an agreed distinction between power and principle. That the new regime had come into being by force was not disputed. Since Augustine it had been almost a truism that new societies are founded in violence and Marvell alludes to this in referring to the 'bleeding head' found under the Roman Capitol (69). The removal of Charles's head was at

> that memorable hour
> Which first assured the forcèd power.
>
> (65–66)

It is not power that is amoral, or 'naked'[17] but its mode of acquisition through force. In the light of such beginnings it had been conventional since the fourteenth century to distinguish tyranny of origin from exercise. Tyrannies of origin would include both Romulus's murder of Remus and Parliament's execution of Charles. Tyranny of exercise, however, was a matter of the systematic abuse of an office, not exercise of power but of force, the very crime of which Charles had been condemned.

On this score, then, de facto origination was not the issue, the contest concerned its implications for moral obligation demanded by the Engagement. This rendered the very distinction between the de facto and the de jure contentious; it was insisted upon by anti-engagers, but resisted by their opponents who, curiously are the ones who have since been described as the de facto theorists. Among them Anthony Ascham regarded the distinction as irrelevant, others explicitly denied its validity.[18] Thus the way in which the debate has been understood by modern scholars inadvertently accepts the issues as drawn up by those sympathetic to Charles. Once these are taken to the poem any discomfort about his execution is bound to be accentuated, and an aesthetic balance of approbation established on the spurious authority of a misread context.

Similarly, among those advocating the Engagement, I have found none who presented a case in purely pragmatic terms, and to have done so would have been strikingly obtuse. For the need to comply with the new men was pretty much accepted on both sides of the dispute; each paraded a concern for *utilitas*, the rhetorical category covering a range of anticipated practical consequences and evoking them to bolster their respective arguments from principle, *honestas*. The Engagers insisted that what was required was a full and proper ethical adherence to the Republic and hence the last thing they would accept was that the issue was might versus right, or that mere compliance out of self-interest was an adequate response. If Marvell, like Hobbes, is to be numbered among them, we need to recognize that the poem is explicating the basis for such a higher commitment. If the new regime was a tyranny by origin, notwithstanding, it ruled by right and it must be judged on the way in which it exercised its office, its power. Thus the elision of modern with seventeenth-century uses of power can create an incoherence in Marvell's poem. The failure, according to Chernaik to reconcile power with right is actually guaranteed by anachronistic expectations, and an indifference to seventeenth-century moral vocabulary.[19]

The main drift of the Engagers' argument, in fact went as follows: all power is of God (which is why it is a moral category) and allegiance is due to the offices themselves irrespective of the contingent personae occupying them.[20] The position took the form of an enthymeme. God instituted the office of rule, this must be exercised; therefore for conscience sake we should obey those in office who are capable of doing as He requires.[21] If officers in an army are killed, stated Joseph Caryl, others must assume the necessary duties.[22] In practical terms, to refuse full moral allegiance to the exercise of office would, as one writer put it, destroy government by a 'lingering consumption'.[23] The ultimately theological rationale for obligation also gave providence a significant place in the debates as John Wallace recognized many years ago.[24] Providential victory, an exercise of God's power, was a moral sanction. As Caryl remarked, because both sides in the civil wars had appealed to providence, it is reasonable to see the outcome in such terms.[25]

Conversely, for the opponents of the Engagement, fealty could only be given to the authentic office-holding *personae*.[26] If a man usurped the position of a husband, a wife might have little choice other than to submit, but this did not make a rapist her spouse. God's injunction to obey the higher powers did not, therefore, mean anyone who might bustle in. Otherwise, rule would be indistinguishable from tyranny and office would be maintained only for so long as one set of swords were long enough and sharp enough to prevail. The purely pragmatic consequences for continuing instability were horrific.[27] So whereas the Engagers insisted on a firm distinction between exercise and acquisition, and the very point of the office of rule, the anti-Engagers, not disputing the rationale and sanctification of office, stressed adherence to its limits as a necessary condition for distinguishing rule from tyranny, and so allegiance from mere compliance; they saw also the mode of acquisition as contaminating exercise. Living under a tyranny took the gloss off an appeal to providence, but it remained a source of warnings; providence, quoth William Prynne, showed that rebels and tyrants were apt to come to the same sticky end. [28] Thus de facto acceptance of the new rulers was one thing, but recognizing right was beyond the pale. To de facto control only de facto compliance can be given.

In the context of such animadversions, Marvell's poem takes on a sharper moral focus, at one with that detected by Norbrook and somewhat alien to modern sensibilities.[29] Cromwell is not simply a primal force of energy and violence, a Nietzschean superman as it were, above mere human moral categories. On the contrary, his ascendency is providential, he is 'The force of angry heaven's flame' (26). In the smoke is certainly a whiff of Margarita Stocker's apocalyptic,[30] and it drifts across all the Cromwell poems. In the Ode, force as energy and strength is itself ethicized because it is heaven's; and it is this that makes it madness 'to resist or blame'(25). Madness conveys more than futility; it is the enormity of confronting the evidence of God's will.[31] Indeed, Marvell makes clear that there is a moral grounding, a rectitude and industry that has made it appropriate for Heaven to choose Cromwell as its purging instrument in the first place. And in Caesar's head blasting through his laurels (23–24), Cromwell's *persona* is transformed and his exercise of office becomes the justificatory focus.

The following lines (37–44) also need shifting beyond the contours of a simple opposition between might and right, de facto or de jure:

Though justice against fate complain,
And plead the ancient rights in vain:

But those do hold or break
As men are strong or weak.
Nature that hateth emptiness
Allows of penetration less:
And therefore must make room
Where greater spirits come.

This passage concerns three inter-related things, the acquisition of office through violence, the reason for there being a ruling office in the first place, namely to provide justice that cannot be sustained without those in power having the strength to exercise their office, and that if this is so, the necessity of continuity becomes the overwhelming imperative. These are all points at one with the promulgation of the Engagement and endorse the casuistic arguments of its defenders.

The lines following and rehearsing the entrapment and execution of Charles (50–60) are elaborations of this moral perspective. The image of Charles as the deer should not be coloured by modern delicacy or sympathy for hunted animals.[32] It expresses his incapacity for the office to which he has been born, he is a royal actor upon the scaffold. And this theatrical image, playing with the double entendre of scaffold could have been meant to convey that he only played at ruling—reason enough in a providential world to explain Heaven's anger. Acting was condemned by some as morally compromising role-play; by others it was elevated to the status of an office in its own right but one involving a pretence of virtues, not their practice. On either understanding of acting, it was discrepant with the responsibilities of rule. According to the conventions of nominal definition, much favoured in seventeenth-century political argument, and persistently relied upon during the controversy, the misfit between *persona* and office carried the strict implication that no true monarch had been executed, for in not ruling, or ruling tyrannically a monarch, being a function of the exercise of office, ceased to be. He who would harm his children, wrote Anthony Ascham, is no longer a father; people owe an ex-ruler no moral obligation; oaths can only be to those in official capacities.[33] The contrast to Cromwell, the once private man who had become a Caesar, is not the captured king but the man or actor Charles, confronting the block. It had been Charles Stuart that Parliament had taken to the scaffold. Irrespective of this, at least it is clear that in being executed Charles played his part well, '*He* nothing common did or mean' (57). Although the point is directly to condemn bloody hand-clapping at his death, it might leave open his conduct on other scenes. Crucially, his decorous performance is necessary to imply, that the de facto acquisition of power has now been transformed to licit exercise. Whether it also carries a stronger resonance of sympathy in alluding to the iconography of the *Eikon Basilike*, requires an arrow from a longer bow.[34]

Nor called the gods with vulgar spite
To vindicate his helpless right (61–62).

Thus 'the forcèd power' is assured (66). Tyranny of acquisition is but a prelude to the moral exercise of office.

That calibrated ethics of office is immediately reinforced with the authority of Roman mythology. Rome might have originated in violence but from that sprang its 'happy fate' (72). And in his actions, Cromwell demonstrates his integrity.

How fit he is to sway
That can so well obey.
He to the Commons' feet presents
A kingdom, for his first year's rents:
And, what he may, forebears
His fame, to make it theirs:
And has his sword and spoils ungirt,
To lay them at the public's skirt. (83–90)

This is the most sustained contrast with the failures of which Charles had been accused at his trial, of being that monster, an unaccountable officer, who acted in a private not a public interest, one incapable of trust who abused his office by breaking it.[35] The sovereign power is now asserted to be Parliament and Cromwell's fitness for highest office comes from what Charles could never do, work within the moral bounds of obedience to something higher. The qualities attributed to Cromwell, then, are precisely those that deny the accusation of tyrannous conduct. And obliquely they make a further contrast with the royal actor. Cromwell synthesizes the attributes of both the active and contemplative lives; setting aside his muses, books and garden, he has proved himself as one who both acts (rather than plays) and knows (76). The implied reluctance to be plucked from the contemplative ambiance accords with a familiar, ultimately Platonic and Ciceronian prejudice, that those most fit for office are least beguiled by its attractions; those wanting or born to rule are least suited to its responsibilities. The poem concludes on the necessity of supporting Oliver's continuing service; for his battle is against 'the spirits of the shady night' (118), the superstitions of Catholicism and its priesthood with both of whom Charles had, for so many, been tainted. These are enemies requiring the same arts, that is virtues and capacities, to hold power as were needed for its acquisition. The quelling of the Irish shows what can and must be done, the 'parti-coloured' Pict (106) is next. And as Cromwell has proved himself worthy, the implicit injunction is for others also to accept the moral reciprocity of obedience to the Commonwealth, the source of continuing justice and law. Little wonder the poem virtually disappeared from the *Miscellaneous Poems* of 1681.[36] It is a celebration of a providentially blessed evangelical republic, threatened but energetic in the processes of reformation and imperial consolidation. Despite the institutional ruptures, there is a continuity of God's office to which allegiance is due; it was probably anathema to almost any self-respecting royalist before the poem became a safe piece of literature.[37]

Many of those arguing for the Engagement alluded to or exploited fears of 'popery' but judiciously, did not go as far as Marvell in placing a demand for commitment within an eschatological and highly divisive framework. Not all showed such heightened enthusiasm for the Commonwealth but they were giving deliberative advice to those who wanted to be relieved of moral perplexity when confronted with a new prince.[38] To do so the Engagers needed to draw on shared perceptions, and resist the sort of inflated claim that might undermine suasive power. They were not involved in formal exhibitions of epideictic rhetoric with their diminished need to stay close to literality. Marvell's images of Charles and Cromwell, transforming *personae* pivoting around the desiderata of the office of rule should not then be measured by historical verisimilitude, but they place the poet with men like Milton and Sidney who believed fervently that Charles had been a tyrant and that an aggressive republic was necessary for the concomitant imperatives of reformation and imperial independence.[39]

We can now reconsider the balance of similarities between Marvell and Hobbes. Unlike the poet, Hobbes had no truck with the intrusions of apocalyptic perspectives, and was particularly chary of appeals to providence and knowledge of God's intentions—except, of course, in the case of obedience to the sovereign. His prominence in the controversy is partially accidental for he had long been developing a considered theory of sovereignty as an office which, irrespective of various mutations, was a necessity for civilization; regardless of personal preference, it was bound to embrace any who could offer effective protection—there was no such governmental form as tyranny. Hobbes's allusions to the controversy in *Leviathan* are designed to clarify this, perhaps because, ironically, his theories were not uniformly seen as supporting the Engagement.[40] The result was to get him accused of the commitments Marvell declaims and to set on its way the baseless myth that the frontispiece was a portrait of Cromwell. Thus allegiance to the exercise of sovereign power amalgamates an appeal to self-interest and what is morally right because authorized by the consent of the would-be protected and required by God. Marvell has little stress on the *utilitas* of accepting the new regime and only at the climax does he invoke the dangers of the shady spirits of priestcraft. For Hobbes, however, both are major preoccupations. His account of human nature was designed to explain the fragility of society and the necessity of obedience to what keeps fellow wolves from the door. Effective rule was thus the *sine qua non* for any workable notion of justice, a point by no means exclusively Hobbesian and close to Marvell's insistence that right and justice

hold or break
As men are strong or weak (39–40).[41]

Neither writer is presenting an image of political society as fundamentally about power in any indiscriminate, modern or amoral fashion. Hobbes's natural condition may indeed concern something like this; but the whole point of political society is to escape the horrors of such an hypothetical situation. It is to convert the inadequacies of power, everyone's ineffective, if not helpless right, into the powers of office, authorized by those made to feel secure.[42]

For Hobbes, among the most pressing dangers to peace lay Roman clerics and as for Marvell, they were shady in the night, the ghostly fathers of the 'Kingdom of Darkness', creeping around graveyards, like fairies in the gloom, they instantiated the propensities of all clergy to subvert sovereignty in the names of conscience and obedience to a divine power of which they claimed to be the mediators.[43] If Marvell is counselling the reader, it is at one with the explicit injunctions of the Engagers and Hobbes, morality and prudence should lead us to accept the powers that be for their work is both onerous and essential.

Contexts are the rolling contours over which the ongoing hunt for meaning and indeterminacy in Marvell's work will no doubt continue to range. Yet there is one scent that leads to a precipice of clarity. If the Engagement debates inform the Ode they suggest that clear commitments cohere it throughout; and even if the potentialities of epideictic allow a distance between voice and encomium, we need to try it with a keener eye than the blunt dichotomies of modern analysis have allowed. To conclude with unseemly directness: the presence of Charles in the poem is no digression, neither is it for ethical balance, aesthetic decorum or nostalgia. It is the reason for Cromwell. That Charles was comely and deer-like is hardly to the point. After all, we are not that far from Milton's composite of Cromwellian apostasy and Carolinian tyranny—Lucifer, who would be comely enough and a bit of a beast to boot.

Notes

1   Annabelle Patterson, *Marvell and the Civic Crown* (Princeton: Princeton University Press, 1978), pp. 67–68; C. J. Wortham, 'Marvell's Cromwell Poems', in Conal Condren and A. D. Cousins eds, *The Political Identity of Andrew Marvell* (Aldershot: Scolar Press, 1990), pp. 18, 24–29 and n. 5 p. 49; citing for example, Margarita Stocker, *Apocalyptic Marvell: The Second Coming in Seventeenth-Century Poetry* (Brighton: Harvester, 1986); Blair Worden, 'The Politics of Marvell's Horatian Ode', *The Historical Journal,* 27.3 (1984), 525–48; David Norbrook, *Writing the English Republic: Poetry, Rhetoric and Politics, 1627–1660* (Cambridge: Cambridge University Press, 2000), p. 245 for telling critique of the royalism in the poem.

2   William Lamont, 'The Religion of Andrew Marvell: Locating the "Bloody Horse"', in *The Political Identity of Andrew Marvell*, p. 135.

3   Wortham, 'Marvell's Cromwell Poems', pp. 24–29.

4   Worden, 'The Politics of Marvell's Horatian Ode', pp. 539–40, 547.

5   Norbrook, *Writing the English Republic*, pp. 252–54; Wortham, 'Marvell's Cromwell Poems', p.18.

6   Lawrence W. Hyman, *Andrew Marvell* (New York: Twayne, 1964), p. 92.

7   Sir William Cornwallis, *Essays of certain Paradoxes* (1616).

8   Worden, 'The Politics of Marvell's Horatian Ode', p. 530; Ron Bedford, 'Historicizing Irony: The Case of Milton and the Restoration', in Philippa Kelly ed., *The Touch of the Real: Essays in Early Modern Culture* (Perth: UWA Press, 2002), pp. 64–83.

9   Worden, 'The Politics of Marvell's Horatian Ode', p. 540; Norbrook, *Writing the English Republic*, p. 268. For a fuller discussion of the controversy, see Conal Condren, *Argument and Authority in Early Modern England: The Presupposition of Oaths and Offices* (Cambridge: Cambridge: University Press, 2006), ch. 14 and the literature there cited.

10 Wortham. 'Marvell's Cromwell Poems', pp. 48–49; see also Patterson, 'Miscellaneous Marvell?' in *The Political Identity of Andrew Marvell*, pp. 206–8 for a more decisive identification of commitment than she had made in *The Civic Crown*; Norbrook, *Writing the English Republic*, pp. 268–70.

11 'An Horatian Ode upon Cromwell's Return from Ireland' (1650), in *Andrew Marvell: The Complete Poems*, ed. Elizabeth Donno (Harmondsworth: Penguin Books, 1978 edn), pp.55–58. Line numbers are given in parentheses in the text.

12 Thomas Washbourne, letter to Robert Sanderson (1650), in 'The Case of the Engagement', Sanderson, *Works*, ed. W. Jacobson (Oxford: Clarendon Press, 1854), vol. 5, pp. 19–21. Modern discussions have been apt to assume that the Engagement was an oath, but its status was in doubt and the terms oath, engagement, vow, promise could have differing meanings and moral implications.

13 See for example, Perez Zagorin, *A History of Political Thought in the English Revolution* (New York: Thoemnes Press, 1954, 1977), pp. 62–67, 70; Sarah Barber, *Regicide and Republicanism: Politics and Ethics in the English Revolution, 1646–59* (Edinburgh: University Press, 1998), pp. 188–90.

14 Worden, 'The Politics of Marvell's Horatian Ode', pp. 533–34.

15 Wortham, 'Marvell's Cromwell Poems', p. 28; for a sustained and standard treatment in these terms see at length, John M. Wallace, *Destiny His Choice: The Loyalism of Andrew Marvell* (Cambridge: Cambridge University Press, 1968).

16 See, for example, John Rocket, *The Christian Subject* (1650), p. 119.

17 Wortham, 'Marvell's Cromwell Poems', p. 40.

18 Anthony Ascham, *On the Confusions and Revolutions of Goverments* (1649), pp. 33, 24–25; Marchamont Nedham, *The Case for the Commonwealth Truly Stated* (1650), p. 40; N. W., *A Discourse concerning the Engagement, or the Northern Subscribers Plea* (1650), p. 16; Joseph Caryl, *A logical Demonstration of the Lawfulness of Subscribing to the New Engagement* (1650), p. 3.

19 Warren Chernaik, *The Poet's Time: Politics and Religion in the Work of Andrew Marvell* (Cambridge: Cambridge University Press, 1983), pp. 21–22.

20 See for example, Francis Rous, *The Lawfulnes of Obeying the Present Government*

(1649) in Joyce Lee Malcolm ed., *The Struggle for Sovereignty: Seventeenth Century English Political Tracts* (Indianapolis: Liberty Fund, 1999), vol. 1, pp. 393–494; Anon., *Conscience Puzzl'd,* (1650) in *ibid.,* pp. 438–43; John Rocket, *The Christian Subject* (1650); John Dury, *A Disengaged Survey* (1650*).*

21   This most evident in Rous, *Lawfulnes,* and Caryl, *A Logical Demonstration.*

22   Caryl, *A Logical Demonstration,* p. 3.

23   Anon., *Memorandums of the Conferences held between The Brethren scrupled at the Engagement and others who were satisfied with it* (1650) p. 8.

24   John Wallace, 'The Engagement Controversy, 1649–52: An Annotated Checklist of Pamphlets', *Bulletin of the New York Public Library,* 68.6 (1964), pp. 384–85.

25   Caryl, *A Logical Demonstration,* pp. 5–6.

26   See for example, Edward Gee, *An Exercitation* (1650); *A Plea* (1650); Anon., *The Westminsterian Iunto's Self-Condemnation* (1649).

27   Anon., *The Grand Case for Conscience Stated* (1649) in Malcolm, *The Struggle for Sovereignty,* vol. 1, pp. 408–33, esp. pp. 409–11.

28   William Prynne, *A Brief Apology for all Non-Subscribers* (1650), pp. 2–6, 12–13.

29   Norbrook, *Writing the English Republic,* pp. 243–71.

30   Wortham, 'Marvell's Cromwell Poems', pp. 46–47.

31   Patterson, *Marvell,* p. 63; Wortham, 'Marvell's Cromwell Poems', p. 20.

32   The White Hart was the heraldic symbol of the previously deposed Richard II.

33   Ascham, *Confusions,* p. 79; *Conscience Puzzl'd,* pp. 442–43.

34   Patterson, *Marvell,* pp. 67–68.

35   See at length, Anon., *A Declaration of the Parliament of England* (1648/9), in Malcolm, *The Struggle for Sovereignty,* vol. 1, pp. 369–90.

36   Patterson, 'Miscellaneous Marvell', reasonably hazards a printer's failure of nerve, the poem is found in two surviving copies, p. 206.

37   Norbrook, *Writing the English Republic,* p. 268; England was an empire in the sense of being independent, especially of Rome, not necessarily in having an empire; Lamont, 'The Religion of Andrew Marvell', at length.

38   Nedham, *The Case for the Commonwealth,* p. 35; Mazzeo, 'Cromwell as Davidic King', pp. 42–45.

39   See, for example, Jonathon Scott, *Algernon Sidney and the English Republic, 1623–77* (Cambridge: Cambridge University Press, 1988), at length.

40   A pirated edition of his 'Elements of Law'and a translation of *De cive* gave Hobbes a disproportionate presence; *Leviathan* (1651), ed. Richard Tuck (Cambridge: Cambridge University Press, 1991), 'Review and Conclusion'; Ascham, *Confusions,* pp. 122–23 considered *De cive* as irrevocably royalist, cf Anon., *Conscience Puzzl'd,* p. 443 sounding much like Hobbes.

41   Norbrook, *Writing the English Republic,* p. 264; Wortham, 'Marvell's Cromwell Poems', pp. 28–29.

42   Hobbes, *Leviathan,* ch. 30.

43   Hobbes, *Leviathan,* ch. 47, pp. 480–82.

Andrew Marvell and the Tree of Life

Victoria Bladen

I. The Language of Trees

Andrew Marvell's (1621–78) epic topographical poem 'Upon Appleton House, to my Lord Fairfax' (1651–2) maps a journey across the country estate of Nun Appleton in Yorkshire (Figure 12). It was written during Marvell's stay at Nun Appleton while engaged as languages tutor to Mary Fairfax, daughter of Thomas, third Baron Fairfax (1612–71), the former commander of the parliamentary army in the English Civil War. Fairfax, who had opposed the execution of Charles I, had retired in 1650 in protest at the proposed invasion of Scotland.

The poem, ambitious in scale and scope, explores both the estate and the worlds of Marvell's patron, while also alluding to contemporary events and biblical episodes. After sixty stanzas of the poem, covering house, Fairfax, family history, the garden and the meadows, Marvell's speaker retreats to the sanctuary of the woods. Constructed as a sacred place of both topographical and

Figure 12: Nun Appleton Estate, Yorkshire; the track towards the forest.

metaphysical terrain, the woods are given shifting roles as ark, world tree, family lines, labyrinths and vegetal cathedral. Marvell's speaker also adopts a series of roles, as natural philosopher, nature priest, vegetal sacrifice and Green Man.

This article seeks to trace in the forest sequence a series of metaphors of sacrificial death and resurrection, presented in arboreal terms. It seeks to relate these metaphors to a recurring tree of life paradigm in Renaissance culture whereby pruning or withering was juxtaposed with, or seen as a pre-requisite to, rejuvenation. Life, spiritual, familial and political, was commonly imagined in vegetal terms in various cultural discourses. This paradigm of arboreal rebirth was of central significance in

Christian doctrine, migrated to political iconography and was blended with classical sources for didactic purposes in the emblem books. Marvell draws from facets of such arboreal symbolism in Renaissance culture in innovative ways and plants them in the poetic topography of a country estate.

The extensive botanical metaphors across Renaissance culture have been explored critically from various perspectives. Gerhard Ladner traced the pruning/ rejuvenation paradigm in Renaissance iconography and sought to link it with the concept of a Renaissance. Rostvig identified and surveyed the vein of mystical experience in landscape and the figure of the 'hortulan saint' in Renaissance literature. More recently Horowitz has traced botanical metaphors of knowledge and virtue.[1] In Marvell criticism, various aspects of the forest episode have been highlighted including the relevance of alchemical tree emblems (Abraham), the implications of druidic references (Larson; Brooks-Davies) and the relevance of pagan forest ritual (Cummings).[2] Marvell's imagery and allusions are sufficiently complex and ambiguously nuanced to support a range of such readings and this essay seeks to add to such readings by considering the forest episode from the perspective of tree of life symbolism, which to date has not been explored.

This essay also seeks to emphasize the significance of visual precedents for Marvell's arboreal imagery. Arboreal iconography was extensively present across Europe in different forms and media, which articulated biblical metaphors in literal ways. A language of trees surrounded a poet such as Marvell and there are porous boundaries between his poetic forest and his material culture.[3]

II. The Verdant Cross

In John 15, the text's author has Christ claim to be 'the true vine', a metaphor that expresses immortality and rebirth through the verdant continuity of the vine. It constructs Christ as a source of spiritual sustenance to whom the faithful either adhere, and are succoured, or otherwise 'cast forth' if they 'beareth not fruit' (i.e. do not perpetuate the faith) (John 15:1–8, 16–17).[4] The vine motif was interchangeable with the tree of life image in its suggestion of unending regeneration and life. It was also associated with the rituals of the Eucharist whereby celebrants drank wine representing Christ's blood

Figure 13: Tree of life design on doors, York Minster (13th c.).

for the salvation of the human soul.[5] This metaphor is one of an extensive body of botanical and horticultural metaphors throughout the Old and New Testament texts that employ arboreal language to express spiritual doctrine.

Visual articulations of the idea are extensively present in medieval and Renaissance European culture. There are numerous examples of foliate crosses where the notion of sacrifice embodied in the cross fuses with the resultant spiritual rejuvenation embodied in the fecund vine.[6] There is also commonly vine imagery without the human figure of Christ. Figure 13 shows a tree of life design in wrought iron on doors in York Minster.

In stanza 77 of the forest episode in 'Upon Appleton House', the poet's speaker imagines his own verdant crucifixion in the forest.

> Bind me, ye woodbines, in your twines:
> Curl me about, ye gadding vines,
> And O so close your circles lace,
> That I may never leave this place.
> But lest your fetters prove too weak,
> Ere I your silken bondage break,
> Do you, O brambles, chain me too,
> And courteous briars nail me through.

$$(\text{ll. } 609\text{--}16).^{7}$$

Most critics recognize the language of crucifixion in this passage.[8] Yet what is generally overlooked is its specifically vegetative nature.[9] Marvell's speaker seeks to be bound with woodbines (honeysuckle) and curled with vines; chained and nailed with brambles and briars. Fecund imagery of curling vines is mixed with the nailing of briars; verdant continuity with sacrifice. In my view the poet's language invokes the image of Christ as the tree of life, recurrent in religious discourse and in contemporary visual culture. It is this traditional motif that gives meaning to an otherwise irrational episode.

What is also striking about Marvell's version of the verdant crucifixion is its theatricality. Marvell's speaker directs nature and imagines a tableaux which imitates the tree of life. While contemporary religious iconography made literal the metaphor of Christ as the true vine by depicting cross and vine, or just vine, Marvell extends the metaphor. He imagines not a 'two-dimensional' image, but a 'three-dimensional' performance of a crucifixion and encircling by botanical vines. Furthermore he relocates an abstract motif into the local landscape of Nun Appleton. At the same time, the performance is not performed as such, but imagined. In the language of the stanza it remains a mere directive by the speaker to the vines and brambles to crucify him.

When Marvell imagines the performance of a verdant crucifixion in the Nun

Appleton woods, fusing traditional Christian symbolism with a local landscape, there are two types of precedent that are significant. A literary precedent is Aemilia Lanyer's mystic episode on the raised wooded area in 'The Description of Cooke-ham' (1611) where a tree is described in iconic terms, strikingly suggestive of the motif of Christ as the tree of life (ll. 53–66).[10] Lanyer merges the abstract symbol with a 'real' tree on the country estate of Cooke-ham.

A second type of precedent is the presence in the early seventeenth century of visual images that place the symbol of the crucified Christ in contemporary landscapes. An example is a painting by Hendrik Goltzius (1558–1617), *Christ on the tree of life* (1610), where the vision of the crucified Christ is placed in a local contemporary landscape, at the base of which is a woman contemplating an open Bible.[11]

A similar idea is articulated in an English emblem from Francis Quarles' (1592–1644) *Emblemes* (London, 1635) where the idea of the cross as a tree and Christ as the tree of life is articulated by placing the tree in a contemporary landscape, at the base of which sits a woman.[12] Such visual ideas were indebted to the biblical passage of the Song of Solomon in which the figure of the Bridegroom (who was typologically interpreted as Christ) is described as an apple tree under which sits the Bride (interpreted as the Church or the individual soul).[13] In the images, the Song of Solomon passage is conflated with the crucifixion image and the idea of Christ as the tree of life. A historical sacred episode becomes mystically present and an event removed in time, place and divinity becomes proximate to the seventeenth-century European believer in a local, if stylized, landscape.

Given these contexts, what meanings arise from Marvell's invocation of such imagery? Why does Marvell place an imagined crucifixion in the forest of Nun Appleton? Ormerod and Wortham suggest reading the imagery in the light of Romans:

For if we have been planted together in the likeness of his death,
we shall be also in the likeness of his resurrection:
Knowing this, that our old man is crucified with him, that the body of sin might be
destroyed, that henceforth we shall not serve sin.

(6:5–6)[14]

In the imitation of Christ it is sin, 'our old man', that is crucified, with the suggestion that a rejuvenated self will emerge. The biblical directive is cast in horticultural language: 'planted' in imitation of the ultimate tree of life.

We could read Marvell's vegetative crucifixion as a form of poetic atonement for the carnage of civil war, perhaps directed at his patron's troubled conscience over the regicide. Marvell expressly equates pre-war England with Eden and civil war with the Fall:

> Oh thou, that dear and happy Isle
> The garden of the world ere while,
> Thou Paradise of four seas ...
> What luckless apple did we taste,
> To make us mortal, and thee waste?

(ll. 321–23, 327–28)

Having made that analogy, the crucifixion performance in the forest could be read as reparation for the fallen state of the nation, just as Christ's death, in New Testament ideology, repaired original sin. Marvell's speaker seeks to imitate the verdant Christ in order to facilitate regeneration.

Marvell may have chosen the woodbine for its pun ('bound to the wood') as well as its connotations of peace. A seventeenth-century emblem in E. M.'s *Ashrea* (1665) employs the woodbine as a symbol of peace.[15] The association supports a reading of the sacrificial performance as addressed at some level at the Civil War. The choice of plant may be a dual reference to the *Pax Romana*, that supposedly followed Christ's appearance on earth, and the hope for a new peace after the turmoil of war. We should also keep in mind that the tree of life in the biblical passage of Revelation 22.1–2 is described as a healing balm for the nations. Marvell's invocation of the tree of life motif may have sought a poetic balm for the fractured nation.

III. The King Tree

The conflation of the Civil War with the Fall is embodied in another literalized metaphor in the falling of an oak tree in the forest, generally read as a reference to the regicide of 1649:[16]

> The good [the hewel] numbers up, and hacks,
> As if he marked them with the axe;
> But where he, tinkling with his beak,
> Does find the hollow oak to speak,
> That for his building he designs,
> And through the tainted side he mines,
> Who could have thought the tallest oak
> Should fall by such a feeble stroke.

(ll. 545–52)

Supporting the reading of the oak tree as the king is the possibility of a pun in the words 'hewel' and 'axe'. The names of the two officers responsible for procuring an executioner for the King were Colonels John Hewson and Daniel Axtel.[17] The poetic possibilities of such names would not have been lost on Marvell. Fairfax himself had used the metaphor of a tree in relation to the king's execution. He wrote:

My afflicted and troubled Mind for it, and my earnest Endeavour to prevent it, will,
I hope, sufficiently testify my dislike and abhorrence of the Fact: And what will they
not do to the shrubs, having cut down the Cedar?[18]

A contemporary image also draws on arboreal iconography in relation to the
execution of the king. The frontispiece by William Marshall to *Eikon Basilike:
The Pourtraicture of his Sacred Majestie in his Solitudes and Sufferings* (London,
1649) depicts Charles I as equated with Christ, taking up a crown of thorns as a
substitute for the worldly crown, with a vision of a promised heavenly crown.[19] To
the left of the picture are two palm trees, the larger hung on either side with weights
with a Latin banner that reads '*crescit sub pondere virtus*'. The palm had classical
associations with victory and strength, appropriated in Christian symbolism for
martyrdom as victory over death. In 'The Explanation of the Frontispice' the author
describes Charles as taking up the crown of thorns and likens him to 'the Palme,
which heavyest weights do try, Vertue oppresst, doth grow more straight and high'.[20]
The visual link between king and tree provides a significant analogue to Marvell's
imagery, even though its purpose is quite different.[21] Rather than equating the king
with the palm of martyrdom, Marvell's felling of the king-tree in the context of the
forest episode as a whole seems a requisite, or at least natural, pruning for the benefit
of the political order as a whole.

In passages of the Old Testament, retribution is articulated as tree-lopping:

Behold, the Lord, the LORD of hosts, shall lop the bough with terror: and
the high ones of stature shall be hewn down, and the haughty shall be humbled.
And he shall cut down the thickets of the forest with iron, and Lebanon shall fall by
a mighty one

(Isaiah 10:33–34)[22]

Marvell may also have been familiar with the biblical passage in Daniel where
the king Nebuchadnezzar has a dream of a tree reaching the sky. It is lopped and
its human heart exchanged for the heart of a beast, leaving only a stump (Daniel
4:7–15). Daniel interprets the tree as the king himself, to be reduced to a beast for
his pride, and the remaining stump as the kingdom, to be kept for him until his
reformation (Daniel 4:16–24). There were also biblical precedents for the metaphor
of tree-felling as beneficial pruning of the spiritually sterile. In Matthew, John the
Baptist warns the Pharisees and Sadducees to 'bring forth therefore fruits meet for
repentance' and that 'now also the axe is laid unto the root of the trees: therefore
every tree which bringeth not forth good fruit is hewn down, and cast into the fire'
(Matthew 3:7–11).[23]

Marvell's felled tree embodies a sense of retribution; lopped for its pride or
political sterility. Yet the stump, like the nation, has the ability to resprout anew.

In Renaissance culture pruning and lopping carried with it the implicit potential of rebirth. The regenerating stump image appears in the biblical passage of Job: 'For there is hope of a tree, if it be cut down, that it will sprout again, and that the tender branch thereof will not cease' (14:7).[24] The motif was well known in religious iconography and appears in a sketch by Leonardo da Vinci, *Sprouting Tree Stump and Falcon* (late fifteenth century).[25] It depicts a cut stump with new foliage sprouting, with the figure of a bird above.[26] The cut stump signified the old tree of sin and the death of Christ as the tree of life, while the new shoot signalled resurrection and salvation, the bird aligning with the redemptive idea of the new shoot. The cut stump also appeared in alchemical emblems as representative of the vessel in which the alchemical process takes place.[27]

Sterility and fecundity were two parts of the same paradigm; twin poles like the two trees of knowledge/death and life. The juxtaposition of dry and verdant trees was common in Renaissance religious iconography, present in background landscapes depicting scenes from the life of Christ.[28] Such visual compositions articulated the Christian doctrine of sacrifice and redemption in arboreal terms. The dry tree had multiple resonances and could be read, like the cut stump, as the original tree of the Fall, spiritual sterility and the crucifixion, the wood of the tree echoing the wood of the cross. The verdant tree represented both the resurrected Christ as the tree of life, new spiritual hope for man and the ultimate tree of life in the future heavenly city (Revelation 22.1–2).

The two trees, of death and life, could also be imagined as different states of the one tree, or as a composite.[29] An example of a composite dry-and-verdant tree appears in the frontispiece to an English Bible published in 1537 which depicts a central tree both barren and verdant.[30] Emerging from the same central trunk, the branches at the top left are dry, aligning with the tree of knowledge/death at the left with Adam and Eve. The branches at the top right are verdant, aligning with the scenes of Christ's crucifixion and resurrection at the right. Tree imagery created a symbolic language to accompany narration and recall biblical metaphors.

The dry-and-verdant paradigm was also drawn on for political symbolism. In Ripa's *Iconologia* (Padua, 1618), the figure of Riforma depicts an old woman holding a scythe in the foreground while behind her are juxtaposed dry and verdant trees.[31] The implication is that the pruning of dead wood will facilitate political rejuvenation. Political pageantry also appropriated religious iconography. One of the emblematic tableaux set up around London for Elizabeth I's first public procession was at Cheapside where two hills were constructed, each with a tree on it. One was withered to represent a 'decayed commonwele', and the other was green to represent a 'flourishing commonwele', and between the two came the figures of Truth and Time.[32] Thus the juxtaposition of the old and new regimes was articulated through a language of trees.

Read in the context of Renaissance discourses of political rejuvenation through a language of trees, Marvell's felling of the oak tree seems a requisite death; a fortunate Fall. The oak, as the tainted political body embodied in the king, needs to fall so that the forest overall will be renewed. The pruning represents the death of the old political order and the potential for rejuvenation seems implicit, particularly given earlier imagery in the forest episode of fallen trees re-shooting:

> The double wood, of ancient stocks,
> Linked in so thick, an union locks.
> It like two pedigrees appears,
> On one hand Fairfax, the other Veres:
> Of whom, though many fell in war,
> Yet more to Heaven shooting are,
> And, as they nature's cradle decked,
> Will in green age her hearse expect.
>
> (ll. 489–96)

The fallen soldier-trees are earlier Fairfaxes lost in previous wars.[33] They re-shoot, with a pun on sprouting rather than firing; thus the forest will rejuvenate. The death of the king too is placed in the context of an overall natural order and the tree 'seems to fall content' (l. 559). Thus political death and rejuvenation are played out in metaphorical and arboreal terms in Marvell's forest.

IV. The Vegetal Cathedral and the Green Man

The forest itself is imagined as a vessel of rejuvenation:

> But I, retiring from the flood,
> Take sanctuary in the wood,
> And, while it lasts, myself embark
> In this yet green, yet growing ark,
> Where the first carpenter might best
> Fit timber for his keel have pressed.
>
> (ll. 481–86)

The forest is a 'green, yet growing ark', another image of re-sprouting wood. The ark was a type, *inter alia*, of the Cross and if we read the verdant crucifixion imagery of stanza 77 as a reference to the tree of life motif, this earlier image of the green ark seems an anticipation of the idea. Marvell's reference to 'the first carpenter', Noah, anticipates the 'second carpenter', Christ. The ark could also represent the Church.[34] Fairfax used the ark in this sense in a couplet: 'I'th' Sacred Arke Reason of State should lye/But rules of state should nott Religion tye'.[35]

The idea of the forest as a mystic space and vessel is further explored in the notion of the 'temple green':

> Dark all without it knits; within
> It opens passable and thin,
> And in as loose an order grows,
> As the Corinthian porticoes.
> The arching boughs unite between
> The columns of the temple green,
> And underneath the winged quires
> Echo about their tuned fires.
>
> (ll. 505–12)

Corinthian columns featured stylized acanthus leaves, which were a symbol of rebirth.[36] The boughs unite, creating a visual image of gothic pointed arches, making the forest a vegetal cathedral, pagan temple or a conflation of both.

In considering how Marvell's forest is described as an alternative cathedral, we should also be cognizant of the extent to which cathedrals were like forests. Leafy columns line the entrance to the Holy Trinity church at Hull, Yorkshire (Figure 14) while carved leafy spires decorate the roof (Figure 15). The poet's imagery creates a relationship of affinity between church and forest as sacred spaces and sites of imagined contact with deity.

Behind the trees, the poem's speaker 'encamps [his] mind' (ll. 601–2). The retreat to this topographical and metaphysical terrain seems also a mystic journey to a form of prelapsarian Adamic state. Here the speaker knows the language of birds and has an omnipotent knowledge of the forest's green life:

Figure 14: Foliate capitals, Holy Trinity church, Hull (15th c.).

Figure 15: Foliate spire, Holy Trinity church, Hull (15th c.).

> Already I begin to call
> In their most learned original,
> And where I language want, my signs
> The bird upon the bough divines ...
> ... No leaf does tremble in the wind
> Which I returning cannot find.
>
> (ll. 569–72, 575–76)

The forest is a place of knowledge, concealed and revealed. In nature's mystic book leaves are sibylline; texts to be read as prophecy (ll. 578, 584). Marvell invokes the idea of man as an inverted tree himself, with his roots in the divine sphere and his branches in the mortal: 'Or turn me but, and you shall see / I was but an inverted tree' (ll. 567–68). This suggests an affinity between the reader (as tree) and the read (leaves). It also recalls the earlier image of the speaker as 'embarked' (l. 483) on entering the wood. Marvell's speaker not only reads the leaves; he becomes covered with them:

> And see how chance's better wit
> Could with a masque my studies hit!
> The oak leaves me embroider all,
> Between which caterpillars crawl;
> And ivy, with familiar trails,
> Me licks, and clasps, and curls, and hales.
> Under this antic cope I move
> Like some great prelate of the grove.
>
> (ll. 585–92)

The encircling ivy anticipates the verdant crucifixion imagery in stanza 77 however the suggestion of a leafy mask/masque and embroidery of leaves invokes a related but distinct figure. In my view Marvell's language conjures up the figure of the Green Man, a figure whose face was formed from leaves, or from whom vine tendrils emerge (Figure 16).[37] The Green Man was extensively present as sculptural decoration in churches and cathedrals throughout Europe, also appearing in illuminated manuscripts and printed book frontispieces. Marvell could have seen such figures in any number of Yorkshire cathedrals, or at Cambridge, where he studied.[38]

Appearing in endless variations, the Green Man was an ambiguous figure whose visual attributes intersected with orthodox Christian tree of life iconography. As a potentially demonic, unpredictable figure he seems a vestige of the pagan vegetation gods which Christianity supplanted. Anderson notes points of similarity with Dionysus, Osirus, Attis, and the Celtic forest god Cernunnos.[39] Yet the Green Man was commonly present alongside central Christian iconography on rood screens, misericords and spires. No mere gargoyle, he is inside the churches and

Figure 16: Green Man (13th c.; York Minster).

survived the iconoclasm of the Reformation.

On one hand he is an anti-type to the orthodox figure of Christ as the tree of life and the eucharistic symbolism of the vine. Yet the vitality of his leaves and curling vines aligns him with the tree of life iconography signifying Christ. A possible interpretation of this enigmatic figure is that he represents the fallen, dead Adam, in whose mouth, according to Christian folklore, were planted the seeds from the tree of life in Eden.[40] These seeds produced a tree that eventually became the cross.[41] The regenerating plant would then represent Adam's and humanity's redemption through Christ, as the life-giving vine.[42] Sometimes the Green Man appears to be Christ himself.[43] Fittingly Marvell places the Green Man imagery within three stanzas of his tableaux of crucifixion. If the forest is a green cathedral then, like the cathedrals Marvell would have been familiar with, there are places for both Green Men and verdant crosses.

V. Conclusions

Marvell's poetic forest traverses a terrain both symbolic and topographical. In this forest of the mind the poet plants a series of symbolic trees and our reading of the episode is illuminated by considering how the tree imagery relates to contemporary cultural traditions from which authors and artists drew. Botanical and horticultural paradigms of sterility and fecundity or pruning and regeneration, were used to express spiritual and political ideas. Visual forms of such ideas in religious and secular iconography gave visual and literal force to metaphors. At the same time, poetry was responding to new empirical and rational forces in the culture, leading to a unique blend of the natural and the supernatural, the symbolic and the observed in the poetic imagination. Abstract symbols could be placed into 'real' landscapes. Marvell drew from the body of Renaissance arboreal symbolism because it enabled a complex poetic fusion between topographical and symbolic landscapes, and offered a paradigm of rebirth as a balm for a fallen post-war world.

In Marvell's forest the world is both retreated from and recreated in arboreal terms. In the forest, all things suffer a tree-change. Here a matrix of linked imagery emerges between the quasi-Adamic figure with knowledge of the unfallen first language, who falls/Falls into nature, becomes the leafy-masked Green Man and a priest of the grove; then imagines himself as verdantly crucified. The Green Man and the crucified Christ as the tree of life are curled with vines in contemporary iconography and in Marvell's poem. In 'falling', to hit the leafy texts, the subject of his study, the Adamic figure replicates the trespass into forbidden knowledge. Transgressive knowledge was bound up with original sin, expulsion from paradise and the loss of immortality. In Marvell's forest suggestions of knowledge and secret language are bound up with imagery of death and rejuvenation.

The mortal and decomposing Adam, embroidered with leaves and caterpillars, requires the verdant figure of Christ for a green rebirth. Likewise the forest requires the tainted king-oak to fall for it to be rejuvenated. This re-enactment of spiritual and political fall and redemption, played out in arboreal imagery, reads as a poetic attempt by Marvell to interpret the rupture of civil war and regicide. His speaker performs a transformative release and atonement for his patron in the mystic space of the forest. Nature in the forest seems both the tree of death/knowledge, with its leaves as text to be read, and the tree of life, the verdant crucifixion to which he seeks to be bound forever. If the forest becomes one wood, a fifth elemental world tree, it is both dry-and-verdant, a tree of death and new life.

At the end of these symbolic sacrifices there is the language of renewal:

For now the waves are fall'n and dried
And now the meadows fresher dyed:
Whose grass, with moister colour dashed,
Seems as green silks but newly washed.
No serpent new, nor crocodile,
Remains behind our little Nile,
Unless itself you will mistake,
Among these meads the only snake.

See in what wanton, harmless folds
It everywhere the meadow holds,
And its yet muddy back doth lick,
Till as a crystal mirror slick ...

(ll. 625–36)

Having crucified the old body of sin Marvell's speaker emerges from the wood newly baptized. Nature, which fell with man, is likewise resurrected. Flood waters have receded, meadows are 'fresher dyed' and the grass, perhaps like man, is redeemed and baptized as 'green silks'. The river is the only snake and Marvell's image of it licking its own back, suggests the *ouroboros* ('the great round'), the snake devouring itself, the symbol of eternal rebirth.[44] Intriguingly, just such a motif appears in a sculptural detail in the Holy

Figure 17: Snake sculptural detail, Holy Trinity church, Hull.

Figure 18: From the edge of the forest at Nun Appleton, looking towards the river.

Trinity church at Hull (Figure 17). In a passage rich in arboreal rejuvenation, the regenerative serpent-river seems a fitting image to greet the new Adam emerging from the woods of Nun Appleton (Figure 18).

Notes

1   Gerhard Ladner, 'Vegetation Symbolism and the Concept of Renaissance', *De Artibus Opuscula 40, No. 1 (Essays in Honor of Erwin Panofsky)*, ed. Millard Meiss (New York: New York University Press, 1961), pp. 303–22; Maren-Sofie Rostvig, *The Happy Man: Studies in the Metamorphoses of a Classical Idea* (Oslo: Norwegian Universities Press, 1962); Maryanne Cline Horowitz, *Seeds of Virtue and Knowledge* (Princeton, NJ: Princeton University Press, 1998).

2   Lyndy Abraham, *Marvell and Alchemy* (London: Scolar Press, 1990); Charles Larson, 'Marvell and Seventeenth-century Trees', *Durham University Journal* (1987), 27–35; Douglas Brooks-Davies, 'Marvell's Political Mysticism: Hermes and the Druids at Appleton House', Studies *in Mystical Literature*, 1 (1980): 97–119; Robert Cummings, 'The Forest Sequence in Marvell's *Upon Appleton House*: The Imaginative Contexts of a Poetic Episode', *Huntington Library Quarterly*, 47 (1984): 179–210.

3   The author gratefully acknowledges the assistance of the University of Queensland's Graduate Student Research Travel Awards which enabled travel to the UK to document examples of tree of life and Green Man iconography in the Yorkshire area.

4   All biblical quotations are taken from *The King James Bible* (1611) [online version produced by the University of Michigan using the Oxford Text Archive: http://quod.lib.umich.edu/k/kjv)].

5   Gertrude Schiller, *Iconography of Christian Art* (London: Lund Humphries, 1971), p. 134.

6   An example of a foliate cross is the thirteenth-century century mosaic in the apse of San Clemente, Rome (reproduced in Ladner, Figure 10) where a large acanthus vine scrolls out from the cross.

7   All quotations are taken from David Ormerod and Christopher Wortham (eds), *Andrew Marvell: Pastoral and Lyric Poems 1681* (Perth, WA: University of Western Australia Press, 2000).

8   Nigel Smith (ed.), *The Poems of Andrew Marvell* (London: Pearson Longman, 2003), p. 235; Rostvig, pp. 185–90; H. M. Richmond, *Renaissance Landscapes: English Lyrics in a European Tradition* (The Hague; Paris: Mouton, 1973), p. 125; William Empson, *Some Versions of Pastoral*, 2nd edn (Harmondsworth: Penguin Books, 1966), p. 102. Cummings claims this is an overreading and sees the passage as erotic metaphor with sinister undertones in a cultic context (p. 201). Larson reads additional nuances of a 'martyrdom for the religion of nature' inspired by druidical ritual (p. 33). Brooks-Davies refers to the 'strange crucifixion imagery', suggesting a druidic nuance (p. 112).

9   An exception is Ormerod and Wortham's reference to the passage in Romans 6:5–6, with its botanical nuance to the imitation of Christ (p. 258).

10 The line reference is taken from Susanne Woods (ed.), *The Poems of Aemilia Lanyer: Salve Deus Rex Judaeorum* (Oxford: Oxford University Press, 1993).

11 Reproduced in Simon Schama, *Landscape and Memory* (London: HarperCollins, 1995), Figure 25.

12 Stanley Stewart, *The Enclosed Garden: The Tradition and the Image in Seventeenth-Century Poetry* (Madison, Milwaukee and London: The University of Wisconsin Press, 1966), Figure 31. This is a copy of an earlier continental model from Herman Hugo's *A Collection of Religious Emblems* (Antwerp, 1624, Figure 29) (Stewart, Figure 29).

13 'As the apple tree among the trees of the wood, so is my beloved among the sons. I sat down under his shadow with great delight, and his fruit was sweet to my taste' (2:3). Fairfax translated a version of the passage: 'I am the Rose of Sharon's fruitfull field / The Lilly wch the humble valleys yield / In midst of thornes as Lilly appear's above / So mongst the youthfull Virgins is my love/ As Apple-trees 'mongst trees o'th Forrest growe / Amongst the sones of Men my love is soe / Under whose shade is my delightfull seat / And to my tast his fruit is pleasant meat', *The Poems of Thomas Third Lord Fairfax*, ed. Edward Bliss Reed (New Haven, Conn.: Yale University Press, 1909), p. 259. See Stewart generally on the interpretation of the Song of Songs.

14 Ormerod and Wortham, p. 258. Also note Fairfax's translation of Moses' Song in Exodus 15 where the Israelites are likened to plants: 'To Zions mount thou didst them bring / Didst plant them in its firtil soyle / The place wher thou delightst in / A sanctuary freed from toyle' (Fairfax 256, ll. 53–56).

15 In E. M.'s *Ashrea* (London, 1665) the seventh emblem is the woodbine with the epigram: 'Blessed are the Peace-makers, for they shall be called the Children of God'. Beneath the image of two trees intertwined with the woodbine are the lines 'Thus, while two foster deadly hate / A third steps in to end debate; Hands, / Makes Peace, unites both Hearts and / How blest is he who makes such bands.'

16 See Ormerod and Wortham (p. 250) and Don Cameron, *Image and Meaning: Metaphoric Traditions in Renaissance Poetry* (Baltimore: The Johns Hopkins Press, 1960), p. 146. Note however that although the oak was commonly associated with royalty, it is possible

that it represents the nation. Abraham notes that the cedar was used more often than the oak to designate royalty and that the new parliamentary seal of 1649 replaced the crosses of monarchy with oak trees, suggesting the oak as a symbol of nationalism (Abraham, p. 150).

17 Graham Edwards, *The Last Days of Charles I* (Stroud: Sutton Publishing, 1999), pp. 172–73.

18 Abraham, pp. 150–51.

19 The image is reproduced in David Howarth, *Images of Rule: Art and Politics in the English Renaissance, 1485–1649* (Berkeley, LA: University of California Press, 1997), p. 149 and located at the Edinburgh University Library.

20 As Howarth notes, the idea of Charles as a Christian martyr took hold (p. 148). The king in his farewell speech invoked the martyr St Stephen: 'I pray God with St. Stephen that this be not laid to their charge, nay not only so, but that they may take the right way to the peace of the kingdom, for my charity commands me not only to forgive particular men, but my charity commands me to endeavour to the last gasp the peace of the kingdom' (Edwards, pp. 179–80, 184).

21 An earlier identification of Charles I with the palm is in Ben Jonson's *Love's Triumph through Callipolis* (1631) in which 'the throne disappears; in place of which there shooteth up a palm tree with an imperial crown on the top' (cited in Abraham, p. 160).

22 Also in Ezekiel 15 the wrath of Yahweh against the Israelites is likened to the discarding of vine wood on the fire for fuel (15:6).

23 Here the sinful are imagined as unfruitful trees that will be cut. An implicit parallel emerges between these human-trees and the original tree of sin, the tree of knowledge of good and evil. The image here of a cut tree, the stump, is a metaphor of retribution. The speaker, John the Baptist, casts God as a gardener or horticulturist who will prune souls like trees that are not spiritually fruitful.

24 The author uses the image of the re-sprouting tree as a figure of comparison with man, who does not come again but 'crumbles away like rotten wood.' Job also contains an allegory of the godless as like withered reeds devoid of water, or plants growing in sterile ground (Job 8:8–20).

25 The image is reproduced in Ladner, Figure 7.

26 Leonardo's sketch has an accompanying note: 'Albero tagliato che rimette—ancora spero' ('the cut tree that reshoots—there's still hope').

27 Abraham, p. 151.

28 An example is Giovanni Bellini's *The Transfiguration* (1480). To the back left is the withered tree, signifying the death of Christ. In the left foreground is the cut stump, signifying the death of sin as well as the cutting of the tree of life (Christ). To the back right is a tree with full foliage, signifying the resurrection and echoing the figure of Christ as the tree of life in the centre.

29 Dante draws on the idea of the regeneration of the dry tree in an episode in *Purgatory*. A griffon (half eagle and half lion), symbolising Christ, ties the pole of the triumphal chariot of the Church to the foot of the dry tree, which is then rejuvenated in canto XXXII *Earthly Paradise—Through the Forest: The Tree of Adam and the Tree of Christ: Wednesday Morning*. *Purgatory* ends with an image of Dante's speaker as the tree of life with new foliage: 'From those most holy waters, born anew / I came, like trees by

change of calendars / Renewed with new-sprung foliage through and through, / Pure and prepared to leap up to the stars', *The Comedy of Dante Alighieri, the Florentine*, trans. Dorothy L. Sayers (Harmondsworth: Penguin Books, 1949), canto XXXIII, ll. 142–45.

30 *The byble, translated by Thomas Matthew* (London & Antwerp: Whitchurch & Grafton, 1537), reproduced in R. B. McKerrow and F. S. Ferguson, *Title-page Borders used in England & Scotland 1485–1640* (London: Oxford University Press, 1932), Figure 32.

31 Cesare Ripa's *Iconologia* was first published in Rome in 1593 and first illustrated in the third edition, published in Rome in 1603. There followed an edition of 1611 published in Padua and a further Paduan edition of 1618, the image from which is reproduced in Ladner (Figure 1).

32 Rosemary Freeman, *English Emblem Books* (London: Chatto and Windus, 1966), p. 49.

33 Ormerod and Wortham, p. 244.

34 Ormerod and Wortham, p. 244.

35 Fairfax, p. 261.

36 Vitruvius related how Callimachus the architect who devized the Corinthian column, was visiting Corinth to fulfill a commission. He came upon the tomb of a young girl, on the top of which were cups and a tile in which an acanthus plant had seeded and grew out from. The acanthus was thus associated with death and rebirth (Anderson, p. 45).

37 For the Green Man figure see William Anderson, *The Green Man: the Archetype of our Oneness with the Earth* (London and San Francisco: HarperCollins, 1990) and Katherine Basford, *The Green Man* (Cambridge: D. S. Brewer, 1978). The suggestion of the Green Man figure in this stanza has been noted by Anderson and Richmond.

38 Many Green Men figures can be seen at Beverley Minster and York Minster. Green Men also appear across the front of the screen at King's College Chapel, Cambridge, dating from the sixteenth century (Anderson, p. 139).

39 Anderson, pp. 38–40. A bearded mask wreathed with vine or ivy leaves was used as a representation of Dionysus in initiation rites (Anderson, p. 40). The Celtic god of the forest Cernunnos, often portrayed with antlers growing from his brow, also likely has a common ancestry with Dionysus (Anderson, p. 40). Anderson's study includes examples of Green Men that he identifies as the horned Cernunnos (pp. 62–63).

40 The story primarily originates from Jacobus de Voragines' *Legenda Aurea* (Golden Legend) a thirteenth-century text (with subsequent translations including one into English published in 1483). Marvell's knowledge of the work is evidenced in 'Upon Appleton House' where it is mentioned at line 122.

41 The account is related by Stewart (p. 79).

42 For the links between Adam and Christ in the tree of life mythology see Schiller, pp. 130–33.

43 An example is the Green Man at Sampford Courtenay, Bow, Devon (fifteenth-century) whose face appears strikingly Christ-like [reproduced in Mike Harding, *A Little Book of the Green Man* (London: Aurum Press, 1998), cover image].

44 Anderson, p. 21; Abraham, pp. 74, 202–3. In Fairfax's translation of Saint-Amant's *La Solitude* the stream also glides under its arbored banks 'As windinge Serpents in the grass' (265).

The Double Strand of Cleopatra Plays

Kay Gilliland Stevenson

Between the late sixteenth and early eighteenth century, Cleopatra VII of Egypt attracted the attention of poets and playwrights in England more than a dozen times.[1] These dramatic versions of her life can be sorted into a double strand, in which recurrent patterns are conspicuous. Two periods of her life appealed to dramatists; soon after her father's death she is paired with Julius Caesar and in later years with Mark Antony. Caesar met her at the crest of his success; Antony stayed as his power waned. At the time of the Alexandrian War she had been wronged by her brother; in maturity she is clearly in the wrong at Actium. Within the plays set in both periods, other binary patterns appear in shifting combinations: ambition and amorousness, wiles and principles, politics and private concerns, male or female dominance, historical accuracy or imaginative embellishment.

There is rarely a hint of the industry, competence, and tenacity Cleopatra exhibited over more than two decades, from her accession to the throne at the age of seventeen to her death at thirty-nine.[2] No playwright alludes to the politically instructive difficulties the Ptolemies faced during her childhood. Her uncle committed suicide after Cyprus was annexed by Rome and her father provoked insurrection by massive debts he owed the Romans, debts ironically related to the expense of hiring troops to control earlier disorder. The most famous of Cleopatras was more astute and more fortunate than her three sisters. The elder two, Cleopatra VI and Berenice IV, reigned while their father was in Rome appealing to Pompey and the Senate for military aid. This Cleopatra somehow disappeared; Berenice was executed on her father's orders when he returned. Although his will left the throne jointly to Cleopatra VII and her brother Ptolemy XIII, seven years her junior, she was driven from power by the young king's ambitious advisers. At this point, there is a memorable intersection between Roman and Egyptian civil wars. In 48 BC when Pompey, defeated at Pharsalia by Julius Caesar, tried to take refuge in Egypt, Cleopatra had managed to raise an army, drawn up near Alexandria against her brother's troops led by Achillas. Arsinoe, Cleopatra's last surviving sister, then attempted to take advantage of the turmoil that followed the murder of Pompey on his arrival in Egypt. When the adolescent Ptolemy XIII drowned after one of the battles, 'the younger daughter of the late king Ptolemy, in the fond hope that the throne was now without an occupant, left her quarters in the palace to join the camp of Achillas' (Caesar, *Civil War*, 218). The victorious Julius Caesar led Arsinoe in triumph when he returned to Rome.

Cleopatra's name does not appear in the titles of dramatic texts set in her youth. On stage, however, she is almost always given a prominent and positive role in these works. Crucial as her determination to regain regal power is, no dramatist shows her encamped against her brother, and some contrive to make her imprisoned by him. Partly motivated by concern for dramatic unity, this modification of the situation serves to make her appealingly vulnerable, a victim of masculine aggression. When Ptolemy XIII is depicted as a child controlled by his regency council, her magnanimity is displayed in the care with which she blames only the advisers, not her brother. When playwrights tinker with fact and increase his age, they provide opportunity for a noble confrontation between equals.

The task of representing young Cleopatra as a heroine is made easier by the fact that the retinue of Ptolemy XIII included a trio of villains: the eunuch Photinus, the king's chief minister, who urged him to kill Pompey; Achillas, captain of the guard; and the Roman soldier Septimius, who assassinated the general in whose forces he once served. It is made harder by the fact that the major source for the plays is Lucan's *The Civil War*, so hostile to Cleopatra that imaginative manipulation of the material is a challenging necessity. In Lucan's epic account she is a menace to Roman virtues. With the rhetorical question 'Who can refuse pardon to the infatuation of Antony, when even the stubborn heart of Caesar took fire?' (10. 70–72)[3] Lucan casts across the young queen the shadow of later tragedy. He paints her as crafty, luxurious, adulterous, incestuous. Presenting her as culpably rather than commendably resourceful, he describes how she uses bribery, first to persuade guards to unlock chains across the harbour so that she can enter the Alexandrian palace (*corrupto custode* 10. 57), and then to buy, with the night spent together, Caesar's support for her cause (*corrupto judice* 10. 106). Almost all the playwrights, however, minimize her wiles. Despite the obvious dramatic appeal of the scene in which she is smuggled into Caesar's presence, only Fletcher and Massinger, in *The False One*,[4] choose to include it. Except in the farce which occupies the final act of Sir William Davenant's *A Playhouse to be Let*,[5] her behaviour is notably decorous. Despite Lucan, Cleopatra at this period of her life is usually presented with sympathy and admiration.

The most ambivalent presentation of the young Cleopatra is the earliest one, the anonymous Trinity College Oxford play called *The Tragedie of Cæsar and Pompey, or Cæsar's Revenge* (1607),[6] which spans events from Pharsalia to Philippi. Given that only four of the twenty-one scenes are set in Egypt, Cleopatra cannot be said to be a major character, but the resonance of mythological allusions expands her place in the drama. In the large cast of twenty-six characters, three are female, with Cleopatra sandwiched between two Roman wives, Cornelia and Calpurnia. While each of the three women has exactly two scenes on stage, Cleopatra has significantly more influence or impact than the Roman matrons. Their action is limited to pleading unsuccessfully with their husbands to avoid danger, mourning for the dead husbands, and dying (in Cornelia's case) or threatening to die (Calpurnia). Off stage, Cleopatra appeals to Caesar to restore her rightful place on the throne; when they first enter, together, the suit is already successful (1. 6. 1–8). She has little to say beyond inviting the Roman generals to a banquet; what is said about her is more important. During her two scenes on stage, this is mainly lyrical praise of her beauty[7] by Caesar and by Antony; in defiance of history but in the interest of dramatic ironies—and in a pattern which other playwrights adopt—the younger soldier has accompanied Julius Caesar to Egypt. Others attendant on Caesar respond to Cleopatra's presence less ecstatically. An unnamed Lord briefly observes, aside, that this fair sorceress melts warriors into wantonness (2. 3. 68–70), and Dolabella cites the threats Circe and Calypso posed to virtuous, active endeavour (2. 3. 95). Caesar implicitly counters such criticism through alternative allusions; he compares himself to Mars resting in Venus' bed after bloody rage and to Hercules returning to Deianira's arms after victories and toil (2. 3. 71–87).

In order to set up contrasts between Caesar and Antony, the playwright ignores events which Lucan explicitly deplored, Caesar's lingering in Egypt and Cleopatra's bearing his son.[8] Only by omitting Cleopatra's two-year sojourn in Rome, during which Caesar installed a statue of her in the temple of Venus, can he invent a scene in which Caesar celebrates having shaken off

> these wommanish links
> In which my captived thoughts were chayned a fore
> By that fayre charming Circe's wandring look.
>
> (3. 2. 1–3)

Antony, who remains obsessed by memories of Cleopatra, is given a supernatural vision in which his guardian spirit compares 'that fatal face' to Helen's, as Lucan had done (10. 70); the scene ends with Antony commenting that this visitation resembles Mercury's coming to Aeneas 'To warne him leave the wanton dalliance' of Carthage (3. 2. 160). Venus and Deianira, Circe and Calypso, Helen of Troy, Dido—the range of mythological allusions creates divided responses. In particular, parallels between Cleopatra and Dido, although embedded in warning, evoke pathos. Few readers of *The Aeneid* fail to sympathize with a north African queen, initially competent in leading her people, who chooses to die for love.

In the panoramic sweep of the Trinity Play, it is easy to overlook an odd adjective in the speech when Caesar promises his protection:

> I will replant thee in the Ægiptian Throne
> And all thy wrongs shall Cæsars vallor right,
> Ile pull thy crowne from the vsurpers head
> And make the Conquered Ptolomey to stoope,

And feare by force to wrong a mayden Queene.

(l. 6. 4–8)

More prominently, the prologue to Fletcher and Massinger's *The False One* (c. 1620), asserts that the audience will see

Young *Cleopatra* here, and her great mind
Express'd to the height, with us a Maid, and free.

(12–13)

What is startling in the prologue is not simply the unqualified admiration or sympathy for Cleopatra, who here and in subsequent plays is made the prisoner of her brother. It is the word 'maid' that gives us pause. Coming to the story, as we are apt to do, through Shakespeare, we remember two passages in *Antony and Cleopatra* attributing to her an early liaison with Gnaeus Pompey, the elder son of Pompey the Great. Shakespeare's source was Plutarch, who assumes Cleopatra was still at court in 49 BC when Gnaeus Pompey visited Egypt, mustering ships and soldiers for his father's cause. Some modern historians suggest she had already been ousted from power.[9] In any case, Fletcher and Massinger emphasize virginity, and go to other lengths to distance Cleopatra from her common association with luxurious extravagance. In an apparently trivial but finally significant modification of Lucan, an entire scene in *The False One* is used to divert blame from her to Ptolemy for the ostentatious Egyptian banquet that whets Roman avarice (3. 3. 1–25). Insistence on this display is the only time the young and generally 'misled' (5. 1. 20) king acts on his own initiative.

As the double plots of *The False One* are developed, the comic ascent of Cleopatra's movement from captivity to confirmation as queen only briefly crosses the descent of the villains who behead Pompey and then turn against Caesar. Photinus begins as a convincingly Machiavellian adviser. When he conspires to form a triumvirate which will dispose of Ptolemy and use Cleopatra as a figurehead, his intent to rid himself quickly of the accomplices and rule alone might be seen as a parody of Roman politics. In Act V, when he approaches Cleopatra with offensive fantasies of their union, followed by threats to have her and her sister Arsinoe raped by common soldiers, he is merely melodramatic. Cleopatra's 'great mind' is established primarily in imperious scorn for Photinus, impatience with Caesar when he is dazzled by mere wealth, and courage when the palace is besieged during the Alexandrian uprising. In that scene, the childish flutter of her attendants sets off her self-possession, and her advice to her sister 'study to dye nobly' (5. 4. 139) evokes the escape from humiliation she was later to choose. One wonders whether Massinger and Fletcher might have intended to clarify the ironic foreshadowing here, reminding an audience that Arsinoe would be led in a Roman triumph.

Oddly, given the general tendency in *The False One* to ennoble Cleopatra, no other play shows her so coolly planning to use her sexual attraction for political purposes. She goes to Caesar counting not only on the justice of her cause but also on his amorous reputation.

> ... though I purchase
> His grace, with losse of my virginity,
> It skills not, if it bring home Majesty.

(1. 2. 104–6)

When, in the 'Examen' of *La mort de Pompée* (1642–43),[10] Corneille specifically notes that his Cleopatra is amorous only through ambition, he is not emphasizing calculation but preserving her from Lucan's accusations of lascivious hedonism. The play, which entered English theatrical history early in the Restoration period when it was twice translated, for productions in Dublin and London,[11] presents her with respect.

In his 'Examen' Corneille is notably scrupulous about how he has conserved or falsified history, cataloguing the alterations he made in the interest of place, time, and confrontations between characters. His changes result in the most favourable view of the young queen thus far. By increasing the boy-king's age, and by shifting the good priest Achoreus to Cleopatra's retinue, Corneille sets up dichotomies as sharp as those in the first act of *King Lear*. Ptolemy's opening speech crisply sets out moral antitheses posed by the arrival in Egypt of Pompey:

> He hazards me, who did my Father save...
> We must now hasten, or prevent his fate,
> His Ruine hinder or precipitate,
> That is unsafe, and this Ignoble is;
> I dread injustice, or unhappiness.

(Philips 1663, 1. 1. 35, 37–40)[12]

On one side in the Egyptian court are Ptolemy and his counsellors, on the other Cleopatra and Achoreus: ingratitude against obligation, politics against justice, expedience against honour. Later in the play Caesar and Cornelia, disdaining treachery, also contrast sharply with Ptolemy. Cleopatra is aligned with Roman virtues rather than with Egyptian decadence.

Historically, and in the earlier plays, there are two episodes involving the young king Ptolemy's injustice, his deposing his sister from the throne and depriving the fugitive Pompey of his life, but these are separate issues. Corneille links them. Cleopatra, as a prisoner in Alexandria, has no power, but when she hears of the decision made at Ptolemy's council to reject Pompey's appeal for asylum, she strongly protests, thus establishing her principle of loyalty over her brother's opportunistic attempt to win favour from the victorious Julius Caesar. Furthermore, Corneille undercuts the potential for self-interest in Cleopatra's plea for Pompey by inventing an earlier relationship with Caesar. Therefore when her brother sneeringly accuses her of favouring Pompey because, as guardian of their father's will, he would be apt to support her claim to joint power, she can reveal that Caesar first admired her when she visited Rome with her father, during his years of exile. Since she is confident of Caesar's affection and attachment, the magnanimity of her support for Pompey is even more admirable.

In a final modification of history, Corneille brings Cornelia to Alexandria. It is true that she was on the same ship with her husband when he reached Egypt, that she witnessed his assassination, and that Ptolemy had her ship pursued. Corneille, by having her captured, opens possibilities for comparison with Cleopatra which underline the spirit and principles of both characters. Pompey's wife is a model of dignity, loyalty, resolution, and even of courageous risk-taking. She scorns to join an Egyptian plot against Caesar but instead warns him of danger, so that he will live until she and the remnant of Pompey's supporters will be able to confront him openly. Cleopatra profits from association with a second noble, defiantly strong, attractive and assertive woman. The two dominate the play, in personality and in line-count. In Katherine Philips' *Pompey*, songs and spectacles added after the acts give the female characters even more prominence. After Act III she has Cornelia comforted by the ghost of her husband, a scene perhaps suggested by the four dreams or visions in Lucan. Only in Philips' version is an actor required for Pompey.[13] For the finale, she emphasizes Cleopatra's coronation with pageantry and the climactic song 'Ascend a Throne Great Queen'.

In the 1660s, a plot concerned with the beheading of a revered hero and with restoration to the throne of a rightful monarch had obvious political appeal. In 1677, when Giocomo Francesco Bussani dedicated his libretto for *Giulio Cesare* (set by Antonio Sartorio and performed in Venice) to the royalist diplomat Thomas Higgins, great-nephew of General George Monck, the compliment implied a parallel between Monck's restoring Charles II and Caesar's returning Cleopatra to a rightful place.[14] Bussani's libretto, along with many other continental versions of Cleopatra's life, would have no place in this discussion except that it was the major source for Handel's *Giulio Cesare in Egitto*, performed in London thirteen times between 20 February and 11 April 1724. This is the first time on the English stage, except for Davenant's spoof in *A Playhouse to be Let*, that Cleopatra's love for Caesar is a prominent theme.[15] Although Handel's librettist Nicola Francesco Haym is not quite as flamboyant as Bussani, he follows him in general outline, exploiting opportunities for the pathetic, passionate, or picturesque.[16] Pompey's widow Cornelia is now accompanied by Sextus, who vows to avenge his father and continue the war against Caesar. Historically, he was her stepson, a seasoned warrior in his late twenties. To set up moving exchanges, he is transformed into a valiant adolescent, Cornelia's true son. When she is not suffering as widow and mother, Cornelia is fending off amorous advances from Achillas or from Ptolemy, whose age is increased as much as Sextus' is diminished. She parallels Cleopatra as a beautiful object of desire and as an imperilled victim of Ptolemy's aggression; Cornelia's scene when forced to labour in the seraglio garden is matched by that of Cleopatra in chains after her brother defies the Romans. Other spectacular scenes include Cleopatra's twice hiding her identity from Caesar in decorative disguises; these episodes provide time for her to find she adores him. In the prefatory Argument of his libretto, Haym claims that he departs from 'Facts' found in the writings of Caesar, Dio, and Plutarch only in making Sextus the instrument of Ptolemy's death.[17] Given Handel's music, the fanciful story hardly matters. Historical absurdity dissolves in the sumptuous arias of lament, love and, finally, triumph.

By December of 1724, Colley Cibber contrived, with *Cæsar in Ægypt*, to tag along on the success of the opera.[18] In his autobiography Cibber comments that he set about making dormant plays of older authors 'fitter for the Stage...as a good Housewife will mend old Linnen, when she has not better Employment' (1740; 1968, 146).[19] While most of his play is stitched together from *The Death of Pompey* and *The False One*, with an occasional shred of Shakespeare, Cibber's embellishments work in Cleopatra's favour. He adds a turn of the plot that heightens her association with the admirable Pompey. She sends a letter of warning to the defeated general, albeit a letter intercepted and used by Ptolemy as proof, to Caesar, that she plotted in opposition to him. In the tensest of the scenes between sister and brother, she accuses him of treason in his failure to protect Pompey; he accuses her of treason in sending the warning. The heroine is, naturally, given the stronger lines:

> You speak, as if my Crimes, like yours, were writ
> In Blood.

> (Cibber 1725, 20)

No frivolous or luxurious servants attend her, to imply imperfection even by association, although Cibber does introduce a mild query by her maid Charmion about impolitic behaviour, in order to motivate Cleopatra's definition of lofty principles which unite her with Caesar:

> My just Concern for *Pompey*, though his Foe,
> Demands his Admiration, not Resentment.
> Soon is the Lover lost, we fear to lose;
> But while, for *Pompey*'s Sake, I brave that Danger,
> *Cæsar* will envy, what a lower Mind
> Wou'd hate.

> (Cibber 1725, 16)

Only once, during a scene with Antony in Act IV, does she descend even to coquettishness and, significantly, by the end of the scene she regrets her flirtation. 'Why did I dally with his gen'rous Flame?' she asks, and vows enduring commitment to 'one Heart of Merit' (Cibber 1725, 59).

Young, vulnerable, spirited or principled or passionate, Cleopatra in her salad days is easily seen as attractive. Innocent of blame for the shocking reception of Pompey, she had herself been wronged when denied joint rule with her brother. She profits from association with Cornelia, also wronged, also spirited and principled. Comparison between Cleopatra and a Roman matron here has a notably different effect from comparison with Octavia in plays about her later life. Although title pages sometimes bear the label 'Tragedy,' for Cleopatra the plot moves toward a fortunate ending; except in the panoramic Trinity College play and Davenant's farce, concluding speeches or songs celebrate her restoration to the throne.

The mature Cleopatra presents a greater challenge to dramatists. By the seventeenth century her name is a byword for the combination of beauty and betrayal, as Amelia Lanyer's poetry indicates.[20] Actium is at the centre of the story of her relationship with Antony, and Actium is a disgrace that cannot be ignored. On the other hand, even a poet writing under Augustus could admire Cleopatra's suicide. Horace's 'Nunc est bibendum' ode (I. 37) modulates from triumph over a mad queen toward tribute to a brave woman who refused to be displayed in triumph. Mary Morrison suggests that the largely sympathetic sixteenth-century plays about Cleopatra which proliferated in Italy, France, and Germany, are linked to the visual arts, and specifically to the discovery of a beautiful piece of sculpture now thought to represent Ariadne sleeping, but for some time, because of a bracelet in the form of a serpent, misinterpreted.[21] Generations of visitors to the Vatican admired what John Evelyn called 'that incomparable figure of the dying Cleopatra' (Evelyn 18 January 1645; 1959, 159). As early as 1512 it was an honoured part of the papal collections and Leo X had it installed in a fountain. Among those moved by it, Castiglione wrote a poem interpreting the flow of water as her tears for Antony. In Alexander Pope's translation, she claims respect from posterity:

> Deny'd to reign, I stood resolv'd to die,
> Such charms has death when join'd with liberty.
> Let future times of Cleopatra tell,
> Howe're she liv'd none ever dy'd so well.
>
> (Pope, 'On the Statue of Cleopatra,' ll. 13–16)

The easiest way to cope with the problem of Actium has the advantage of dramatic unity, along with considerable other advantages. Except for Shakespeare's and May's plays, all begin after the battle, so that the dramatic curve is upward, from a nadir of recrimination toward reconciliation and reunion. Although indubitably tragic, the conclusion involves a strong current of triumph. Suicide becomes almost as ceremonial and celebratory, in its restoration of the lovers' faith, as the coronation that provides dramatic climax in plays on her earlier days. There is a current of triumph, too, in Cleopatra's success in outmanoeuvring Octavius and evading the humiliation of being led captive through Rome.

Given the familiarity of Shakespeare's *Antony and Cleopatra* and of Dryden's *All for Love*,[22] this discussion will give primary attention to a pair of extraordinarily sympathetic Elizabethan closet dramas, to Thomas May's scholarly work,[23] and to Sir Charles Sedley's complex and energetic pair of plays.[24] One text is tantalizingly missing from the cluster of Elizabethan tragedies. Two years after Mary Sidney Herbert, Countess of Pembroke translated Robert Garnier's *Marc-Antoine* (1578),[25] as *The Tragedie of Antonie* (1592), Samuel Daniel provided a complementary *Tragedie of Cleopatra* (1594).[26] Fulke Greville followed his friend Daniel by writing a play called *Antony and Cleopatra*, but he destroyed the manuscript after the death of Essex in 1601, his characters 'having some childish wantonnesse in them, apt enough to be construed, or strained to a personating of vices in the present Governors, and government'.[27]

Private concerns dominate the extant plays of the Sidney circle. In *The Tragedie of Antonie* a completely loyal Cleopatra is ready to sacrifice all for love of Antony, 'More deare then Sceptre, children, freedome, light'.[28] As Mary Ellen Lamb has commented, despite the play's title, it is Cleopatra who provides dramatic tension.[29] At some length her attendants marshal arguments for her abandoning Antony. She should save the realm and herself; her children will suffer (2. 289–412); her loyalty is useless to Antony—who himself realistically notes that Octavius Caesar could not afford to leave him alive (3. 167–68). Throughout the play, Garnier largely invites respect for a noble figure, resolute for death, her steadfastness set off against choruses concerned with lament and mutability. In a tender scene of farewell between Cleopatra and her children, when she bids them remember 'That this great *Antony* your father was / *Hercules* bloud, and more than he in praise' (5. 63–64), the playwright ignores the existence of Caesarion, her son with Julius Caesar. Perhaps the motive was historical accuracy, since Caesarion was not then in Alexandria; more probably the intent was to preserve a simple focus on Cleopatra as Antony's faithful 'wife', a title she claims in her first scene (2. 320).

In *The Tragedie of Cleopatra* (1594), Daniel pays homage to the Countess of Pembroke by imitating the organisation of *The Tragedie of Antonie* and expanding some of its themes. Making even more prominent Cleopatra's role as mother, he absolves her of negligence. In the opening act, she postpones following Antony in death only out of protective concern for her offspring, 'to purchase grace / For my distressed seede after my death' (77–8). A long scene in Act IV (and in later revisions, material added to Act I) recounts her attempt to send her eldest son to

India for safety under the protection of his tutor Rodon; Rodon's penitence at betrayal of Cleopatra's trust further elevates her stature. In developing the question of motherhood, Daniel sets up contrasts between Cleopatra's protective care and Octavius' ruthless ambition. Caesarion posed a particular threat to Octavius, great-nephew to Julius Caesar, adopted only in the will that made him heir. He carefully cultivated a public image as Julius Caesar's true son.[30] There is thus chilling point to a line in Act III, 'Plurality of *Cæsars* are not good' (582).

In a subtle handling of the reputation of Cleopatra, Daniel develops her dignity, honour, and self-analysis. Taken out of context, lines in her opening monologue seem a confession of wrong:

> ...even affliction makes me truly love thee.
> Which Antony, I must confesse my fault
> I never did sincerely untill now.

> (Daniel, 150–52)

This is, however, part of a movingly introspective, reflective passage in which she surveys the past, when she took for granted that all wooed her, and leads to appreciation that Antony found her in 'This Autumne of my beauty' (181) and truly loved her.

Cleopatra is not in the cast of *The tragicomœdi of the vertuous Octavia* (1598) by the justly obscure Samuel Brandon, although she is of course as important here as Pompey is to Corneille. Most of the charges against 'Egypt's craftie Queene' (Brandon 1598, D4)[31] are predictable, with an added reminder that suicide is sinful; in Act III Octavia rejects that high Roman fashion for the patient endurance a Christian audience could approve. Alongside the *Tragicomœdi,* Brandon's dogtrot epistles between Octavia and Antony similarly rest on stark antitheses between virtue and vice. In a rare vivid image, Octavia imagines Antony, after his death, standing with her 'wronged ghost' on his right hand, and 'that queen' on his left (G8v). A much more appealing spin-off from drama to Ovidian epistle is Daniel's 'Letter sent from Octavia to her husband Marcus Antonius into Ægypt' (1599), which widens the issues to thoughtful discussion of what women can accomplish.[32]

Thomas May evidently read Daniel's epistle and play with appreciative attention. In his full translation of Lucan's epic, May adopts phrases from the second stanza of the 'Letter sent from Octavia,' where Cleopatra is reviled as 'that incestuus Queene, / The staine of Ægypt and the shame of Rome.'[33] In Act V of *The Tragœdy of Cleopatra Queene of Ægypt* (1626), May echoes *The Tragedie of Cleopatra,* although in a different tone. 'I come', says the queen, 'Never till now thy true and faithfull love'. She anticipates that she will follow Antony in tears:

And begge thy pardon in the other world.
All crimes are there for evermore forgott.
There *Ariadne* pardons *Theseus* falsehood,
Dido forgives the perjur'd Prince of Troy,
And *Troilus* repentant *Cressida.*
Though false to thee alive, I now am come
A faithfull lover of thy dust and tombe. *Exit.*

(5. 3. 108–9, 116–22)

Damning as the confession is, May's Cleopatra has considerable force. Although
one of those begging pardon is the pliant Cressida, the other two are male. In the
other world, Cleopatra stands with the great heroes Theseus and Aeneas. 'Queene'
is the key word in the title of May's play; no other playwright preserves so much
of Plutarch's evidence about her competence as a monarch, one who adroitly
regained some of the territories earlier ruled by the Ptolemies. The first member of
her Greek-speaking royal family to learn Egyptian, she could communicate with
diplomats from neighbouring states in at least six other languages (Plutarch, *Antony*
27; [34] May 1. 1. 70–82). Although she feared a reconciliation between Antony and
Octavia, her case for accompanying Antony to war rests also on having supplied
men and ships (Plutarch, *Antony*, 56; May 2. 220–26, 91–95).[35] While in Garnier,
Daniel, and Shakespeare, the queen regards duty to her country with magnificent
irresponsibility; May shows her controlling matters as trivial as a banquet (1. 2) and
as important as rendering the city of Pelusium to Octavius (4. 2). Most playwrights
ignore, and Shakespeare condenses into a brief casual comment, Cleopatra's having
studied 'easy ways to die' (5. 2. 350); May dares showing her try fatal poisons on
condemned criminals (Plutarch, *Antony* 71, May 4.1.1–73). In an astonishing tour
de force, he makes her more admirable here than in many other scenes of the play.
Her handling of the situation deserves a place in a management manual on difficult
interviews. Both experimental subjects happily accept the chance to die privately;
when the prisoner who drew the short straw dies easily, she frees the other.

Steeped in the classical authors who saw Cleopatra as a threat to Rome, with
numerous marginal citations of Cassius Dio along with Plutarch, May presents the
conflict between Antony and Octavius as parallel to that between Julius Caesar
and Pompey. He even has Antony assemble a senate of expatriates in Alexandria,
promising that two months after war with Octavius is concluded he will 'resigne
my power againe / Unto the Senate and the people of Rome' (2. 1. 91–2).[36] As the
table of characters in his manuscript shows, May divided a large cast into three
almost equal groups, 8 Antoniani, 8 Aegyptii, 7 Caesarii.[37] Thus he begins with a
nice equilibrium of partisan forces, and when two of Antony's followers go over to
Caesar early in Act II, the slight imbalance rocks significantly the other way. More
cynical than romantic, May has Antony roused from his depression after Actium not

by affection but by reminders of his own callous disposal of opponents during the triumvirate. Throughout, there is substantial discussion of Roman domination from the perspective of those dominated; Egyptians are understandably unhappy about Rome's domestic quarrels spilling over into slaughter elsewhere (2. 4). Conversely, at a lavish banquet where Antony presents Cleopatra with the crowns of Cyprus, Phoenicia, and Coelosyria, Romans complain not simply about their general's personal dotage but about 'Three wealthy kingdomes gott with Roman blood, / And our Forefathers valour, giv'n away' (1. 167–68). The closing lines of the play are not, as in many versions of Antony and Cleopatra, a tribute to their glory, but a materialistic colonial triumph:

> Advance, brave friends,
> Our prosperous Eagles home to Italy,
> To reape the fruit of all oure warre and toiles,
> And fill great Rome with conquer'd Aegypts spoiles.

                                                                                  (5. 5. 117–20)

The play is an affront to those who assume Antony and Cleopatra's story is, or should be, more about passion than about politics.

After the Restoration, Sir Charles Sedley's *Antony and Cleopatra* (1677) reinstates the balance between personal and public issues. As one of the five court wits who translated an act of *La mort de Pompée,* Sedley has a particular place in a study of how Cleopatra appeared on the Restoration stage, since he had a hand in plays on both periods. Like May, he mingles materials from sources about Cleopatra's youth and about her maturity. Specifically, as in *Pompey the Great*, the Egyptian queen holds loyalty higher than political expedience. She scornfully describes Rome as favouring the victor, whoever that might be (Sedley 1677, 26). Secondly, Sedley borrows from Lucan (directly or via Corneille) both name and function of the unscrupulous courtier, Photinus, who plots the death of Caesar's rival (1677, 55—with the Caesar in question now Octavius rather than Julius. From the first act onward, it is clear that Cleopatra is no household dove; in the aftermath of Actium, she announces that she has tried the captain of her gallies and had him executed for cowardice. In the final act, false news of her death motivates, as usual, Antony's suicide, but as Sedley rewrites the story, she is here blameless. It is not Cleopatra who sends the fatal message; instead, it is a final exhibition of Photinus' villainy. He melodramatically gloats:

> Know that the Queen yet lives, thou loving Fool,
> And I the Story of her Death contriv'd,
> To make thee kill thy self, which has arriv'd
> Just as I wish't...

                                                                                  (Sedley 1677, 53)

His motive is ambition; he expects (with the folly common to such characters on stage) to be rewarded by Caesar with the sceptre of Egypt, and to make Iras his queen.

The multiple plotting of Sedley's play is a source of its energy. Whereas Dryden, later in 1677, simplifies, Sedley complicates. He introduces debates about love, ambition and the decline of Roman republicanism, thus widening the background of Antony and Cleopatra's personal stories, expanding the scope of the play as choruses in the Garnier/Pembroke and Daniel plays do. Parallel and parodic episodes within the play provide a way of evaluating the central figures. Well before the final acts, suicide is a prominent motif. In ways that invite comparison or contrast with the usual report of Cleopatra's death, Cornelia and Antony use the threat or promise of taking their own lives as a tactical counter, while Photinus fails to carry through a suicide attempt purely from lack of Roman resoluteness. Sedley multiplies the pairs of lovers. Alongside the mutual passion of Antony and Cleopatra he introduces Mecoenus' hopeless love for Octavia and Photinus' wooing of Iras. Perhaps, when he made Iras easily tempted to believe she could become queen, Sedley was remembering Shakespeare's Charmian, when she playfully instructs the soothsayer, 'Find me to marry me with Octavius Caesar, and companion me with my mistress' (1. 2. 25–26). Most interestingly, Sedley invents a repetition of Antony's disastrous action at Actium, placing in Act IV a battle scene in which Antony has sallied forth from Alexandria and beaten back the Roman forces, but abandons his victory when he hears that Cleopatra too has left the city and been surrounded. Her plan to join him in battle is foreseen in Act I as a gesture of commitment, and accepted as such by Antony:

> *Cleo.* When you attaque, we'l sally from the Town
> And blood instead of *Nile* our Plain shall drown.
> We'l in the midst of *Cæsar*'s Army meet,
> And like *Bellona* I my *Mars* will greet.
> *Ant.* Would Goddesses themselves to me endear,
> In *Cleopatra*'s shape they must appear.
>
>   (Sedley 1677, 10)

The intricacy which is part of the interest of this play is, however, also its weakness. Sedley himself seems to have recognized this. As capable of learning from Dryden, as Dryden was capable of borrowing from him,[38] Sedley reshaped his plot in *Beauty the Conquerour: or, The Death of Marc Antony* (1702). While retaining much of the political and military interest which Dryden's *All for Love* jettisoned, Sedley sharpens the focus on the central pair of lovers. He reduces activities of his devious villain, and deletes scenes in which Octavia appeared. Brief choruses added between the acts carry some of the thematic material. The complete reshaping of

Act II gives greater point to Iras's response to the villain's wooing; the scene in which she ignobly falls to his promise to set her on the throne is now juxtaposed to a scene in which two ministers urge Cleopatra to save her crown by betraying Antony to Octavius. In this scene and throughout the play, Sedley expands the speeches in which Cleopatra expresses both regality and love, sometimes like seventeenth-century royalists defining in the face of defeat an exuberant cavalier spirit. One such additional speech, at the climax of Act I, could be printed as an independent song:

> *Cleo.* Like Prodigals, already half Undone,
> We'll waste the Wealth of many Years in one:
> Pleasures shall flow, and Joys about us throng:
> Life is not happier made by being long.
> We'll drink the sprightly Draught while it runs clear,
> And break the Cup when the first Dreggs appear.
> Together we will Live, together Die,
> And thus resolv'd, we tread on Destiny.
>
> (1702, 11)

The final lines of Act V are a tribute from Octavius Caesar to the 'Great Minds' (1677) or 'High Minds' (1702) of the lovers.

Notes

1   Lucid surveys of the numerous continental plays about Cleopatra can be found in Marilyn L. Williamson, *Infinite Variety: Antony and Cleopatra in Renaissance Drama and Earlier Tradition* (Mystic, Connecticut: Lawrence Verry, 1974); Mary Morrison, 'Some Aspects of the Theme of Antony and Cleopatra in Tragedies of the Sixteenth Century', *Journal of European Studies*, 4 (1974), 113–25; J. Douglas Canfield, 'The Jewel of Great Price: Mutability and Constancy in Dryden's *All for Love*', *ELH: A Journal of English Literary History*, 42 (1975), 38–61; and Derek Hughes, 'Art and Life in *All for Love*', *Studies in Philology* , 80 (1983), 84–107. How important these plays are to English dramatic history is debatable: Hughes mildly observes that Canfield 'exaggerates the number of plays probably known to Dryden' (p. 84).

2   The family history of Cleopatra VII is complicated by the fact that the Ptolemies rival the Stuarts in consistent choices of names, and the Borgias in family harmony. Nonetheless, it is worth trying to sort out the final chapters of the dynasty in order to recognize how freely playwrights deal with available classical materials, omitting, compressing, and modifying facts as much as, say, Shakespeare does in the English history plays or *Macbeth*. Consider, among other gaps in the story, the fact that in Cleopatra's series of consorts, her second brother, Ptolemy XIV, who formally succeeded Ptolemy XIII as her husband and co-ruler, is regularly ignored. Although Winton Dean comments that 'classically-trained audiences…might have objected if the stage blatantly contradicted the facts as they knew

them' ('Handel's 'Julius—a first among equals', BBC Proms programme (London: 23 August 2005), pp. 10–16 (pp. 11–12), he underestimates the manipulation of history.

3   Quis tibi vaesani veniam non donet amoris, / Antoni, durum cum Caesaris hauserit ignis / pectus?

4   John Fletcher and Philip Massinger, *The False One* (c. 1620), in *The Dramatic Works in the Beaumont and Fletcher Canon*, ed. Fredson Bowers (Cambridge: Cambridge University Press, 1966–96), vol. 8.

5   Sir William Davenant, *The Play-House to be Let*, in *The Works of Sir William Davenant* (London: Henry Herringman, 1673).

6   *The Tragedie of Cæsar and Pompey, or Cæsar's Revenge*. Privately acted by the Studentes of Trinity Colledge in Oxford (London, 1607; Tudor Facsimile, 1913; repr. New York: AMS Press, 1970).

7   Although Dio, in his Roman History, asserts that 'she was a woman of surpassing beauty' (41. 34), the British Museum exhibition of 2001 showed how little evidence supports such a judgement. There is considerable difficulty in identifying genuine portraits, because during her two years in Rome with Caesar, many matrons adopted Egyptian hair styles, in what Peter Higgs has called the Princess Diana phenomenon. The most reliable depictions, on coins, are unflattering (Susan Walker and Peter Higgs eds, *Cleopatra of Egypt: from History to Myth* (London: The British Museum Press, 2001), pp. 200–14), confirming Plutarch's comment that 'in itself her beauty was not absolutely without parallel, not the kind to astonish those who saw her' (*Life of Antony*, 27).

8   Lucan. *The Civil War*. Loeb Classical Text, with trans. J. D. Duff (Cambridge: Harvard University Press, 1928, repr. 1997). Trans. Thomas May under title *Pharsalia, or The Civill Warres of Rome, betweene Pompey the great and Julius Cæsar*. London: Thomas Jones and John Marriott, 1627), 10. 77–81.

9   Michael Grant, *Cleopatra* (London: Weidenfeld & Nicolson, 1972; repr. London: Phoenix Press, 2000), pp. 49–52.

10 Pierre Corneille, *Pompée* [early title *La mort de Pompée*] (1642–43), ed. H. T. Barnwell (Oxford: Oxford University Press, 1971). Trans. Katherine Philips, *The Death of Pompey* (1663), in *The Complete Works*, ed. Patrick Thomas et al. (Stump Cross: Stump Cross Books, 1990-93). Trans. Edmund Waller, Charles Sackville, Charles Sedley et al., *Pompey the Great* (London, 1664).

11 Both her letters (Philips 1992, pp. 68–71, 103, 111–114) and her text show that Katherine Philips, in Ireland, tried harder than the established court poets who divided the task of translation in London. Waller, at the height of fame, took Act I; Sackville (Lord Buckhurst, later 6th Earl of Dorset), Act IV; Filmer, Sedley, and perhaps Godolphin, the rest. A minor example of Philips' care is the awkward word 'déplorable' in 'Ce déplorable chef du parti le meilleur' (l. l. 15). Philips describes Pompey as 'That distress'd Leader of the Juster Side' (1. 1. 15); Waller takes the easy option and calls him 'the pitied leader,' although how the Egyptians will respond to his pitiable state is precisely in question.

12 Katherine Philips, *The Collected Works of Katherine Philips: The Matchless Orinda*, ed. Patrick Thomas, G. Greer and R. Little (Stump Cross: Stump Cross Books, 1990–93).

13 'Il y a quelque chose d'extraordinaire dans le titre de ce poëme, qui porte le nom d'un héros qui n'y parle point; mais il ne laisse pas d'en être, en quelque sorte, le principal acteur, puisque sa mort est la cause unique de tout ce qui s'y passe' (Corneille, Examen).

14 Craig Monson, '"Giulio Cesare in Egitto": from Sartorio (1677) to Handel (1724)', *Music and Letters*, 66 (1985), 313–43 (pp. 313–15).

15 Davenant's farce reduces Caesar, Antony, and Cleopatra to a jolly amorous triangle; Cordelia is eventually convinced, by the argument that all flesh is grass, to share their carefree attitudes.

16 Monson, p. 323; Winton Dean and John Merrill Knapp, *Handel's Operas 1704–1726* (Oxford: Clarendon Press, 1995), pp. 486–89.

17 Nicola Francesco Haym, *Giulio Cesare in Egitto* (London: T. Wood, 1724), A4v.

18 Theatrical histories or critical surveys often dismiss *Cæsar in Ægypt* as a failure (Dorothea Frances Canfield, *Corneille and Racine in England* (New York: Columbia University Press, 1904), p. 223; Helene Koon, *Colley Cibber: A Biography* (Lexington: The University Press of Kentucky, 1986.), pp. 107–9. In December 1724, however, it had a run of five nights, by no means contemptible at the time. Some popular success is suggested by a reprint of the 1725 edition in 1736. At first I suspected that this might have been a publisher's attempt to unload old stock with a new title page, but on examination it proves to be a genuine new edition, in duodecimo rather than in the quarto of the first printing.

19 Colley Cibber, *Cæsar in Ægypt: A Tragedy* (London: John Watts, 1725). Cibber's modestly domestic self-depreciation contrasts with Pope's attack in The Dunciad: 'A past, vamp'd, future, old, reviv'd, new piece, / 'Twixt Plautus, Fletcher, Shakespeare, and Corneille, / Can make a Cibber, Tibbald, or Ozell.'

20 Aemilia Lanyer, *The Poems: Salve Deus Rex Judæorum* (1611), ed. Susanne Woods (New York and Oxford: Oxford University Press, 1993), ll. 209–16, 1409–49.

21 Mary Morrison, 'Some Aspects of the Theme of Antony and Cleopatra in Tragedies of the Sixteenth Century', *Journal of European Studies* , 4 (1974), 113–25.

22 John Dryden, *All for Love, or the World Well Lost* (1677), in *The Works of John Dryden*, vol 13, ed. Maximilian E. Novak et al. (Berkeley: University of California Press, 1984).

23 Thomas May, *The Tragœdy of Cleopatra Queene of Ægypt* (London, 1639 [acted 1626]), ed. Denzell S. Smith (New York: Garland, 1979).

24 Sir Charles Sedley, *Antony and Cleopatra: A Tragedy* (London: Tonson, 1677. Facsimile London: Cornmarket, 1969); *Beauty the Conquerour,* in *Miscellaneous Works* (London: John Nutt, 1702).

25 Robert Garnier, *Marc-Antoine* (1578), trans. as *The Tragedie of Antonie* (1592) by Mary Sidney Herbert, Countess of Pembroke, in *Three Tragedies by Renaissance Women*, ed. Diane Purkiss (London: Penguin, 1998).

26 Samuel Daniel, *The Complete Works in Verse and Prose*, ed. Alexander B. Grosart (1885, repr. New York: Russell and Russell, 1963).

27 Greville, in Geoffrey Bullough ed., *Narrative and Dramatic Sources of Shakespeare*, vol. 5 (London: Routledge and Kegan Paul, 1964), p. 217. In contrast to Greville, both Sedley and Dryden may have deliberately invited topical readings of Antony and Cleopatra's story (Richard Braverman, *Plots and Counterplots: Sexual Politics and the Body Politic in English Literature, 1660–1730* (Cambridge: Cambridge University Press, 1993), pp. 134–52; Novak ed., *Works*, 1984, pp. 373–74).

28 Pembroke, *Three Tragedies*, 2. 174. Her catalogue anticipates the list of roles that Dryden's Antony finally abandons: 'Emperor! / Friend! Husband! Father!' (Dryden 3. 362–63).

29 Mary Ellen Lamb, *Gender and Authorship in the Sidney Circle* (Madison: The University of Wisconsin Press, 1990), p. 130.

30 Williams, in Walker and Higgs (eds), *Cleopatra of Egypt*, p. 190.

31 Samuel Brandon, *The Tragicomoedi of the vertuous Octavia*. Bound with his pair of Ovidian verse letters, 'Octavia to Antonius' and 'Antonius to Octavia' (London: William Ponsonbye, 1598, repr. Tudor Facsimile Texts, 1912, 1970).

32 The first person singular pronominal adjectives frequent in stanzas 4–13 (my heart, my selfe, my love) give way to first person plurals. 'Our' in stanza 13 defines a privileged social class, the great whose virtues should stand bright above the base; 'our' for the next eleven stanzas means womankind, as Octavia considers 'the reputation to our sexe assign'd' (st. 15) in an energetic analysis of gender, freedom, and justice. The final stanzas circle back to a specific 'inchantresse' and a prophetic dream about Actium: a mighty hippopotamus swimming from the Nile into the sea, with a wanton mermaid steering its course.

33 'The staine of Ægypt, Romes pernicious / Fury, unchast to Italyes disgrace' (May, *Pharsalia* 1627, X. 70–71).

34 Plutarch, *Roman Lives*, trans. Robin Waterfield (Oxford: Oxford University Press, 1999).

35 Only Shakespeare, in *Antony and Cleopatra* I. 3. 3, dramatizes the bitter experience behind Cleopatra's fear that Antony would betray her.

36 Dio, *Roman History*, Loeb Classical Text, with trans. Earnest Cary (9 vols, Cambridge: Harvard University Press, 1961–69).

37 As the facsimile page included in Smith's edition (1979) shows, May prefaced his text with Lucan's bitter comparison between Cleopatra and Helen. May quotes the Latin text (Lucan, 10. 60–62); in his own full translation, *Pharsalia*, the lines read 'As much as Helena's bewitching face / Fatall to Troy, and her own Greekes did proove, / As much Romes broiles did Cleopatra moove.'

38 H. Neville Davis, 'Dryden's "All for Love" and Sedley's "Antony and Cleopatra"', *Notes and Queries,* 212 (June 1967), 221–27; Peter Caracciolo, 'Dryden and the "Antony and Cleopatra" of Sir Charles Sedley', *English Studies,* 50 (1959), 50–55.

Disgrace as J. M. Coetzee's *Tempest*

Laurence Wright

In recent times, the notion of the literary source has undergone a metamorphosis almost as radical as that attributed to the literary work in postmodern culture.[1] Where once source-hunting was a matter of diligently tracking down localized textual borrowings and influences—an enterprise often regarded as a worthy but unexciting contribution to conventional literary history, somewhat removed from literature's contemporary interpretive potential—the literary work is today seen as inhabiting fields of heterogeneous discourse, a virtually limitless extension of 'amorphous textuality'.[2] We have sidelined such limited textual categories as 'sources', 'traditions', 'backgrounds', 'antecedents', 'precursors', 'origins', 'subtexts', 'contexts' and 'analogues'[3] for something much more radical. It is now regularly argued that entire episodes, whole plot structures even, are driven by processes of textual incursion. On this view, proverbial, iconographical, analogical, and rhetorical tropologies hitch works of literature to pre-existing discursive energies, literary and non-literary, already at play across time. Authors figure and reconfigure these energies to create a momentary stay honoured in the frail stability of a discrete text.

Given that the older, defined sense of literary influence is partially overshadowed at present, it becomes feasible to recognize that a work may engage the energies of a precursor, deliberately and powerfully, without signalling this engagement through the venerable mechanisms of sources and influences. This seems to be the case with J. M. Coetzee's most ideologically challenging novel, *Disgrace* (1999).[4] Amid the deluge of criticism and commentary the work has evoked, quite remarkably nobody has noticed that the book re-engages exactly the energies Shakespeare deployed in *The Tempest*, a play which has become an icon, if not *the* icon, of colonial and postcolonial studies.

Coetzee's *Tempest*, if I may be allowed for the moment to beg the question, is at once an echo, a revision and an updating of Shakespeare's. David Lurie is a professor in the humanities, a student of literature, working at a lineal derivative of those same 'liberal arts' which so engrossed Prospero that he lost control of his dukedom (I. 2. 66–87).[5] Of course, Lurie's studies are not directed towards occult knowledge or control over the forces of nature. History has all but demolished the pre-scientific, alchemical synthesis within which Prospero operates. But Lurie's quest for intellectual transcendence may still to an extent be regarded, quite legitimately, as a pale descendent of Prospero's, especially when one considers controversial materialist indictments of the role played by the western humanities in general, and Shakespeare in particular, in subduing the colonial populace in South Africa. Scholars such as Martin Orkin, David Johnson, Leon de Kock and Bhekisizwe Peterson echo and extend the charges so memorably articulated by Nosipho Majeke (pseudonym of Dora Taylor), in *The Role of the Missionaries in Conquest* (1952), her groundbreaking critique of colonial education in the country.[6]

Prospero's dukedom was usurped solely in consequence of his preoccupation with the liberal arts. Neglecting his princely role, the duties of a ruler, in the quest for occult mastery and supernatural powers, he lost his kingdom. Similarly, in a sense, Lurie's quest for personal transcendence in sifting through the relics of Romantic aspiration, an exploration documented in the subjects of his research (Boito's *Mefistofele*, Richard of St Victor, Wordsworth and now Byron), has by implication abstracted him from South Africa's hard-won democratic revolution. The parallel with Prospero's neglect of political duty, in favour of his selfish devotion to esoteric studies, is patent. The sea-change in tertiary education so deplored by Lurie, the move towards crass vocationalism, emphasizing 'communication' rather than literature, is a form of intellectual usurpation that pronounces de facto judgement on the inadequacy of the liberal arts, the tradition to which Lurie has devoted his life. There is no indication in the novel that Lurie contributed in any way to the South African political transformation of which he is the thankless heir. Indeed, it could be argued that the relegation of literary studies to an 'optional extra', a mere sop to superannuated humanities academics in a department now orientated to 'Communication Skills' (3), is the verdict of the incoming educational regime on just this political ineffectuality. Yet, stubbornly, Lurie's implicit plaint persists that humane studies have unfairly lost their status and audience in the new, philistine, South Africa.[7]

Prospero escapes to exile on a magical island whose landscapes and ambiance shift and vary, as has often been noted, according to the disposition of the perceiver. Gonzalo, for instance, finds there 'everything advantageous to life'; for Adrian 'The air breathes on us here most sweetly'; but Sebastian chimes in, 'As if it had lungs, and rotten ones' and bad brother Antonio concurs, 'Or as if 'twere perfumed by a fen' (II. 1. 47–50). Following the debacle at the University, David Lurie escapes from the city of Cape Town to his daughter's smallholding at Salem in South Africa's Eastern Cape Province. While Lurie's emotions do indeed oscillate wildly in response to events during his sojourn there, Salem is no enchanted isle. The rural pole of this apparently conventional pastoral binary is cast in a mode of spare and uncompromising realism.[8] Yet this seemingly unproblematic *verismo* is in another way as deceptive, and almost equally as disconcerting, as the qualities of Shakespeare's island. *Disgrace* is an overtly realist novel. True to the genre, the manipulation of verisimilitude, that lust for contingent empirical detail, at once supports and undercuts the literal 'truth' of the presented fiction, but in a manner perhaps especially cogent for South Africans.

Salem is described in the novel as a 'town' (59). The real Salem would be hard put to lay claim to village status: it is little more than a sprawling collection of scattered farmsteads grouped round a Wesleyan 1820 Settler church, with a school hall and a cricket ground. There is one store, a general dealer, and a few houses undergoing sporadic gentrification. (I am reliably informed that Coetzee admitted in conversation he had never been to Salem.) Lurie muses about the smallholding being located in 'old Kaffraria' (122). The territory of British Kaffraria, the colonial province fleetingly established from 1848, lies 120 kilometres to the east of Salem, and is centred on King William's Town. Old Kaffraria itself is further east still, the vast traditional heartland of the Xhosa-speaking people in the nineteenth century before colonial incursion. The real Donkin Square, supposedly the name of the market in Grahamstown where Lucy and Petrus sell their garden produce, is actually in Port Elizabeth, and is known as the Donkin Reserve. There is no regular Saturday market in Grahamstown. You might come across a SAPPI 'No Trespassing' sign in the Hogsback Mountains, 140 kilometres to the north-east, but there is no timber reserve in the immediate vicinity of Salem.[9] One is reminded of Coetzee's remark in *Youth* (2002) that 'if to make his book convincing, there needs to be a grease-pot swinging under the bed of the wagon as it bumps along the stones of the Karoo, he will do the grease-pot' (138).[10] The purpose of this spatial, geographical derangement, a writerly dispensation directed it would seem to a specifically South African readership, is to unsettle pre-judgement, or prejudice. To know a place, so the claim goes, is to know its people. As a metafictional 'Prospero', Coetzee must undermine that conviction if his fabulation is to work. The pastoral setting of *Disgrace* offers the rough magic of a fictive world, not merely a fictionalized reality.

The archetype underlying the story of Prospero's usurpation in Shakespeare's play is of course the sack of Troy, in which a traitor, Sinon, lets loose the enemy concealed in the wooden horse at night inside the walled gates of the city. The essence of the story is one of betrayal from within. In Prospero's case, the betrayal is one of intellectual displacement or escapism on the part of a ruler, the substitution of contemplation for action, the preference for personal enlightenment and magical transcendence over inherited social duty—the predicament, say, of a Faust trapped in political office. The usurpation follows. But in Coetzee's novel, Lurie is expelled from the city not because of his intellectual irrelevance to current political revolution or reform—though that is generally implied—but because of his sexual attack on a student and his refusal to make even procedural, axiomatic amends for it. His betrayal is cast in terms of libidinal revolt against civilized conduct and appears at first to be a psychological emendation or supplement to Prospero's story. In fact Coetzee is underlining *ab initio* the sexual problematic which is at the heart of Shakespeare's play, the necessary source of our 'disgrace'.

Exiled to the island, that mysterious pastoral enclave of wish-fulfilment and stringent moral discipline whose *raison d'être* appears to be restitution of the golden age longed for by Gonzalo, Prospero's dominion appears absolute, his omniscience almost so. He falters only once, providing that moment which Morton Luce has described as perhaps 'the most striking rhetorical achievement in all literature' (114, note 151).[11] Prospero's crisis is precipitated by a moment of profound reverie, of distraction from practical affairs, occasioned by the masque-like entertainment he himself conjures up to celebrate his daughter's betrothal, symbolizing the pinnacle of his magical and dynastic aspirations.[12] In Prospero's speech, originally delivered from the stage of the Globe theatre, the cloud-capped towers and gorgeous palaces of Troy, Carthage, and Rome pass once again before imagination's eye in a paean to mutability, reprising that *translatio imperii* which was so much a part of the Elizabethan and Stuart iconography, and perhaps anticipating the fate of another doomed empire-in-the-making, whose centre would indeed be the towers, solemn temples and gorgeous palaces of London, or 'Troynovant', rising majestically on the far bank of the river Thames.

The speech is disrupted at the memory of 'the foul conspiracy / Of the beast Caliban and his confederates against my life' (IV. 1. 139–41). Prospero's mental upheaval assimilates an earlier disruptive moment in Virgil, where Aeneas stands veiled from sight in Dido's temple at Carthage, with the construction of her new city going on around him, as his own life's tragedy passes once more before his eyes in the frescos depicting the destruction of Troy.[13] His mind is deep in reverie when he is disturbed by the entry of the warrior-queen herself, Dido, or 'widow Dido', as Gonzalo calls her (II. 1. 75). Aeneas's reflections in Juno's temple—Juno, patroness of marriage and protectress of women, the sworn enemy of Troy—are shattered by this forsaken temptress who later, following the seduction in the cave, almost succeeds in diverting him from his divinely ordained mission to found Rome. Aeneas's reverie is disturbed by Dido; Prospero's by the memory of Caliban. There is a curious kinship between these two figurations of disruptive energy, Dido and Caliban. In Prospero's masque, the libidinal energies that almost derailed Aeneas's imperial project are programmatically curbed. His insistence on sexual chastity in Miranda's courtship and betrothal is marked, even fierce. Cupid is barred from the celebrations, and he is safely on the way to the island of Paphos with his mother Venus, before Ceres consents to respond to Juno's summons (IV. 1. 91). In separating Juno from Venus, Prospero indicates that Miranda and Ferdinand will be protected from the powerful alliance of goddesses which conspired to bring about the passionate encounter of Dido and Aeneas in the cave. Indeed, the sexual energies that threatened Aeneas's imperial project are contained so successfully in Prospero's that when this young betrothed couple are discovered in Prospero's cell, the equivalent of Virgil's cave, they are chastely engaged in a game of chess (V. 1. 172), at once an intellectual trope for the mating game and a symmetrical figuration of the broader political power-plays their dynastically appropriate union foreshadows. Chastity is crucial to

Prospero's magical and dynastic power.

In complete contrast, David Lurie in his role as postcolonial Prospero admits himself utterly compromised in the sexual dimension. Far from seeking to banish or curb Cupid he regards himself as a 'servant of eros', as he repeatedly tells us (52, 89). He wants to speak up for the 'rights of desire' (89). Regular, vaguely affectionate, impersonal sex contents him profoundly, as his arrangement with the prostitute Soraya clearly demonstrates (5). He quotes Blake to his daughter— ('Sooner murder an infant in its cradle than nurse unacted desires'(69)—and, more tellingly, agonizes over the cruel treatment accorded the next-door neighbour's dog at his former marital home in Kenilworth. The poor animal is routinely chastized to thwart its natural copulatory urges (89–90). On his own admission, he well-nigh rapes one of his own students, Melanie Isaacs (25)—a 'betrayal from within' if ever there was one, as far as the university is concerned. Later, lamenting his failing powers of sexual attraction, he yields to the gauche advances of the unattractive Bev Shaw almost out of habit or duty (148–50); on his return to Cape Town he casually procures a 'blow job' on Signal Hill from a prostitute (194); and most striking of all, immediately after his silent prostration before Mrs Isaacs and her younger daughter at the family home in George, his act of deep penitence for the 'rape' he has committed on the older daughter, as he looks from the one to the other, 'again the current leaps, the current of desire' (173). There is an intriguing contrast here with Prospero, whose neglect of his dukedom is presented as conventionally culpable, a matter of wrong choice, failure of duty. As we have seen, Lurie has lost his institutional kingdom—the university study of literature—as an indirect consequence of political transformation, something outside his control; but he is also far along in the ordinary biological process of losing his sensual kingdom, too, another factor beyond his control. Age is diminishing his sexual powers and attractiveness, yet it is made insistently clear that Lurie is not only incapable of resisting sexual urges, he is unwilling to; indeed, he deems any such restraint vaguely immoral. The effect of this portrayal of Lurie's mundane sexual predicament is to underline *Disgrace*'s commitment to the libidinal drive as fundamental, unmanageable and inescapable, a disgraceful assumption recognized only fitfully in the history of western philosophy, profoundly and perversely in Pauline Christianity, and obsessively in the rigid Calvinism which infected apartheid's originators. *Contra* Prospero, Venus and Juno cannot be so easily separated. The repressed and exiled will return. By superimposing the disruptive energies of Caliban and Dido, Shakespeare hints at the imperative and undifferentiated character of our animal drives, expressed in political, social and sexual energies. Coetzee's novel underlines this reductive assumption, one deeply subversive to the founding impulses of western civilization in its high regard for moral order, as is recognized in different ways from Plato to Schopenhauer and Freud.

Immediately prior to the gang rape in *Disgrace*—which, significantly, is the only moment of real, immediate action in the novel, just as Prospero's dispersal of the masque is the only moment of immediate (unmagical) action in *The Tempest*—Lucy ventures an anthropological description of her father's moral plight, one in which he concurs, but with some supplementary historical updating:

> 'Your colleagues can breathe easy again, while the scapegoat wanders in the wilderness.'
> A statement? A question? Does she believe he is just a scapegoat?'
> 'I don't think scapegoating is the best description,' he says cautiously. 'Scapegoating worked in practice while it still had religious power behind it. You loaded the sins of the city on to the goat's back and drove it out, and the city was cleansed. It worked because everyone knew how to read the ritual, including the gods. Then the gods died, and all of a sudden you had to cleanse the city without divine help. Real actions were demanded instead of symbolism. The censor was born, in the Roman sense. Watchfulness became the watchword: the watchfulness of all over all. Purgation was replaced by the purge.' (90–91)

Lurie is pointing to more than a retreat from religious superstition. Where once city and country, art and nature, law and tradition, sophistication and simplicity, domesticity and the wilderness, enjoyed a symbolic geographical or territorial demarcation, at least in literary tradition if not in fact, now they compete for ascendancy within each of us. The contest between nature and civility has become an inner conflict, essentially 'private'—something Lucy insists upon to Lurie's puzzlement after the gang rape has occurred (112)—and inaccessible to public scrutiny without personal confession. Yet Lurie was only too ready to evade the attempt of the disciplinary review to coax from him more than a mere acknowledgement of procedural transgression in the case of his assault on Melanie Isaacs. He leaves the university, exiling himself, but will not admit real moral culpability nor make a public apology. Only when his own daughter suffers a parallel fate, in a rural environment bare of effective public criminal or civil justice, does the consequence of his own beliefs dawn on David Lurie. It is as if by leaving the city he has tried to exact upon himself the symbolic punishment accorded in ancient times to those who transgress the laws of civility, only to find that the pastoral mythography has become outmoded. The ancient binary is dissolving. 'Inexorably, he thinks, the country is coming to the city: soon there will be cattle again on Rondebosch common' (175). On his arrival in Cape Town, he finds his home has been ransacked (176). Unsupported by civic convention humanity is at the mercy of the wilderness within. It is the traitor inside the gates, Sinon, the one who lets the enemy loose in the sleeping city, who is the real enemy.

The Troy story replays itself in *The Tempest* in complex ways. The first duty of a ruler is to protect and defend his subjects. The analogical conspiracies on the island, both the plot of Antonio and Sebastian to overthrow Alonso, and Caliban's farcical scheme to kill Prospero and take over the island with the help of Stephano and Trinculo, each require Prospero's magisterial intervention to save vulnerable, sleeping persons from attack, so that in this special, magical domain he effortlessly repairs the failure of his actual rule in Milan. What is the story at base? It has its roots in ancient middle-eastern mythography concerning the origins of civilization. Settled cultivators built cities to defend themselves against hungry, swift-moving nomads. Jacob Bronowski affirms that:

> …war, organized war, is not a human instinct. It is a highly planned and cooperative form of theft. And that form of theft began ten thousand years ago when the harvesters of wheat accumulated a surplus, and the nomads rose out of the desert to rob them of what they themselves could not provide.[14]

Cities evolved from agricultural surplus. The frail defences of settled cultivators, originally mazes, meanders or labyrinths,[15] gradually developed the formidable character of walled cities. The literal rape and pillage that routinely follows breaching of the city wall, as the nomads struggle to lay hold of the economic surplus, becomes mystically associated with the need to preserve economic, social and sexual integrity. Cities in western legend are generally female. It is worth recalling that the classical earth goddesses of vegetation, grain and agriculture in general—Phyrgian Cybele, Greek Demeter and Roman Ceres—are often represented in visual art by the figure of a high-born woman, her head crowned like a turreted city—the so-called mural crown. The iconography commemorates that natural abundance, native to the fertile deltas and flood-plains of rivers like the Nile, the Tigris-Euphrates and the Indus, which first allowed large communities to congregate in cities. The physical defences of these cities were enhanced by mystical practices relating to the celebration of agricultural abundance, presided over by the earth goddesses. Prospero's conventional obsession with preserving Miranda's virginity until marriage, with all its patriarchal, dynastic and political implications, as opposed to Caliban's attempt to rape her and people the isle with Calibans (I. 2. 348–49), reflects the play's concern with defending the magical wall of western civilization. Miranda becomes the maiden goddess of the city, the emblem of imperial civilization.

Lucy is David Lurie's Miranda. Why is she lesbian? An odd question, and the answer is either one of mere contingency—she is lesbian because that is the way things are—or she is so constituted in order that Lurie's stake in patriarchal order can be thwarted. In *The Tempest*, Prospero's interest in Miranda's betrothal is both filial and political. Lucy's erstwhile partner, Helen, is kept carefully offstage for the duration of the story, and Lurie is to have no Prospero-like control over his daughter's reproductive power. In terms of the novel's re-writing of *The Tempest*'s concerns, Lucy's sexual orientation looks very much like an authorial device to free her from Miranda's historical positioning. Lucy earns her living through market gardening and running dog kennels. These are not 'pet' dogs, but working dogs, guard dogs employed in the area, part of the mechanism of social control and defence left over in an untransformed South Africa. Just as Prospero magically evokes the Ovidian hounds to punish and reprimand the comic would-be revolutionaries, so these dogs are employed by farmers and the owners of small-holdings to defend themselves and their property from theft, attack, and more recently, land invasion. In *Disgrace*, the trio of rapists, the 'gang of three' (199) (Coetzee elides the two *Tempest* subplots, the revolution attempted by the three 'men of sin' and the comic insurrection instigated by Caliban, Stephano and Trinculo) callously destroys the dogs in an act of repellent vengefulness. Their motives are never spelt out but clearly are not gratuitous. The slaughter takes place because of the role such dogs had been made to play in the colonial enterprise. These are not magical hounds, and the bullets that kill them are not the 'invisible bullets' of Greenblatt's famous essay, but real ones wielded by Petrus's informal army, his 'people' (201).[16]

Similarly, the moment in *Disgrace* equivalent to Prospero's upheaval in the 'cloud-capp'd towers' speech is no mere internal mental struggle for self-control, sparked by sudden recollection of Caliban's trivial insurrection. Petrus's Saturday evening party, the plebeian version of the magician's masque, celebrates his acquiring formal ownership of a portion of Lucy's land, as a result of a Government land-grant. It is a moment of explicit political triumph, of counter-conquest, of restitution. The figure of Petrus is a radical take on the shepherd of the green world who re-educates urban sophisticates in the verities of nature. This party, too, is a pastoral celebration. Two sheep are to be slaughtered, sacrificed. Why two? Could they represent, metafictionally, Lurie and his daughter? And, as with Prospero's betrothal masque, this celebration is also disrupted. Not long into the proceedings, Lucy suddenly recognizes one of her rapists. Here the upheaval is far from private, though the extent to which those present are aware of what has unfolded over the previous few days is left disturbingly opaque. Prospero's masque is disrupted by his private memory of a would-be rapist, and an absurd if desperate counter-revolutionary plot doomed to failure. Petrus's party is disrupted by the presence of an actual rapist, and the dynastic, political celebration following successful revolutionary action continues undisturbed by the perturbation exhibited by David Lurie and his daughter. The defeat is total. Later, Lurie also fails a Prospero-like trial of Olympian self-mastery when he lashes out ineffectually at the boy-rapist: 'This is what it is like to be a savage!' (206). It is no accident that he wants to put into Byron's mouth Aeneas's desolate words before Dido's frescos at Carthage portraying the destruction of Troy: *Sunt lacrimae rerum, et mentem mortalia tangunt* (162): 'Tears are shed for things even here and our mortal ways touch the soul.'

Like Prospero, Petrus is a taciturn figure who never betrays his intentions to his 'audience'—his companions, or David and Lucy, or the reader. When we first meet him, Petrus occupies a Caliban-like position: the stereotypical South African 'farm boy', trusted to a degree, intimate up to a limit, but never 'one of us', in Conrad's phrase. Like Caliban showing Prospero 'the qualities o'th' isle' (I. 2. 337), he shows David Lurie, as he had earlier shown Lucy, the properties of the land. He calls himself, wryly, the 'dog-man' (64): the man who looks after the dogs, but also the man who is treated like a dog, and the man whom apartheid ideology has proclaimed to be less than fully human. Like Caliban, his people were 'not honoured with / A human shape' (I. 2. 283–84). Lurie's rebarbative remarks regarding the apparent failure of missionary education to achieve anything significant towards the education of the Xhosa (95) are reminiscent of Miranda's self-righteous complaint concerning the failure of her efforts to educate Caliban (I. 2. 350–61). But there is in fact no sign that Petrus's education is in any way deficient in relation to the demands of his own agenda. This particular Caliban has learned to do a great deal more than curse. Curiously, too, where David starts out simply helping Petrus with his duties as an employee of Lucy's, he ends by assisting Petrus with the irrigation piping for Petrus's own farm. Not only is it Petrus who has the knowledge and superior skills in this regard (just as Prospero has the advantage of superior knowledge over Caliban) but, earlier, David has actually performed the kind of willing service that Prospero imposes on Ferdinand to prove himself a sound suitor for Miranda: 'All right, I'll handle the dog-meat, I'll offer to dig for Petrus' (77). Considering that we are left to suppose that for her 'protection' Lucy will be taken under the wing of Petrus as an additional wife (the sexual arrangements accompanying this move are left ambiguous: 204), the intertextual implications are deliberately disturbing. David Lurie is caught in the role of a perverse pander, unwittingly working to bestow his daughter on a polygamous patriarch. Where *The Tempest*'s magical achievement of political and sexual civility embodied in the betrothal of Miranda and Ferdinand receives symbolic confirmation in the vignette of them flirtatiously playing chess together, in a moralizing re-write of Virgil, Lurie has to admit the absolute failure of any Prospero-like ambitions he might have entertained:

> Against this new Petrus what chance does Lucy stand?…Where is Lucy going to find someone to dig, to carry, to water? Were this a chess game, he would say that Lucy has been outplayed on all fronts. (151)

Prospero's period of exile serves to fulfil (and to test) his dream of a magical solution to the problem of civilization. He indulges seemingly at will his powers to contain, effortlessly, the claims of those 'beyond the pale'—outside the parameters of civilization. His moment of crisis in the 'cloud-capp'd towers' speech remains intensely private. The momentary mental reflux of the Dido/Caliban complex, sufficiently arcane to be inaccessible to the other characters on stage, is all we are given by way of explanation. Yet its import is sufficiently powerful to undermine quite radically Prospero's dream of universal civility imposed from on high by those in power. In complete contrast, David Lurie's pastoral sojourn becomes a prolonged and devastating immersion in the tough realities of life beyond the confines of colonial order, where the civic capability of the new public dispensation is very much in question. In the major chiasmic movement of the novel, Lurie (the Prospero figure) and Petrus (the Caliban figure) change places. This lends a new inflection to Caliban's song of freedom: ''Ban, 'Ban, Ca-Caliban / Has a new master—get a new man!' (II. 2. 179–80). Sending a quirky note of metafictional commiseration across the textual and temporal divide, Lurie remarks, 'He would not wish to be marooned with Petrus on a desert isle' (137). And, indeed, from one perspective, Lurie's predicament is far more painful than his predecessor's. Where Prospero's magical sovereignty had been more than adequate to protect his daughter from rape and pillage, Lurie must suffer not only the searing knowledge of his physical, moral and intellectual ineffectuality in this regard, but the dawning realization that Lucy's best chance of survival, given that she is intent on staying, is indeed to submit to a form of patriarchy more stifling and oppressive than that of colonial society. The unborn child, which is one outcome of the rape, represents her best hope of security under the new dispensation, cementing her alliance of convenience under the uncertain aegis of Petrus. This is in effect Miranda raped and then protected by Caliban. Where Prospero confronts the perennially base, universal, Caliban-like impulses of humanity fleetingly but profoundly in the 'cloud-capp'd towers' speech, Lurie becomes increasingly moved by our common animal inheritance, our kinship with other life forms, specifically dogs. 'A dog-man, Petrus once called himself. Well, now he has become a dog-man: a dog-undertaker; a dog psychopomp; a *harijan*' (146). Dogs in *Disgrace* represent among other things a lowest common denominator, 'ground level' (205), the innocent animal heritage upon which civility must build, that which is never to be relinquished or transcended. This is something upon which David and Lucy for once agree:

> 'How humiliating,' he says finally. 'Such high hopes, and to end like this.'
> 'Yes, I agree, it is humiliating. But perhaps that is a good point to start from again. Perhaps that is what I must learn to accept. To start at ground level. With nothing. Not with nothing but. With nothing. No cards, no weapons, no property, no rights, no dignity.'
> 'Like a dog.'
> 'Yes, like a dog.' (205)

The passage upends Gonzalo's imaginary commonwealth of the golden age (II. 1. 145–62), and Lurie has no concealed, private ambitions to 'be king on't' (154).

As with Prospero, who is artist, dramatist and fantasist before he is anything else, Lurie's real domain is the imagination.[17] His quest for some kind of harmonious resolution to the predicament of his importunate gendered sexuality is expressed mainly in his ambition to compose '*Byron in Italy*, a meditation on love between the sexes in the form of a chamber opera' (4). In all his manifold sexual shenanigans, it was in Byron's liaison with Contessa Teresa Guiccioli that the poet came closest to achieving emotional stability and fulfilment.[18] Lurie seeks similar salvation from Teresa, but can do so only in the least physical form of the arts, music. In the course of the novel, the initially social, dramatic character of Lurie's chamber opera thins in conception, first, to a duet, a musical dialogue between Teresa in her fifties and the shade of the dead Byron, and finally to a one-sided, all-absorbing 'inner duet' in which Lurie hears only the music of Teresa. The longed-for resolution subsists, apparently, only in imagination, and is thoroughly undermined by Lurie's poignant, persistent awareness that any actual release from sexual impulse is a physiological response to ineluctable biological process. All he can do is to relinquish his physical being-in-the-world for imaginative satisfaction; but there is no release, no resolution in the realm of nature's bodies. Like Prospero he must acknowledge 'this thing of darkness … mine' (V. 1. 275–76), and then give it up.

At one level *Disgrace* is indeed a postcolonial updating of *The Tempest* and its concerns. More than that, it is the kind of contribution to western tradition identified by T. S. Eliot in his once-famous essay of 1919, 'Tradition and the Individual Talent',[19] one which adds something new but sends a reorienting shiver back through the literary heritage. The two works stand as matching book-ends, bracketing the colonial experience—*The Tempest* anticipating it, *Disgrace* conferring a baleful valediction. In both instances, the protagonist's relation to the *status quo ante* is disillusioned, sardonic and withdrawn, and the future deeply troubling. 'Oh brave new world / That has such people in't', cries Miranda. ''Tis new to thee', responds Prospero (V. 1. 183–84). David Lurie is more forthright: 'Lucy's future, his future, the future of the land as a whole—it is all a matter of indifference, he wants to say; let it all go to the dogs, I do not care' (107). Lucy, who has jettisoned the afflatus and pretensions of western civilization, along with many of its amenities, emerges as a stoic, tranquil and determined survivor. Lurie's final, seemingly incurable vision of her is as an idealized figure of the eternal feminine, at one with nature in a painterly romantic landscape:

> The wind drops. There is a moment of utter stillness which he would wish prolonged forever: the gentle sun, the stillness of mid-afternoon, bees busy in a field of flowers; and at the centre of the picture a young woman, *das ewig Weibliche*, lightly pregnant, in a straw sunhat. A scene ready-made for a Sargent or a Bonnard. City boys like him; but even city boys can recognize beauty when they see it, can have their breath taken away. (218)

The visual surface of pastoral is restored to Lurie, its inner meaning gone forever. Lurie cannot make the transition Lucy is attempting. He recalls Rilke: '*Du must dein Leben ändern!*: you must change your life. Well, he is too old to heed, too old to change. Lucy may be able to bend to *the tempest*; he cannot, not with honour' (209, emphasis mine).

Prospero and Lurie retire from the scene, the one to his recovered dukedom, where every third thought will be his grave, the other to the dog yard to resume his otherworldly, musical intercourse with the shade of Teresa Guicciolli, a dream of impossible sexual harmony. Their imaginary worlds of desire and aspiration leave to others—as they always have done—the primary human task of achieving an inclusive civic accommodation with nature, with those biological drives which ensure our individual and collective survival. Their's is the contribution of the artist, one sort of artist. In a broader historical frame it is clear that these particular protagonists are not the sturdy, violent types who built the Empire, nor the mixed crew that dismantled it from within and without, but prime examples of what C. S. Lewis famously described as 'men without chests':[20] the head (imagination and intellect) is intact, their heart's affections capricious but sound (they are deeply devoted to their daughters), their genitals in working order; but they lack 'magnanimity' and the central human emotions of the chest, that passion which impels humans to act with courage and vision in the practical, political world in order to realize the values they profess.

Needless to say, *Disgrace* is much more than a postcolonial commentary on *The Tempest*, but I hope I have said enough to indicate that the intertextual engagement is more than circumstantial, if less than fully determinative. One of the perils of postmodernism's boundless textuality is that it may encourage pursuit of an impossible comprehensiveness. The lesson of our predicament is that the old virtues of critical tact and judgment remain as ever our only defence against the mare's nest.

Notes

1   See William Paulson, *Literary Culture in a World Transformed: A Future for the Humanities* (Ithaca and London: Cornell University Press, 2001) for relevant discussion.

2   The phrase is from Stephen J. Lynch, *Shakespearean Intertextuality: Studies in Selected Sources and Plays* (Westport, CT, and London: Greenwood Press, 1998), p. 1.

3   The list is adapted from Robert S. Miola, 'Shakespeare and his Sources: Observations on the Critical History of *Julius Caesar*', *Shakespeare Survey*, 41 (1988), 69–76.

4   J. M. Coetzee, *Disgrace* (London: Vintage, 2000). In-text page references are to this edition.

5   References to *The Tempest* are from Stephen Orgel's Oxford World's Classics edition (Oxford and New York: Oxford University Press, 1987).

6   Martin Orkin, *Shakespeare Against Apartheid* (Johannesburg: Ad. Donker, 1986); David Johnson, *Shakespeare and South Africa* (Oxford: Clarendon Press, 1996); Leon De Kock, *Civilising Barbarians: Missionary Narrative and African Textual Response in Nineteenth-Century South Africa* (Johannesburg: Witwatersrand University Press, 1996); Bhekizizwe Peterson, *Monarchs, Missionaries and African Intellectuals: African Theatre and the Unmaking of Colonial Marginality* (Trenton, NJ: Africa World Press, 2000); Nosipho Majeke (pseud. of Dora Taylor), *The Role of the Missionaries in Conquest* (Cape Town: Society of Young Africa [1952]).

7   Coetzee offers Lurie's jaundiced response to this fictive educational reform with satirical intent. Clearly, Lurie's is not the most adequate or informed perspective on what is going on in South African tertiary education. I raise this mundane issue because *Disgrace*, like any major imaginative work, implicates its readers in manifold perceptions and judgements which are questionable, partial and need to be challenged. This in part is what art is for.

8   See Gareth Cornwell, 'Realism, Rape, and J. M. Coetzee's *Disgrace*', *Critique: Studies in Contemporary Fiction*, 43.4 (2002), 307–322.

9   SAPPI stands for South African Pulp and Paper Industries (see page 69 of the text).

10 J. M. Coetzee, *Youth* (London: Secker & Warburg, 2002).

11 See his Arden Shakespeare edition of *The Tempest* (London: Metheun, 1901), p. 114, n. 151.

12 Glynne Wickham has argued that Prospero should be seen as James I in his role as marriage broker for his daughter Elizabeth, the Princess Royal, here represented as Miranda, with Juno as Queen Anne, 'Masque and Anti-masque in *The Tempest*', in *Essays and Studies 1975*, ed. Robert Ellrodt (London: Routledge & Kegan Paul, 1975). With three potential candidates already discarded by 1611, the king of Sweden, the Duke of Brunswick and the Prince of Nassau, two others were still in contention, the Protestant Elector Palatine, supported by James, and the Catholic Prince of Piedmont, favoured by Anne. Court rumour also lighted on the recently widowed King Philip of Spain as an outside possibility. Clearly, it would be both impossible and tactless for Shakespeare to prejudge so delicate a diplomatic question: the emphasis must fall on the anticipation of a brilliant outcome thanks to the King's skill as diplomat, peacemaker and dynastic architect.

13 Cumulative discussion on this issue can be sampled in work by J. M. Nosworthy, 'The Narrative Sources of *The Tempest*', *Review of English Studies*, 24 (1948), 280–94; John Pitcher, 'A Theatre of the Future: The *Aeneid* and *The Tempest*', *Essays in Criticism*, 34.3 (1984), 193–295; and Heather James, *Shakespeare's Troy: Drama, Politics, and the Translation of Empire* (Cambridge: Cambridge University Press, 1997).

14 Jacob Bronowski, *The Ascent of Man* (London: British Broadcasting Corporation, 1973), p. 88.

15 The notions of 'maze' and 'meander' occur in *The Tempest* at 3. 3. 1–3, suggesting a form of metatheatrical comment on the play's episodic plot structure, in which successive efforts at revolt and rebellion are stifled by magical intervention. *The Tempest* substitutes Prospero's metaphysical magic for the physical defences of civility.

16 Stephen J. Greenblatt, 'Invisible Bullets', in *Shakespearean Negotiations: The Circulation of Social Energy in Renaissance England* (Oxford: Clarendon Press, 1988), pp. 21–65. The episode is a devastating negation of the myth of Actaeon [see Ovid, *Metamorphoses III*, ed. A. A. R. Henderson (Bristol: Bristol Classical Press, 1979), pp. 138ff]. In Ovid, the hounds belong to the huntsman, and Diana turns their power against him in effortless reprisal for his act of inadvertent, unseemly voyeurism. Rape is scarcely on the agenda. She transforms him into a stag so that he is destroyed by his own dogs—male power imploding. In *The Tempest* the visionary hounds (4. 1. 256ff) wreak comic revenge on Caliban, Stephano and Trinculo with a swift dunking in the horse pond as punishment for their political gall, not to mention their cheeky appropriation of royal apparel. In *Disgrace*, the dogs are wantonly slaughtered by the intruders, even though they are caged in Lucy's kennels and unable to prevent rape and plunder of this rural 'Diana'. This is Ovid re-written, so to speak, by the Clint Eastwood character, Dirty Harry!

17 A point well made in Mike Marais, 'J. M. Coetzee's *Disgrace* and the Task of the Imagination', *Journal of Modern Literature*, 29.2 (2006), 75–93.

18 A judgement sustained in current biography. See Fiona MacCarthy, *Byron: Life and Legend* (London: John Murray, 2002).

19 T. S. Eliot, 'Tradition and the Individual Talent', in *Selected Essays*, third edn (London: Faber and Faber Limited, 1951), pp. 13–22.

20 C. S. Lewis, *The Abolition of Man* (London: Oxford University Press, 1944), p. 14.

King Lear and Film Genres

Robert White

G. Wilson Knight was one of my personal heroes. I sent him a copy of a book of mine which had been largely inspired by his vision of Shakespeare, and for whose cover he had kindly supplied a phrase. It reached him on the morning of his death. I often wonder if he had time to glance at it. I admired Knight's commitment to each of Shakespeare's plays, as both an ethical and theatrical experience, and his notion of the play as an organic whole, a 'spatial metaphor', a 'visionary whole',[1] in which narrative, themes, thought and imagery supported each other. He was my embodiment of a Keatsian reader, and indeed Keats was another of his literary loves. His distinction between 'interpretation' and 'criticism' seemed to me an important and valuable one for a teacher of literature, faced at that time with Leavisite injunctions to 'judge' works from a lofty vantage point and rank them in a rigid canon. The world has moved on, Wilson Knight is no longer with us, we can now place his work as high modernism,[2] driven by a need to find unity in diversity, concord in discord, an aim which postmodern theory regards as, if anything, the wrong way around. That I should begin an essay for Chris Wortham by recalling this revered figure in my intellectual development may be no coincidence, but I mention him for more anecdotal reasons. I once had afternoon tea with Wilson Knight, some forty years after he had published *The Wheel of Fire*. Clearly he was not one for small talk, so I dived into the deep end with some question about *King Lear*. 'King Lear', he said, and paused for some time, deep in thought. 'I don't think I've ever read *King Lear*.'

Knight's comment, delivered with honesty, makes me remember my own first reading of the play. I expected a lot, primed by critical fashion declaring it to be Shakespeare's greatest creation,[3] but I was disappointed. It was completely confusing in every way. The first scene, admittedly, was clear and spellbinding, and I felt on firm ground with my bearings set for a particular kind of narrative leading to the 'promised end' of a recognisable folk tale, a variation on the 'three caskets' test in *The Merchant of Venice*, spliced with *Cinderella*. However, I was then sidetracked from Cordelia's story which was surely set up as central, into a loosely integrated subplot, disconcerted by an inappropriate Fool, taken through rantings and ravings in a storm and nocturnal rings of incoherent and 'mad' chatter between men feigning beggary and insanity, appalled by the visible cruelty of Gloucester's blinding, and by the degrading presentation of an old man clearly suffering from senile dementia, and eventually dumped on an ending that completely reversed my expectations. It was a mess. Fuelled by its powerful verse, it seemed a magnificent wreck, a set of fragments defying order. However, over some years I was convinced, or convinced myself, that the kind of unity Knight searched for could indeed be found in the play. Paradoxes like 'folly is wisdom, wisdom folly' and 'blindness is sight, sight is blindness' took me part of the way, and I could recognize some parallels between the Gloucester family and the Lears. Even the ending could be accommodated into the tonal and atmospheric exhaustion of 'the full close', as if Shakespeare were not compromising with his material, and his final moments could be seen as an Aristotelian accountability for a character who had committed a moral crime as a result of a 'fatal flaw', more or less like Othello. But still, even now that I have finally sorted out the plot, some things still rankle—that Shakespeare added a Fool to this solemn tragedy, without precedent from his sources and, most notoriously, he changed the ending of all his sources, from one that was 'happy' to one that was 'sad'. At certain moments I can see precisely why Samuel Johnson was so disconcerted, why Charles Lamb declared this play of plays to be 'unstageable', and why Nahum Tate had been earlier driven to rewrite the play along the lines of its sources, in an attempt to 'rectify what was wanting in the Regularity and Probability of the Tale … This method necessarily threw me on making the Tale conclude in a Success to the innocent distrest Persons' (1681).[4]

Even textual criticism, considered in earlier times of Gregg and Fredson Bowers to be a science which could clarify and elucidate narrative problems, has now come to acknowledge the kind of fundamental indeterminacy that underpinned my own initial confusion. Nowadays editors have come around to a new orthodoxy that *King Lear* should be seen not as one play but as two, signalled in shorthand as the 'Quarto' of 1608 and the 'Folio' of 1623, each of which is significantly different, and unlikely to be indebted to a lost manuscript. Which is the 'director's cut' and which the actual stage version cannot be answered, and they may both be stage versions of exactly equal status. Chris Wortham has brilliantly contributed to this debate by comparing the *Lear* texts with the undoubtedly discrete versions of *Doctor Faustus*. Daring to hypothesize that the Quarto text came after the Folio (which is not implausible since it is common for writers to add rather than subtract material), Wortham suggests that 'the figure of Albany is rewritten [in the Quarto] to accommodate James I in quite a literal way'.[5] But the fundamental question raised by the existence of the two texts has perhaps not yet been squarely faced. Even when editors acknowledge that there are two, they locate the differences in general tone and emphasis. The Quarto in general is more humane with its examples of compassionate behaviour, while the pared down Folio text is more austere and harsh in its economy. The usual reason given for the existence of two is that the Folio is a shortened version of the Quarto because of theatrical exigencies of some kind, although a minority, as mentioned, suggest the Quarto is a lengthened version of the Folio, again for theatrical or artistic reasons. (The older view, that both are based on a lost original which can be recovered by a conflated version, cannot entirely be ruled out either.) However, it is less often granted that the respective titles suggest a much more unsettling problem, that they are two different *kinds* of plays, belonging to different genres. The Quarto is titled *The History of King Lear* (recalling the immediate source, *The True Chronicle History of King Leir*) while in the Folio *Lear* is firmly placed amongst the tragedies by those great classifiers, Heminges and Condell, who confidently entitled it *The Tragedy of King Lear*. It looks like the purchaser of the Quarto was meant to be kept in suspense about how the play will end, while by the time of the Folio, long after the writer's death, the ending would be well known. The matter is not trivial, since chronicle plays and tragedies, although they could draw on the same material, were different genres, and *Richard III* and *Richard II*, both described as 'tragedies' in their quartos, are structured differently from the Henriad. After history, life goes on, after tragedy, it does not, and it would be difficult to conceive of sequels to *Lear* in the way that there are so many sequels to Shakespeare's chronicle history plays. A play which we regard as archetypically tragic, the touchstone of all tragedy, may not have been anything of the kind in the mind of its creator or first audience. It is possible that the text as Shakespeare originally conceived and wrote it, is unsure of its genre or at least uneasily contains the potential for several contradictory genres (history, tragedy, tragi-comedy), and that it was his posthumous editors who made the decision. In short, the unthinkable is possible—that Shakespeare, in Olivier's famous phrase about Hamlet, 'was a man who simply could not make up his mind'.

Internal evidence might support these unsettling possibilities, quite apart from my own initial confidence that the play was in structure a folk tale. In a somewhat strange way, each character seems to know he or she exists in a play, at the mercy of its plot and genre, but each has a different notion of what kind of play they are in and even what the plot is. Lear sees himself in an autobiography, writing the last chapter, or at least he is now concluding a 'great man' drama, ensuring his epitaph will tell his tale correctly. For those who make history, history ends with them, and what comes after is the beginning of somebody else's life-story. He has lived four score years and upwards, and has, according to his own lights, ruled wisely and well, dispensing justice fairly and without fear or favour. This he chooses as the theme for his denouement. He effects the succession of the nation equally amongst his three daughters, 'that future strife may be prevented now', thus ensuring the peace of a happily ever after tale. Our Act One, Scene One, is his intended final scene of Act Five. The rest is silence. And so it would have been but for one word that is only a breath away from silence, the word 'Nothing'. From this insignificant non-signifier unravels a family civil war which Tennessee Williams and Edward Albee internalized and reproduced. Anatomy of a family disintegration is another genre available in this sprawling play.

The Jacobean purchaser of the 1608 Quarto would have had more than an inkling from the title page that the play was amongst the most popular genres in the 1590s by the dramatist whose name was synonymous with the chronicle history play:

> Master William Shakespeare: his chronicle history of the life and death of King Lear and his three daughters. With the unfortunate life of Edgar, son and heir to the Earl of Gloucester, and his sullen and assumed humour of Tom of Bedlam.

It is not so different from the bill of fare offered on the title page of the Quarto of *2 Henry IV*: 'The Second part of henrie the fourth, continuing to his death, and coronation of Henrie the fift. With the humours of sir Iohn Falstaffe, and swaggering Pistoll'.[6] Like all Shakespeare's history plays, it deals centrally with political dynasties and succession to the kingdom. The fact that the king's death is mentioned would not immediately suggest the play is a tragedy, for we see the death of Henry IV in his play, yet it finishes triumphantly with the accession of the new king, and the subplot concerning Edgar mirrors the fortunes of either Hotspur in *1 Henry IV* or Falstaff in both parts. However, once the astute buyer began reading, he or she would have reassessed, and realized the play was in fact not a history, since after the first few minutes or so attention switches away from events of the kingdom, and strong signs indicated that it belonged to the genre much more popular by 1608, family romance of reconciliation.[7] The subplot would have clinched this, coming as it does from the most famous prose romance of the whole age, Sidney's *Arcadia*, but even the main plot is clearly in the territory. In fact, its almost startling resemblance to the plot of *The Winter's Tale* which Shakespeare went on to write just three years later, reinforces the impression for us. In both plot and subplot a ruler renounces a family member for the wrong reasons, and is warned by a chorus of loyal counsellors that the consequences will be disastrous, which immediately proves true. The 'promised end' is clear: in both plays, after a period of suffering and penitence, the ruler is reunited with a long-lost, loving daughter (and in Leontes' case, his wife), and lives on with her. Again, the astute Jacobean reader would have known from the familiar chronicle sources that this is indeed exactly what will happen, and it is what Cordelia seems to expect. Right up until her death this pattern and set of expectations is available. The play is a romance which will deliver a happy ending, akin to the genre's cousin, romantic comedy, where 'the whirligig of time brings in its revenges'. Characters within the plot have preconceptions about how it will all end, and given that the self-evidently 'good' characters maintain an optimistic stance, there seems internal evidence to support the view that the material will end happily. Edgar's disguise is comparable to that of Antipholus of Syracuse, and he sees his inexplicable situation as part of a comedy of errors which will eventually be resolved:

To be worst,
The lowest and most dejected thing of fortune,
Stands still in esperance, lives not in fear.
The lamentable change is from the best,
The worst returns to laughter.

(Scene 15, 2–6)[8]

His 'esperance' may be immediately contradicted by the entrance of his blinded father, but he continues to hope for a happy ending, educating his father out of despair, and it may be some personal reward to know that at least his father dies 'smilingly'. Edgar then turns his attention to rectifying the wrong his brother has perpetrated, and changes his genre-expectations to that other popular standby of the period, revenge tragedy. Edgar orchestrates the chivalric joust between himself as anonymous knight and his evil brother Edmund, as carefully as Titus had prepared the meal for his enemies, or Hieronimo had plotted his revenge.[9] The two most clearly trustworthy characters of all, Cordelia and Kent, are in no doubt about future happiness. Kent maintains his disguise, even after it is unnecessary in Cordelia's judgement, because he too expects a miraculous revelation scene in which, as at the end of *Twelfth Night*, providence and a 'natural perspective' created by Cordelia, will prevail:

Good King, that thou must approve the common say,
Thou out of heaven's benediction com'st
To the warm sun.
        [*He takes out a letter*]
Approach, thou beacon to this under globe,
That by thy comfortable beams I may
Peruse this letter. Nothing almost sees miracles
But misery. I know 'tis from Cordelia,
Who hath now fortunately been informed
Of my obscured course, and shall find time
For this enormous state, seeking to give
Losses their remedies. All weary and overwatched,
Take vantage, heavy eyes, not to behold
This shameful lodging. Fortune, good night,
Smile; once more turn thy wheel.

(Scene 7, 150–64)

Cordelia herself, judging from her words in the first scene and her actions later, must assume she is in a kind of morality play, where inner virtue will eventually prevail over hypocrisy and flattery, good over evil. The reconciliation with her father and their touching forgiveness of each other is her promised end, and, believing in 'kind gods' and 'restoration', she draws the appropriate moral conclusion from a story of patient virtue rewarded: 'We are not the first / Who with best meaning have incurred the worst' (Scene 24, 3–4). She is faithful at least to the play's sources. This scene should have been the one to end a romance. Unfortunately, defying its historical antecedents, this play goes on. Perhaps Shakespeare, faced with so many loose ends, reversed his judgement at the end of *Love's Labour's Lost*, and thought to himself, 'That's too short for a play.'

Other characters have their own views and expectations about what kind of play they are acting in. The Fool, another character who is clearly loyal to his master and set up as a moral spokesman, acts as though he believes that Lear will come to 'see better' and all will be mended. The fact that he disappears in the 'noon' of the play when he chooses to 'go to bed', is ominous, but not conclusive since we expect his reappearance when the problems are solved, but hopes are dashed with 'And my poor fool is hanged' (Scene 24, 299).[10] At the very least, his tone is one indicating he is witnessing a farce turning on 'errors', at worst a black comedy, but not a tragedy. Even the illegitimate nihilist Edmund, judging from his aside on his brother's entrance, 'Pat, he comes like the catastrophe of the old comedy', is at the very least thinking along the lines of a Iago who plots his own comic vindication.

However, generic certainties begin to disintegrate in different ways as the plot seems to lose its way by straying into subplots. Goneril and Regan become involved in a love romance with Edmund, parallelling in a perhaps negative light the cameo romance of Cordelia and France, who marry for the right reasons. Only Albany's sublimely banal line, 'great thing of us forgot!—' (Scene 24, 231) refocuses attention on the narrative confusion of a play which has 'forgotten' its major plot, protagonist, and heroine, in the distractions of other matters concerning the Gloucester family. However, rather than deliver us the happy ending that all expect, the play instead shocks us beyond belief by killing off the heroine, offstage and unlamented by anyone except her father. Even the charity of calling the play a chronicle history is demolished, not only because it violates its own chronicle sources, but also because the issue of succession to the kingdom, the overriding preoccupation of all history plays, is left in complete disarray. Constitutionally Albany inherits the crown but he immediately abdicates (here we go again?) bestowing it in a power-sharing arrangement on Edgar and Kent (here we go again?) neither having any family claim unless it is tenuously based on Edgar being Lear's godson. Kent, deciding he is not in a comedy or a romance but a Roman tragedy, exits to commit suicide like Enobarbus, in loyalty to his dead master. The one who is technically next in line to the throne, the King of France, is not even mentioned, let alone, like Fortinbras, Octavius, or Malcolm, appearing on stage to restore some stability.[11] At this point many readers, such as our Jacobean buyer of the script, Nahum Tate, and Samuel Johnson in the eighteenth century, Coleridge in the nineteenth, and innocent readers today, can be forgiven for saying with Goneril, 'No more, the text is foolish', and turning away in either bemusement or disgust at a writer who simply does not know what genre his material inhabits. The storm has blown away more than the old king's clothes. It has blown away any claim the play may have had to the unity that genre bestows. The Folio version eliminates at least some of the more blatant ambiguities by announcing itself as a tragedy and being placed by the editors amongst the tragedies, and even by eliminating some of the more romance—like gestures of compassion and kindness by minor characters like the three Servants who tend the blinded Gloucester and apply flax and whites of eggs to his bleeding face (Quarto, III. 7. 97–111). However, by stripping the play so unremittingly of all 'comfort',[12] the 1608 editors, in their zeal to impose a genre, risk turning it into a grim parody of the form of tragedy. 'What learn we by that?' the moral theorist of literature, Sir Philip Sidney, could well ask, when he contemplates the violations of poetic justice and wandering plots of 'mongrel' tragi-comedy which he found fashionable in the 1580s.[13]

If *Love's Labour's Lost* is Shakespeare's comic experiment in disrupting generic expectations, *King Lear* is his tragic equivalent, and the reasons may be surprisingly similar. In the former, after verbally balletic courtship inevitably leading to marriage, the action 'doth not end like an old play' because 'real life', in the reported news of an offstage death, intervenes and the lovers must part, the men forced to do 'community work' and to confront the kind of serious issues that Biron, for one, will find in a hospice. In *Lear* any possible expectation of a comic or romance ending is thwarted likewise, by news of an offstage death, and then an undeniably visual confrontation with the reality of that death, with the entrance of a father with his dead daughter in his arms, followed by his own death. We might note with some irony, that an anonymous contemporary of Nahum Tate changed the ending of *Love's Labour's Lost* to conform with what could be seen as its true generic promised end. In this play, *The Students* (1762), the wooing *doth* end like an old play: Jack *hath* Jill, and the ladies' courtesy makes their sport a comedy. More ironically, even in our own days of lynx-eyed textual finesse, Kenneth Branagh has done exactly the same at the end of his film. Shakespeare's very point, however, in both *Lear* and *Love's Labour's Lost*, like Milton's in his grief-stricken anti-elegy *Lycidas*, is that any formal boundaries of literature, such as those imposed by genre, prevent the artist achieving his own priority of 'imitating nature'.[14]

I. Cinematic Genres and *King Lear*

The desire to categorize literary works into kinds is as old as Aristotle, who created the tripartite scheme of epic, dramatic and lyric. Shakespeare's first editors, Heminges and Condell, spoke for their age in proposing the dramatic genres of comedy, history and tragedy, the elastic generic markers parodied by the player in *Hamlet*. Others have been added along the way, such as romance, pastoral, and tragi-comedy. Film theorists resisted the temptation until the 1960s, when they proceeded to take the plunge. Some chose to follow the custom of creating three—drama, documentary and avant-garde—but most favoured groupings that reflected subject matter, setting, or affect, like the western, musical, epic, romantic comedy, family saga, horror, thriller, gangster, *film noir*, heritage, and so on. In all cases, it was audience expectation that lay behind the impulse. Audiences are assumed to be entitled to know what kind of film they have chosen to attend, and to know where they stand, from the early moments of a film.

> Stated simply, genre movies are those commercial feature films which, through repetition and variation, tell familiar stories with familiar characters in familiar situations. They also encourage expectations and experiences similar to those of similar films we have already seen.[15]

If we think of genre as a 'vehicle' in a literal sense, we might make the loose analogy that the same people can travel in either a car, a train, or an aeroplane. And that *King Lear* can travel in a family saga or a western. I should say that stage performances could be taken equally as evidence of the play's plural possibilities, since it has enjoyed periods of being structured around the dialogue between Lear and the Fool and played like *Waiting for Godot*, and of being rewritten as Artaudian Theatre of Cruelty based on the atrocities of Gloucester's blinding, in plays like Edward Bond's *Lear*, Howard Barker's *Seven Lears: The Pursuit of the Good*, and Elaine Feinstein's *Lear's Daughters*. But it is film genres which I shall be discussing here.

It is a long-term project of mine to explore the deep connections between Shakespeare and Hollywood (which I use as shorthand for 'mainstream' Anglo-American commercial films made for mass distribution), though I have not yet decided whether Shakespeare invented Hollywood or Hollywood reinvented Shakespeare. The fact of the intertwined fortunes is not surprising, since Hollywood is full of graduates from ivy-league universities eager to put their expensive education in the classics to lucrative use in writing scripts. Their contribution of overt and covert references to Shakespeare sprinkles films from *noir* of the 1940s to *The Simpsons* and *The Lion King* (where, I would argue, *Hamlet* and Milton's *Paradise Lost* vie for prime billing).

My argument is that it is at the level of genre, or formal expectations and 'shells' of Hollywood films that Shakespeare has his most ubiquitous presence. *The Tempest* gave us a classic science fiction film, *Forbidden Planet* (1956), and this intriguing link leads us to speculate that the play laid down the prototype for the genre, just as, in its subplot of Miranda and Ferdinand it gave us a cameo glimpse of the possibilities in a 'summer beach romance' or rite of passage film for teenagers. *Macbeth* was frequently quoted in gangster films in the 1940s, and its plot can be seen as their *ur-*

text. It has the raw narrative components of murder, guilt, conscience and retribution, and even anticipates the developed genre of 'gangster-couple' movies popular in the 1960s, after *Bonnie and Clyde* (1967) and *Badlands* (1973). Macbeth and Lady Macbeth are, after all, the most notorious of all partner murderers, the original Bonnie and Clyde. In Hollywood there are plenty of philosophical, witty but troubled and melancholy heroes like Hamlet who, if he were reborn today would surely seek 'analysis' to explore his relationship with his mother, dead father, and step-father. Woody Allen is just one amongst many Hamlets, and here the connection comes through the Freudian psychoanalyst Ernest Jones and Laurence Olivier. Most roads from the modern romantic comedy and 'chick-flick' genres can be traced straight back to *A Midsummer Night's Dream*, and many cinematic star-crossed lovers are variations on Romeo and Juliet. Kenneth Branagh cleverly recognized and exploited the fact that war films take their format from *Henry V*, and it is difficult to imagine his own film being so extraordinarily popular in any year other than 1989, the fiftieth anniversary of the start of World War Two, when British media were saturated with memorabilia and nostalgia. How else can we explain the frequent broadcasting of Branagh's music-soaked, stirring rendition of 'Once more unto the breach' on BBC radio, alongside Beethoven and Elgar during that year? Branagh's *Love's Labour's Lost* points towards an explicit if unacknowledged link between Busby Berkeley and song-filled Shakespearean comedies (via the explicit evidence of Reinhardt's *Dream* [1935]), and more generally suggests that Shakespeare laid down a blueprint for the musical. For decades film theorists have argued over whether film genres exist, as anthropologists suggest, because their stories are contemporary versions of collective social myths embedded in the culture or, as materialists argue, whether they are created as a result of the Hollywood system of production and distribution of films which assumes a contract between producers and consumers that the product will confine surprise within consistent and predictable product descriptions.[16] The same questions could be asked of the editors of the First Folio.

My argument here is more specific, that the genre indeterminacy built into the play *King Lear* by Shakespeare has led to films that are adapted to surprising structures, each of which can be traced back to the conflicting audience expectations generated in the early stages of the play. The diverse range of films influenced by the play may support the conclusion which I have advanced above, that the play's writer was not at all sure at the outset where his narrative would lead him.

Of course 'Shakespeare' is a film genre in itself with literally thousands of entries if we include offshoots, an international subset of English 'heritage film' which is often based on literary adaptation. Even restricting ourselves to the plays more conservatively packaged as 'versions' of his plays, there are well over 600 listed on the Internet Movie Database. Of these, since the first silent version (1909), there are about sixteen 'straight' *King Lears* listed, a number fewer than *Hamlet* (56) and the

Dream (25) but still placing it amongst the more filmogenic plays in the canon. In terms of genre, these are all identifiable as tragedies, at least in terms of their endings, as one would expect from works which use modern conflated playtexts which are always titled and packaged as having tragic endings. However, the parameters and latitudes of genre given to *King Lear* exceed those in film versions of any other play by Shakespeare. Even the most well-known and conservatively packaged of these reflect something of the original's ambiguity, since the narrative is deployed for some ulterior directorial motive. For Orson Welles the central thread is Lear himself as fatally flawed hero of an Aristotelian tragedy. The production was 'staged by' Peter Brook for the C.B.S. television programme, *Omnibus*, in 1953, a rather courageous decision given the limitations of the medium at that early stage in its development. Welles often spoke of *Lear* as a play which is elementally simple in its structure, and this is certainly observable in Welles' own performance, if in few other productions. He and Brook have cut the play to the bone, probably to fit an allotted time span of just over an hour but perhaps also with integrity to a concept. There is no Edgar at all, and Edmund is retained with very few lines to speak and his presence seems to be merely to explain the deaths of Goneril and Regan. Gloucester's role is simply to help the king and have his eyes thumbed out for this, and 'Poor Tom' is a character in his own right, played by Micheál Macliammóir. The intention of the restructuring is to place the complete focus on Lear himself, and to a lesser extent on his Fool. In a self-fulfilling prophecy, Welles makes the play into a structurally straightforward one, the fall of the great man, an *Oedipus Rex* for his times. Peter Brook returned time and again to directing *Lear* and each result reflects cultural preoccupations of the time in which it was made. His 1970 version, starring Paul Scofield, is the most well known and easily available. Directing at the height of Samuel Beckett's stage popularity and in the wake of the highly influential book by Jan Kott, *Shakespeare Our Contemporary*,[17] Brook turns the play into a bleak contemplation of the futility of 'nothing' set in the frozen Scandinavian winter. The insistent chorus is the sardonic black comedian, the Fool, while Lear is a dangerous, crew-cutted autocrat, not because he is out of control in his anger and madness but because he is over-controlled and menacingly obessional. While black comedy is not quite the right term, grotesquerie (following Wilson Knight's lead) and existential absurdism (following Beckett's and Kott's) are suggestive of the film's style.

Famously, as Grigorii Kozintsev made clear in his book,[18] his film *Korol Lir* (1970), based on Pasternak's translation, is something of an allegory of the Russian Revolution. Its stunning opening shows hundreds of beggars converging for a quiet protest march up the hill to the palace, which is guarded by armed soldiers on horseback and reminiscent of a police state. The king is a small, bird-like man, an unknown actor with a strong regional Georgian accent, giggling with his fool in full view of a solemnly black aristocracy, later shown to be corrupt and liable to civil war and overthrow. Edgar increasingly emerges as Lenin-like leader of the disaffected peasantry, taking them through to the fires of revolution where decadence is purged. The film takes its cue from Lear's social conscience awakened to the needs of 'poor naked wretches' whose beggary is the casualty of a preoccupied and unjust aristocracy, and also to Gloucester's similar awakening. 'Political parable' and 'national epic' are more descriptive of the film's genre than 'the tragedy of a king'. The old Russia is swept away and the new ushered in. The same can be said of Akira Kurosawa's *Ran* (1985), its plot following closely the contours of Shakespeare's play even if the daughters are replaced by sons, and the road to Dover in Celtic times is transposed to the snow-clad mountains of Japan in the Samurai times, Kurosawa's favoured period and setting. The ending of this film is as purgative as Kozintsev's, as a spectacular fire burns out the *ancien regime* in another progressive, national epic, paralleling the disarmed Japan's enforced transition from a war culture to industrialism after World War Two. Apparently the castle was built under the brow of Mount Fuji especially for the film, and was then incinerated, just as the bridge over the River Kwai was constructed and then exploded for the sake of that film.

The quintessentially British Lear, Laurence Olivier, as was his wont, makes the play into one about Lord Olivier—forgivably, since he was financing the film himself and had been declared uninsurable because of his advanced years, unreliable health, and erratic temper. The onset of senility and dementia in the central character was, according to backstage anecdotes, mirrored in the star's deteriorating physical and mental condition during the filming (the early 1980s, when he was in his mid-seventies). In other ways the film belongs to him, as he adapts the play into one largely purged of political content about authority and the kingdom, centring instead on his own patriarchal position in British stage and film, and the inheritance he wishes to leave behind him. The opening scene shows him as the grand old man, avuncular, relaxed and genially capricious, setting up a love-test between representatives from three generations of actresses with whom he had worked. Dorothy Tutin was fifty-three when the film was released, Diana Rigg was forty-five, and Anna Calder-Marshall thirty-six. The gestures of personal rebuff from his 'daughters' fuel what is essentially presented as a bourgeois family saga centring on the aging individual's obsession with his will, in the vein of *The Forsyte Saga* or *Brideshead Revisited* (1981) in which Olivier had recently acted. The tragedy belongs to those left behind after the final exit of the Great Man, lamenting the vacuum left in British stage and Hollywood cinema.

Without having seen more than a fraction of the 'Shakespeare films' made, I would suggest it is difficult to think of any other play that has been presented as political parable, family saga, national epic, theatre of cruelty, and black comedy. In whatever setting or time *Hamlet* is placed, it is still the tragedy of Hamlet—or a parody of the tragedy of Hamlet. Yet with *King Lear*, even amongst directors apparently striving to be 'faithful' to 'the text', we do find such latititude. The generic variations become even more diverse when we look at films which have become known as 'offshoots'. This is most interesting because such films are by definition less reverential to the text or received wisdom about the text, and they often begin by setting up the initial premise of the play and then seeing where it can lead—just as, I have suggested, Shakespeare in this play sets up a premise and then witholds until the very ending a confident audience expectation as to where it will lead.

It comes as no surprise that *A Thousand Acres* (1997), the film made from Jane Smiley's novel which was itself modelled on *King Lear*,[19] was directed by Jocelyn Moorhouse who had already made *How to Make an American Quilt* (1995). Both films dwell on the special knowledge stitched from generation to generation by women, both show sisters finding out unpleasant surprises about each other, and both are plays about families rather than a nation or an individual. *A Thousand Acres* gives a distinctively female perspective on Shakespeare's play. Goneril and Regan (Ginny and Rose), far from being evil, are married farm women who have very plausible grievances against their tyrannical and abusive father, and also their younger sister Caroline, who avoided the family conflicts and the father's whims by leaving the rural Iowa farm in the midwest to become a lawyer. There is a suggestion she has come back only for the inheritance, and that she is tactically holding out for the lot. The focus is on ancient tensions and betrayals between the siblings, and the aged father's distribution of land is an occasion or a catalyst for these smouldering resentments to explode in revelations of childhood abuse and later adultery. Shakespeare's initially straightforward discrimination between good and evil is problematized in a set of paradoxes, and it becomes impossible to judge characters in such simple terms in the film.

King of Texas (2002) was a western made for television and it is without any doubt at all meant to be seen as a version of *King Lear* (Shakespeare is credited as co-writer). The tagline used to publicize it was 'Between land and power lies the frontier of greed...the saga of family...the heart of drama'. John Lear (Patrick Stewart) owns a large ranch in Texas and, just like King Lear, tries to divide it among his three daughters (Susannah, Rebecca and Claudia) in order to stop them squabbling after his death, with exactly the same disastrous results. There is even a relatively 'faithful' subplot of Gloucester (Henry Westover) and his good and evil sons, of whom Thomas (Edgar) seems to take control at the end. There is a Fool who is an Afro-American named Rip, although for economy he also plays Kent's role and stays around to see his master die. The King of France is a Mexican, Menchaca, who lives on adjoining land and welcomes Claudia and her father at the end. Events unfold exactly as they do in Shakespeare's play, including the storm and a ghastly blinding, yet in the American West. Why? Only the director (Uli Ede) could fully know, but we can speculate. There was an antecedent, Dmytryk's *Broken Lance*

(1954), starring Spencer Tracy as a cattle baron whose three sons turn against him, in a role billed as a 'Western King Lear'. The film drew from the play themes of conflict between generations and a frontier culture clashing with industrial. But even so, the question can be asked also of this film—why? The initial stimulus may have been the heath, a frontier wilderness which, as it was transposed to the Russian steppes by Kotsintsev, (and the Namibian Desert in *The King is Alive* [2002]) is here transported onto the wide open range. As well, the story can hold the mythic evocation of a period before the 'civilizing' stability of land ownership legislation, when rugged, masculine individualism resisted women's notions of settlement and family (Susannah and Rebecca are not quite so unsympathetic as Goneril and Regan), and also stood out against the niceties of land law and lawmaking in general. The western also depends on unsubtle moral categories embodied in characters who are identifiably good and evil, another characteristic of *King Lear*, although the western takes a firm stance on the ending as a restoration of order. John Lear and Claudia are reconciled in their moments of death, ensuring that the future of the family saga is in the reliable hands of Menchaca, who has remained true to his word. A tendency to emotional melodrama accompanies the stereotypical characterisation, and love interest in both versions is kept at the margins of our attention. Coming as late as 2002, we might also deduce that the film also is set at the end of the true western era when expansion was hitting borders and the cowboy ethic was waning just as chivalry waned at the end of the fifteenth century. John Lear is the last of the old brigade, just as King Lear is seen by Albany or Edgar (depending on whether we use the Quarto or the Folio) as the last of his kind who will never be duplicated: 'We that are young shall never see so much, or live so long'. And so, since *Lear* anticipates all these basic conventions of the western, why not make it into a western?

Few would suspect *The Godfather* (1972) of being an offshoot of *King Lear*, but the fact is confirmed by the film's director, Francis Ford Coppola:

> I have a belief with so-called work-for-hire movies that you should fall in love with the movies you have to make. You find what about that film that you love. And so with *The Godfather* I said, this is a classic story, this is like Shakespeare. I'm gonna do it like a king he has three sons and each son has gotten some part of his talent. One is cunning and cold, and one is violent and emotional, and the third is sweet but sorta dumb, and the godfather the father had all of those qualities and that's why he was a great king. And I'm gonna tell it like a story of succession and it must be classical and so out of whatever you've chosen to fall in love with comes the style.[20]

I am not the first to note this connection, since Tony Howard has done so in *The Cambridge Companion to Shakespeare on Film*,[21] but whereas his analysis focuses on *Godfather III* (1990), where admittedly the *Lear* signals are very explicit, yet the analogy seems to have been present in Copolla's mind from the outset. It may well have been the promise of a Shakespearean model that lured Marlon Brando, the best Mark Antony ever in Joseph L. Mankiewicz's *Julius Caesar* (1953), out of reclusive retirement, since the prospect of playing King Lear is especially appealing to aging male actors. When we look closely, Coppola's perception about his film is indeed suggestive. The Corleone family, while all-male, does make a close fit with the Lear dynasty, and the Godfather, 'Don' Vito Corleone, is in character a New York Italian equivalent of King Lear. The roles and characters of his three sons, Michael, Sonny and Fredo, loosely resemble those of Goneril, Regan and Cordelia. As we witness the family tearing itself apart, we begin to see that Shakespeare's film, quite apart from being the progenitor of film tragedy, national epic, family saga, western, theatre of cruelty, and absurdist comedy, is also the godfather of all mafia movies.

The godfather image has a link with my last and strangest example, perhaps the exception that proves the rule. Genre in French films in their witty, subtle and self-parodying style is very different from Hollywood's conventions. Just as they have resisted Hollywood genres, so the proudly nationalistic French have always harboured suspicions of a bard who is unfortunate enough to have been born English and equally unfortunate in being so eagerly embraced by German writers from Goethe and Brecht and by Russians like Pasternak. Jean-Luc Godard, whose flirtation with Hollywood was notorious, is the exception. This in turn may explain why Godard has been so popular with Anglo-American New Wave critics and film-makers, while being treated with détente by the industry in his own country. He made a version of *King Lear* (1987), alternatively named *King Lear: Fear and Loathing*, which is regarded variously as profundity or as a joke.[22] Its central connection with Shakespeare's play comes from the pivotal word 'Nothing' and the film is set after a post-Chernobyl destruction of the world, certainly the end of written culture, and perhaps at the end of meaning. With some uneasiness, one presumes, it is categorized by the IMDb as 'sci-fi, drama', and Shakespeare is given the writer's credit. Amongst others, it has appearances from Woody Allen as 'Professor Alien', a dread-locked Godard himself as 'Professor Pluggy', Norman Mailer as 'The Great Writer' and an American Peter Sellars (sic) as 'William Shakespeare Junior the Fifth', who, promisingly for my longer argument on the cultural ubiquitousness of Shakespeare, announces himself as the last person alive. Drawing perhaps on the subtext of Coppola's film, Godard's central character is an aging Mafioso called Learo. If a genre exists to accommodate Godard's *Lear*, it would be in the vicinity of deconstructive, comic absurdism, and the evidence suggests this is what Godard intended.

This essay has canvassed only well-known films that are adaptations of King Lear. I have not been able to view, let alone analyse, the many ethnic films such as *The Yiddish King Lear* (1935), *The Jewish King Lear* (1912), and the Yiddish *Mirele Efros*; the Telegu *Gunsundari Katha* (1949) and its Tamil remake *Gunsundari* (1955). But I am privileged to have seen filmed versions of three staged, Indian-language

Lears in Shakespeare in India (2004) on a CD-ROM compiled by Poonam Trivedi, each of which has very different effects springing from indigenous dramatic forms, different dramatic kinds, and different languages (Gujerati, Hindi and Marathi).[23] Just as Shakespeare seems to have kept his generic options open until the very end of his play, so the diversity of stage and film adaptations prove its potential for filling very different genres. The play, or rather plays, remain a quarry, an inviting potential, whose real power is to compel the imagination in apparently endless ways, as evidenced by the bewildering diversity of filmed versions. Like Wilson Knight, I am left feeling that I have never read Shakespeare's *King Lear*. At least I know now what he meant.

Notes

1   G. Wilson Knight, 'On the Principles of Shakespeare Interpretation', *The Wheel of Fire* (Oxford: Oxford University Press, 1930), ch. 1.

2   See Hugh Grady, *The Modernist Shakespeare* (Oxford: Clarendon Press, 1991), ch. 2.

3   See, for example, R. A. Foakes, *Hamlet versus Lear* (Cambridge: Cambridge University Press, 1993), arguing that the two World Wars in the twentieth century came to make *Lear* seem a more contemporary play than *Hamlet*.

4   Quoted in Frank Kermode, *Shakespeare: King Lear* (London: Macmillan, 1969), p. 25.

5   Christopher Wortham, 'Ghostly Presences: Doctor Faustus meets King Lear', *Meridian*, 14 (1995), 59–66 (p. 64).

6   E. K. Chambers, *William Shakespeare: A Study of Facts and Problems* (Oxford: Oxford University Press, 1930), vol. I, p. 378.

7   For this approach, see L. G. Salingar, 'Romance in *King Lear*', *English*, 27 (1978), 5–21; see also Howard Felperin, *Shakespearean Romance* (Princeton: Princeton University Press, 1972), ch. 4.

8   Unless otherwise noted, I quote from *The History of King Lear* in Stanley Wells and Gary Taylor (eds), *The Complete Oxford Shakespeare* (Oxford: Oxford University Press, 1987).

9   For an analysis showing that elements of revenge tragedy are used in unexpected places by Shakespeare, see Linda Anderson, *A Kind of Wild Justice: Revenge in Shakespeare's Comedies* (Newark: University of Delaware Press, 1987). See also Harry Keyishian, *The Shapes of Revenge: Victimization, Vengeance, and Vindictiveness in Shakespeare* (New Jersey: Humanities Press, 1995), esp. pp. 67–79.

10   Some critics have argued the line refers to Cordelia: see, for example, Ralph Berry, 'Woman as Fool: Dramatic Mechanism in Shakespeare', *Shakespearean Structures* (London: Macmillan, 1981), pp. 12–23.

11   For another consideration of this issue, see R. S. White, '*King Lear* and Philosophical Anarchism', *English*, 37 (1988), 181–200.

12   The critic who most forcibly insisted on the play's bleakness, in the face of a tradition of fairly cheerful Christian criticism, was Barbara Everett in 'The New *King Lear*', *Critical Quarterly*, 2 (1960), 325–39.

13 Sir Philip Sidney, *A Defence of Poetry*, in *Miscellaneous Prose of Sir Philip Sidney*, ed. Katherine Duncan-Jones (Oxford: Oxford University Press, 1973).

14 Stephen Greenblatt, in his biography of Shakespeare, sees *King Lear* as 'a tremendous explosion of rage, madness, and grief', although he can find 'no easy, obvious link' with 'the known circumstances of his own life'. He does point out that Shakespeare's father died three years before he apparently began writing the play. See Stephen Greenblatt, *Will in the World: How Shakespeare Became Shakespeare* (London: Jonathan Cape, 2004), p. 356.

15 Barry Keith Grant, 'Introduction', *Film Genre Reader*, ed. Barry Keith Grant (Austin: Univesity of Texas Press, 1993), p. xi.

16 Works that shift between genres can be seen as parodically derivative and disunified, like the Bollywood musical, or, occasionally, as highly innovative, like the Australian film *Japanese Story* which jumps from romantic comedy to tragedy in a split second.

17 Jan Kott, *Shakespeare Our Contemporary*, transl. Boleslaw Taborski (London: Methuen, 1964).

18 *King Lear, the space of tragedy: the diary of a film director*, Grigori Kozintsev; translated by Mary Mackintosh; with a foreword by Peter Brook (Berkeley: University of California Press, 1977).

19 For contextual information on the writer and her script, see Susan Farrell, *Jane Smiley's 'A Thousand Acres'* (New York and London: Continuum, 2001).

20 DVD *A Decade Under the Influence: The 70's films that changed everything*, dir. Richard Lagravanese and Ted Demme (2000), ch. 6.

21 Tony Howard, 'Shakespeare's cinematic offshoots', *The Cambridge Companion to Shakespeare on Film*, ed. Russell Jackson (Cambridge: Cambridge University Press, 2000), p. 299.

22 For analysis of this film as Godard's deliberate 'mess', see Douglas Morrey, *Jean-Luc Godard* (Manchster: Manchester University Press, 2005), pp. 168–72.

23 Poonam Trivedi, 'Multi Shakespeare: Performing *King Lear* in India,' in *The International Shakespeare Yearbook 2005*, ed. Graham Bradshaw (London: Ashgate, 2005).

Fragments Recollected from Two Lives

Christopher and Anne Wortham

During the early part of the Second World War our lives began at much the same time on two different continents. Anne was born first, in June 1940, Chris a few months later in November of that year. She was born in Adelaide, South Australia; he in a small town in the northern Transvaal province of South Africa. Despite the accidental differences of place and parental background, our early lives had much in common. To begin with, we were both war babies. As we grew to consciousness in the 1940s we became war children. And as we grew towards adulthood in the 1950s we became post-war adolescents. At the time, war seemed to have little to do with anything; looking back we now see that it had everything to do with how we had begun and with who we were to become. Only by recognizing that overwhelming circumstance have we been able to get beyond the limitations it imposed on development, behaviour and values.

From the beginning there was sunlight in our lives, a sunlight that could not be dispelled or overcome by the overwhelming grey gloom. The lives of our parents and their parents had been irremediably blighted by the Boer War, the First World War and the Great Depression, ever before we arrived. It would be our good fortune to see the world with fresh eyes and to enter into life with a capacity for joy from which previous generations had been excluded. When the Hippie movement came in the 1960s and we first met—young and free in a London that was suddenly bursting with a new and inexplicable vitality—we were able to enter into its glory and its folly without inhibition and with very little sense of guilt. At the secondary modern school where we met and taught in the London semi-slum of Harlesden there was rejoicing among the children when the Beatles were conjointly awarded the MBE. Apoplectic ex-servicemen were not pleased, however, and some sent back their medals and decorations in protest. That moment, some time in mid-1965, marked the watershed of difference between generations. And we had just made it into the new one! But only just: we could not really remember the war, but we could remember its atmosphere and its aftermath only too well.

Let us take you back towards our early recollections. Here is a little of what Anne has written. This and all the passages of quotation that follow have been drawn from our joint memoirs, as yet unpublished:

> Intermarriage has always been at the heart of all social history. In the second generation of my English/Australian maternal family, intermarriage started to become

a factor in family life. Two of my great-aunts married into the families of German wine-producers. The German grape-growers had been in South Australia almost from the beginning of the colony. It was fairly inevitable that contact should occur, but by the forties when my memories begin, there were some tensions as well. One of the great-aunts took to the 'new' culture with zeal: I myself have faint memories of sailor suits and dirndls being worn at the Christmas afternoon tea that occurred each year. My parents felt that the cultural statement being made was not necessary, but they did not initially feel very bothered by it. As the war went on, year after year, I have a slight memory that we ceased to see these wearers of dirndls and sailor suits at Christmas. The boxes of wine did not cease to arrive on the doorstep, since that was the usual way in the family. Whatever one produced was shared by all. However, the fact of the German element in the family was not much commented on and was certainly not rejoiced at. Decades later in Rhodesia, when the Huchzermeyer family took Chris and me into their hearts, home and choir, I found it hard to shake off feelings of profound guilt that I think originated in Adelaide, and the fact that we had quietly distanced ourselves from German relatives.

Chris experienced cultural difference in a more obscure way. Though his Dutch grandfather and German great-grandfather had fought as Boers in the Boer War, this information had been largely elided from family history. For, after leaving their farm in the Orange Free State, the family had Anglicized to the point where his father spoke mainly English, attended St John's College, a posh Anglican school in Johannesburg, became an Anglican and Anglicized his name from Wertheim to Wortham. Though his grandmother's native tongue was German, Chris never heard her speak it, or Dutch or Afrikaans or French, in all of which she was equally fluent. His second intimation of the war was playing with other young children in a pit that had been hollowed out as an air-raid shelter somewhere in remote rural Natal. Apparently fear of the enemy had engendered extreme alarm. Two or three years before that, his first intimation had been in incident that occurred while his mother and the children had been staying at a guest house in the Cape province while the husband and father of the family was away at the war:

There was a white woman who also helped with the children of residents. Nothing about this woman lasts in my mind except her stern injunction to me as she put me down to sleep in my cot one evening. Evidently she was afraid that a child lying face downwards might suffocate, for she spat out: 'Don't lie on your stomach. Germans lie on their stomachs!' I had no idea what a German was, but I knew it must be very bad. It would be many years before I would become aware that there was a corollary to the importance of not being German: it was important not to be Jewish either. From scraps of adult conversation gathered during those war years I was in no doubt that Germans must be evil. They must at best be foreign, and that was bad enough. Foreignness was a problem ...

It would take a long time for Chris to unravel the complexities. Only in his teenage years would he learn that his Dutch grandfather had been a Jew.

Both the Osborne family in Australia and the Wortham family in southern Africa shared a common thread of experience in their post-war lives. They were ever on the move. The Osbornes moved from genteel Adelaide to the rough mining town of Broken Hill when Anne was in primary school. Frederick Osborne was a bank manager and, like all bank employees of his generation, he worked his way up the ladder by accepting transfers approximately every three years to wherever the General Manager's office decreed. Banks gave no thought to family disruption.

During the war years, Chris's mother, Vi, had moved with the children at least three times: from the northern Transvaal to the hinterland of Natal, near the great Drakensberg mountains and thence to the Transkei coast in the Cape. After his father, Leonard, came back from the war, there were more moves. The most significant of these came at much the same time that the Osbornes had travelled from Adelaide to Broken Hill. After the Afrikaner Nationalists took power in 1948, the new government, which was well laced with former Nazi supporters, made its opponents feel that they were enemies. There were incidents. One of them tellingly involved the family dog:

> To some of the Afrikaners in the district my father was seen as one who had turned against his own. Cars had driven through the dusty roads of the neighbourhood proclaiming by megaphone the victory of Afrikaner nationalism. However, one of the cars driving past was not carrying a megaphone but a rifle. My beloved dog, Gyp, a Doberman-Pointer cross, was mooching in the garden near me. There was a crack of rifle fire and in an instant he lay with a gaping wound in his side as gobbets of blood gurgled from his mouth. He died in my arms. It was about this time that my parents decided to leave South Africa and to head north to Rhodesia.

Throughout the childhood and adolescent years and into the university experience we both knew personal desolation. Although we both came from families in which there was intellect and some cultural breadth, we each felt we were rather odd fish, out of our depth in a world we did not understand or accept. We had friends, but we had to learn the emotional weight of loss. In part, it was to do with the moves our two families made. For Anne there were many more of these: from Adelaide to Broken Hill, thence to Bendigo, to Sydney, where she stayed while her family moved on yet again to Wagga Wagga and then back again to Sydney. For Chris, after the immense upheaval of leaving Johannesburg for Salisbury in Rhodesia, there was only one other major transition, from Salisbury to the border town of Umtali. We each sought friendship during our families' sojourns, only to have to break old relationships and seek new ones when the time came to move on. This was painful, for we were two rather timid and tentative children, but isolation taught us independence and forced us into learning to tolerate change. Those qualities have supported us ever since.

Our university experiences were utterly diverse. Anne went to the University of Sydney at a time when it was at its most intellectually challenging and daring. Among her contemporaries there were many who would soon famously became part of that international phenomenon of The Sixties. Germaine Greer, Robert Hughes, Clive James, Les Murray and Bob Ellis were already campus notables by the time she finished her degree there in 1961. Sydney was very much a city university, with all the opportunities and limitations of such an institution. Chris, on the other hand, had spent five years at Rhodes University in the small educational centre of Grahamstown in the eastern Cape of South Africa. It was a very sheltered environment, almost entirely residential, and with a highly active but inwardly-turned cultural life. Rhodes was not out of touch with the wider world, however, for it gave rise to many vigorous demonstrations of protest against the Apartheid regime in South Africa and a number of its most distinguished alumni from that time would courageously give their careers—and in some cases their very lives—to the cause of social and political justice. One such, John Conradie, would later become godfather to Chris and Anne's elder child, Miranda; though he would be unable to attend the baptismal ceremony because he was serving a twenty-year prison sentence for his political activities. Ultimately, the very differences in our university experiences would bring us closer together, for by sharing our experiences and the attitudes gained from them we would each become able to accommodate to wider views of the human condition.

We met in London, early in 1965. For both Australian and South African youngsters who had completed their first degree, going to London was almost an imperative. It was certainly an immense and wonderful attraction in all sorts of ways. Anne had gone there some eighteen months before and was studying the history of art at London University, which provided lecturers from the Courtauld Institute. During the day she was working on a number of teaching jobs. Chris, having gained a particular interest in modern American writing during his Honours degree, had decided to write a Master's degree on contemporary drama, with special reference to Arthur Miller. London was obviously the place to go in order to foster his interest. Rhodesia in 1965 was obsessed with the grave political issues confronting its future and at the time was not the place to encounter a theatrical experience much more immediate than the plays of Terence Rattigan, though within a few years there would be some very exciting developments, especially at the Reps Theatre in Salisbury and on the campus of the University of Rhodesia.

The educational establishment at which we met in London as temporary supply teachers was a church-aided secondary modern school called The Cardinal Hinsley School in Harlesden. 'Secondary Modern' was the euphemism applied to describe the 80% of children who had been unable to get into Grammar Schools on the results of their Eleven-Plus exams. The headmaster there had given up a position of considerable prestige at Finchley Grammar School in order bring new life and light to the boys of an area that at the time was particularly deprived and depraved. Both the school and the area are probably very different today, but we have not sought to find out. Chris's first impressions were callow and judgmental, perhaps, but not without their validity:

The building itself, a square construction several storeys high, breathed post-war utility: glass, plastic and grey concrete seemed to be the chief structural components. There was no attempt at any kind of finish that would soften the environment or make it more comforting. It was more than one step up from the horrors of slum life in the London in the previous century as depicted by Charles Dickens, but that was about the best one could say for it.

This was Harlesden in 1965. Most of its population were immigrants. This suburb, and the adjoining one of Willesden, had once been lower-middle-class and firmly English, built in the great urban expansion of the nineteenth century. The area consisted mainly of endless terraces of red-brick houses, mostly identical in shape and every visible aspect. To my eye these terraces were like so many enormous and elongated loaves of bread, all thinly sliced into compartments, each of which would squeeze at least one family within its narrow walls. I wanted to live somewhere near the school, so I looked at hand-written cards stuck up on the public notice boards at tube stations. Many rooms seemed to be on offer, but at that time public racial discrimination had not yet been outlawed, which meant that many of the notices advertising accommodation had 'Sorry NO Blacks' written across the top of them. Having been appalled by racism in South Africa, I was aghast to find it alive and well in Britain, but I was determined not to submit to it and so only answered the adverts that didn't say 'Sorry NO Blacks.' After I had knocked at half-a-dozen doors, it began to dawn on me that the absence of the 'Sorry NO Blacks' prohibition meant that the landlords *were* black. Each time I knocked and was greeted by a black face, that face registered stark disbelief when it saw me.

One could tell endless stories about Cardinal Hinsley School. The most poignant of these for me was the day when I walked into a classroom and found young Philip Roach of class 2S standing in the midst of an admiring circle of boys. Philip may well have grown into a decent young man, but at that stage he was a thug and ordinarily too rough and tough for most of the other boys to go anywhere near him. Like the fathers of many boys at the school, his father was in prison at Wormwood Scrubs. When I finally managed to break through the hubbub and restore something approaching silence, there was Philip standing an an aura of praise with a seraphic smile across his broad and usually threatening face. I asked him what it was all about. He replied: 'Me dad's been made captain of the Scrubs football team.' Philip came from a poor Irish family that had drifted from the country to Dublin, thence to Liverpool and had finally filtered down to London. This little piece of hard-earned dignity was as much as he could muster. Other immigrant groups represented there included West Indians and Asians from Catholic enclaves such as Sri Lanka. Little Edmund Wombeeck, originally from Colombo, would sit silently in my art classes, his eyes filled with tears, drawing only palm trees, blue sky and a golden sun. None of these would he be likely to see again, certainly not all together. Then there was Gerald Auld, an emaciated thirteen-year-old, who seemed like a wizened grandfather. After the fortnight-long Easter holidays, I asked him how he had spent the time. 'In bed,' her replied. ' Oh,' said I thoughtlessly, ' Were you sick?' 'No,' he replied without emotion, 'My mum went away with a new uncle. There was no food, so I went to bed.' Not everything at the school was by any means as bad as these few examples might suggest. However, this was another London altogether from the one I saw three or four nights a week in the rosy glow of theatre foyers.

In this desolate environment there was little we could do to alleviate the situation. But we also learned there to appreciate more fully our own good fortune. We enjoyed to the utmost our almost nightly visits to the theatre or cinema or to concerts on the south bank. To begin with we reported to each other in the school staffroom during the lunch break on what we had each done the night before. Soon we began to go out together in the evenings and occasionally we would have Sunday lunches together. It was at one of our Sunday lunches that we began to discuss what were—up to then—our separate plans for travel to Europe during the summer holidays.

To our own surprise, though probably not to anyone else's we found ourselves planning to go to Europe together—purely for mutual convenience and protection, of course. In the end, during July and August of 1965 we travelled together through France, Switzerland and Italy. Chris had to get back to Rhodesia to fulfil a teaching commitment in terms of a contract he had signed years earlier in order to gain the scholarship that had paid for his university education. Anne had already worked off a similar scholarship commitment before leaving Australia. The problem was that by this time we did not want to be parted and had in fact agreed to marry. The situation was accentuated by two factors: the first was that Chris was returning to a deepening political crisis that would soon result in the infamous Unilateral Declaration of Independence; and the second was that Anne knew she must go back to Australia and spend time with her parents and family before going to Africa. We said goodbye in Rome, Chris to catch a plane to Salisbury, Anne to catch a train to London. It was a bleak moment for both of us.

In January 1966, two months after UDI and in the face of economic and possible military sanctions against Rhodesia, Anne arrived there. Her family had said that she was mad and her father had said that she clearly had a well-developed death wish to be travelling to such a place at such a time. Anne recalled that in her school days he had often looked over his newspaper at breakfast to declare ominously: 'Mark my words: there's going to be a bloodbath in Africa.' Of this moment in personal and political history we have written:

We were married on 15 January, 1966, a few weeks after Ian Smith had unilaterally declared independence from Great Britain. A detachment from the RAF had been sent to Lusaka, possibly in preparation to bomb Salisbury. The port of Beira had been blockaded. Sanctions had been imposed by the United Nations. The world was watching Rhodesia and Rhodesia was watching TV, assured of its centrality in the universe. Mind you, the RAF could not possibly have bombed Salisbury without having been guided in from the control tower in Salisbury itself and, besides, many of the serving officers had been trained in Rhodesia during the Second World War. Furthermore, any invading force making its way into Rhodesia by any means would have within it personnel with close personal ties to people actually living within the country. Thus the kith-and-kin argument was beginning to raise its head in the more conservative areas of British society and was well understood in white Rhodesia.

In this tense political situation, full of 'ifs' and 'buts', our wedding went ahead. Chris had started the business of the banns being read in the Cathedral before Anne had actually arrived. We had ten days living in Chris's parents' house out in the bush outside Umtali before the wedding actually took place. We were not idle during these ten days. Chris had already rented part of a grand house and garden on the edge of Murambi Gardens, an elegant suburb just below the line of high hills to the north of the town. To Anne, the setting was glorious because the vegetation was thick and tropical and the greens were outside her experience, except by reference to Queensland. Directly behind the house was Cecil Kop, where we walked, marvelling at the landscape and the view below. We took with us little Chipo, Anne's first and only animal acquisition in Rhodesia. When Chris first saw Chipo he said to Anne: 'You've gone and got an alley cat.' But eventually he fell in love with this little black cat and its white ear feathers. Chipo would be with us wherever we went for the next ten years. His name was Shona for 'gift'.

We were not rich. We had no immediate prospects of academic careers in Rhodesia and anyway we knew that in all likelihood we would have to leave the country sooner rather than later. For the rest of that year Chris was to teach at Umtali Boys High School, which he himself had attended, in fulfilment of his contractual obligation. And Anne, having been offered three jobs, chose to join the staff of the Umtali Teachers Training College. The choice she made was unwittingly a contentious one: all the students at UTTC were black and, in the eyes of many white Rhodesians, education for the blacks was precisely the cause of the racial unrest that had become a serious issue in the country a few years earlier. For some of these—among them close friends of Chris's parents—teaching Africans was akin to sleeping with the enemy. Very precisely, in fact, as it turned out at one of the frequent weekend house parties:

One such Sunday, we were guests of friends of Chris's parents. We were being as cautious as we were capable of being, knowing that at any moment we might offend. The trouble started in this way. One woman addressed Anne from across the lawn.

This woman was wearing a demurely outmoded cotton dress of ankle length, gathered at the waist and covered in frilly bows. To Anne she said sweetly: 'But how are you coping, dear, in *that place*?' She meant, of course, the African teacher training college down the road. Anne, sensing imminent trouble, smiled back and said: 'I'm finding it really interesting and so far I have not run into any difficulties. I find the students courteous and hard-working.' Anne was trying to head her interlocutor off at the pass. Unsuccessfully. The woman continued: 'But would you let your daughter *marry* one?' Anne replied, giving the question serious thought: 'Well, I've never had any children and it's hard to say what I might or might not do in the future. However, it seems likely that I would allow my children to make their own choices in life.' The woman uncoiled and spat: 'In this country, that is *filth*!' Anne realized that this had never been a fair contest: she had been deliberately set up. In the world she had come from guests were never openly attacked. Chris and Anne realized that the parental friends had now to be avoided at all costs. It was the beginning of a rift and a new era.

You will readily understand, gentle reader, that we soon began to feel isolated in the small town where Chris had grown up and to which he had now returned with his foreign bride who had so little understanding of what it meant to bear the white man's (or woman's) burden in Africa. Together we were deemed to be letting the side down.

As it happened, relief was soon in sight. Before the year had ended both Chris and Anne had been offered teaching appointments at what was then the University College of Rhodesia. Prior to 1952, when the college opened, black people who were prospective university students had to travel to South Africa, where opportunities for that country's own black populations were already extremely limited. In fact, very few received a proper university education. Approved by the University of London, with UCR in Salisbury established as a constituent college of the University from 1956, education in Africa was given a great boost. By the time we arrived there in 1967, UCR had Faculties of Arts, Science, Agriculture, Commerce, Law, Medicine, Veterinary Science, and Engineering well established. The majority of students were still white and overall numbers were low, probably less than 2000, but the place was beginning to grow and many more black students were coming into the system. UCR became the independent University of Rhodesia in 1971, though for some years afterwards the University of London continued to underwrite its degrees. Today what is now the University of Zimbabwe has well over 10,000 undergraduate students and over 500 postgraduates, almost all of whom are black.

Our ten years at the University in Salisbury (not to be renamed Harare until after we left) were very happy ones, despite all sorts of difficulties and setbacks, and when the time came for us to leave the wrench would prove an almost physical rending. Those years have been covered by Geoff Cooper in his sensitive and generous Introduction to this volume. But there is more that we would like to add. Externally we were embattled, but within the broad campus we felt the warm reassurance of many like-minded people of dedication and good will toward all the people of the country, not just one racial group. As Geoff Cooper has pointed out, many fine academics with established reputations were there during our time and by the time we left many younger one who had been our contemporaries were beginning to make themselves known internationally. There was Geoff himself, who ultimately rose to Professorial rank at The University of Western Australia, where he initiated some radical and vitally important developments in academic areas of student support; Conal Condren, later to become Professor of Political Science at the University of New South Wales; Linda Kirk, who went on to lecture with distinction in History at the University of Sheffield; Norman Austin, later to become Professor at Massey University in New Zealand; David Pike, would become Head of the Department of Classics at the University of Natal (Pietermaritzburg); and Anthony Chennells, one of the few who elected to stay through all the troubles and has remained a Professor at what is now the University of Zimbabwe, while also fulfilling many periods of teaching at the University of California. These, and many others we could name, have all made their significant mark. However, there were others whose careers or lives or both were cut short by the troubles one way or another: among these were Duncan Middleton, a child prodigy who died young; John Conradie, Miranda's godfather, who would be the only white man to be buried in Heroes' Acre after the end of the guerrilla war; and the promising young black novelist Charles Marechera.

We both taught in the English Department at first, though Anne subsequently moved to Linguistics and by the time we left was lecturing in the Faculty of Education. The University was partially in the mould of the South African universities and the Scottish universities upon which the South African degrees had been largely modelled: accordingly, it offered Pass Degrees in which students studied several subjects in each year. For the Pass Degree there were set courses in English literature of all genres, largely British literature, in survey form, giving a sweep that went from Chaucer to the present day. However, in addition the University offered Honours degrees on the English model of a single subject studied in depth for three years; and the English Department notably participated in that programme too. So those of us who were teaching there gained wonderful education ourselves in the process of delivering one to our students! We had to be generalists, able to teach in all periods and genres for the Pass Degree, and also specialists in particular areas for our Honours students. The Honours programme culminated in a fearsome regimen of ten three-hour papers, written over a fortnight.

Our lives were full. We shared literature; we had similar cultural interests, ranging from ancient indigenous rock art to contemporary European experimental works; we diversely participated in music-making, in orchestras and in house music groups; for Chris there was active involvement in sport, where he represented the University at cricket and tennis; and for both of us there were warm and creative friendships with people of diverse callings and backgrounds. Among the last group there were Jacqui and Jimmy Carstairs—she an Australian artist and her husband a doctor—and Harry and Lina Kantor, prominent members of the Jewish community. We had first met Harry through his *pro Deo* work as a lawyer, which included acting for John Conradie through his trial and prison years, but we later got to know his whole delightful family. Lina was a fine concert pianist, though profoundly deaf because of a bomb blast in the water near the rowing boat in which her parents were escaping the Nazis from the Island of Rhodes during the Second World War. Lina performed several Mozart piano concertos with the chamber orchestra we established on campus. And then there were our dearest friends, Mike and Liz Saunders, with their four young children. Mike had been at school with Chris in Umtali, back in the 1950s and he had gone to England to study engineering. He had met Liz, who had a degree in Russian, at university and together they had come back to Africa in the mid-1960s. He worked as a consultant engineer in Salisbury. Liz was an accomplished violinist and played in the Salisbury Municipal Orchestra with Chris; and they both played house music with us as well. Mike had taken up the clarinet late and described himself as 'a senile prodigy'.

Yes, our lives were full but also very uncertain. As Anne has sometimes remarked in later times: 'Everywhere there was the clatter of typewriters as young members of staff hastily knocked out the PhD theses that would provide passports to academic jobs elsewhere when the political situation inevitably collapsed.' We had no money—academics in Rhodesia earned missionary salaries—and no prospect of ever being able to buy a house: in ten years we moved ten times from one rented house or flat to the next. We had theoretical permanency in our academic positions, but in practical terms that counted for little in the face of the country's overall instability. Paradoxically, as the university grew and flourished, so the political situation declined; and as the guerrilla war became more and more of a civil war, so students would mysteriously disappear from class. Then we would be told in whispers that they had gone to join the guerrillas. As a daily reminder to us, angry-sounding helicopters laden with corpses would overfly the university in the late afternoon as they flew back from the war zone to the north to the morgue at the barracks near the university. Their mighty engines and swooshing rotors, as they flew meaningfully low over us, would drown out lectures and seminars for minutes at a time. Part of the paradox was that the University still received substantial funding and other support from its mother institutions, the Universities of London and Birmingham, while the country as a whole was suffering slow economic constriction as the noose of sanctions imposed by the United Nations in retribution for the white government's Unilateral Declaration of Independence in 1965 inexorably tightened.

In our first days together in Rhodesia, there had been a frisson of excitement.

Nobody knew then what would happen. Would Britain invade? Would there be a spontaneous uprising? Would the country suddenly grind to a halt? None of these things transpired. At a personal level we exercized a little daring by teaching in an unauthorized, and therefore illegal, night school for African adults in Umtali's black township of Sakubva. Would we be arrested? Again nothing happened. For some months we were being watched very overtly by the Special Branch of the Police, who were keeping an eye on us for being supposedly feckless and dangerous dissidents. But eventually they got bored and went away. Later, at the University, we would be under a degree of surveillance, though in that enclave there was enough mutual reinforcement, born of a deep commitment to an utterly worthwhile project in African education, to keep us from feeling embattled.

Towards the latter end of our time in Rhodesia, however, the situation in the country as a whole began to impinge. Dangers became more real, more immediate, and much more deadly. There was the short but intensely unsafe period of Chris's conscription into the Department of Internal Affairs as a wartime auxilliary: he would end up in charge of a so-called 'Protected Village', in which most of the locals had been won over to the guerrilla cause. It was that which necessitated his resignation from the University: he wrote in his letter of resignation that, even though peace talks were going on sporadically, he could not again be involved in propping up a political regime that he could not endorse and that he would simply have to go. By the end of 1976, when we left, guerrilla bands had penetrated much of the country and were quietly moving in and out of village communities within striking distance of the capital. Chris's mother—his father had died some years before—was living alone in a house at Christon Bank, almost a dormitory suburb, but also well detached and quite thinly populated as a settlement of small holdings rather than suburban blocks. This was about twenty kilometres from the centre of Salisbury and the last seven kilometres or so were on dirt roads susceptible to land mines. To our knowledge, no mines were ever detonated on that stretch of road, but by that time we had a precious baby daughter and were not going to expose her life to unknown quantities of risk. So we stopped driving out to see Chris's mother at weekends, and for us that disruption really marked the end.

About this time Anne had another decisive experience. She tells the story:

Jacqui Carstairs had introduced us to a famous potter, Violet Ndoro. We would go out to visit her in her little village. She lived quite near the city and for those who know Rhodesia, in the shadow of Domboshawa (meaning 'red/ brown rock'). It is a site famous for its ancient rock art. Violet made many artefacts for us, small African candlesticks, two lighthouse candlesticks—from a sketch: Violet had never seen a lighthouse—and huge beerpots which we used for growing bougainvilleas in. We were fascinated by the fact that Violet worked according to traditional methods, moulding the objects by hand and then firing them in a deep hole in the ground, the heat coming from dried mealie-stalks which were packed over and around the objects before a fire was started and the entire arrangement turned into a conflagration. The artefacts bear evidence of this method of firing: black shadows, or marks perhaps, sear the red-brown pottery.

Shortly before we left, I made my last visit out to see Violet. It was towards the end of 1976. Jacqui was painting that day, and Chris was teaching, but I was determined to go out and say goodbye. So I left baby Miranda in the care of Anna, since it was too dangerous to take her beyond the city limits. I took the Domboshawa Road, then turned up the narrow, winding track that would lead me to Violet's village. It was in its usual tranquil state. As usual, the ground had been swept, but the little thatched houses were strangely quiet. The well, where villagers were normally gathered, was deserted. Violet had heard the car coming up the track and she emerged from her thatched hut looking agitated. She only said one word to me: 'Go, go!' I realized in an instant that I had put both our lives in jeopardy. She could no more afford to be seen fraternising with me than I could afford to be seen alone and unprotected in that African village. The guerrillas were there in the village or at least within the vicinity. I do not know how I turned the car round. The track was so narrow and the edges so soft with mud that I knew my car could easily become bogged. Somehow, anyhow, I don't remember how, I was in an instant heading back down the track. I was shaking from head to foot and could barely control the car. I myself was completely out of control and in a state of sheer terror.

As I turned right onto the main road which led back to the city, I saw a chameleon on the road, making its slow, elegant way across. I would normally have slowed or stopped to avoid it. But fear took over and I crushed it beneath the wheels. As I looked back through the rear-vision mirror, I saw the poor thing alive but terribly stricken. The best part of me wanted to go back and kill it but the coward sped off to the city. I did not even alert the authorities to my experience because I feared that Violet's village would be raided and razed by the army. I did nothing as the best thing I could do. Thereafter, the mechanics of packing up and saying goodbye were somehow achieved by a robot. My real life in Africa had come to an end on the Domoshawa Road with a mangled chameleon feebly writhing in the dust.

There could be no turning back. Or not for us. There were talks, and talks about talks. Henry Kissinger finally impressed upon Ian Smith and his government that they had reached the end of their road, but by that time we had both resigned and Chris had been offered lectureships at two universities in Australia and one in New Zealand. Gratefully, but with heavy hearts, we began to shut down our lives in Africa.

We were saying goodbye to a beautiful country, to many delightful friends, to worthwhile occupations in the community, and most of all we were farewelling ten years of exhilarating experience in teaching at the University of Rhodesia. While our personal departure may have meant little, we were in a tide of emigration that would, in the end, leave the country impoverished. The Rhodesian/Zimbabwean diaspora consists today of millions of people, black and white, who have left behind them their most cherished hopes and dreams. Those who have been exceptionally lucky, like ourselves, have found abundant opportunity for fulfilment in their new lands. For Anne the coming to Australia has been a return to her native land after a long absence; for Chris it has been a fresh start and, sometimes, a painful one of necessary adjustment through finding new outlooks and discarding old ones. Given the choice, we would now not live anywhere other than Perth, which has been our home for thirty blessed years. Our daughter, Miranda, was one year old when we came in 1977 and Nicholas was to be born here a year later. They are both well-travelled and have broad outlooks, but, like us, they are aware always of their special privilege in being Perth-bred Australians.

To begin with, our new life in Perth was a long, slow struggle. The head and the heart were at odds. Though homesick and lonely, we accepted with gratitude the great good fortune we had been offered in the form of a lectureship for Chris at the University of Western Australia. He found himself in a fine department, much larger than the one he had left behind and buzzing with excitement. Whereas he had had to cover all periods and genres of literature in Rhodesia, here the diversity of courses and the size of the department meant that he could specialize alongside a few like-minded colleagues in his favourite area of medieval and Renaissance studies. We were warmly welcomed by most, though a few people set out to discomfit us, and for a variety of motives. Friendship here could never be what it had been in Rhodesia, simply because the situation was so different: uncertainty mixed with danger had given a spice to human relationships; now we were in a place where the greatest crises seemed to us minimal by comparison.

For Anne, settling in was more problematical because, although an Australian herself, she had long been away and was returning to the other side of the country from that she had known in childhood, youth and young adulthood. She had no relatives in Perth, no pre-existing friends of network of acquaintance, and no status as a professional in her own right. Furthermore, she was looking after very young children in an environment wherein the other young mothers were primarily interested in sustaining the friendship groups they had enjoyed throughout their lives in Perth from cradle to the present. Unlike Chris, she had no framework to support her, apart from those other mothers who were kind enough to let her into their Kindy groups: not all the Cottesloe mums were so welcoming! While Anne has never sought to re-establish her academic career here, she has been for many years associated with English language and literature at a variety of levels, ranging from teaching on-arrival English to refugees to coaching very bright students in literature in preparation for their entry to University.

Conversely, at the University of Western Australia, Chris found affirmation and support. Thus encouraged, he inaugurated the Perth Medieval and Renaissance Group (around the beginning of 1980) that was to become central to the consolidation of early

European studies throughout the Faculty of Arts in later years. Out of the influence of PMRG grew a new interdisciplinary MPhil degree that would see many successful students, a number of whom would go on to PhDs within the same field and become major figures in scholarship. The MPhil was supported by input from colleagues in the Departments of English, History, Philosophy, Political Science, Classics, Italian, French, German, Fine Arts and Music. In 1984 Chris was elected President of the Australian and New Zealand Association for Medieval and Renaissance Studies (ANZAMRS) and hosted its conference at UWA in the following year. Ten years later, having co-edited Renaissance texts, he was invited to take on the editorship of ANZAMRS's journal, *Parergon*. By the time of his retirement in 2005, a new initiative from academics within the UWA-based group of scholars in the field, who had worked together in the MPhil programme and on the editorial committee of *Parergon*, would see the foundation of an ARC-funded Network for Early European Research. This last project was a vindication of thirty years of work largely spent in bringing together scholars into a constructive interdisciplinary relationship of exceptional value and productivity. Looking back, he is proud to have been associated with the development of an area of study that has become prominent at UWA and well-known not only in the Australasian region but throughout the world.

Over the years our attachment to Perth has become a deeply abiding love. After our first five years or so we began to find friendships of quality among like-minded people from many walks of life. Our circle has grown to the point where we host several large garden parties a year in addition to meeting in smaller groups at restaurants and for cultural events. From our initial loneliness we have gone to a richness in friendship beyond our imagining. We also get a lot of what may be called passing trade, in that old friends from our days in England and Africa as well as from other parts of Australia pass through Perth on their way to somewhere else. While our own children have now grown up and have found their own rewarding lives in Perth in new family units, we continue to live in the little house we have occupied since just a few weeks after our arrival thirty years ago. Our children and their children visit us frequently, and we them. Our daughter Miranda, now a teacher in her own right, is married to Robert Selman and at the time or writing they have two children, Olivia (aged almost three) and the newly-born Thomas. She has a BEd degree in Early Childhood Studies from Edith Cowan University (one of the five universities in the metropolitan area). Our son, Nicholas, is studying history and anthropology at Curtin University, following a successful period in the University's administration. He and his partner Josie have a six-year-old daughter, Rachael.

In our long and fortunate lives we have learned to value the past, to rejoice in the present, and to look forward to the future. We are grateful for the many beautiful experiences that have come our way and for having had mercifully few of those sad reverses that come into all our lives. It was a tremendous opportunity for Chris that at the moment of his retirement from UWA, the Anglican Cathedral offered him the position of Scholar in Residence. Also, as Emeritus Professor and Senior Honorary Research Scholar he continues to contribute to the life of UWA by supervising postgraduate theses and by continuing with his own research.

We are grateful for the most generous and unexpected festschrift that has been gathered by Andrew Lynch and Anne Scott to mark a retirement that has so far proved as fruitful for both of us as did our earlier working lives. To all who have wished us well we offer in thanksgiving this chronicle and brief abstract of our lives together.

Notes on Contributors

Victoria Bladen completed undergraduate studies in Arts and Law at UWA. Inspired for life by Christopher Wortham, she has pursued Andrew Marvell, Renaissance gardens and interdisciplinary approaches ever since. She is currently completing her PhD at the University of Queensland on the tree of life and arboreal symbolism in English Renaissance literature and its relationship to early modern visual culture.

Ann Blake is an Honorary Associate of La Trobe University, Melbourne, and formerly a Senior Lecturer. She has published articles on Shakespeare and other dramatists, on crime fiction and on Christina Stead. She is the author of *Christina Stead's Politics of Place* (1999) and co-author of *England through Colonial Eyes in Twentieth-Century Fiction* (2001). Her latest publications are new editions of Sheridan's *The School for Scandal* and Farquhar's *The Beaux' Stratagem* for the New Mermaid series.

Helen Vella Bonavita completed her undergraduate and postgraduate degrees at the University of Western Australia, where Chris Wortham was among her most inspirational lecturers. She is currently head of the English department at the University of Wales, Lampeter.

Graham Bradshaw is Professor of English at Chuo University, in Tokyo, and an Honorary Professor of English at the University of Queensland, but prefers to live, whenever or if ever he can, at his home in Jimbaran, Bali. He is or at least was the author of *Shakespeare's Scepticism*, *Misrepresentations: Shakespeare and the Materialists*, *Shakespeare in Japan* (written with Tetsuo Kishi), *Shakespeare's Peculiarity* (forthcoming); he and the younger, smarter Tom Bishop also edit the *Shakespearean International Yearbook*. The older, ailing Bradshaw is now more than ever inclined to write about other authors (and composers), since he knows he is then less likely to repeat himself, like Polonius: recent non-Shakespearean efforts have included essays on J. M. Coetzee, Giuseppe Verdi, Joseph Conrad, cognitive linguistics, metrics, John Donne and Ted Hughes. But (*caveat lector*) these six disparate subjects are all threatening to turn into books, if he lives much longer.

Conal Condren is a Fellow of both The Academy of the Humanities and of The Social Sciences in Australia, an Associate of The Erasmus Centre for Early Modern Studies, Erasmus University of Rotterdam and a member of Churchill College Cambridge. An Emeritus Scientia Professor at UNSW, he is about to take up an appointment as an Honorary Professor at The Centre for the History of European Discourses, The University of Queensland. His most recent book is *Argument and Authority in*

Early Modern England, (Cambridge University Press, 2006). His current work is on Shakespeare and the history of political thought, and on early modern satire of science and metaphysics.

Geoff Cooper (BA Hons, MA, Birmingham; PhD Queen's, Canada) has taught at many levels, first at Queen's University, and then the Universities of Alberta, Rhodesia and Western Australia where he specialised in Old and Middle English language and literature. Subsequently, he taught English at the Perth schools Scotch College and Guildford Grammar where he was also head of English. A final career move was as Learning and Research Skills Advisor in Student Services at UWA whence he retired as an Associate Professor. He received two Excellence in Teaching Awards at UWA and was made a Fellow of the Higher Education and Research Society of Australasia. Besides a number of articles medieval and educational, he has published two very different books, *The Summoning of Everyman,* and *The Intelligent Student's Guide to Learning at University.*

Joost Daalder is a Professor of English attached to Flinders University. His chief research interest is English Renaissance literature, an area in which he has widely published, both on verse and on drama. Favourite authors on whom he has worked include Sir Thomas Wyatt; Middleton and Rowley; Shakespeare, and Thomas Dekker, whose *The Honest Whore, I and II,* he is currently editing for the Revels Plays.

Heather Dubrow, Tighe-Evans Professor and John Bascom Professor at the University of Wisconsin-Madison, is the author of six books, most recently *The Challenges of Orpheus: Lyric Poetry and Early Modern England* (Johns Hopkins, 2008). Her other publications include collections of essays, two chapbooks of poetry as well as poems in numerous poetry journals, and articles on early modern literature and pedagogy.

Brett D. Hirsch has published articles on early modern drama and culture in *The Ben Jonson Journal, Early Modern Literary Studies,* and *Parergon,* and is co-editing a collection of essays with Christopher Wortham to be published jointly by Brepols and the UCLA Center for Medieval and Renaissance Studies. He is the general editor of the *Digital Renaissance Editions,* co-convenor of *Early Modern Drama in the Electronic Age,* a research cluster funded by the Australian Research Council Network for Early European Research, and the editorial assistant for the international scholarly journal of the British Shakespeare Association, *Shakespeare.* He has taught at The University of Western Australia and the University of Otago.

Philippa Kelly lives in California and is a Visiting Senior Research Fellow at the University of New South Wales. With Ron Bedford and Lloyd Davis she published

Early Modern Autobiography: Theories, Genres, Practices (Michigan) in September 2006, and will publish *Early Modern English Lives* in 2008 (Ashgate). Besides working on theories of individuality in early modern England, she has also published extensively on Shakespeare and in particular *King Lear*.

Andrew Lynch teaches in English and Cultural Studies at UWA and writes on medieval, medievalist and Australian literature, with a special interest in the ideology of war and peace. In 2002 he succeeded Chris Wortham as editor of *Parergon: Journal of the Australian and New Zealand Association for Medieval and Early Modern Studies*, which he now co-edits with Anne Scott.

Alicia Marchant took a degree in History and English at the University of Western Australia and is now completing a PhD in History also at UWA. Her thesis is on the revolt of Owain Glyndŵr in fifteenth-century English historiography. She is currently a visiting researcher at the University of Ghent, Belgium.

Anthony Miller is Honorary Associate Professor of English at the University of Sydney, where he was Chair of Department in 2003–6. He holds degrees from Western Australia, Cambridge and Harvard, and was a colleague of Christopher Wortham at Western Australia in 1975–8. He is the author of *Roman Triumphs and Early Modern English Culture* (Palgrave, 2001) and is working on a study called *The Poetics of Vulcan: Mining and Metallurgy in the Early Modern Imagination.*

Paige Newmark has taught and guest lectured at numerous renowned academic institutions including Stanford University, Williams University, UCLA, USC, Rhodes University in South Africa, University of Western Australia, and his present residence, Oxford University. In addition to his academic work, Paige is also a theatre director. He is currently the Artistic Director of the national touring Shakespeare company in South Africa called 'Shakespeare SA.' He has directed theatre all over the world including England, Australia, South Africa, and throughout the USA.

Kate Riley studied medieval and Early Modern history and literature as an undergraduate, culminating in an Honours dissertation on Marvell supervised by Chris Wortham. Reading seventeenth-century poets led, via Herbert, to a doctorate in History on the Ferrar family of Little Gidding. She maintains an interest in medieval and early modern history and the intellectual, religious, literary and visual cultures of the period, and enjoys teaching across disciplinary borders.

Anne M. Scott is Convenor of the Australian Research Council Network for Early European Research, as well a being an honorary research fellow in the Discipline of English and Cultural Studies at The University of Western Australia. Her field of research is in fourteenth-century English Literature, and her monograph, '*Piers Plowman* and the poor', was published in 2004. Work is currently in progress for a book on the iconography and representations of poverty in medieval English literature and art. Among other literary diversions, she is co-editor, with Andrew Lynch, of *Parergon*, the journal of the Australian and New Zealand Association for Medieval and Early Modern Studies, now available as part of the Project Muse database.

Jane Southwood is a lecturer in French at the University of New England, Armidale, New South Wales. Her passion for sixteenth-century literature began at The University of Western Australia under the expert guidance of Beverley Ormerod (Noakes), with whom she undertook her Master of Arts thesis on the collection of love poems treated here, the *Délie* of 1544, written by the Lyon poet and scholar, Maurice Scève. Though her doctoral thesis was on literature from a later period, she continues to be passionately interested in all aspects of the sixteenth century. This *Festschrift* for her friend and colleague, Chris Wortham, has given her a further opportunity to return to a period and a work she finds fascinating.

Kay Gilliland Stevenson, Reader in the Department of Literature, Film and Theatre Studies at the University of Essex, is author of *Milton to Pope: 1650–1720* (2001) in Palgrave Macmillan's 'transitions' series. She is co-author, with Clive Hart, of *Heaven and the Flesh: Imagery of Desire from the Renaissance to the Rococo* (1995) and, with Margaret Seares, of *Paradise Lost in Short: Smith, Stillingfleet and the Transformation of Epic* (1998).

Karina Welna is currently a PhD student at The University of Western Australia. Her thesis explores the portrayal of greed, wealth and profit in Mystery plays, Morality drama and early Tudor interludes. Her work is particularly focused on how drama articulates, shapes and forms moral ideas within its social and historical context. While currently focusing on the medieval, Karina is also interested in the modern drama of Brecht and Beckett. In further work she hopes to explore the connections between modern and medieval literary and dramatic works.

R. S. White became Professor of English, Communication and Cultural Studies at the University of Western Australia, after teaching at the University of Newcastle upon Tyne from 1974 to 1988. He was for several years Vice President of the Australian and New Zealand Shakespeare Association and was awarded an Australian Centenary Medal for service to Australian society and the humanities through the study of English. He has published many books, articles and chapters on Shakespeare, including *Innocent Victims: Poetic Injustice in Shakespearean*

Tragedy (1986) and also *Keats as a Reader of Shakespeare. Natural Law in English Renaissance Literature* (1996) has led to a sequel, *Natural Rights and the Birth of Romanticism in the 1790s* (2005). For five years he wrote the 'Contributions to Critical Studies' for *Shakespeare Survey* and also the chapter 'Twentieth Century Criticism' for the Cambridge Companion to Shakespeare Studies. His latest book is *Pacifism in English Literature: Minstrels of Peace* (London: Palgrave Macmillan, 2008).

Laurence Wright is Director of the Institute for the Study of English in Africa at Rhodes University. His research interests include African literature in English, Shakespeare and the history of Shakespeare in South Africa, South African Language Policy, and language education for teachers. He is Honorary Life President of the Shakespeare Society of Southern Africa and a Governor of the National Arts Festival.